VMware® ESXi: Planning, Implementation, and Security

Dave Mishchenko

Course Technology PTR

A part of Cengage Learning

COURSE TECHNOLOGY
CENGAGE Learning™

Australia • Brazil • Japan • Korea • Mexico • Singapore • Spain • United Kingdom • United States

COURSE TECHNOLOGY
CENGAGE Learning™

VMware® ESXi: Planning, Implementation, and Security
Dave Mishchenko

Publisher and General Manager, Course Technology PTR: Stacy L. Hiquet

Associate Director of Marketing: Sarah Panella

Manager of Editorial Services: Heather Talbot

Marketing Manager: Mark Hughes

Acquisitions Editor: Heather Hurley

Project Editor: Karen A. Gill

Technical Reviewer: Charu Chaubal

Copy Editor: Andy Saff

Interior Layout Tech: MPS Limited, a Macmillan Company

Cover Designer: Mike Tanamachi

Indexer: Sharon Shock

Proofreader: Sue Boshers

For product information and technology assistance, contact us at **Cengage Learning Customer & Sales Support, 1-800-354-9706.**

For permission to use material from this text or product, submit all requests online at **cengage.com/permissions.**
Further permissions questions can be e-mailed to **permissionrequest@cengage.com.**

VMware is a registered trademark of VMware, Inc. in the United States and/or other jurisdictions. Microsoft Windows and SQL Server are registered trademarks of Microsoft Corporation in the United States and/or other countries. All other trademarks are the property of their respective owners.

All images © Cengage Learning unless otherwise noted.

Library of Congress Control Number: 2010932782

ISBN-13: 978-1-4354-5495-8

ISBN-10: 1-4354-5495-2

Course Technology, a part of Cengage Learning
20 Channel Center Street
Boston, MA 02210
USA

Cengage Learning is a leading provider of customized learning solutions with office locations around the globe, including Singapore, the United Kingdom, Australia, Mexico, Brazil, and Japan. Locate your local office at: **international. cengage.com/region.**

Cengage Learning products are represented in Canada by Nelson Education, Ltd.

For your lifelong learning solutions, visit **courseptr.com.**

Visit our corporate Web site at **cengage.com.**

Printed in the United States of America
1 2 3 4 5 6 7 12 11 10

To Marcia, beautiful wife, wonderful mother, best friend.

Acknowledgments

A book typically carries one name on the cover, but in reality it would not be possible without so many people. I first thank God for both this opportunity and the wonderful people He has placed in my life who have made this project a reality.

My virtualization journey started with VMware Workstation 3.0 and ESX 1.5, and I soon became familiar with the VMware Communities forums. In that community I was able to learn so much from others and in turn contribute back to others as they started their own journeys. I would like to thank community leaders Robert Dell'Immagine, Badsah Mukherji, and most recently Alex Maier. Also, thank you to John Troyer, who has contributed his leadership to this community and the VMware vExpert program. In addition, thanks to the numerous VMware Communities moderators, both past and present, who have contributed to making the forums such a wonderful community to be a part of.

The staff at Cengage Learning has been an absolute pleasure to deal with. I would like to thank Heather Hurley for her support, Andy Saff and Sue Boshers who worked to ensure that my mistakes did not make it past the editing process, and in particular Karen Gill who has guided me through this entire process.

I would like to thank Charu Chaubal from VMware for contributing his time to provide the technical review for this book. His experience with the virtualization market and with VMware ESXi has contributed significantly to this book. Charu is the name behind much of the information you see for ESXi, such as the system architecture documents for ESXi, the vSphere Hardening Guide, and the VMware ESXi Chronicles blog (blogs.vmware.com/esxi/).

Lastly, I would like to thank my family for their support. For my children Ariana, Karis, Luke, and Yerik, who sacrificed a summer while I was busy writing, and to my wife Marcia who kept things running, I thank you and could not have done this without you.

About the Author

Dave Mishchenko has been in the IT industry for 13 years and is currently a technical consultant with ProServeIT Corporation, a top-rated professional technology services company. He provides consulting services to ProServeIT's customers and focuses on network infrastructure and security, thin client computing, database tuning, server hardware, and virtualization. Dave is actively involved in the VMware Community forums, where he is a user moderator and in particular focuses on VMware ESXi. Dave was awarded the vExpert status by VMware in 2009 and 2010. He is a coauthor of *vSphere 4.0 Quick Start Guide: Shortcuts Down the Path of Virtualization*.

Contents

Introduction. xiii

Chapter 1
Introduction to VMware ESXi 4.1   1

Understanding the Architecture of VMware ESXi 3
Managing VMware ESXi 6
Comparing ESXi and ESX 8
    Common Features and Capabilities 9
    Product Differences 12
What's New with vSphere 4.1 16
Conclusion 23

Chapter 2
Getting Started with a Quick Install   25

Determining Hardware and Software Requirements 25
Installing VMware ESXi 27
Configuring the DCUI 32
Installing the vSphere Client and Initial Configuration 37
Conclusion 44

Chapter 3
Management Tools   45

Managing Your ESXi Host with the vSphere Client 45
    Using the Host Configuration Tab 46
    Viewing Resource Allocation 53
    Viewing Events and System Logs 56

Managing Your Hosts with vCenter Server 56
  Ensuring Configuration Compliance with Host Profiles 57
  Managing VMs with vSphere Web Access 60
Getting Started with PowerCLI and the vCLI 62
  Getting Started with the vCLI 63
  Getting Started with PowerCLI 64
Configuring and Troubleshooting ESXi with the DCUI 67
  Restarting and Shutting Down the Host 67
  Configuring the DCUI Keyboard Language 70
  Configuring a Password for the Root Login 71
  Enabling Lockdown Mode 72
  Configuring the Management Network 73
  Restarting the Management Network 79
  Testing the Management Network 79
  Disabling the Management Network 80
  Restoring the Standard vSwitch 81
  Viewing Support Information 82
  Viewing System Logs 82
  Troubleshooting Mode Options 84
  Resetting Your System Configuration 86
  Removing Custom Extensions 86
Using Third-Party Products to Manage Your Hosts 87
  RVTools 87
  Veeam FastSCP 88
  Xtravirt vSphere Client RDP Plug-In 89
  Vizioncore vFoglight 90
  ManageIQ EVM Control 91
Conclusion 91

Chapter 4
Installation Options   93

Using ESXi Embedded 93
ESXi Installable Media and Boot Options 99
  Creating a Network Media Depot for VMware ESXi 101
  PXE Booting the ESXi Installer 104
  Installing VMware ESXi 4.1 Using Graphical Mode 117
  Installing VMware ESXi 4.1 Using Scripted Mode 124
Conclusion 143

Chapter 5
Migrating from ESX   145

Prerequisites 145

Upgrading to vCenter Server 4.1 147

    Migrating the VirtualCenter Database to a Supported Version 150

    Backing Up vCenter Server Configuration Data with the
    Data Migration Tool 151

    Restoring the vCenter Server Configuration Data and Installing
    vCenter Server 4.1 153

    Installing the License Service on the New vCenter Server Host 158

Upgrading Datastore and Network Permissions 159

Migrating ESX Hosts 164

Upgrading Virtual Machines 170

    Performing an Interactive Upgrade of VMware
    Tools with the vSphere Client 172

    Automating the Upgrade of VMware Tools with the vSphere Client 174

    Upgrading Virtual Hardware 177

    Using PowerCLI to Upgrade VMware Tools and the Hardware Version 177

    Using vCenter Update Manager to Upgrade VMware Tools and
    the Hardware Version 178

Conclusion 179

Chapter 6
System Monitoring and Management   181

Configuring Active Directory Integration 181

    AD Integration Prerequisites 182

    Configuring AD Integration with the vSphere Client 182

    Configuring AD Integration with Host Profiles 184

    Configuring AD Integration with the vCLI 185

    Assigning AD Permissions on VMware ESXi 186

Enabling Time Synchronization and NTP 189

    Configuring NTP with the vSphere Client 189

    Configuring NTP with Host Profiles 190

    Configuring NTP with PowerCLI 192

Redirecting ESXi Logs to a Remote Syslog Server .193

    Configuring Syslog Settings with the vSphere Client 195

    Configuring Syslog Settings with PowerCLI 195

    Managing ESXi Syslog Data 197

Monitoring ESXi and vCenter Server with SNMP 200
    Configuring SNMP on ESXi and vCenter Server 201
    Configuring Your SNMP Management Server .203
Monitoring Your Hosts with vCenter Server 205
    Working with Alarms 207
    Working with Performance Charts 215
    Working with Storage Views 226
    Hardware Management 229
Integration with Server Management Systems 235
Host Backup and Recovery 238
    ESXi Backup and Recovery 238
    Backup and Recovery for Virtual Machines 240
Conclusion 245

Chapter 7
Securing ESXi   247

ESXi Architecture and Security Features 247
    Security and the VMkernel 248
    Security and Virtual Machines 249
    Security and the Virtual Networking Layer 250
Network Protocols and Ports for ESXi 252
Protecting ESXi and vCenter Server with Firewalls 256
Using ESXi Lockdown Mode 260
Configuring Users and Permissions 265
    Managing Permissions on a Standalone VMware ESXi Host 266
    Managing Permissions with vCenter Server 274
Securing VMware ESXi and vCenter Server with SSL Certificates 283
    Types of SSL Certificates 284
    SSL Certificates Used by ESXi and vCenter Server 285
    Replacing the SSL Certificates Used by vCenter Server and ESXi 286
    Enabling Certificate Checking and Verifying Host Thumbprints 293
Configuring IPv6 and IPSec 293
Securing Network Storage 305
    Securing FC SAN Storage 305
    Securing NFS Storage 306
    Security iSCSI Storage 306
Securing Virtual Networking 309
    Security Virtual Networking with VLANs 309
    Configuring vSwitch Security Properties 310

Security and Clustering 314
Isolating Virtual Machine Environments 316
Conclusion 318

Chapter 8
Scripting and Automation with the vCLI   321

Installing the vCLI on Linux and Windows 321
Installing and Configuring the vMA 325
Running vCLI Commands 329
Configuring vMA Components 335
    Configuring vi-fastpass Authentication 335
    Capturing ESXi Logs with vi-logger 340
Managing vSphere with the vCLI 344
    Managing ESXi Hosts 346
    Managing Virtual Machines 351
    Managing Host Networking 354
    Managing Host Storage 357
    Managing Files 363
    Monitoring Performance with resxtop 364
Scripting with the vCLI and the vSphere SDK for Perl 366
Conclusion 367

Chapter 9
Scripting and Automation with PowerCLI   369

Installing vSphere PowerCLI 369
    Accessing the vSphere Managed Object Browser 370
    Installing and Testing PowerCLI 372
Understanding the Basics of PowerShell and PowerCLI 374
    PowerShell Objects and Pipelines 374
    PowerShell Variables 375
    Formatting Output 377
    Managing Connections 378
    Developing Scripts with WhatIf 379
    Finding PowerCLI Cmdlets 379
Using PowerShell Drives 380
Managing Virtual Machines with PowerCLI 382
    Creating Virtual Machines 383
    Creating Virtual Machines from Templates .384

Managing Virtual Machine Snapshots 385
Interacting with VMware Tools 386
Managing ESXi Hosts and vCenter Server with PowerCLI 390
Configuring Your ESXi Hosts with a PowerCLI Script 390
Managing Host Profiles with PowerCLI 394
Integrating PowerCLI with vCenter Server Alarms 395
Troubleshooting Your ESXi Hosts 396
Extending PowerCLI with Other Tools 398
The Integrated Shell Environment 398
VMware Project Onyx 399
PowerWF 402
Conclusion 403

Chapter 10
Patching and Updating ESXi 405

Installing Patches for ESXi 405
Patching ESXi with the vCLI Command vihostupdate 407
Patching ESXi with the vCenter Update Manager 408
Installing vCenter Update Manager 409
Configuring vCenter Update Manager 413
Creating a vCenter Update Manager Baseline 416
Scanning and Remediating ESXi with vCenter Update Manager 419
Patching ESXi with PowerCLI 424
Updating a Host with Install-VMHostPatch 424
Updating a Host with VUM PowerCLI 426
Conclusion 427

Chapter 11
Under the Hood with the ESXi Tech Support Mode 429

Accessing Tech Support Mode 429
Auditing Tech Support Mode 433
Exploring the File System 436
Understanding System Backups and Restores 443
Repairing ESXi and Restoring from Backups 444
Troubleshooting with Tech Support Mode 448
Conclusion 453

Index

Index. 455

Introduction

VMware ESXi is the easiest way to get started with virtualization. It has been steadily growing in popularity since it was released in the free VMware vSphere Hypervisor edition. As part of the vSphere family, it can be licensed at the same levels as VMware ESX and provides the same functionality that you're accustomed to with ESX.

With the release of vSphere 4.1, VMware has stated that there will be no future releases of ESX. VMware ESXi is now the flagship hypervisor for the vSphere product family. This book will cover installation, management, security, and integration of ESXi into your current environment to provide a seamless migration from ESX to ESXi.

Who This Book Is For

This book is targeted to current VMware VI3 and vSphere administrators who may be planning their migration to vSphere ESXi. These users may have some experience with ESXi but not yet have it deployed within their production environment. This book provides the guidance to implement ESXi in their environment, ensuring a smooth transition from their current deployment of ESX.

How This Book Is Organized

This book covers the following aspects of migrating a VI3 or vSphere ESX environment to vSphere ESXi:

- **Chapter 1, "Introduction to VMware ESXi 4.1,"** provides an introduction to VMware ESXi, including some of the aspects of managing ESXi, comparing it with ESX, and new features in ESXi 4.1.

- **Chapter 2, "Getting Started with a Quick Install,"** reviews the hardware requirements for ESXi, walks through an interactive installation, and outlines post-installation tasks to perform.

- **Chapter 3, "Management Tools,"** reviews the management tools available for ESXi. These tools include the vSphere client, vCenter Server, the vSphere command-line interface (vCLI), PowerCLI, the Direct Console User Interface (DCUI), and a few other tools.

- **Chapter 4, "Installation Options,"** discusses the installation options for ESXi. VMware ESXi is available in both an Embedded edition and an Installable edition. New for ESXi 4.1 is the option to perform scripted installations.

- **Chapter 5, "Migrating from ESX,"** covers migration options from your current environment to vCenter Server 4.1 and ESXi 4.1. You'll read about the various steps for upgrading vCenter Server, your vSphere hosts, and virtual machines in this chapter.

- **Chapter 6, "System Monitoring and Management,"** introduces various aspects of system monitoring and management. New for ESXi 4.1 is Active Directory integration. The chapter also includes configuring vCenter alarms, performance charts, storage views, and host backup.

- **Chapter 7, "Securing ESXi,"** discusses the various aspects of securing your ESXi hosts. This includes coverage of the architecture and security features of ESXi, protecting your ESXi hosts and virtual machines, and configuring authentication for your hosts.

- **Chapter 8, "Scripting and Automation with the vCLI,"** talks about the vCLI. The vCLI was released as the Remote Command-Line Interface (RCLI) and is a replacement mechanism for administrators accustomed to using the Service Console on ESX.

- **Chapter 9, "Scripting and Automation with PowerCLI,"** covers VMware PowerCLI. PowerCLI is a VMware extension to Microsoft PowerShell that allows you to automate all aspects of managing your vSphere environment.

- **Chapter 10, "Patching and Updating ESXi,"** discusses various aspects of patching and upgrading ESXi hosts. VMware ESXi can be patched with a number of tools including the vCLI, PowerCLI, and vCenter Update Manager.

- **Chapter 11, "Under the Hood with the ESXi Tech Support Mode,"** introduces ESXi Tech Support Mode (TSM). TSM provides direct access to the VMkernel of ESXi and is used for advanced configuration tasks and troubleshooting.

Note: The scripts used in this book are available for download from http://www. vm-help.com/esxi_book.zip and http://www.courseptr.com/downloads.

---

1 Introduction to VMware ESXi 4.1

VMware was formed as a company in 1998 to provide x86 virtualization solutions. Virtualization was introduced in the 1970s to allow applications to share and fully utilize centralized computing resources on mainframe systems. Through the 1980s and 1990s, virtualization fell out of favor as the low-cost x68 desktops and servers established a model of distributed computing. The broad use of Linux and Windows solidified x86 as the standard architecture for server computing. This model of computing introduced new management challenges, including the following:

- **Lower server utilization.** As x86 server use spread through organizations, studies began to find that the average physical utilization of servers ranged between 10 and 15 percent. Organizations typically installed only one application per server to minimize the impact of updates and vulnerabilities rather than installing multiple applications per physical host to drive up overall utilization.

- **Increased infrastructure and management costs.** As x86 servers proliferated through information technology (IT) organizations, the operational costs—including power, cooling, and facilities—increased dramatically for servers that were not being fully utilized. The increase in server counts also added management complexity that required additional staff and management applications.

- **Higher maintenance load for end-user desktops.** Although the move to a distributed computing model provided freedom and flexibility to end users and the applications they use, this model increased the management and security load on IT departments. IT staff faced numerous challenges, including conforming desktops to corporate security policies, installing more patches, and dealing with the increased risk of security vulnerabilities.

In 1999, VMware released VMware Workstation, which was designed to run multiple operating systems (OSs) at the same time on desktop systems. A person in a support or development type position might require access to multiple OSs or application versions, and prior to VMware Workstation, this would require using multiple desktop systems or constantly restaging a single system to meet immediate needs. Workstation significantly reduced the hardware and management costs in such as scenario, as those environments could be hosted on a single workstation.

1

With snapshot technology, it was simple to return the virtual machines to a known good configuration after testing or development, and as the virtual machine configuration was stored in a distinct set of files, it was easy to share gold virtual machine images among users.

In 2001, VMware released both VMware GSX Server and ESX Server. GSX Server was similar to Workstation in that a host OS, either Linux or Windows, was required on the host prior to the installation of GSX Server. With GSX Server, users could create and manage virtual machines in the same manner as with Workstation, but the virtual machines were now hosted on a server rather than a user's desktop. GSX Server would later be renamed VMware Server. VMware ESX Server was also released as a centralized solution to host virtual machines, but its architecture was significantly different from that of GSX Server. Rather than requiring a host OS, ESX was installed directly onto the server hardware, eliminating the performance overhead, potential security vulnerabilities, and increased management required for a general server OS such as Linux or Windows. The hypervisor of ESX, known as the VMkernel, was designed specifically to host virtual machines, eliminating significant overheard and potential security issues.

VMware ESX also introduced the VMware Virtual Machine File System (VMFS) partition format. The original version released with ESX 1.0 was a simple flat file system designed for optimal virtual machine operations. VMFS version 2 was released with ESX Server 2.0 and implemented clustering capabilities. The clustering capabilities added to VMFS allowed access to the same storage by multiple ESX hosts by implementing per-file locking. The capabilities of VMFS and features in ESX opened the door in 2003 for the release of VMware VirtualCenter Server (now known as vCenter Server). VirtualCenter Server provided centralized management for ESX hosts and included innovative features such as vMotion, which allowed for the migration of virtual machines between ESX hosts without interruption, and High Availability clusters.

In 2007, VMware publicly released its second-generation bare-metal hypervisor VMware ESXi (ESX integrated) 3.5. VMware ESX 3 Server ESXi Edition was in production prior to this, but this release was never made public. ESXi 3.5 first appeared at VMworld in 2007, when it was distributed to attendees on a 1GB universal serial bus (USB) flash device. The project to design ESXi began around 2001 with a desire to remove the console operating system (COS) from ESX. This would reduce the surface attack area of the hypervisor level, make patching less frequent, and potentially decrease power requirements if ESXi could be run in an embedded form. ESXi was initially planned to be stored in the host's read-only memory (ROM), but the design team found that this would not provide sufficient storage; so, early versions were developed to boot from Preboot Execution Environment (PXE). Concerns about the security of PXE led to a search for another solution, which was eventually determined to be the use of a flash device embedded within the host. VMware worked with original equipment manufacturer (OEM) vendors to provide servers with embedded flash, and such servers were used to demonstrate ESXi at VMworld 2007.

The release of VMware ESXi generated a lot of interest, especially due to the lack of the COS. For seasoned ESX administrators, the COS provided an important avenue for executing management scripts and troubleshooting commands. The COS also provided the mechanism for third-party applications such as backup and hardware monitoring to operate. These challenges provided some significant hurdles for administrators planning their migration from ESX to ESXi. VMware released the Remote Command-Line Interface (RCLI) to provide access to the commands that were available in the ESX COS, but there were gaps in functionality that made a migration from ESX to ESXi challenging.

With the release vSphere 4.0 and now in 2010 of vSphere 4.1, VMware has made significant progress toward alleviating the management challenges due to the removal of the COS. Improvements have been made in the RCLI (now known as the vSphere Command-Line Interface [vCLI]), and the release of PowerCLI, based on Windows PowerShell, has provided another scripting option. Third-party vendors have also updated applications to work with the vSphere application programming interface (API) that ESXi exposes for management purposes.

VMware has also stated that vSphere 4.1 is the last release that includes VMware ESX and its COS. For existing vSphere environments, this signals the inevitable migration from VMware ESX to ESXi. The purpose of this book is to facilitate your migration from ESX to ESXi. With ESXi, you have a product that supports the same great feature set you find with VMware ESX. This chapter discusses the similarity of features and highlights some of the differences in configuring and using ESXi due to its architecture. The chapters in this book review the aspects of installation, configuration, management, and security that are different with ESXi than they are when you manage your infrastructure with ESX.

In this chapter, you shall examine the following items:

- Understanding the architecture of ESXi

- Managing VMware ESXi

- Comparing ESXi and ESX

- Exploring what's new in vSphere 4.1

Understanding the Architecture of VMware ESXi

The technology behind VMware ESXi represents VMware's next-generation hypervisor, which will provide the foundation of VMware virtual infrastructure products for years to come. Although functionally equivalent to ESX, ESXi eliminates the Linux-based service console that is required for management of ESX. The removal from its architecture results in a hypervisor without any general operating system dependencies, which improves reliability and security. The result is a footprint of less than 90MB, allowing ESXi to be embedded onto a host's flash device and eliminating the need for a local boot disk.

The heart of ESXi is the VMkernel shown in Figure 1.1. All other processes run on top of the VMkernel, which controls all access to the hardware in the ESXi host. The VMkernel is a POSIX-like OS developed by VMware and is similar to other OSs in that it uses process creation,

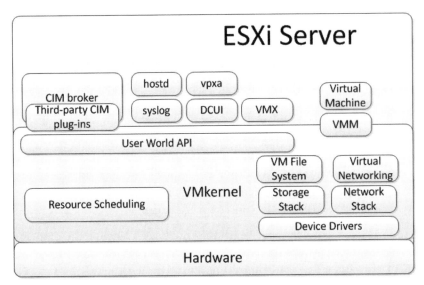

Figure 1.1 The architectural components of VMware ESXi.

file systems, and process threads. Unlike a general OS, the VMkernel is designed exclusively around running virtual machines, thus the hypervisor focuses on resource scheduling, device drivers, and input/output (I/O) stacks. Communication for management with the VMkernel is made via the vSphere API. Management can be accomplished using the vSphere client, vCenter Server, the COS replacement vCLI, or any other application that can communicate with the API.

Executing above the VMkernel are numerous processes that provide management access, hardware monitoring, as well as an execution compartment in which a virtual machine operates. These processes are known as "user world" processes, as they operate similarly to applications running on a general OS, except that they are designed to provide specific management functions for the hypervisor layer.

The virtual machine monitor (VMM) process is responsible for providing an execution environment in which the guest OS operates and interacts with the set of virtual hardware that is presented to it. Each VMM process has a corresponding helper process known as VMX and each virtual machine has one of each process.

The hostd process provides a programmatic interface to the VMkernel. It is used by the vSphere API and for the vSphere client when making a direct management connection to the host. The hostd process manages local user and groups as well as evaluates the privileges for users that are interacting with the host. The hostd also functions as a reverse proxy for all communications to the ESXi host.

VMware ESXi relies on the Common Information Model (CIM) system for hardware monitoring and health status. The CIM broker provides a set of standard APIs that remote management applications can use to query the hardware status of the ESXi host. Third-party hardware vendors are able to develop their own hardware-specific CIM plug-ins to augment the hardware information that can be obtained from the host.

The Direct Console User Interface (DCUI) process provides a local management console for ESXi. The DCUI appears as a BIOS-like, menu-driven interface, as shown in Figure 1.2, for initial configuration and troubleshooting. To access the DCUI, a user must provide an administrative account such as root, but the privilege can be granted to other users, as discussed in Chapter 11, "Under the Hood with the ESXi Tech Support Mode." Using the DCUI is discussed in Chapter 3, "Management Tools."

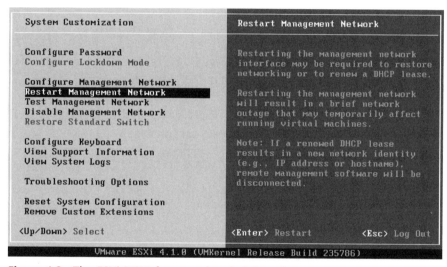

Figure 1.2   The ESXi DCUI for console administration.

The vpxa process is responsible for vCenter Server communications. This process runs under the security context of the vpxuser. Commands and queries from vCenter Server are received by this process before being forwarded to the hostd process for processing. The agent process is installed and executes when the ESXi host is joined to a High Availability (HA) cluster. The syslog daemon is responsible for forwarding logging data to a remote syslog receiver. The steps to configure the syslog daemon are discussed in Chapter 6, "System Monitoring and Management." ESXi also includes processes for Network Time Protocol (NTP)–based time synchronization and for Internet Small Computer System Interface (iSCSI) target discovery.

To enable management communication, ESXi opens a limited number of network ports. As mentioned previously, all network communication with the management interfaces is proxied via the `hostd` process. All unrecognized network traffic is discarded and is thus not able to reach other system processes. The common ports including the following:

- **80.** This port provides access to display only the static Welcome page. All other traffic is redirected to port 443.

- **443.** This port acts as a reverse proxy to a number of services to allow for Secure Sockets Layer (SSL) encrypted communication. One of these services is the vSphere API, which provides communication for the vSphere client, vCenter Server, and vCLI.

- **902.** Remote console communication between the vSphere client and ESXi host is made over this port.

- **5989.** This port is open to allow communication with the CIM broker to obtain hardware health data for the ESXi host.

Managing VMware ESXi

Rather than relying on COS agents to provide management functionality, as is the case with ESX, ESXi exposes a set of APIs that enable you to manage your ESXi hosts. This agentless approach simplifies deployments and management upkeep. To fill the management gap left by the removal of the COS, VMware has provided two remote command-line options with the vCLI and Power-CLI. These provide a CLI and scripting capabilities in a more secure manner than accessing the console of a vSphere host. For last-resort troubleshooting, ESXi includes both a menu-driven interface with the DCUI and a command-line interface at the host console with Tech Support Mode.

ESXi can be deployed in the following two formats: Embedded and Installable. With ESXi Embedded, your server comes preloaded with ESXi on a flash device. You simply need to power on the host and configure your host as appropriate for your environment. The DCUI can be used to configure the IP configuration for the management interface, to set a hostname and DNS configuration, and also to set a password for the root account. The host is then ready to join your virtual infrastructure for further configuration such as networking and storage. This configuration can be accomplished remotely with a configuration script or features within vCenter Server such as Host Profiles or vNetwork Distributed Switches. With ESXi Embedded, a new host can be ready to begin hosting virtual machines within a very short time frame. ESXi Installable is intended for installation on a host's boot disk. New to ESXi 4.1 is support for Boot from storage area network (SAN), which provides the capability to function with diskless servers. ESXi 4.1 also introduces scripted installations for ESXi Installable. The ESXi installer can be started from either a CD or PXE source and the installation file can be accessed via a number of protocols, including HyperText Transfer Protocol (HTTP), File Transfer Protocol (FTP), and Network File System (NFS). The installation file permits scripts to be run pre-install, post-install, and on first boot. This enables advanced configuration, such as the creating of the host's virtual networking, to be performed as a completely automated function. Scripted installations are discussed further in Chapter 4, "Installation Options."

For post-installation management, VMware provides a number of options both graphical and scripted. The vSphere client can be used to manage an ESXi directly or to manage a host via vCenter Server. To provide functionality that was previously available only in the COS, the vSphere client has been enhanced to allow configuration of such items as the following:

- **Time configuration.** Your ESXi host can be set to synchronize time with a NTP server.

- **Datastore file management.** You can browse your datastores and manage files, including moving files between datastores and copying files from and to your management computer.

- **Management of users.** You can create users and groups to be used to assign privileges directly to your ESXi host.

- **Exporting of diagnostic data.** The client option exports all system logs from ESXi for further analysis.

For scripting and command-line–based configuration, VMware provides the following two management options: the vCLI and PowerCLI. The vCLI was developed as a replacement to the esxcfg commands found in the service console of ESX. The commands execute with the exact same syntax with additional options added for authentication and to specify the host to run the commands against. The vCLI is available for both Linux and Windows, as well as in a virtual appliance format known as the vSphere Management Assistant (vMA). The vCLI includes commands such as vmkfstools, vmware-cmd, and resxtop, which is the vCLI equivalent of esxtop. PowerCLI extends Microsoft PowerShell to allow for the management of vCenter Server objects such as hosts and virtual machines. PowerShell is an object-orientated scripting language designed to replace the traditional Windows command prompt and Windows Scripting Host. With relatively simple PowerCLI scripts, it is possible to run complex tasks on any number of ESXi hosts or virtual machines. These scripting options are discussed further in Chapter 8, "Scripting and Automation with the vCLI," and Chapter 9, "Scripting and Automation with PowerCLI."

If you want to enforce central audited access to your ESXi through vCenter Server, ESXi includes Lockdown Mode. This can be used to disable all access via the vSphere API except for vpxuser, which is the account used by vCenter Server to communicate with your ESXi host. This security feature ensures that the critical root account is not used for direct ESXi host configuration. Lockdown Mode affects connections made with the vSphere client and any other application using the API such as the vCLI. Other options for securing your ESXi hosts are discussed in Chapter 7, "Securing ESXi."

For third-party systems management and backup products that have relied on a COS agent, VMware has been working with its partners to ensure that these products are compatible with the vSphere API and thus compatible with ESXi. The API integration model significantly reduces management overhead by eliminating the need to install and maintain software agents on your vSphere host.

The Common Information Model is an open standard that provides monitoring of the hardware resources in ESXi without the dependence on COS agents. The CIM implementation in ESXi consists of a CIM object manager (the CIM broker) and a number of CIM providers, as shown in Figure 1.3. The CIM providers are developed by VMware and hardware partners and function to provide management and monitoring access to the device drivers and hardware in the ESXi host. The CIM broker collects all the information provided by the various CIM providers and makes this information available to management applications via a standard API.

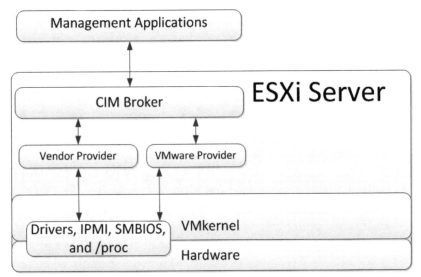

Figure 1.3 The ESXi CIM management model.

Due to the firmware-like architecture of ESXi, keeping your systems up to date with patches and upgrades is far simpler than with ESX. With ESXi, you no longer need to review a number of patches and decide which is applicable to your ESX host; now each patch is a complete system image and contains all previously released bug fixes and enhancements. ESXi hosts can be patched with vCenter Update Manager or the vCLI. As the ESXi system partitions contain both the new system image and the previously installed system image, it is a very simple and quick process to revert to the prepatched system image.

Comparing ESXi and ESX

Discussions of ESXi and ESX most often focus on the differences in architecture and management due to the removal of the COS. The availability of ESXi as a free product also leads some to believe that ESXi may be inferior or not as feature-rich as ESX. As discussed in the previous sections, the architecture of ESXi is superior and represents the future of VMware's hypervisor design. The following section explores the features of vSphere 4.1 that are available and identical with both ESXi and ESX.

Common Features and Capabilities

The main feature set for vSphere 4.1 is summarized in Table 1.1. Items listed in this table are available in both ESXi and ESX. The product vSphere hypervisor refers to the free offering of ESXi. This edition can be run only as a standalone host and the API for this edition limits scripts to read-only functions. With the other license editions, you have the option of running ESXi or ESX. This allows you to run a mixed environment if you plan to make a gradual migration to ESXi. If you are considering the Essentials or Essentials Plus license editions, these are available in license kits that include vCenter Server Foundation; they are limited to three physical hosts.

Beginning with host capabilities, both ESXi and ESX support up to 256GB of host memory for most licensed editions and an unlimited amount of memory when either is licensed at the Enterprise Plus level. Both editions support either 6 or 12 cores per physical processor slot depending on the license edition that you choose. As support for ESXi has increased, hardware vendors have improved certification testing for ESXi, and you'll find that support for ESXi and ESX is nearly identical. With the exception of the free VMware hypervisor offering, all license additions include a vCenter Server Agent license. The process of adding or removing host to vCenter Server is identical between ESXi and ESX, as is the case for assigning licenses to specific hosts in your datacenter.

Tip: If you plan to install ESXi with hardware components such as storage controllers or network cards that are not on VMware's Hardware Compatibility List (HCL), you should check with the vendor for specific installation instructions. ESXi does not enable you to add device drivers manually during the installation process as you can with ESX.

The following are some of the common features worth mentioning. When you are configuring these features with the vSphere client, in almost all cases you won't see any distinctions between working with ESXi and ESX. Thin Provisioning is a feature designed to provide a higher level of storage utilization. Prior to vSphere, when a virtual machine was created the entire space for the virtual disk was allocated on your storage datastore. This could lead to a waste of space when the virtual machines did not use the storage allocated. With Thin Provisioning, storage used by virtual disks is dynamically allocated, allowing for the overallocation of storage to achieve higher utilization. Improvements in vCenter Server alerts allow for the monitoring of datastore usage to ensure that datastores retain sufficient free space for snapshot and other management files. vSphere also introduced the ability to grow datastores dynamically. With ESXi and ESX, if a datastore is running low on space, you no longer have to rely on using extents or migrating virtual machines to another datastore. Rather, the array storing the Virtual Machine File System (VMFS) datastore can be expanded using the management software for your storage system and then the datastore can be extended using the vSphere client or the vCLI.

Table 1.1 vSphere Feature List

	vSphere Hypervisor	Essentials	Essentials Plus	Standard	Advanced	Enterprise	Enterprise Plus
Host Capabilities							
Memory per Host	256GB	256GB	256GB	256GB	256GB	256GB	Unlimited
Cores per Processor	6	6	6	6	12	6	12
vCenter Agent License	Not Included	X	X	X	X	X	X
Product Features							
Thin Provisioning	X	X	X	X	X	X	X
Update Manager		X	X	X	X	X	X
vStorage APIs for Data Protection		X	X	X	X	X	X
Data Recovery			X	Sold separately	X	X	X
High Availability			X	X	X	X	X
vMotion			X	X	X	X	X
Virtual Serial Port Concentrator					X	X	X
Hot Add Memory or CPU					X	X	X
vShield Zones					X	X	X
Fault Tolerance					X	X	X
vStorage APIs for Array Integration					X	X	X

vStorage APIs for Multipathing	X	X
Storage vMotion	X	X
Distributed Resources Scheduler	X	X
Distributed Power Management	X	X
Storage I/O Control	X	
Network I/O Control	X	
Distributed Switch	X	
Host Profiles	X	

Update Manager is a feature to simplify the management of patches for ESXi, ESX, and virtual machines within your infrastructure. Use of this feature is covered in Chapter 10, "Patching and Updating ESXi." While the patching processes for ESXi and ESX are significantly different, Update Manager provides a unified view to keeping both flavors of vSphere up to date.

vMotion, High Availability (HA), Distributed Resource Scheduler (DRS), Storage vMotion, and Fault Tolerance (FT) are some of the features included with vSphere to ensure a high level of availability for your virtual machines. Configuration of HA and DRS clusters is the same regardless of whether you choose ESXi or ESX, and you can run mixed clusters to allow for a gradual migration to ESXi from ESX.

The VMware vNetwork Distributed Switch (dvSwitch) provides centralized configuration of networking for hosts within your vCenter Server datacenter. Rather than configuring networking on a host-by-host level, you can centralize configuration and monitoring of your virtual networking to eliminate the risk of a configuration mistake at the host level, which could lead to downtime or a security compromise of a virtual machine.

The last feature this section highlights is Host Profiles. This feature is discussed in subsequent chapters. Host Profiles are used to standardize and simplify how you manage your vSphere host configurations. With Host Profiles, you capture a policy that contains the configuration of networking, storage, security settings, and other features from a properly configured host. That policy can then be applied to other hosts to ensure configuration compliance and, if necessary, an incompliant host can be updated with the policy to ensure that all your hosts maintain a proper configuration. This is one of the features that, although available with both ESXi and ESX, reflects the architectural changes between the two products. A Host Profile that you create for your ESX host may include settings for the COS. Such settings do not apply to ESXi. Likewise, with ESXi, you can configure the service settings for the DCUI, but these settings are not applicable to ESX.

Product Differences

When ESXi was first released, VMware documented a comparison between the two hypervisors that highlighted some of the differences between the products. New Knowledge Base (KB) articles were published as subsequent versions of ESXi were released. The following list documents the Knowledge Base articles for each release:

- ESXi 3.5: http://kb.vmware.com/kb/1006543

- ESXi 4.0: http://kb.vmware.com/kb/1015000

- ESXi 4.1: http://kb.vmware.com/kb/1023990

These KB articles make worthwhile reading, as they highlight the work that VMware has done to bring management parity to VMware ESXi. The significant differences are summarized in Table 1.2.

Table 1.2 ESXi and ESX Differences

Capability	ESX 3.5	ESX 4.0	ESX 4.1	ESXi 3.5	ESXi 4.0	ESXi 4.1
Service Console (COS)	Present	Present	Present	Removed	Removed	Removed
Command-Line Interface	COS	COS + vCLI	COS + vCLI	RCLI	PowerCLI + vCLI	PowerCLI + vCLI
Advanced Troubleshooting	COS	COS	COS	Tech Support Mode	Tech Support Mode	Tech Support Mode
Scripted Installations	X	X	X			X
Boot from SAN	X	X	X			X
SNMP	X	X	X	Limited	Limited	Limited
Active Directory Integration	3rd Party in COS	3rd Party in COS	X			X
Hardware Monitoring	3rd Party COS Agents	3rd Party COS Agents	3rd Party COS Agents	CIM Providers	CIM Providers	CIM Providers
Web Access	X	X				
Host Serial Port Connectivity	X	X	X		X	
Jumbo Frames	X	X	X		X	X

The significant architectural difference between ESX and ESXi is the removal of the Linux COS. This change has an impact on a number of related aspects, including installation, CLI configuration, hardware monitoring, and advanced troubleshooting. With ESX, the COS is a Linux environment that provides privileged access to the ESX VMkernel. Within the COS, you can manage your host by executing commands and scripts, adding device drivers, and installing Linux-based management agents. As seen previously in this chapter, ESXi was designed to make a server a virtualization appliance. Thus, ESXi behaves more like a firmware-based device than a traditional OS. ESXi includes the vSphere API, which is used to access the VMkernel by management or monitoring applications.

CLI configuration for ESX is accomplished via the COS. Common tasks involve items such as managing users, managing virtual machines, and configuring networking. With ESXi 3.5, the RCLI was provided as an installation package for Linux and Windows, as well as in the form of a virtual management appliance. Some COS commands such as `esxcfg-info`, `esxcfg-resgrp`, and `esxcfg-swiscsi` were not available in the initial RCLI, making a wholesale migration to ESXi difficult for diehard COS users. Subsequent releases of the vCLI have closed those gaps, and VMware introduced PowerCLI, which provides another scripting option for managing ESXi. The COS on ESX has also provided a valuable troubleshooting avenue that allows administrators to issue commands to diagnose and report support issues. With the removal of the COS, ESXi offers several alternatives for this type of access. First, the DCUI enables the user to repair or reset the system configuration as well as to restart management agents and to view system logs. Second, the vCLI provides a number of commands, such as `vmware-cmd` and `resxtop`, which can be used to remotely diagnose issues. The vCLI is explored further in Chapter 8, and relevant examples are posted throughout the other chapters in this book. Last, ESXi provides Tech Support Mode (TSM), which allows low-level access to the VMkernel so that you can run diagnostic commands. TSM can be accessed at the console of ESXi or remotely via Secure Shell (SSH). TSM is not intended for production use, but it provides an environment similar to the COS for advanced troubleshooting and configuration.

Two gaps between ESXi and ESX when ESXi was first released were scripted installs and Boot from SAN. ESX supports KickStart, which can be used to fully automate installations. As you will see in subsequent chapters, ESXi is extremely easy and fast to install, but it was initially released without the ability to automate installations, making deployment in large environments more tedious. While the vCLI could be used to provide post-installation configuration, there was not an automated method to deploy ESXi until support for scriptable installations was added in ESXi 4.1. With ESXi 4.1, scripted installations are supported using a mechanism similar to KickStart, including the ability to run pre- and post-installation scripts. VMware ESX also supports Boot from SAN. With this model, a dedicated logical unit number (LUN) must be configured for each host. With the capability to run as an embedded hypervisor, prior versions of ESXi were able to operate in a similar manner without the need for local storage. With the release of ESXi 4.1, Boot from SAN is now supported as an option for ESXi Installable.

ESX supports Simple Network Management Protocol (SNMP) for both get and trap operations. SNMP is further discussed in Chapter 6. Configuration of SNMP on ESX is accomplished in the COS and it is possible to add additional SNMP agents within the COS to provide hardware monitoring. ESXi offers only limited SNMP support. Only SNMP trap operations are supported and it is not possible to install additional SNMP agents.

It has always been possible to integrate ESX with Active Directory (AD) through the use of third-party agents, allowing administrators to log in directly to ESX with an AD account and eliminating the need to use the root account for administrative tasks. Configuration of this feature was accomplished within the COS. With vSphere 4.1, both editions now support AD integration and configuration can be accomplished via the vSphere client, Host Profiles, or with the vCLI. This is demonstrated in Chapter 6.

Hardware monitoring of ESX has been accomplished via agent software installed within the COS. Monitoring software can communicate directly with the agents to ascertain hardware health and other hardware statistics. This is not an option with the firmware model employed with ESXi, and as discussed earlier, hardware health is provided by standards-based CIM providers. VMware partners are able to develop their own proprietary CIM providers to augment the basic health information that is reported by the ESXi standard providers.

The initial version of ESX was configured and managed via a Web-based interface with only a simple Windows application required on a management computer to access the console of a virtual machine. This feature was available in later versions of ESX, and via Web browser plug-ins, it was possible to provide a basic management interface to ESX without the need for a client installation on the management computer. Due to the lean nature of the ESXi system image, this option is not available. It is possible to provide this functionality to ESXi hosts that are managed with vCenter Server.

Via the COS, ESX has supported connecting a host's serial ports to a virtual machine. This capability provided the option to virtualize servers that required physical connectivity to a serial port–based device connected to the host. This option has not been available with ESXi until the release of ESXi 4.1. When configuring a serial port on a virtual machine, you can select between the option of Use Physical Serial Port on the Host, Output to File, Connect to Named Pipe, and Connect via Network. The Connect via Network option refers to the Virtual Serial Port Concentrator feature that is discussed in the "What's New with ESXi 4.1" section. If you require connectivity to serial port–based devices for your virtual machines and the ability to migrate virtual machines, you should investigate using a serial over IP-device. With such a device, a virtual machine is no longer tethered to a specific ESXi host and can be migrated with vMotion between hosts, as connectivity between the serial device and the virtual machine occurs over the network.

The last item mentioned in Table 1.2 is support for jumbo frames. The initial release of ESXi supported jumbo frames only within virtual machines and not for VMkernel traffic. Other minor network features, such as support for NetQueue and the Cisco Discovery Protocol, were also not available. These gaps in functionality were closed with ESXi 4.0.

As you have seen in the preceding section, in terms of function, there is no difference between ESXi and ESX, and the great features such as vMotion and HA that you've used function the same as you migrate to ESXi. The removal of the COS could pose a significant challenge in your migration. Over the last few releases of ESXi, VMware has made significant progress to provide tools that replicate the tasks that you have performed with the COS. If you have made heavy use of the COS, you should carefully plan how those scripts will be executed with ESXi. Subsequent chapters look more closely at using the vCLI and PowerCLI to perform some of the tasks that you have performed in the COS. You should also review any COS agents and third-party tools that you may utilize to ensure that you have a supported equivalent with ESXi. Lastly, because of the removal of the COS, ESXi does not have a Service Console port. Rather, the functionality provided to ESX through the Service Console port is handled by the VMkernel port in ESXi.

What's New with vSphere 4.1

Each new release from VMware of its virtual infrastructure suite has always included innovative new features and improvements to make management of your infrastructure easier. The release of vSphere 4.1 is no different and includes over 150 improvements and new features. These range in improvements to vCenter Server, ESXi, and virtual machine capabilities. Comprehensive documentation can be found at the link http://www.vmware.com/products/vsphere/midsize-and-enterprise-business/resources.html.

One significant change is that vCenter Server ships only as a 64-bit version. This reflects a common migration of enterprise applications to 64-bit only. This change also removes the performance limitations of running on a 32-bit OS. Along with other performance and scalability enhancements, this change allows vCenter to respond more quickly, perform more concurrent tasks, and manage more virtual machines per datacenter. Concurrent vMotion operations per 1 Gigabit Ethernet (GbE) link have been increased to 4 and up to 8 for 10GbE links. If your existing vCenter installation is on a 32-bit server and you want to update your deployment to vCenter 4.1, you have to install vCenter 4.1 on a new 64-bit server and migrate the existing vCenter database. This process is documented in Chapter 5, "Migrating from ESX." For existing vCenter 4.0 installations running on a 64-bit OS, an in-place upgrade may be performed.

vSphere 4.1 now includes integration with AD to allow seamless authentication when connecting directly to VMware ESXi. vCenter Server has always provided integration with AD, but now with AD integration you no longer have to maintain local user accounts on your ESXi host or use the root account for direct host configuration. AD integration is enabled on the Authentication Services screen as shown in Figure 1.4. Once your ESXi host has been joined to your domain, you may assign privileges to users or groups that are applied when a user connects directly to ESXi using the vSphere client, vCLI, or other application that communicates with ESXi via the vSphere API.

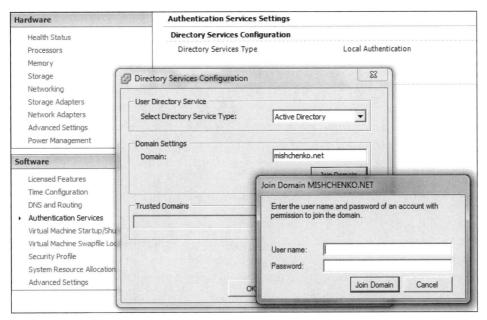

Figure 1.4 Configuring Active Directory integration on VMware ESXi.

A number of enhancements have been added to Host Profiles since the feature was introduced in vSphere 4.0. These include the following additional configuration settings:

- With support for configuration of the root password, users can easily update this account password on the vSphere 4.1 hosts in their environment.

- User privileges that you can configure from the vSphere client on a host can now be configured through Host Profiles.

- Configuration of physical network interface cards (NICs) can now be accomplished using the device's Peripheral Component Interconnect (PCI) ID. This aids in network configuration in your environment if you employ separate physical NICs for different types of traffic such as management, storage, or virtual machine traffic.

- Host Profiles can be used to configure AD integration. When the profile is applied to a new host, you only have to supply credentials with the appropriate rights to join a computer to the domain.

A number of new features and enhancements have been made that impact virtual machine operation. Memory overhead has been reduced, especially for large virtual machines running on systems that provide hardware memory management unit (MMU) support. Memory Compression provides a new layer to enhance memory overcommit technology. This layer exists between the use of ballooning and disk swapping and is discussed further in Chapter 6. It is now possible to pass through USB devices connected to a host into a virtual machine. This could include devices such as security dongles and mass storage devices. When a USB device is connected to an ESXi host, that device is made available to virtual machines running on that host. The USB Arbitrator host component manages USB connection requests and routes USB device traffic to the appropriate virtual machine. A USB device can be used in only a single virtual machine at a time. Certain features such as Fault Tolerance and Distributed Power Management are not compatible with virtual machines using USB device passthrough, but a virtual machine can be migrated using vMotion and the USB connection will persist after the migration. After a virtual machine with a USB device is migrated using vMotion, the USB devices remain connected to the original host and continue to function until the virtual machine is suspended or powered down. At that point, the virtual machine would need to be migrated back to the original host to reconnect to the USB device.

Some environments use serial port console connections to manage physical hosts, as these connections provide a low-bandwidth option to connect to servers. vSphere 4.1 offers the Virtual Serial Port Concentrator (vSPC) to enable this management option for virtual machines. The vSPC feature allows redirection of a virtual machine's serial ports over the network using telnet or SSH. With the use of third-party virtual serial port concentrators, virtual machines can be managed in the same convenient and secure manner as physical hosts. The vSPC settings are enabled on a virtual machine as shown in Figure 1.5.

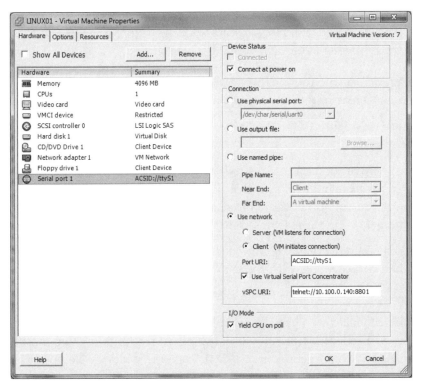

Figure 1.5 Enabling the Virtual Serial Port Concentrator setting on a virtual machine.

vSphere 4.1 includes a number of storage-related enhancements to improve performance, monitoring, and troubleshooting. ESXi 4.1 supports Boot from SAN for iSCSI, Fibre Channel, and Fibre Channel over Ethernet (FCOE). Boot from SAN provides a number of benefits, including cheaper servers, which can be denser and require less cooling; easier host replacement, as there is no local storage; and centralized storage management. ESXi Boot from iSCSI SAN is supported on network adapters capable of using the iSCSI Boot Firmware Table (iBFT) format. Consult the HCL at http://www.vmware.com/go/hcl for a list of adapters that are supported for booting ESXi from an iSCSI SAN. vSphere 4.1 also adds support for 8GB Fibre Channel Host Bus Adapters (HBAs). With 8GB HBAs, throughput to Fibre Channel SANs is effectively doubled. For improved iSCSI performance, ESXi enables 10GB iSCSI hardware offloads (Broadcom 57111) and 1GB iSCSI hardware offloads (Broadcom 5709). Broadcom iSCSI offload technology enables on-chip processing of iSCSI traffic, freeing up host central processing unit (CPU) resources for virtual machine usage.

Storage I/O Control enables storage prioritization across a cluster of ESXi hosts that access the same datastore. This feature extends the familiar concept of shares and limits that is available for the CPU and memory on a host. Configuration of shares and limits is handled on a per-virtual-machine basis, but Storage I/O Control enforces storage access by evaluating the total share allocation for all virtual machines regardless of the host that the virtual machine is running on. This ensures that low-priority virtual machines running on one host do not have the equivalent I/O slots that are being allocated to high-priority virtual machines on another host. Should Storage I/O Control detect that the average I/O latency for a datastore has exceeded a configured threshold, it begins to allocate I/O slots according to the shares allocated to the virtual machines that access the datastore. Configuration of Storage I/O Control is discussed further in Chapter 3.

The vStorage API for Array Integration (VAAI) is a new API available for storage partners to use as a means of offloading specific storage functions in order to improve performance. With the 4.1 release of vSphere, the VAAI offload capability supports the following three capabilities:

- **Full copy.** This enables the array to make full copies of data within the array without requiring the ESXi host to read or write the data.

- **Block zeroing.** The storage array handles zeroing out blocks during the provisioning of virtual machines.

- **Hardware-assisted locking.** This provides an alternative to small computer systems interface (SCSI) reservations as a means to protect VMFS metadata.

The full-copy aspect of VAAI provides significant performance benefits when deploying new virtual machines, especially in a virtual desktop environment where hundreds of new virtual machines may be deployed in a short period. Without the full copy option, the ESXi host is responsible for the read-and-write operations required to deploy a new virtual machine. With full copy, these operations are offloaded to the array, which significantly reduces the time required as well as reducing CPU and storage network load on the ESXi host. Full copy can also reduce the time required to perform a Storage vMotion operation, as the copy of the virtual disk data is handled by the array on VAAI-capable hardware and does not need to pass to and from the ESXi host.

Block zeroing also improves the performance of allocating new virtual disks, as the array is able to report to ESXi that the process is complete immediately while in reality it is being completed as a background process. Without VAAI, the ESXi host must wait until the array has completed the zeroing process to complete the task of creating a virtual disk, which can be time-consuming for large virtual disks.

The third enhancement for VAAI is hardware-assisted locking. This provides a more granular option to protect VMFS metadata than SCSI reservations. Hardware-assisted locking uses a storage array atomic test and set capability to enable a fine-grained block-level locking mechanism. Any VMFS operation that allocates space, such as the starting or creating of virtual machines, results in VFMS having to allocate space, which in the past has required a SCSI reservation to ensure the integrity of the VMFS metadata on datastores shared by many ESXi hosts. Hardware-assisted locking provides a more efficient manner to protect the metadata.

You can consult the vSphere HCL to see whether your storage array supports any of these VAAI features. It is likely that your array would require a firmware update to enable support. You would also have to enable one of the advanced settings shown in Table 1.3, as these features are not enabled by default.

The storage enhancements in vSphere 4.1 also include new performance metrics to expand troubleshooting and monitoring capabilities for both the vSphere client and the vCLI command resxtop. These include new metrics for NFS devices to close the gap in metrics that existed between NFS storage and block-based storage. Additional throughput and latency statistics are available for viewing all datastore activity from an ESXi host, as well as for a specific storage adapter and path. At the virtual machine level, it is also possible to view throughput and latency statistics for virtual disks or for the datastores used by the virtual machine.

vSphere 4.1 also includes a number of innovative networking features. ESXi now supports Internet Protocol Security (IPSec) for communication coming from and arriving at an ESXi host for

Table 1.3 Advanced Settings to Enable VAAI

VAAI Feature	Advanced Configuration Setting
Full Copy	DataMover.HardwareAcceleratedMove
Block Zeroing	DataMover.HardwareAcceleratedInit
Hardware-Assisted Locking	VMFS3.HardwareAcceleratedLocking

IPv6 traffic. When you configure IPSec on your ESXi host, you are able to authenticate and encrypt incoming and outgoing packets according to the security associations and policies that you configure. Configuration of IPSec is discussed in Chapter 7. With ESXi 4.1, IPSec is supported for the following traffic types:

- Virtual machine

- vSphere client and vCenter Server

- vMotion

- ESXi management

- IP storage (iSCSI, NFS)—this is experimentally supported

IPSec for ESXi is not supported for use with the vCLI, for VMware HA, or for VMware FT logging.

Network I/O Control is a new network traffic management feature for dvSwitches. Network I/O Control implements a software scheduler within the dvSwitch to isolate and prioritize traffic types on the links that connect your ESXi host to your physical network. This feature is especially helpful if you plan to run multiple traffic types over a paired set of 10GbE interfaces, as might be the case with blade servers. In such a case, Network I/O Control would ensure that virtual machine network traffic, for example, would not interfere with the performance of IP-based storage traffic.

Network I/O Control is able to recognize the following traffic types leaving a dvSwitch on ESXi:

- Virtual machine

- Management

- iSCSI

- NFS

- Fault Tolerance logging

- vMotion

Network I/O Control uses shares and limits to control traffic leaving the dvSwitch. These values are configured on the Resource Allocation tab as shown in Figure 1.6. Shares specify the relative importance of a traffic type being transmitted to the host's physical NICs. The share settings work the same as for CPU and memory resources on an ESXi host. If there is no resource contention, a traffic type could consume the entire network link for the dvSwitch. However, if two traffic types begin to saturate a network link, shares come into play in determining how much bandwidth is to be allocated for each traffic type.

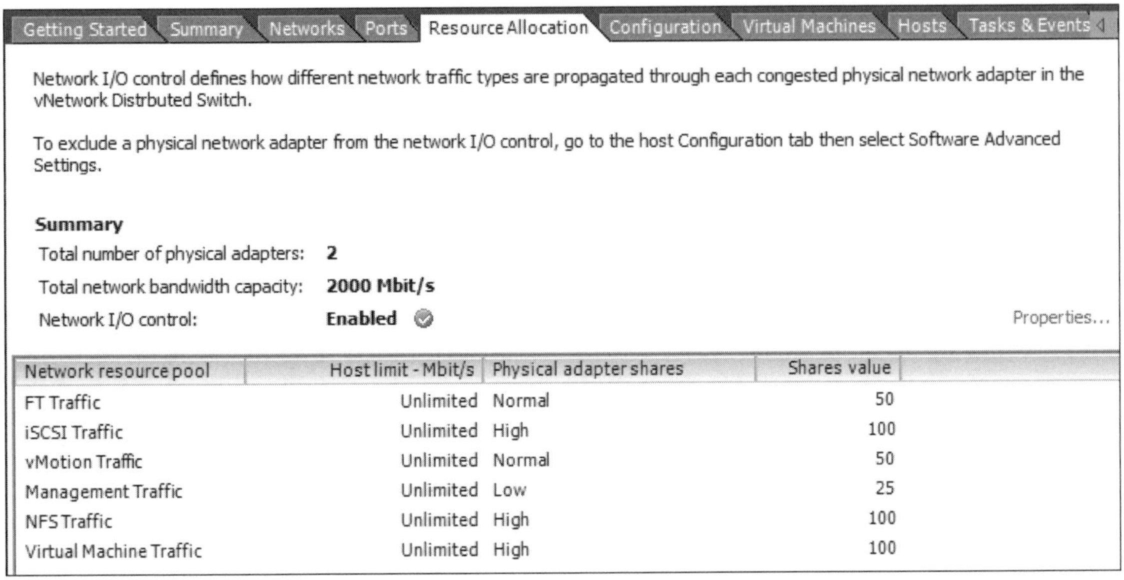
Getting Started
Summary
Networks
Ports
Resource Allocation
Configuration
Virtual Machines
Hosts
Tasks & Events
Network I/O control defines how different network traffic types are propagated through each congested physical network adapter in the vNetwork Distrbuted Switch.
To exclude a physical network adapter from the network I/O control, go to the host Configuration tab then select Software Advanced Settings.
Summary
Total number of physical adapters: 2
Total network bandwidth capacity: 2000 Mbit/s
Network I/O control: Enabled
Properties...
Network resource pool | Host limit - Mbit/s | Physical adapter shares | Shares value
FT Traffic | Unlimited | Normal | 50
iSCSI Traffic | Unlimited | High | 100
vMotion Traffic | Unlimited | Normal | 50
Management Traffic | Unlimited | Low | 25
NFS Traffic | Unlimited | High | 100
Virtual Machine Traffic | Unlimited | High | 100

Figure 1.6 Configuring shares and limits for Network I/O Control.

Limit values are used to specify the maximum limit that can be used by a traffic type. If you configure limits, the values are specified in megabits per second (Mbps). Limits are imposed before shares and limits apply over a team of NICs. Shares, on the other hand, schedule and prioritize traffic for each physical NIC in a team.

Note: Configuration of iSCSI traffic resource pool shares do not apply to iSCSI traffic generated by iSCSI HBAs in your host.

The last new networking feature that this section highlights is Load-Based Teaming (LBT). This is another management feature for dvSwitches designed to avoid network congestion on ESXi physical NICs caused by imbalances in the mapping of traffic to those uplinks. LBT is an additional load-balancing policy available on the Teaming and Failover policy for a port group on a dvSwitch. This option appears in the list as "Route Based on Physical NIC Load." LBT works to adjust manually the mapping of virtual ports to physical NICs to balance network load leaving and entering the dvSwitch. If ESXi detects congestion on a network link signified by 75 percent or more utilization over a 30-second period, LBT attempts to move one or more virtual ports to a less utilized link within the dvSwitch.

Note: The vSphere client is no longer bundled with ESXi and ESX builds. Once you have completed an installation of either product, the link on the Welcome page redirects you to a download of the vSphere client from VMware's Web site. The vSphere client is still available for download from the Welcome page for vCenter Server.

Conclusion

VMware ESXi represents a significant step forward in hypervisor design and provides an efficient manner for turning servers into virtualization appliances. With ESXi, you have the same great features that you've been using with ESX. Both can be run side by side in the same clusters to allow you to perform a gradual migration to ESXi. With the removal of the COS, ESXi does not have any dependencies on a general operating system, which improves security and reliability. For seasoned COS administrators, VMware has provided two feature-rich alternatives with the vCLI and PowerCLI. ESXi includes the vSphere API, which eliminates the need for COS agents for management and backup systems. ESXi also leverages the CIM model to provide agentless hardware monitoring.

2 Getting Started with a Quick Install

In Chapter 1, "Introduction to VMware ESXi 4.1," you had a broad overview of VMware ESXi, including its architecture and management model. You also reviewed how VMware ESXi compared to and differed with VMware ESX. In this chapter, you will learn how to begin using VMware ESXi. This will include a discussion of:

- Hardware requirements for running VMware ESXi

- A basic installation of VMware ESXi Installable

- Postinstallation configuration for VMware ESXi

- Installation of the vSphere Client

Determining Hardware and Software Requirements

One of the critical decisions you'll make in implementing VMware ESXi is the hardware you'll use for your project. If you've worked with earlier versions of ESX, you'll be aware that the Hardware Compatibility List (HCL) for VMware vSphere is much stricter than for that of other operating systems that you might install, such as Linux or Windows. VMware tends not to support a broad range of hardware for vSphere; the support offered instead focuses on a smaller number of systems and devices that have been thoroughly tested, resulting in end-user experiences of higher hardware stability.

The best place to start your search for hardware is the HCL at www.vmware.com/go/hcl. Many vendors have systems listed, and you're likely to find a number of systems that have been certified by your preferred hardware vendor. Some vendors will also maintain their own specific HCL for vSphere ESX and ESXi, so it is worthwhile to check their Web sites to have access to the latest hardware support data. When you review a system on VMware's HCL, you will want to check the notes for the system to see whether there are any special requirements and verify that the system has been certified with ESXi. In some cases, the system may be certified for either ESXi or ESX but not both.

Sizing a server is beyond the scope of this book, but the process you use to select your hardware will be the same as it would be if you were selecting a system for vSphere ESX. VMware

ESXi 4.1 will run on 64-bit CPUs with a 1 CPU core all the way up to systems with 64 logical processors (the logical processor count per host is defined as CPU sockets × cores/socket × threads/core). Likewise, for memory ESXi can scale from a minimum of 2GB to 1TB for host memory. Thus, you'll be able to make a choice between scaling out with more systems that have fewer CPUs and memory or scaling up with fewer systems with more CPUs and memory. As you'll find on the HCL, ESXi is also supported on all form factors, including rack mount, blade, and pedestal.

Your choice of storage architecture is also an important part of your hardware decision. Many advanced features of vSphere, such as vMotion and Fault Tolerance, require shared storage, so you will be looking at Fibre Channel, Internet Small Computer System Interface (iSCSI) or Network File System (NFS) storage for your ESXi hosts. The HCL lists the supported storage options and compatibility for host bus adapters as well. As with selecting a server, it is import that you review the notes for your potential storage solution to check specific compatibility with ESXi and to see whether there are any specific requirements for an officially supported system.

Your networking hardware is also an important part of your hardware decision. Practically, you'll just require a single network interface card (NIC) port to get started, but if you are deploying in a rack server environment with 1GB network links, your ESXi deployment will typically use six NIC ports to allocate to management traffic, virtual machine traffic, and storage traffic allowing for redundant network links. In a blade server environment, you may have fewer network ports per server, so you may have to combine network types onto a fewer number of NICs using virtual local area networks (VLANs). Likewise, as 10GB networking becomes a more viable option, you may design your host with two network ports and separate your network traffic types solely with VLANs. Although it won't be required for most deployments of ESXi, your networking hardware must be capable of supporting up to 32 NIC ports depending on the model of network card selected. With ESXi, you won't be configuring any Service Console ports as you would with ESX, but you will still want to separate the VMkernel port used for management either physically with additional NIC ports or logically with VLANs from the virtual machine network load as well as isolating VMkernel ports used for storage, vMotion, and Fault Tolerance.

VMware ESXi does depart in similarity with ESX on a few installation disk options. Unlike ESX, ESXi is only experimentally supported for installation on a storage area network (SAN) logical unit number (LUN). However, ESXi is supported for installation on flash devices. ESXi Embedded is deployed on a flash drive device and, starting with ESXi Installable 4.0, you can now install ESXi onto a supported flash device. Should you want to install ESXi Installable onto a flash device, you should verify the vender's support of this option. With Hewlett Packard (HP), for example, you can install ESXi onto an HP 4GB SD Flash device (HP part number 580387-B21). If you choose HP's BL460 G6 blade models, you can simply slide a blade out of the chassis, insert the SD card, and be ready to install ESXi onto a diskless server. Using a flash device may not be seen as such a reliable choice for a local install of ESXi as using physical disks, but it is important to note that once ESXi has booted, most of its system disk activity occurs within the RAM drive that is created each time that ESXi boots and not to the universal serial bus (USB) device. Likewise, if you plan to use only local storage with ESXi, you need not split disk input/output (I/O) for your VMFS datastore and the ESXi install, because ESXi does not impose a significant load on the physical disks for system I/O.

Tip: When you start your deployment of VMware ESXi, you'll ideally start with a lab environment to get familiar with the software. You may not have HCL hardware for that purpose, but that shouldn't stop you from getting a lab environment up and running. If you have some older 64-bit servers around that have been on the HCL in the past, those might work fine with ESXi or you can check out VMware's Community Hardware list at http:// communities.vmware.com/community/vmtn/general/cshwsw. If you have the right workstation, you can also run VMware ESXi within a virtual machine on VMware Workstation. With sufficient CPU resources and 8GB of memory, you can create an ESXi environment on your PC including two ESXi virtual machines and one virtual machine for running vCenter Server and iSCSI or NFS for shared storage. Chapter 4, "Installation Options," will include some instructions for running ESXi as a virtual machine should you choose to go this route for a training environment.

Installing VMware ESXi

As noted in the introduction, VMware ESXi is available in the following two different versions: VMware ESXi Embedded and VMware ESXi Installable. Both versions function identically but have different deployment methods. This quick install with VMware ESXi will use the Installable version. The installation CD-ROM (ISO) image can be downloaded from VMware's download site at http://www.vmware.com/downloads. The download for VMware ESXi is available as part the vSphere product downloads. You select to download the ISO image for VMware ESXi and after accepting the End User License Agreement, you can download the image via your Web browser or with VMware's download manager.

Tip: The download page for the VMware ESXi ISO image lists both an md5sum and sha1sum checksum for the download. To ensure that the download was successful, it is worthwhile to verify the checksum. On a Linux PC, you can run md5sum <filename> to generate the value, or for a Windows PC, a number of shareware downloads, such as MD5summer from http://www.md5summer.org/, are available to generate a checksum. If the value generated does not match the value posted on the download page, you should download the VMware ESXi image again.

If you are planning to install VMware ESXi on a Dell, HP, or IBM server, you need to download a customized install image for those brands. These customized installation images include enhanced Common Information Model (CIM) providers that can collect information on the following:

- **Software inventory.** CIM provider versions, Basic Input/Output System (BIOS) versions, and Ethernet adapter driver versions.

- **Storage providers.** Redundant Array of Independent Disks (RAID) controllers, enclosures, physical drive status, and logical volume information.

- **Networking providers.** Ethernet ports, port link status, statistics, Internet Protocol (IP) and Media Access Control (MAC) addresses.

- **PCI providers.** Peripheral Component Interconnect (PCI) devices, adapter card and slot information.

- **Sensor providers.** Server intrusion, system temperature for components such as central processing unit (CPU) and memory, system board voltage, and system fan speeds.

The customized images also provide improved integration for VMware ESXi with these vendors' system management packages, such as HP Systems Insight Manager or Dell OpenManage Server Administrator, and enables better monitoring and management of your host. When a new version of VMware ESXi is released, for example ESXi 4.1, a vendor customized image is released as well. That is also the case for update releases that represent a minor version change for VMware ESXi. When ESXi 4.1 Update 1 is released, you will also see a vender release for that specific update. These customized releases can sometimes lag behind the general release for a VMware ESXi version, but improvements in the CIM providers make the delay worthwhile and it's best to check with the vendor's Web site to see whether the current VMware ESXi release has a customized version released.

Adding CIM Support to the Generic ESXi Installable Image Some hardware vendors have begun to release offline update packages that add CIM support to the generic ESXi installation image. These offline bundles can also include support for new storage and networking devices. The bundles utilize the vSphere Installation Bundle (VIB) format, a new patch format from VMware that is intended to provide a common patch and update format across all VMware platforms. These offline bundles can be used to add vendor-specific CIM providers to the generic ESXi image, or to update a vendor-specific install image so that your host is running the latest CIM providers and drivers.

The vSphere Command-Line Interface (vCLI) command set allows you to run common administrative commands for the VMware ESXi host from any management PC with network access to the host. The vCLI will be explored in depth in Chapter 8, "Scripting and Automation with the vCLI," but throughout the book relevant examples will be provided.

To update your ESXi host with an offline bundle, you'll use the `vihostupdate` command. To begin the update process, you'll need to download the appropriate offline bundle to update the CIM providers on your ESXi host. For this example, HP's bundle will be used; you can find the latest version by searching for `ESXi offline bundle` on HP's Web site. Once you have downloaded the update bundle, you can update your ESXi host with the following process:

1. Once you have downloaded the offline bundle zip to the workstation where you have the vCLI installed, you'll first want to power down all running virtual machines on the ESXi host and put the host in maintenance mode. You can put a host in maintenance mode with the vSphere client or using the `vicfg-hostops` command in the vCLI as follows:

    ```
    vicfg-hostops --server esx05.mishchenko.net --operation enter
    Host esx05.mishchenko.net entered into maintenance mode successfully.
    ```

2. You can then use the `vihostupdate` command with the `list` and `scan` options to check the offline bundle. The `list` option shows the bulletins that are contained within the bundle. The `scan` option shows you which bulletins will apply to the host you want to patch, as follows:

    ```
    vihostupdate --server esx05.mishchenko.net --scan
        --bundle c:\tmp\hp-esxi4.0uX-bundle-1.2.zip
    ---------Bulletin ID----------   ---------------Summary----------------
    hpq-esxi4.0uX-bundle-1.2         HP ESXi Bundle 1.2
    ```

3. To install the bundle, run the `vihostupdate` command again with the `install` option. Once the operation has completed, you will need to reboot the host.

4. Once the host has rebooted, you need to take it out of maintenance mode. Otherwise you will not be able to start any virtual machines. This can be done in the vSphere client or using the `vicfg-hostops` command with the `exit` option. To query your ESXi host to see whether the offline bundle was installed, use the `vihostupdate` command with the `query` option.

Once you have downloaded the VMware ESXi ISO image, you can burn it to a CD or mount it to the server's remote control card if it is equipped with one. VMware ESXi is supported for remote installation with Dell Remote Access Card (DRAC) 4/ 5, HP Integrated Lights-Out (iLO), and iLO2 and IBM Remote Supervisor Adapter (RSA) cards. If you choose to install via a remote management card, you should ensure that the card has been upgraded to a recent firmware release, as only specific versions are supported for remote installations.

To begin the installation process, ensure that the server is set to boot from the host's CD-ROM or the remote control card's virtual CD-ROM. If you are reconfiguring the host's BIOS, it is a good

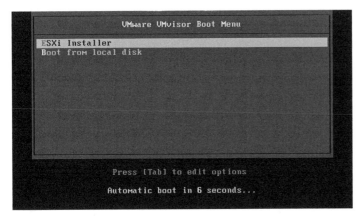

Figure 2.1   The VMware VMvisor boot menu.

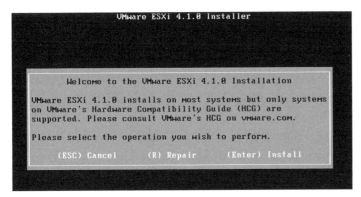

Figure 2.2   Installation welcome screen showing the three installation options.

opportunity to check other BIOS settings such as Intel Virtualization (VT-x) or Intel Directed I/O (VT-d). You should enable the VT-x option if you intend to use 64-bit operating systems in your virtual machines. You will want to enable the VT-d option if you want to use VMDirectPath with your virtual machines. Once the host begins to boot from the VMware ESXi Installable CD, the VMware VMvisor boot menu appears, as shown in Figure 2.1. At this screen, it is possible to add pass boot options to the VMkernel that will boot for the install process. This may be necessary to support installation on your hardware, or it can be used to start an installation script.

The installer welcome screen shown in Figure 2.2 will be displayed once the VMkernel has completed the boot process. Pressing the Esc key will cancel the install process, shut down the VMkernel, and restart the host. The Repair option will perform a repair process on the system partitions for VMware ESXi; this process will be covered later in Chapter 11, "Under the Hood with the ESXi Tech Support Mode." Press the Enter key to proceed with the installation process.

The next screen displays the End User License Agreement (EULA) for VMware ESXi. You can use the arrow keys to scroll through the EULA and then press F11 to continue the installation process. The VMkernel will then scan the storage connected to the host and present visible disks on the

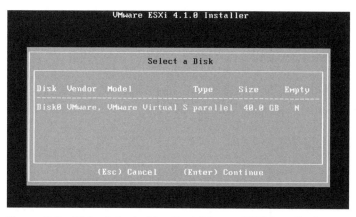

Figure 2.3   Disks detected by the VMware ESXi installation process.

Select a Disk screen displayed in Figure 2.3. If your host is connected to network storage, you might consider disconnecting it, as this will decrease the time required for VMware ESXi to scan available storage. When selecting a disk to use for the installation, note that the disk order is determined by the BIOS and may be out of order. As the installation process will wipe the entire installation disk, ensure that the correct disk is being chosen and then press Enter to continue the process. Should the VMware ESXi installer find existing disk partitions, the Confirm Disk Selection screen will appear with a warning about deleting existing partitions (see Figure 2.4). Press the Enter key to continue.

The Confirm Install screen will then be displayed as shown in Figure 2.5. If you press the Backspace key, you will be able to select another disk to use for the installation. Press the F11 key to begin installing VMware ESXi to the selected disk.

Figure 2.4   The Confirm Disk Selection warning screen.

Figure 2.5   The Confirm Install screen.

The install process will proceed quickly and typically be completed in less than 90 seconds. The installation process will then display the status of the installation and request that you press the Enter key to restart the host. At this point, the host will operate in a 60-day evaluation mode and be licensed at the vSphere Enterprise Plus licensing level. Remove the installation CD and reboot the host. You may have to enter the BIOS of the host and set the installation drive used as the primary boot device. Your host will now be ready for configuration with the Direct Console User Interface (DCUI).

Configuring the DCUI

When VMware ESXi boots for the first time after an installation, the host is given a default configuration. The remaining space on the installation drive will be formatted with a 1MB block size and allocated as Datastore1. The network interface identified as vmnic0 will be added to vSwitch0 and both a VMkernel port called Management Network and a virtual machine port group called VM Network will be created in vSwitch0.

When the VMware ESXi host has completed booting, the DCUI screen will be displayed on the host as shown in Figure 2.6. The first post-installation task is to set the password for the root login, because this will be blank after the install.

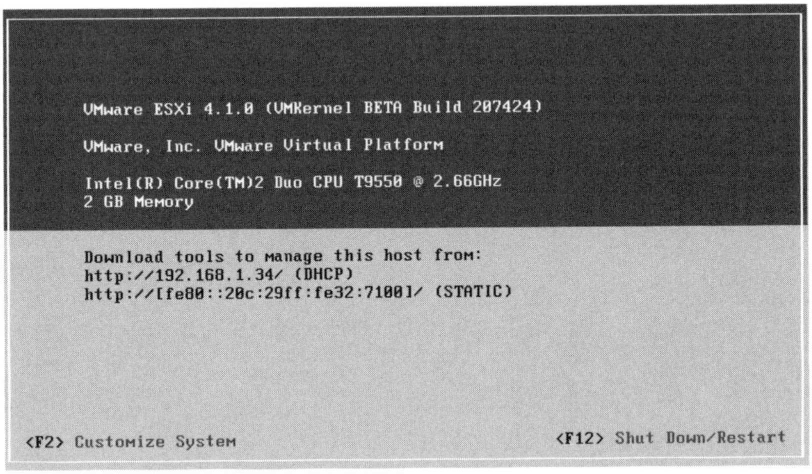

```
VMware ESXi 4.1.0 (VMKernel BETA Build 207424)

VMware, Inc. VMware Virtual Platform

Intel(R) Core(TM)2 Duo CPU T9550 @ 2.66GHz
2 GB Memory

Download tools to manage this host from:
http://192.168.1.34/ (DHCP)
http://[fe80::20c:29ff:fe32:7100]/ (STATIC)

<F2> Customize System                        <F12> Shut Down/Restart
```

Figure 2.6   The Direct Console User Interface (DCUI) Welcome screen.

Press the F2 key to select the Customize System option and you will then be presented with a login screen. The Login Name will be set to root and you can press the Tab key to switch to the Password field and then press Enter to log in. On the System Customization screen that is displayed in Figure 2.7, the first configuration option is Configure Password. The option description on the right side of the screen shows the password status as Not set. Press the Enter key to change the password for the root account, as shown in Figure 2.8. Once the password has been set, the status will be displayed as Set on the System Customization screen.

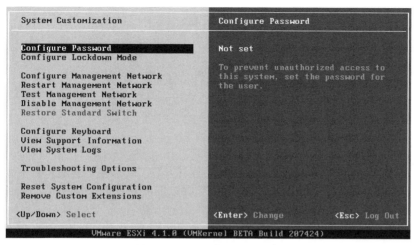

Figure 2.7   The DCUI System Customization menu.

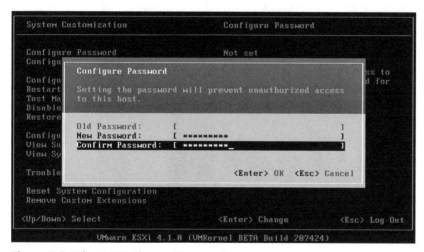

Figure 2.8   The DCUI Change Password screen.

Note: When setting the password for the root account, keep in mind that VMware ESXi has certain password requirements. A valid password for the local accounts on the host requires a mix of the following four character classes: uppercase letters, lowercase letters, digits, and other characters. Should you choose a seven-character-long password, it would require use of three of the four classes, while a six-character-long password would require all the classes. If you select an eight-character-long password, you will only require a single character class. Keep in mind that an uppercase letter that begins a password and a digit that ends it do not count toward the character class count.

The next step in the DCUI is to set the IP address that will be used to manage the host. By default, VMware ESXi is configured to use Dynamic Host Configuration Protocol (DHCP) for the management IP address. If a DHCP server is available on the network to which vmnic0 is attached, an IP address is obtained, as shown in Figure 2.6. If no DHCP server is present, the host assigns itself a link local IP address that is on the 169.254.x.x/16 subnet. In such a case, you will need physical access to the VMware ESXi host to access the DCUI or you can configure the host via the server remote control card.

On the main DCUI screen, press F2 to select the Customize System option. If you have set the password for the root account, you will be prompted to log in. On the System Customization screen, select the Configure Management Network option. The display on the right side of the DCUI shows the current hostname, which may be obtained from the domain name service (DNS) server assigned by DHCP, the current IP and IPv6 addresses for the host, and the DHCP server used if one could be contacted. Press the Enter key to access the Configure Management Network screen shown in Figure 2.9. On this screen, you can view the network adapters that are present in the VMware ESXi host, set a virtual local area network (VLAN) ID for the management network VMkernel port, set the IP or IPv6 addresses for the host, and set the DNS configuration and suffixes to use.

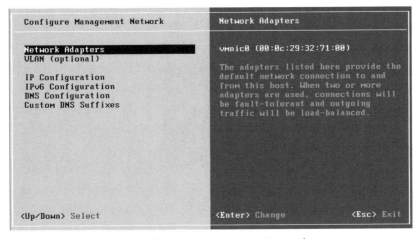

Figure 2.9 The DCUI Configure Management Network screen.

These options will be further discussed in Chapter 3, "Management Tools," but for now, you can select the IP Configuration option to access the IP setting for the VMware ESXi host. The screen shown in Figure 2.10 appears. Choose the static IP address option and then enter in the appropriate IP address, subnet mask, and gateway for the network. Press Enter to save the changes and return to the Configure Management Network screen.

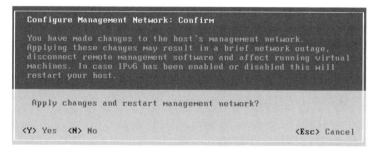

```
IP Configuration

This host can obtain network settings automatically if your network
includes a DHCP server. If it does not, the following settings must be
specified:


( ) Use dynamic IP address and network configuration
(o) Set static IP address and network configuration:

IP Address                                      [ 192.168.1.34      ]
Subnet Mask                                     [ 255.255.255.0     ]
Default Gateway                                 [ 192.168.1.1       ]

<Up/Down> Select   <Space> Mark Selected          <Enter> OK   <Esc> Cancel
```

Figure 2.10   The DCUI IP Configuration screen.

```
Configure Management Network: Confirm

You have made changes to the host's management network.
Applying these changes may result in a brief network outage,
disconnect remote management software and affect running virtual
machines. In case IPv6 has been enabled or disabled this will
restart your host.


 Apply changes and restart management network?

<Y> Yes   <N> No                                  <Esc> Cancel
```

Figure 2.11   The DCUI Configure Management Network Confirm screen.

If you have completed your changes on the Configure Management Network screen, press Esc to return to the System Customization screen. Doing so will bring up the confirmation screen shown in Figure 2.11. Selecting Yes commits the network changes made and restarts the management network. Doing so will disrupt any existing connections made to the host via the vSphere client, vCenter Server, or other management tools. Select No to discard the changes you made on the Configure Management Network screen or press Esc to return to the Configure Management Network screen to make further changes. Once you have set the IP address for the host, you'll be ready to download the vSphere client and to begin to work with your VMware ESXi host.

Setting the Root Password and IP with the vCLI The following two examples will demonstrate the vCLI commands to set the root password on the VMware ESXi host and to change the IP address of the management port.

The command `vicfg-user` is used to create, manage, and delete local users and groups on your host. The `-server` option specifies the host to run the command against. The `-entity` and `-operation` options inform the command that it will be run against a user and that the operation will update the target entity. No login credentials are specified in the command, so the user enters those when prompted. The example that follows updates the password of the root login to 0e493tac32 and a successful status is returned for the command.

```
vicfg-user --server esx05.mishchenko.net --entity user --operation modify
   --login root --newpassword 0e493tac32
Updated user root successfully.
```

To update the IP address used for the management port, you'll use the vicfg-vmknic command. The following command shows the current configuration of the management port:

```
vicfg-vmknic --server esx05.mishchenko.net --list
Interface  Port Group/DVPort         IP Family IP Address
   Netmask        MAC Address        MTU    Type      vMotion
vmk0    Management Network           IPv4    192.168.1.34
   255.255.255.0    00:0c:29:32:71:00 1500   DHCP      Disabled
```

To set the IP address, you use the ip and netmask options:

```
vicfg-vmknic --server esx05.mishchenko.net --portgroup "Management Network"
   --ip 192.168.1.34 --netmask 255.255.255.0
Set IP address successfully
```

As mentioned earlier in the chapter, installation and management of VMware ESXi are supported with a number of remote management cards, including DRAC 4 and 5, HP iLO and iLO2, and IBM Management Module (MM) and RSA II. If you are using another brand of hardware, you'll likely find that the remote card will work just fine with ESXi. A remote card is beneficial for the install process and DCUI management for servers at remote sites or when you don't have easy physical access to a host.

When using a remote access card, it is recommended to have the latest firmware installed for the best results with the card. But if the network stability is poor, you may find that an install using the virtual CD feature will fail, in which case you'll have to consider an alternative such as using ESXi Embedded or installing ESXi from a Preboot Execution Environment (PXE) server.

With some remote access cards, you may find that the default color scheme for the DCUI does not display that well within the remote management application. If you experience this problem, you can change the DCUI display to high contrast mode. At the DCUI Welcome screen, press the F4 key to switch to high contrast mode as shown in Figure 2.12. You can press F4 again to switch back to the regular display mode again. You will only be able to change the display mode at the Welcome screen. If you have already logged in to the DCUI, you will need to press the Esc key to log out, switch to high contrast mode, and then log in again. You should also note that after you restart your VMware ESXi, the display reverts back to the default display mode.

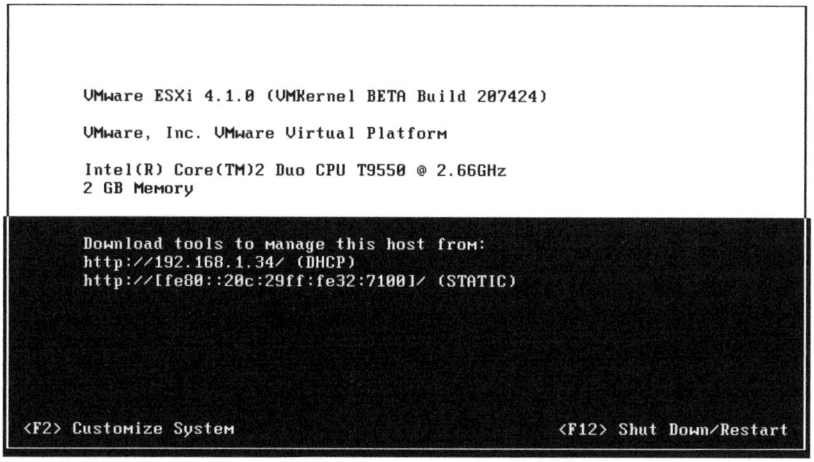

```
      VMware ESXi 4.1.0 (VMKernel BETA Build 207424)

      VMware, Inc. VMware Virtual Platform

      Intel(R) Core(TM)2 Duo CPU T9550 @ 2.66GHz
      2 GB Memory

      Download tools to manage this host from:
      http://192.168.1.34/ (DHCP)
      http://[fe80::20c:29ff:fe32:7100]/ (STATIC)




 <F2> Customize System                        <F12> Shut Down/Restart
```

Figure 2.12   The DCUI Welcome screen in high contrast mode.

Installing the vSphere Client and Initial Configuration

The VMware vSphere client is a Windows application that provides a graphical user interface (GUI) environment for managing your VMware ESXi host. You can connect directly to your ESXi host and authenticate with either a local account or your Active Directory (AD) login if the ESXi host has been set up for use with AD Integration. Because this will be an initial install of ESXi, AD Integration will not be configured; therefore, you will only be able to log in with the root login. In Chapter 3, you will learn how to create additional local accounts on ESXi. Chapter 6, "System Monitoring and Management," covers the setup steps that allow you to use your AD login to connect to your host. Additionally, once you have deployed vCenter Server, you can connect to it with the same vSphere client using your AD login and manage all of your VMware ESXi hosts via a single management point. Some vSphere features, such as cloning and vMotion, are available only when the vSphere client is connected to vCenter Server.

The vSphere client can be installed from the vCenter Server installation media, but the simplest method is simply to download the client from the VMware ESXi host. To download the vSphere client from your ESXi host, follow these steps:

1. From your Windows host open a Web browser.

2. Type in the URL for the ESXi host. You may use the IP address that you configured for the management port earlier or enter the fully qualified domain name (FQDN) if you have configured your DNS servers with the hostname of your ESXi host. A welcome page should appear.

Tip: If the welcome page appears but does not contain text, as shown in Figure 2.13, edit the security options for your Web browser to add the host's IP address or domain name to the Trusted or Local Intranet sites.

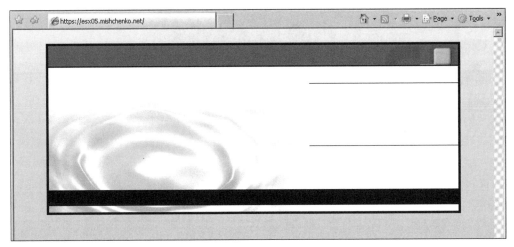

Figure 2.13 A VMware ESXi welcome page that is empty due to incorrect browser security settings.

3. Click on the Download vSphere Client link under Getting Started. With ESXi 4.1, the vSphere client download is now hosted on VMware's Web servers.

4. A security dialog box appears. Depending on your browser security settings, the dialog box will offer an option to Save or Run the VMware-viclient.exe download.

5. Once the installer begins for the VMware vSphere Client 4.1, you will be asked to select the language for the installer and you'll have the choice between Chinese (Simplified), English (United States), German (Germany), and Japanese. Select the appropriate language and click OK.

6. You can click on Next on the Welcome screen to continue with the installation.

7. Click on the radio button labeled I Agree to the Terms in the License Agreement and then click Next.

8. Enter a username and organization and then click Next.

9. Select the destination folder for the installation and then click Next.

10. Click on Install to begin the installation and then Finish to complete the process.

Note: Each version of ESXi and ESX requires a specific version of the vSphere or virtual interface (VI) client. You cannot connect to an ESX 3.5 host with version 4.1 of the vSphere client. However, a single management PC can have multiple versions of the client installed, and examining Add/Remove Programs in Control Panel will show the various versions installed. When you need to connect directly to a host or to vCenter Server, you need only start the VMware vSphere client shortcut that exists on your desktop or in the VMware program group. Once you have entered in the host IP address or hostname and your login credentials and clicked Login, the vSphere client determines the version of the host or vCenter Server to which you are connecting and launches the appropriate client version. If you attempt to connect to a version of host or vCenter Server for which you do not have a matching vSphere or VI client installed, you will be prompted to download and install that client.

Once the vSphere client has been installed, you are ready to launch it and use it to manage your VMware ESXi host. Your client requires IP connectivity to the IP address configured for the management port. The required ports for managing your VMware ESXi host directly or as part of vCenter are discussed in Chapter 7, "Securing ESXi." Use the following steps to log in to your ESXi host.

1. To start the vSphere client, click the Start menu and run the VMware vSphere Client from the VMware program group.

2. On the login screen shown in Figure 2.14, enter the IP address for your ESXi host or its FQDN. Enter the username root and the password that you configured earlier in the DCUI. If you have not yet set a password for the ESXi host, leave the field blank. You can use the Use Windows session credentials option if you have enabled AD Integration on your VMware ESXi host or if you are connecting to vCenter Server.

3. Click on the Login button to connect to the host.

4. The Security Warning screen appears as shown in Figure 2.15. Click the Ignore button to continue connecting to the host.

Tip: The vSphere client, other vSphere products, and third-party tools communicate with the VMware ESXi host over HTTPS and by default the host will be configured with a self-signed certificate for the host localhost.localdomain. For a highly secure environment, the Secure Sockets Layer (SSL) certificate used by the host can be changed; this is covered in Chapter 7.

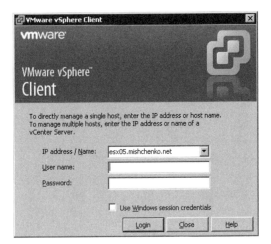

Figure 2.14   The vSphere login screen.

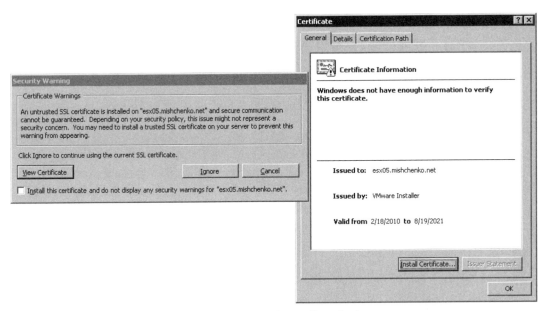

Figure 2.15   SSL security warning during the vSphere client login process.

Once you have connected to the VMware ESXi host, the VMware Evaluation Notice screen appears, informing you that the evaluation license will expire in 60 days. After you clear the message, you can select the Summary tab for the host to view any configuration issues. In Figure 2.16, the vSphere client has detected that the password has not yet been set for the host and that no datastore exists. If you have already set the root password in the DCUI, you will not see the

Figure 2.16   Two configuration issues have been detected for the VMware ESXi host.

password warning. The Configuration tab shows a related error that The VMware ESX Server does not have persistent storage. You can correct the datastore error when using VMware ESXi Embedded, as ESXi will be booting from a USB flash drive, not a hard drive.

Take the following steps to set the password for the root account that has not been changed with the DCUI or vCLI:

1.   In the vSphere client, select the Local Users & Groups tab.

2.   Right-click on the root user and select Edit.

3.   Check the Change password option and then enter the password in both the Password and Confirm fields.

4.   Click the OK button to save the password change.

You can also use the vSphere client to make these networking changes. Select the Configuration tab and then click Networking. The default network configuration of a single vSwitch with vmnic0 discussed earlier can be seen in Figure 2.17.

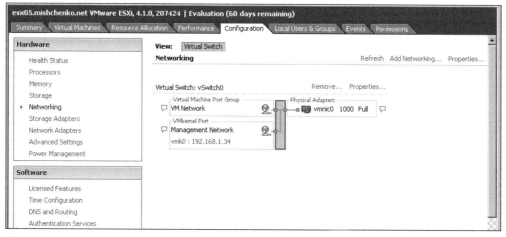

Figure 2.17   The default networking configuration for VMware ESXi.

To change the IP address for the management network, follow these steps.

1. Click on the Properties link for vSwitch0.

2. In the vSwitch0 Properties window, select the Management Network port and then click Edit.

3. Select the IP Settings tab on the Management Network Properties window.

4. Check the radio button labeled Use the Following IP Settings and then set the IP address and subnet mask.

5. To change the VMkernel default gateway, click the Edit button, enter the new gateway, and then click OK to return the IP Settings tab.

6. Click the OK button to commit your change. The Recent Tasks pane will show the Update Virtual NIC task. If the IP address of the host has changed, you will need to exit the vSphere client and connect to the new IP address.

Using the vSphere client with VMware ESXi is similar to using VMware ESX 3.0, 3.5, and 4.0. But there are noticeable differences when navigating the vSphere client. When you view the Memory page on the Configuration tab, only the values for Total, System, and Virtual Machines are displayed. As VMware ESXi does not have the service console that is a part of VMware ESX, an entry for Service Console is not displayed, nor is the Properties link to change the Service Console memory settings. Likewise, the Security Profile page displays only services configured to run on VMware ESXi rather than the firewall settings that configures the Linux iptables-based firewall running in Service Console.

As the reason for deploying VMware ESXi is to create and manage virtual machines, the following steps will walk through the process of deploying a new virtual machine (VM) from an Open Virtualization Format (OVF) template. Given the importance of the vCLI for managing your host, the vSphere Management Assistant (vMA) OVF will be imported to the VMware ESXi host.

1. Select File and then choose Deploy OVF Template.

2. The vMA template can be deployed from a URL or from a file. Enter the URL http://download3.vmware.com/software/vma/vMA-4.1.0.0-268837.ovf or browse to the location of the OVF file on your management PC. The download OVF for the vMA will include both the OVF file and the associated Virtual Machine Disk (VMDK) file.

3. Review the details of the OVF package as shown in Figure 2.18 and then click the Next button to continue.

4. Click on the Accept button after reviewing the EULA and then click Next to continue.

5. Specify the name for the VM and then click the Next button.

6.   Select the datastore on which to store the VM files and click Next.

7.   Select between thin and thick provisioned for the disk format and then click Next.

8.   Click Finish to import the vMA to your host.

Note: The OVF is a standard that describes the metadata about a virtual machine in the format of an Extensible Markup Language (XML) file. Rather than distributing a VMDK file for import to a host, the OVF virtual machine metadata includes configuration settings for the VM such as CPU, network, and storage. The OVF can also include other components, such as an EULA, minimum requirements, and security features. The OVF is also not limited to just a single VM, but can deploy multiple VM configurations for multitiered services that require interdependent VMs.

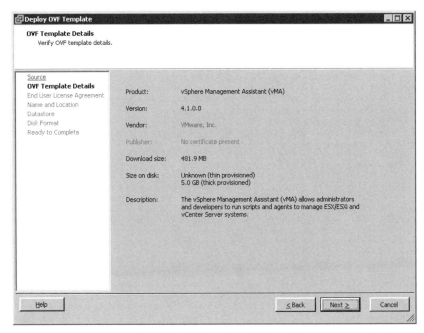

Figure 2.18   OVF template details for the vSphere Management Assistant (vMA).

Once the import of vMA template has completed, you should be able to see the virtual machine listed in the inventory for your ESXi host. You can right-click on the virtual machine and then select Power > Power On. The virtual machine will start up and you can click on the Console tab for the vMA appliance to gain access to the initial configuration screen for the vMA. After a short process, your vMA appliance will be ready for use and you can begin trying some of the vCLI commands discussed in this chapter.

Conclusion

With the growing acceptance of VMware ESXi, there is broad hardware support for ESXi. Also, the same server that you might choose to use with ESX is likely supported for use with ESXi. ESXi is quickly installed on your hardware, and within a short period, you can be using the familiar vSphere client to configure and manage your ESXi host. ESXi includes the DCUI for basic management and configuration, and you can download the vMA appliance, which includes the vCLI. With the vCLI, you have access to a command set similar to that which you have used with the ESX service console.

3 Management Tools

In Chapter 2, "Getting Started with a Quick Install," you learned about the hardware requirements for VMware ESXi; how to perform a simple, interactive install for ESXi; and how to perform some basic configuration steps necessary to begin using the host. In this chapter, you will learn a bit more about the management tools used to manage your ESXi environment. This will include the following listed elements. This chapter does not focus on tasks that you will already be familiar with, such as creating virtual machines (VMs) or configuring virtual switches (vSwitches). Rather, it reviews elements of management that you may not be that familiar with or that have changed with the release of vSphere 4.1.

- Managing a standalone ESXi host

- Managing your hosts with vCenter Server

- Getting started with PowerCLI and the vCLI

- Managing your host with the Direct User Console Interface (DCUI)

- Using third-party products to manage your hosts

Managing Your ESXi Host with the vSphere Client

In some cases, you may find yourself managing a single ESXi host, in which case you'll connect directly to it with the vSphere client. This could be the case if you are working with a test environment, at a single server deployment in a remote site, or if your vCenter Server is unavailable for use. Whichever situation you find yourself in, you can use the vSphere client to manage and configure your host. Certain features of vSphere functionality, such as cloning and vMotion, are not available without vCenter Server, but you can still configure and manage a number of aspects on your host.

When you first connect to your host, the vSphere client displays the Home view, showing the icons in Figure 3.1. These represent the configuration and management options appropriate to single-host management. The following section reviews some of these options. As you explore the vSphere client, you may notice that several options, such as Active Directory Integration, Time Configuration, and Permissions, are not discussed. Those items are reviewed in later chapters on systems management and security.

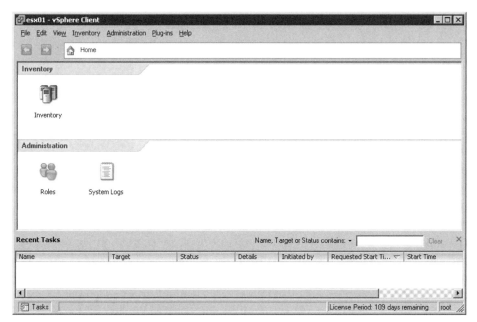

Figure 3.1   The vSphere Client Home screen.

Using the Host Configuration Tab

Most of the elements available to configure your ESXi host are found on the Configuration tab. These options are available when you connect to your host directly with the vSphere client or through vCenter Server. When you select the Configuration tab, the configuration options shown in Figure 3.2 are shown.

- **Health Status.** When you select the Health Status link, the hardware status of various components of your ESXi host is shown. The data displayed on this page depends on the Common Information Model (CIM) providers that are installed with ESXi. As you'll see in Chapter 6, "System Monitoring and Management," you do not need to install hardware agents onto ESXi as you would with ESX.

- **Processors.** This page displays information about the processors in your system. This includes the processor model, socket count, cores per socket, and whether Hyperthreading is enabled. If you click the Properties link, you can enable or disable Hyperthreading. A change on that screen requires a restart of the host. The Processors page shows some information about the host's motherboard, including vendor name, model, and Basic Input/Output System (BIOS) version.

- **Memory.** The host's total memory is shown on this page. Also displayed is the memory allocated to system processes, such as the VMkernel, drivers, and the virtualization layer, and the memory available to VMs. The value for Virtual Machines shown on this page is more than the Total Capacity memory value shown on the Resource Allocation page. The

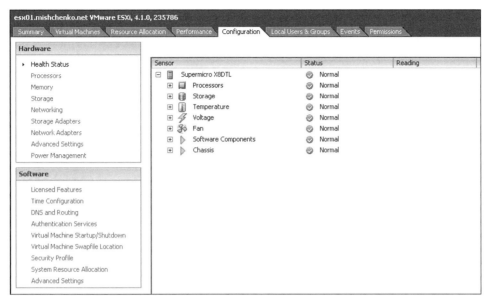

Figure 3.2   The ESXi Configuration screen.

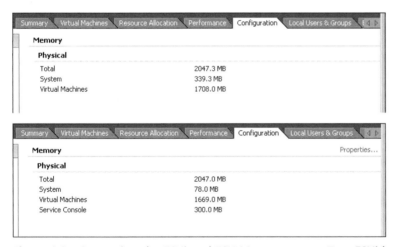

Figure 3.3   Comparing the ESXi and ESX Memory pages. Top: ESXi host. Bottom: ESX host.

Total Capacity value reflects the memory available for use by the guest operating systems. The Virtual Machines value includes that memory and additional memory to handle the overhead of running VMs. You will notice the absence of an option to configure memory. Figure 3.3 shows the memory page for both an ESXi and ESX host. As there is no Service Console with ESXi, there is no Properties link on that page.

■ **Storage, Networking, Storage Adapters, and Network Adapters.** These pages display the current configuration for your host's networking and storage setup. As this book focuses on migrating from ESX to ESXi, it does not deal with end-to-end configuration of these components. But elements of configuration are discussed in later chapters dealing with security and scripting.

- **Advanced Settings (Hardware).** On this page, you can enable VMDirectPath. The host must support Intel Directed input/output (I/O) (VT-d) or Advanced Micro Devices (AMD) Input/Output Memory Management Unit (IOMMU). If you have enabled VT-d or IOMMU in the host's BIOS, you can select this page and click Configure Passthrough. You can then enable devices for VMDirectPath on the Mark Devices for Passthrough screen. Changes on this page require a host restart.

- **Power Management.** VMware ESXi supports both AMD PowerNow! and Enhanced Intel SpeedStep central processing unit (CPU) power management technologies. Configuration on this page is described in the next section, "Setting a Power Management Policy."

- **Licensed Features.** As shown later in this section, you can configure the license key for your host on this page.

- **Time Configuration.** On this page, you can enable Network Time Protocol (NTP) for your host. As your guest operating system may depend on the host for time synchronization, it is important to configure NTP for your host. This is discussed in Chapter 6.

- **DNS and Routing.** On this page, as you'll see later in this chapter, you can configure the hostname, management interface Internet Protocol (IP) address, and other networking elements. A significant difference on this page between ESXi and ESX, as you'll see, is the lack of any Service Console settings.

- **Authentication Services.** With this option, you can enable Active Directory Integration. This will be discussed in Chapter 6.

- **Virtual Machine Startup/Shutdown.** You can configure the behavior of VMs at host startup and shutdown on this screen. This can be particularly useful with a standalone host in that you would want any hosted VMs to start automatically when the host is powered on or restarted.

- **Virtual Machine Swapfile Location.** By default, the VM swapfile is created when a VM is powered on in the same folder as the configuration (VMX) file for the VM. You can change this to another datastore for performance reasons and you can set this at the VM, host, or cluster level. If vCenter Server manages your host, you cannot configure the swapfile location when connected directly with the vSphere client.

- **Security Profile.** On an ESX host, this page displays the settings for the Service Console firewall. As you will see later in this chapter, on ESXi this is significantly different and the page shows the services running on the host.

- **System Resource Allocation.** On this page, you can choose between a simple and advanced view. In the simple view, you can change allocations for memory and CPU resources used by the VMkernel. With the advanced view, you can change resource allocations for specific system processes.

■ **Advanced Settings** (Software). On the Advanced Settings page, you can set a number of configuration options. Throughout this book, you will see a number of examples for both PowerCLI and the vSphere Command-Line Interface (vCLI) in which Advanced Settings are configured.

Setting a Power Management Policy

To improve CPU power efficiency and reduce power load, ESXi supports both AMD PowerNow! and Enhanced Intel SpeedStep CPU power management technologies. With this support, ESXi can change CPU frequency based on the host's workload. When you select the Power Management option on the Configuration tab, the Technology field displays the detected power management technology. If a status of Not Available is shown and you know that your host supports one of these power modes, you should check the BIOS of the host to ensure that the feature is enabled. You can set the Power Management Policy to one of the following options:

■ **High Performance (Default).** With this option, the VMkernel will not use power.

■ **Balanced Performance.** The VMkernel will use the power management features to reduce host power consumption without negatively impacting VM performance.

■ **Low Power.** The VMkernel will aggressively reduce power use at the risk of slightly lower VM performance.

■ **Custom.** With this option, the VMkernel uses the configured Power parameters from the Advanced Settings screen to set power management characteristics. These parameters can be set with the vSphere client or using the vCLI command `vicfg-advcfg`.

To configure the Power Management Policy for your host, follow these steps. Changes made to the policy do not require a host reboot.

1.   In the Inventory view, select your host and then click the Configuration tab.

2.   Select Power Management and then click Properties.

3.   Choose the desired policy for your host.

4.   Click OK to save your change.

Configuring DNS and Routing Settings

On the DNS and Routing page, you can configure a number of networking options for the VMkernel. As noted earlier, ESXi differs from ESX in that there are no Service Console settings, as the management interface is handled by the VMkernel for ESXi. Figure 3.4 shows the summary of information for the DNS and Routing page as well as some of the options you can configure if you click Properties. On the Routing tab of the DNS and Routing Configuration

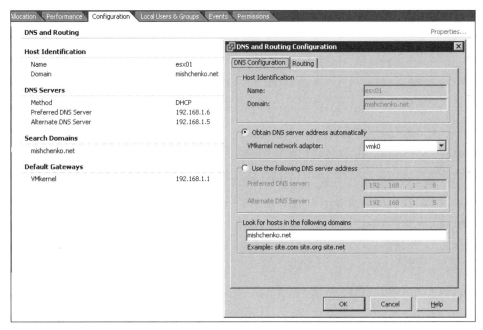

Figure 3.4   Setting VMkernel IP address and hostname options.

screen, you can set the default gateway for the VMkernel. Later in this chapter, you will see how to configure these settings with the DCUI. As was shown in Chapter 2, you can use vCLI commands such as `vicfg-vmknic` to change these same settings.

Configuring Licensing on Your Host

The default licensing mode for VMware ESXi after an installation is to run in evaluation mode for 60 days licensed at the vSphere Enterprise Plus licensing level. In the case of a standalone host, you must license the host before the evaluation has expired; otherwise, you no longer will be able to power on your VMs. If you have installed your ESXi host with an installation script, you may have specified a serial number to use, in which case you will not have to change the licensing for the host. Licensing your ESXi hosts with vCenter Server is covered later in this chapter.

To license your standalone host, you can follow these steps. You do not need to reboot your host after making this change.

1. After you have connected to the ESXi host with the vSphere client, select the Inventory icon to display the Inventory view. This view shows your host in the navigation pane along with any VMs and resource pools that you have created.

2. Select the host and then choose the Configuration tab.

3. Select the link Licensed Features and the license summary for the host will be displayed.

4. Click the Edit link to change the license for the host.

5. Click the radio button Assign a New License to This Host.

6. Add your license serial number in the Add License Key window as shown in Figure 3.5 and then click OK.

7. The Product, Capacity, and other license fields should be updated to reflect the licensed features of the license key. Click OK to close the Assign License window.

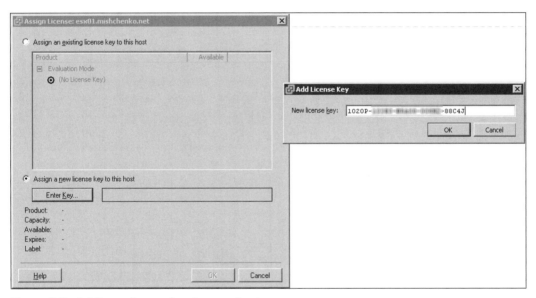

Figure 3.5   Adding a license key to your host.

Managing Your Host's Security Profile

If you look at the Security Profile page for both ESX and ESXi, the architectural differences between the two products clearly emerge. Figure 3.6 shows the Security Profile page for both ESX and ESXi. With ESX, you can see the configuration of the Service Console firewall. If you select Properties, you can see a list of preconfigured services and select which traffic types to allow through the firewall.

With ESXi, there is no firewall, so the Security Profile page displays a list of services that are available on the host, as shown in Figure 3.6. You can click Properties to see whether the service is running, as shown in Figure 3.7. You can then click options to start, restart, and stop the

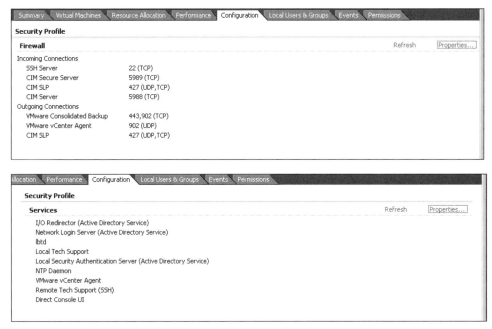

Figure 3.6   Comparing the ESX and ESXi Security Profile page. Top: ESXi Security Profile page. Bottom: ESX Security Profile page.

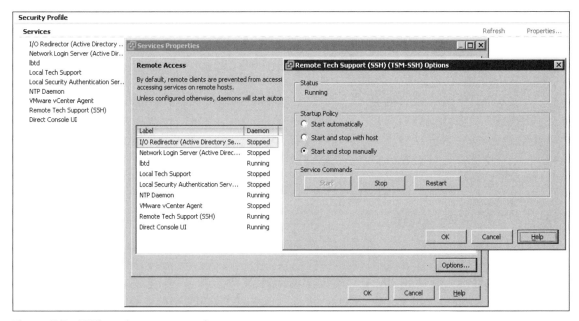

Figure 3.7   ESXi service startup options.

service. You can also set the Startup Policy for the service to be Start Automatically, Start and Stop with Host, and Start and Stop Manually.

Caution: You should note that the Start and Stop Manually policy behaves differently than a service on a Windows server. If you have a Windows service configured for manual startup and then restart the server, the service will not be running when the host has rebooted. In the case of the Start and Stop Manually policy, the service will continue to run until it is manually stopped. If the ESXi host is restarted, the service restarts and continues to run until you have stopped the service.

Viewing Resource Allocation

To view rudimentary information about processor and memory usage, you can use the Summary page at the ESXi host, Resource Pool, or Virtual Machine level. The Resource Allocation and Performance tabs provide more in-depth information about your host's resource usage and allow you to fine-tune resources for best overall performance. For a thorough understanding of resource management, it is worthwhile to review the *VMware vSphere Resource Management Guide*.

Figure 3.8 shows the Resource Allocation tab at the host level. The CPU summary shows the total capacity available to resource pools and VMs. In this case, there are no CPU reservations set for running VMs or resource pools, so the Reserved Capacity value is zero. Thus the Available Capacity for CPU is also equal to the Total Capacity. The Memory Total Capacity value shows the total memory available for allocation to VMs. In Figure 3.8, a number of VMs are running, so a certain amount of memory is now set as Reserved Capacity, leaving the Available Capacity as the difference between those two values. When you are viewing the Resource Allocation tab at the resource pool level, the CPU and memory values reflect the reservation values

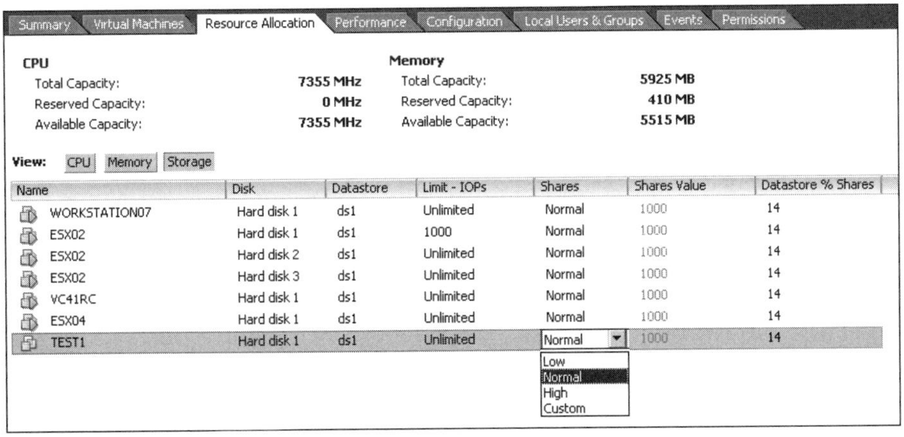

Figure 3.8 The Resource Allocation tab at the host level.

configured for the resource pool. The Resource Allocation tab for a VM displays the CPU and memory usage for the VM as well as configured reservation, share, and limit values.

To change the values for share, limits, or reservation, you either right-click the VM or resource pool and select Edit Resource Settings or you simply fill in a value on the Resource Allocation tab, as is shown in Figure 3.8 with Shares settings on the Storage resource view.

Configuring Storage I/O Control Storage I/O Control is a new feature of vSphere 4.1 that allows you to configure host and clusterwide storage prioritization. In the same way that limits and shares can be used for CPU and memory resources to control resource allocation during times of congestion, Storage I/O Control provides the same level of control for I/O congestion.

When Storage I/O Control is enabled for a datastore, your VMware ESXi begins to monitor the latency that is experienced during communication with the datastore. Should that latency exceed a specified threshold, the datastore is considered congested and VM I/O is controlled in accordance to the Share Disk settings for the VMs on that datastore.

There are a number of requirements to be aware of when configuring Storage I/O Control:

- The ESXi host must be managed by vCenter Server to use Storage I/O Control. Although the values for Shares and Limits I/O operations per second (IOPs)—can be set with the vSphere client connected directly to the host—it is possible to enable Storage I/O Control only when the vSphere client is managing the host through vCenter Server.

- Storage I/O Control is supported only on Fibre Channel and Internet Small Computer System Interface (iSCSI) storage. It is not available for Network File System (NFS) or supported for local storage.

- Datastores with multiple extents are not supported.

- If your storage supports automated storage tiering, you should check VMware's storage area network (SAN) compatibility guide to ensure your system is supported for storage I/O control. If your SAN does not support the ability to move logical unit numbers (LUNs) between different types of storage such as solid-state drives (SSDs), Fibre Channel (FC), serial attached SCSI (SAS), or SATA, no special certification is required for Storage I/O Control.

To use Storage I/O Control, you first need to enable the option on your datastore. You connect your vSphere client to vCenter Server and then find the Configuration tab for the host using the datastore on which you want to enable Storage I/O Control. Select the

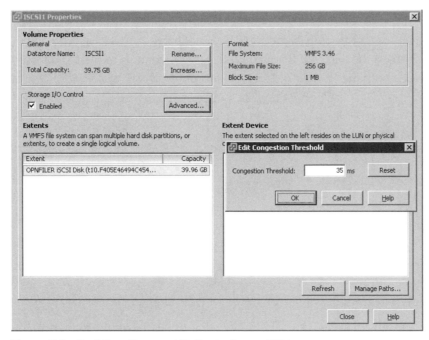

Figure 3.9   Enabling Storage I/O Control on a LUN.

Storage view, right-click on the datastore, and select Properties. Enable the Storage I/O Control option as shown in Figure 3.9. You can also click the Advanced icon to set a Congestion Threshold manually. The threshold takes a time value in milliseconds (ms) and the default value is 35 ms.

When you have enabled Storage I/O Control for a datastore, you can then set shares and limits for the VMs that use the datastore. Note that you can set limits for each virtual disk on the datastore. Storage I/O shares work the same way as shares for CPU and memory. If the resource is constrained, virtual disks with a higher share value than other disks will have greater access to the datastore I/O resources. You can also set a limit for a virtual disk. By default, the limit for a virtual disk is set to unlimited, but you can set it to an appropriate value in I/O operations per second (IOPS). Keep in mind that you may be measuring disk performance within the VM at megabytes per second, so you'll have to take into account the typical I/O size used by the guest operating system to convert the disk requirements into IOPS.

You can set the shares or limit for a virtual disk on the Resource Allocation tab, as shown in Figure 3.8, or individually for a VM with the following steps:

1.   In the vSphere Client inventory view, select the VM.

2.   Right-click on the VM and select Edit Settings.

3. Select the Resources tab and then click Disk.

4. Select the virtual disk to update and then click on Shares. You can select among Low (500 shares), Normal (1000), High (2000), or Custom. With the Custom option, you specify the number of shares to assign to the virtual disk.

5. Click the Limit—IOPS column to change the disk limit. You can enter a value in IOPS.

6. Click OK to save your changes and to close the Virtual Machines Properties window.

Viewing Events and System Logs

The last item that this section covers is viewing the Event tab and accessing system logs when managing a standalone host. After using the vSphere client with a standalone ESXi server, you'll have seen other configuration and management options such as setting permissions and configuring Active Directory Integration, which is covered in later chapters.

When you are managing a standalone host, the Event tab is available on the host, resource pool, and VM objects. An event can be generated by a user or host action and will occur, for example, when a user powers on a VM or when a host has lost a network connection to an iSCSI or NFS datastore.

The Event tab shows a description of the event, the type (info, warning, or error), the time of the event, the target, and, if applicable, the related task and user. If you select a specific event, the Event Details pane displays a summary of the event, as shown in Figure 3.10. In some cases, you may see a link to Ask VMware, as is shown for the NFS error in the figure. This links to a VMware Knowledge Base article that provides assistance with that particular problem. In other cases, you will see a link to Submit Error Report, in which case the data of the event is sent to VMware's secure support servers. This data is collected to report the issue and display a Knowledge Base article should one exist for that topic. A summary of the data to be transmitted is shown on the Submit to VMware screen.

Managing Your Hosts with vCenter Server

The difference between managing ESXi directly with the vSphere client and with vCenter Server is like the difference between night and day. vCenter Server adds so many features that make your life as a vSphere administrator so much easier it's hard to deal with a standalone host after you've used vCenter Server. As the chapters in this book deal with topics such as security, performance, and monitoring, the features of vCenter Server will be explored in more detail. But for now, this section highlights two features of vCenter Server that help ease your management load for ESXi. These features are Host Profiles and vSphere Web Access.

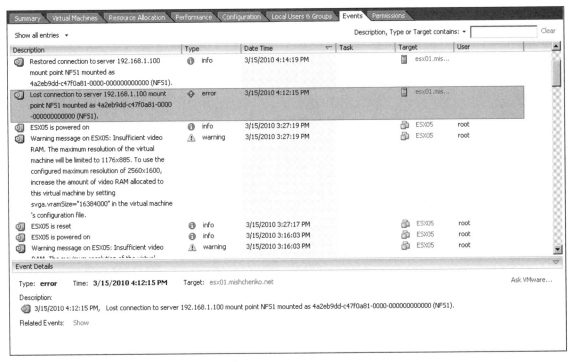

Figure 3.10 The vSphere Client Event tab.

Ensuring Configuration Compliance with Host Profiles

Host Profiles is a new feature with vCenter Server 4.0. This feature was designed to eliminate the need to configure on a per-host basis using the vSphere client, scripts, or other tools. Once a profile is created, it can be applied to your ESXi hosts or clusters. You can then check a host or cluster for any deviations from the preferred configuration in the profile. If the host is not in compliance, you can enforce the settings in the profile to bring the host back into compliance.

To begin using Host Profiles, you start by configuring your reference host. The configuration of the host that is imported into the host profile includes items such as the following:

- NFS storage configuration

- Networking configuration including vSwitches, VM port groups, management IP address configuration, and vNetwork Distributed Switch setup

- NTP server configuration

- Management of the root password

- Configuration of services found on the Security Policy page

- User, group, and permission configuration

- Advanced settings

- Active Directory Integration settings

To create a new host profile, you can right-click on the host and select Host Profile > Create Profile from Host. You can start with the view Home > Management > Host Profiles and then follow this process:

1. Click the Create Profile icon to start the Create Profile wizard.

2. Select the option to Create Profile from Existing Host.

3. Browse through your vCenter hierarchy to find the server that will serve as the reference host.

4. Enter a Name and Description for the new profile and click Next.

5. Click Finish after you have viewed the summary information for the new profile.

Note: You can also import and export Host Profiles. When you export a Host Profile with administrator passwords, they are not exported, as the data in export file is stored in clear text. When you import the profile, you are prompted to enter the passwords again. To export a profile, right-click on the profile and select Export Profile. The profile is stored in the VMware profile format (.vpf). To import a profile file, click on Create Profile on the Host Profiles view and select the Import Profile option.

Once you have created a host profile, you may want to edit it to customize the settings or make them more appropriate for deployment to many hosts. In the Host Profile view, right-click on the profile and select Edit Profile. You will see the Edit Profile window shown in Figure 3.11. If you expand the profile, you will see the subprofiles for the previously listed components. You can browse each subprofile and update policies to best match your environment. In Figure 3.11, the policy to set the management interface IP address for the hosts is set to the option User Specified IP Address to Be Used While Applying the Configuration.

When you are editing a profile, you can also specify whether a policy will be checked for compliance. On the Compliance Details tab, you can disable the check box for that specific policy. Other policies set in the profile are still enabled for compliance unless you specifically disable them.

The next step for Host Profiles is to apply the profile to a host or cluster. When you attach a profile to a cluster, all hosts in the cluster will need to be compliant for the cluster to be compliant. As Host Profiles is not supported for VMware ESXi and ESX 3.5, you should not attach a

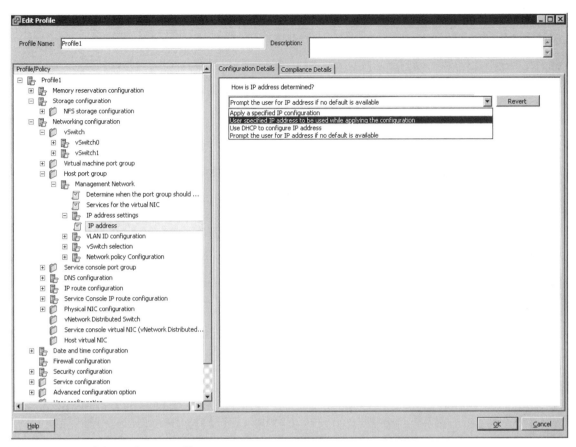

Figure 3.11   Editing a host profile.

profile to a mixed-version cluster. You can attach a profile to a cluster or host in the following ways:

- In the Host Profile view, right-click on the profile and select Attach Host/Cluster.
- Right-click on the host and select Host Profile > Apply Profile.
- Right-click on the cluster and select Host Profile > Manage Profile.
- Select the cluster's Profile Compliance tab and click the Click Here to Attach a Host Profile link.

Once the profile has been attached to a cluster or host, you can check compliance of that object against the host profile. Figure 3.12 shows this process for a cluster. After the profile has been attached to the cluster, you click Check Compliance Now. Figure 3.12 shows that the cluster is

Figure 3.12   Checking a cluster for host profile compliance.

noncompliant as a least one host in the cluster has been found to be noncompliant with the profile.

To correct this situation, select the noncompliant host and click on the link Apply Profile. Note that you have to place the host into Maintenance Mode before you can apply the profile. The Apply Profile wizard starts, which begins by prompting you to enter any required parameters for the profile. When configuring the profile in Figure 3.11, the policy for the management IP address was set to prompt for an IP address to be used. After entering that information, you then click Next and a list of configuration changes is generated for the host. Click Finish to apply the changes and an Apply Host Configuration task is created to update the host. Once the task has completed, the Host Profile Compliance status should change to Compliant, as will the status for the cluster if all hosts are now compliant. You need to take the host out of maintenance mode after you have completed applying the profile.

Tip: PowerCLI includes a number of cmdlets (pronounced *commandlets*) for managing Host Profiles. These include the cmdlets `New-VMHostProfile`, `Test-VMHostProfile-Compliance`, and `Apply-VMHostProfile`. Chapter 9, "Scripting and Automation with PowerCLI," reviews the process of managing and applying host profiles with these and the other profile-related cmdlets.

Managing VMs with vSphere Web Access

Long-term users of ESX will be familiar with the Web-based management interface that has been a part of that product. This Web interface has allowed users to manage VMs easily; for example, they can gain console access without requiring the installation of the vSphere client. This is convenient for end users of VMs who might need to access the console or control the power status for a VM, but don't need to get bogged down with running the vSphere client.

VMware ESXi has not been developed with this ability, but vCenter Server provides an Apache Tomcat–based Web service that allows for the remote management of VMs. The vCenter Web service provides support to the following Web browsers: Firefox, Internet Explorer, Mozilla, and Netscape Navigator.

When you log in to the Web Access, your access to objects is governed by the same roles and permissions that have been configured in vCenter Server. If a user does not have permission to control the power for a VM in the vSphere client, he or she will have the same restrictions in the Web client.

Some of the options for controlling a VM are shown in Figure 3.13. In this case, the login has full permission for the VM and can thus control the power status, reconfigure the virtual hardware, and manage snapshots. The user can also access the console and view alarms, tasks, and events that are related to the VM.

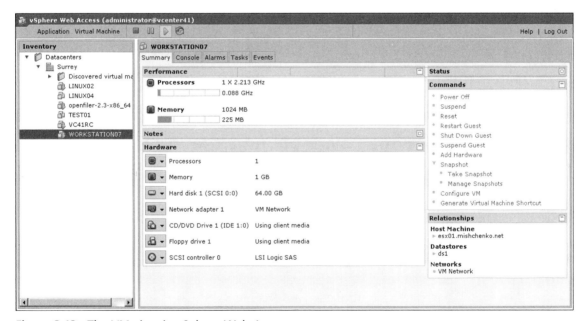

Figure 3.13 The VM view in vSphere Web Access.

One of the commands available is Generate Virtual Machine Shortcut. This can be used to generate a URL that provides an end user with access to the VM's console. You can customize the uniform resource locator (URL) with the following options:

■ **Limit the Workspace View to the Console.** This limits the user's view to just the VM console. Other details such as the Events tab are hidden.

- **Limit View to a Single Virtual Machine.** This option disables the user from viewing other VMs, as is the case with Figure 3.13.

- **Obfuscate This URL.** This option makes the URL difficult to read or change.

The following URL is a sample created by the Generate Virtual Machine Shortcut option:

```
https://vcenter41/ui/?wsUrl=http://localhost:80/sdk&mo=VirtualMachine
    |vm-24&inventory=none&tabs=hide_
```

This option also includes the ability to create a Windows desktop shortcut.

You will notice that the sample vSphere Web Access view in Figure 3.13 does not include any information about the ESXi hosts or clusters that are running the VMs. The Web Access view does not provide any interface to manage those objects. The Datacenters object, folder objects, and child datacenter objects all display the following tabs: Summary, Alarms, Tasks, and Events. For Alarms, Tasks, and Events, all data is shown for the specific object type and all child objects. On the Summary tab, the DataCenters object and any folder objects displays a summary of the objects below it. The Summary tab for a child datacenter object does provide a useful view to gauge the overall health of your datacenter. This summary view provides the overall status for the child datacenter, the number of networks, and number of datastores. A list of datastores in this object is also shown with both the individual datastore capacities and available space for each.

Getting Started with PowerCLI and the vCLI

For the seasoned ESX administrator, one of the significant challenges to migrating VMware ESXi is the inability to run scripts in the Service Console. As you've seen in the proceeding material, the functionality of the major vSphere options, such as vMotion and High Availability, is identical in both products, but you may have developed a number of console scripts that you use to manage your hosts or rely on console commands for maintenance and troubleshooting.

When VMware ESXi 3.5 was introduced, VMware also released the Remote Command-Line Interface (RCLI), which was available for Linux and Windows as well as in a virtual appliance format. The RCLI contained a number of esxcfg commands that you could use in the ESX Service Console except for the fact that the lack of complete command parity made switching to ESXi and the RCLI difficult. For example, the esxcfg commands for iSCSI configuration were not yet implemented in the RCLI and esxtop (or resxtop) was missing in the Windows RCLI. With the release of vSphere, VMware changed the name of RCLI to the vSphere Command-Line Interface and added a number of new commands to increase the vCLI's capability as a replacement using the Service Console.

Microsoft PowerShell was first released in 2006 to replace Microsoft Windows Script Host. PowerShell is integrated with the Microsoft .NET Framework and is an extensible command shell designed to automate a wide range of Windows administrative tasks. VMware first released the VI Toolkit for Windows in 2008 to provide an easy-to-use PowerShell interface to the VMware Infrastructure application programming interface (API). The product was renamed PowerCLI in 2009 and released to provide support for VMware vSphere.

Later chapters provide more details about the installation and use of the vCLI and PowerCLI, and throughout the book there are relevant examples to accompany the equivalent graphical user interface (GUI) configuration. In the following pages, you'll see a few simple examples of how these products can help you automate your management of VMware ESXi and assist in migrating from use of the Service Console.

Getting Started with the vCLI

The vCLI was designed to provide a common set of commands for system administration tasks for managing both ESXi and ESX hosts. For ESX administrators, this provides the opportunity to use existing management scripts with the associated risk of running commands in the Service Console.

The vCLI is available in installation packages for Linux and Windows as well as a preconfigured VMware appliance that can be imported to your host directly from VMware, as was shown in Chapter 2. Once you have one of the options installed, you are ready to start running vCLI commands. The list that follows summarizes the commands that you can use. As you'll see from the list, VMware has started to prefix commands with `vicfg-`, but the prefix `esxcfg-` still exists for old commands. The commands are identical regardless of the prefix used, but as you create new scripts or update existing ones, it is best to begin using the `vicfg-` commands.

```
esxcli.exe                              vicfg-ntp (esxcfg-ntp)
resxtop                                 vicfg-rescan (esxcfg-rescan)
svmotion                                vicfg-route (esxcfg-route)
vicfg-advcfg (esxcfg-advcfg)            vicfg-scsidevs (esxcfg-scsidevs)
vicfg-authconfig (esxcfg-authconfig)    vicfg-snmp (esxcfg-snmp)
vicfg-cfgbackup (esxcfg-cfgbackup)      vicfg-syslog (esxcfg-syslog)
vicfg-dns (esxcfg-dns)                  vicfg-user (esxcfg-user)
vicfg-dumppart (esxcfg-dumppart)        vicfg-vmknic (esxcfg-vmknic)
vicfg-hostops                           vicfg-volume (esxcfg-volume)
vicfg-ipsec (esxcfg-ipsec)              vicfg-vswitch (esxcfg-vswitch)
vicfg-iscsi (esxcfg-iscsi)              vifs
vicfg-module (esxcfg-module)            vihostupdate
vicfg-mpath (esxcfg-mpath)              vihostupdate35
vicfg-mpath35 (esxcfg-mpath35)          vmkfstools
vicfg-nas (esxcfg-nas)                  vmware-cmd
vicfg-nics (esxcfg-nics)
```

Tip: When you are running these commands on the Windows version of the vCLI, you need to add the extension `.pl`. The exception to this is the `esxcli` command.

The command syntax for the vCLI follows this pattern:

```
command - connection info - options
```

If you want to run the `vicfg-vswitch` command directly against your ESXi host, the command looks like the following:

```
vicfg-vswitch --server hostname --user login --password yourpassword options
```

The hostname is either the IP address or DNS name for the host, and the user and password are for an account defined locally on the host. A common option for the vCLI commands is `-list`, which in this case will provide a list of all vSwitches configured on the host.

You can also run the same command against your vCenter Server, but that requires that you add the `--vihost` option. In the following example, the hostname for the `--server` option will be your vCenter Server and the `--vihost` will be the specific ESXi host that the command will be run against:

```
vicfg-vswitch --server hostname --user login --password yourpassword
   -vihost hostname options
```

Note: The preceding examples used the password parameter. In Chapter 8, "Scripting and Automation with the vCLI," you will learn about using session files or the `vi-fastpass` authentication component to remove the need to enter a password each time you execute a vCLI command.

Getting Started with PowerCLI

The power of PowerShell is that it is an object-oriented scripting language rather than just one that produces text output. With the addition of VMware's PowerCLI, the objects that you can use include number vCenter Server and host items such as VMs, Host Profiles, vSwitches, and permissions. With PowerCLI, you can build a pipeline of cmdlets that can process complex tasks within a single line of code.

The installation of PowerShell and PowerCLI will be covered in Chapter 9. Once you have these items installed, you can begin to use PowerCLI. On the computer where you have installed PowerCLI, click Start and select All Programs > VMware > VMware vSphere PowerCLI > VMware vSphere PowerCLI. Once PowerCLI has started, you'll see the welcome message as shown in Figure 3.14 and be ready to enter commands at the PowerShell prompt.

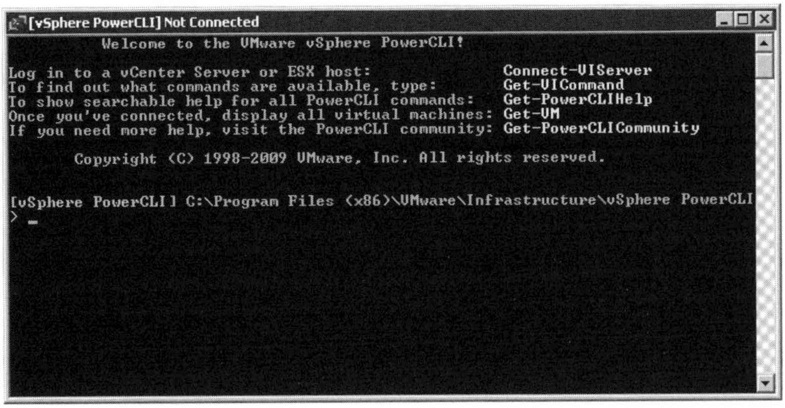

Figure 3.14   The PowerCLI welcome screen.

Tip: You may need to set the PowerShell execution policy if you start the PowerCLI short-cut and get this error: File C:\Program Files (x86)\VMware\Infrastructure \vSphere PowerCLI\Scripts\Initialize-VIToolkitEnvironment.ps1 cannot be loaded because the execution of scripts is disabled on this system. Start the Windows PowerShell application and run the cmdlet Set-ExecutionPolicy RemoteSigned. You can then restart VMware vSphere PowerCLI.

To start using PowerCLI commands you'll first want to connect to a host or vCenter Server with the Connect-VIServer command. The syntax for this command is as follows:

Connect-VIServer -Server <hostname> -User <username> -Password <password>

If you're just starting with PowerCLI, two commands that will help are Get-VICommand and Get-Help. Get-VICommand provides a list of PowerCLI commands. You'll find that there are quite a few cmdlets, so you can reduce that list to Get cmdlets by running the following command, which uses the Where-Object cmdlet to filter the output:

Get-VICommand | Where-Object { $_.Name -like "Get*" }

Get-Help can be used to provide help information about the various commands that are available; it is similar to the man command on a Linux system. If you run Get-Help Get-VMHost, you will see the help file for the Get-VMHost command. You can also use the switches -detailed and -example to see more information or just examples of the command.

Get-Help Get-VMHost -example

If you start to run a command, such as Get-VMHost or Get-VM, the output is fairly explanatory. If you combine these two cmdlets into a pipeline, you can query for a list of VMs running on a specific host with the following command:

```
Get-VMHost <hostname> | Get-VM
```

When you specify the hostname variable, you'll want to use the name of your ESXi host as it appears in vCenter Server.

Now if you want to find out which VMs have snapshots, you can run this command:

```
Get-VMHost <hostname> | Get-VM | Get-Snapshot
```

Lastly, if you want to export the list of VMs with snapshots to a file, you can use the PowerShell cmdlet Export-CSV. The command you started with would now be the following:

```
Get-VMHost <hostname> | Get-VM | Get-Snapshot |Export-CSV
   "C:\data\snapshot_report.csv"
```

This command produces a comma-separated value (CSV) file that you can import into any spreadsheet application.

Table 3.1 summarizes a number of common Get cmdlets that you can use to retrieve information about objects in your vCenter environment.

Table 3.1 Common Get Cmdlets Used to Query Objects in Your vCenter Server Environment

PowerCLI Cmdlet Name	vSphere Object
Get-Cluster	Cluster
Get-Datastore	Datastore
Get-HardDisk	VM hard drive
Get-NetworkAdapter	VM network card
Get-Snapshot	VM snapshot
Get-VirtualSwitch	vSwitch
Get-VM	VM
Get-VMHost	ESXi or ESX server

Configuring and Troubleshooting ESXi with the DCUI

The Direct Console User Interface (DCUI) provides a BIOS-like interface to the console of VMware ESXi. You access the DCUI either at the console of the physical host or via a remote management card such as a Dell Remote Access Card (DRAC), HP Integrated Lights-Out (iLO), or IBM Remote Supervisor Adapter (RSA) card. The DCUI can be used to interact with the host to perform tasks such as the following:

- Setting the root password

- Configuring the IP address and network interface card (NIC) for management traffic

- Restarting the management services on the host

- Reviewing system logs

Caution: By default, only the root account is set up with access to log in to the DCUI. You can change this to allow other users to log in without the root account. Care should be taken in granting access to the DCUI as it is possible to change the management network settings, change the root password, or shut down the host. Security for the DCUI is discussed in Chapter 7, "Securing ESXi."

Table 3.2 describes the keys you can use to navigate and make changes within the DCUI.

When your VMware ESXi host has booted, you will find yourself at the DCUI welcome screen, as shown in Figure 3.15. The screen displays the build of VMware ESXi that is running, as well as the detected server hardware, CPU, and memory. If your DCUI session has been active for more than one minute, the display switches to the black and white sleep mode. Press any key to activate the DCUI session. On the DCUI welcome screen, you then can press F2 to begin configuring the ESXi host or press F12 to restart or shut down the host.

Restarting and Shutting Down the Host

To shut down or restart your ESXi host, follow this procedure:

1. Press F12 at the DCUI welcome screen to shut down or restart your ESXi host.

2. Authentication is required to perform a reboot or shutdown, so you are prompted to provide a login name and password.

3. After you have been authenticated, you are given the option to press F2 to shut down the host. Press F11 to restart the host or press the Esc key to cancel the operation, as shown in Figure 3.16.

Table 3.2 Navigating the DCUI

Key	Action
F2	View or change the host's configuration
F4	Change the display to high contrast mode
F11	Confirm significant configuration changes
F12	Restart or shut down the host
Arrow keys	Move between selection fields
Enter	Select a menu item as well as save and exit a menu
Spacebar	Toggle a value
Esc	Exit without saving
q	Exit system logs
Alt+F1	Access the tech support console
Alt+F2	Return to the DCUI screen
Alt+F11	View summary information for the host (ESXi version, server, CPU, and memory)
Alt+F12	View the VMkernel log

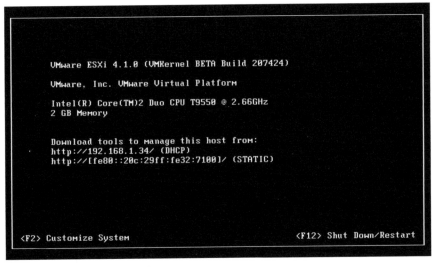

Figure 3.15 The DCUI welcome screen.

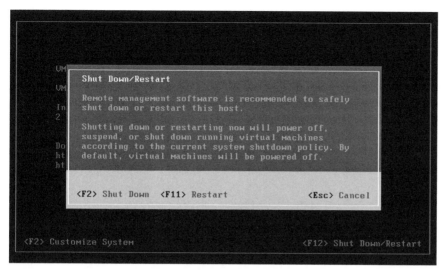

Figure 3.16   The DCUI Shutdown/Restart screen.

Configuring Virtual Machine Automatic Startup and Shutdown Options When you start up or shut down your VMware ESXi host, the Virtual Machine Startup and Shutdown settings on the host control the startup and shutdown of your VMs. By default, these settings are disabled, so when you shut down the ESXi host, the VMs running on the host are terminated, potentially creating problems in the guest operating systems.

Within the vSphere client, you can select the Configuration tab for the host and then click Virtual Machines Startup/Shutdown. After you click Properties, you can enable the option Allow Virtual Machines to Start and Stop Automatically with the System. You can then select Default Shutdown Delay as well as the Shutdown Action for VMs.

These options can also be configured with PowerCLI. To query the status of the Allow Virtual Machines to Start and Stop Automatically with the System option, you can run the cmdlet Get-VMHostStartPolicy. To get the current configuration of your host, you can run the following command:

```
Get-VMHostSTartPolicy -VMHost esx01.mishchenko.net
VMHost              Enabled StartDelay StopAction StopDelay WaitForHeartbeat
--------            -------- ---------- ---------- --------- ----------------
HostSystem-host-18 True     120        PowerOff   120       True
```

You can then use Set-VMHostStartPolicy to configure your host.

To enable automatic startup on all your ESXi hosts, you would use the following command:

```
Get-VMHost | Get-VMHostStartPolicy | Set-VMHostStartPolicy -Enabled:$true
```

The output for this command shows the status for each host as well as the other columns returned by the Get-VMHostStartPolicy cmdlet.

Configuring the DCUI Keyboard Language

When you log in at the DCUI, you are prompted for a login name and password, as shown in Figure 3.17. Note also that it is possible to configure a keyboard language to be used in the DCUI. The DCUI supports the following keyboard language layouts:

■ English (this choice is displayed as Default)

■ French

■ German

■ Japanese

■ Russian

Changing the keyboard language does not change the display language of the DCUI, which remains in English; the layout settings only change the layout of the keyboard input.

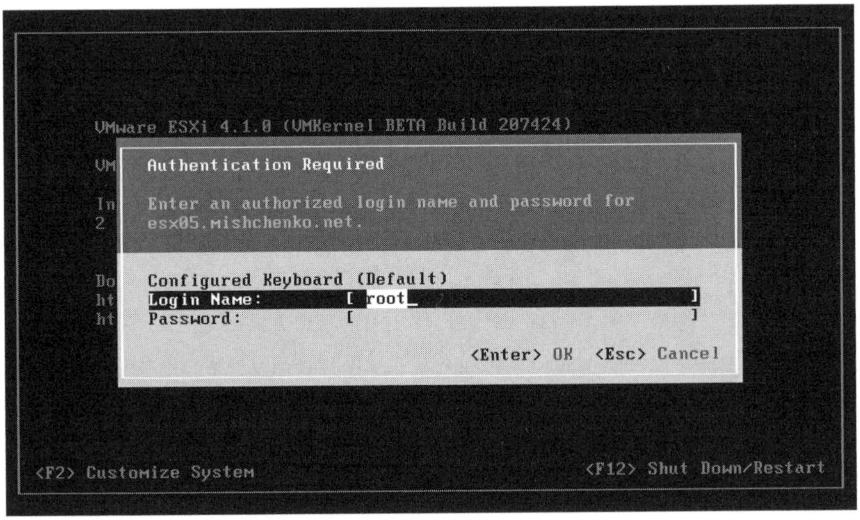

Figure 3.17 The DCUI login screen.

Caution: It is recommended to change the keyboard language used prior to setting the password for the root account. If you change the password and then modify the keyboard language, you may not be able to log in to the DCUI again if you have used a password that cannot be reproduced with the new keyboard language.

You can change the keyboard language on either the login screen shown in Figure 3.17 or with the Configure Keyboard option on the DCUI System Customization screen. To use the latter option, follow these steps:

1.   Select Configure Keyboard on the DCUI Authentication screen or the System Customization screen and press Enter.

2.   Use the arrow keys to scroll to the language you want to select and then press the spacebar to enable that choice.

3.   Press the Enter key to save the configuration change.

Configuring a Password for the Root Login

The most important task in the DCUI is to set the password for the root login. After a default installation, the password for root is blank, opening the host to the potential of unauthorized access. You can use a scripted install to remove that risk, but in cases where that is not possible, your first task in the DCUI should be to set a password for root:

1.   On the DCUI System Customization screen, select Configure Password. If you are setting the password for the first time, you will not be able to enter anything in the Old Password field. If you are changing the password, you must enter the old password before you can switch to the New Password field.

2.   Enter your new password, select the Confirm Password field and retype the new password.

3.   Press Enter to save the password change or Esc to cancel.

VMware ESXi has specific password complexity requirements, which were discussed in Chapter 2. If your new password does not meet those requirements, you will receive the password error shown in Figure 3.18. Once you have set a password for the root account, the option summary for the Change Password option should have a status of Set.

Configure the Password for Root with PowerCLI In Chapter 2, you saw how to change the root password with the vCLI. Now you'll see how to accomplish that with PowerCLI. The first part of this process is to connect to the ESXi server with the `Connect-VIServer` command:

```
Connect-VIServer <hostname> -username root
```

The preceding command is sufficient to connect to a host that has not had the root password set. If you're trying to change the password, you can omit the -username option and you'll be prompted for a login. To change the password, run the following command:

```
Set-VMHostAccount -UserAccount root -password <new password>
```

If you try to change the password to one that does not meet the password complexity requirements for ESXi, you will receive an error similar to the following:

```
Set-VMHostAccount : 3/16/2010 6:41:46 PM   Set-VMHostAccount
    524aec7c-f92e-bd9a-c119-80d5f5233329   A general system error
    occurred: passwd: Authentication token manipulation error
passwd:
At line:1 char:18
+ set-vmhostaccount << << -useraccount root -password short
```

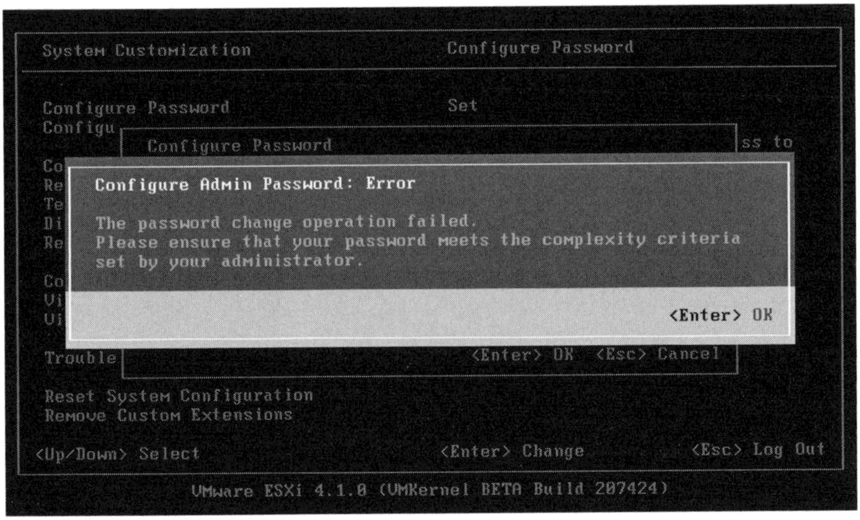

Figure 3.18 Root password complexity error.

Enabling Lockdown Mode

To enhance the security of your VMware ESXi host, you can enable Lockdown Mode. This restricts which accounts are able to manage the host via the following host services: the vSphere API that is used by the vSphere Client, the vCLI and other API clients, Common Information Model (CIM), Tech Support Mode, and the DCUI. After you enable Lockdown Mode, no account other than vpxuser will have authentication permission or be able to perform operations directly on the host. This requires that you manage your ESXi host using vCenter Server rather than connecting directly with your management tools. Lockdown Mode is discussed further in Chapter 7.

Caution: If you are configuring a VMware ESXi host that will not be managed by vCenter Server, you should not enable Lockdown Mode. If you attempt to enable Lockdown Mode on a VMware ESXi host that is not managed by vCenter in the DCUI, the configuration change will not be accepted. Although it may appear that the change has been made, the Lockdown Mode option summary will still display a status of Disabled.

To enable Lockdown Mode, follow these steps:

1. On the DCUI System Customization screen, select the Configure Lockdown Mode option and press Enter.

2. Press the spacebar to enable Lockdown Mode and then press Enter.

Enabling Lockdown Mode with the VI Toolkit for Windows Community Extensions Power-CLI does not have a cmdlet to enable Lockdown Mode, but a third-party extension called the VI Toolkit for Windows Community Extensions provides support for this. To enable Lockdown Mode with this extension, you run the following command.

```
Get-VMHost | Set-TkeVMHostLockdown $True
```

If you try to connect directly to the host with the root login, you will now get the following error.

```
Connect-VIServer : Permission to perform this operation was denied.
At line:1 char:17
+ connect-viserver << << esx05.mishchenko.net
```

Once you have enabled Lockdown Mode, the configuration change takes effect immediately. If you try to connect directly to the ESXi host with the vSphere client, you receive the following error:

```
You do not have permission to login to the server: <hostname>
```

Connecting with other management tools such as PowerCLI or vCLI scripts generates a similar error.

Configuring the Management Network

During the autoconfiguration phase of setup for a new VMware ESXi host, the host is set to use Dynamic Host Configuration Protocol (DHCP) for the IP address. If no DHCP servers are available, ESXi assigns itself a link local IP address on the 16.254.x.x/16 subnet. The autoconfiguration phase also creates a management interface with vmnic0 on vSwitch0. The Configure Management Network screens within the DCUI allow you to set the IP configuration for your host, DNS settings, the virtual local area network (VLAN), and vmnic to use for management traffic.

Caution: If you plan to run VMware ESXi in a high security environment, you may not be allowed to boot an unconfigured host on the network. In such a situation, you should boot ESXi for the first time with no network cables attached to the host. You can then use the following procedures to configure the IP address for the host, VLAN ID to use for management traffic if required, the root password, and the network card to use for management traffic.

When you select the Configure Management Network option, the DCUI screen displays the current IP addresses and hostname, as shown in Figure 3.19. With VMware ESXi, only a single VMkernel port can be dedicated to management traffic. When you are creating a new VMkernel connection with the vSphere client, the Connection Settings screen allows you to set properties for the port group. One of the options is Use This Port Group for Management Traffic. There are also options to enable the port group for vMotion or Fault Tolerance logging. You can also enable this option when you edit the properties for the vSwitch being used for management. If you make changes in the vSphere client, these may not be reflected in the DCUI until you have restarted the management network.

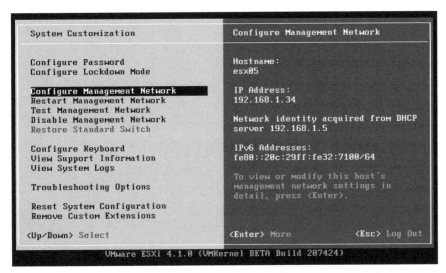

Figure 3.19   The Configure Management Network DCUI menu option.

To begin making networking changes on your VMware ESXi host, select the Configure Management Network option and press Enter. You will have the following configuration options. Selecting each option will display the current settings for that option.

- **Network Adapters.** This screen lists the network adapters that are available to the VMkernel and allows you to configure which are used with the management VMkernel port.

- **VLAN (Optional).** A VLAN ID can be set for the management network. The default setting is none (0).

- **IP Configuration.** On this screen, you can choose between DHCP and a static IP address as well as set a static IP address, subnet mask, and default VMkernel gateway.

- **IPv6 Configuration.** This screen allows you to enable or disable IPv6 for the VMkernel and lets you configure IPv6 settings.

- **DNS Configuration.** You can set the DNS settings for the VMkernel and the hostname with this option.

- **Custom DNS Suffixes.** With this option, you can configure additional DNS suffixes, which the VMkernel uses when attempting to resolve short, unqualified hostnames.

The autoconfiguration process of using vmnic0 for vSwitch0 and the management VMkernel port may not be appropriate to your setup, or you may want to add redundancy to vSwitch0 by adding another network port. In either case, select the Network Adapters option and press Enter. The DCUI Network Adapters screen will show the list of adapters that are available to the VMkernel, as shown in Figure 3.20. The screen shows the physical Media Access Control (MAC) address for each network adapter port as well as a status of Connected or Disconnected. In the case of vmnic2 and vmnic3 in Figure 3.20, the status also appends (...). This indicates that the network port is bound to a vSwitch other than vSwitch0. If you select a network port attached to another vSwitch, you will receive a warning message that the adapter will be removed from its existing connection when you press Enter to save the change on the Network Adapters screen. However, the change will not actually take effect until you press Esc on the

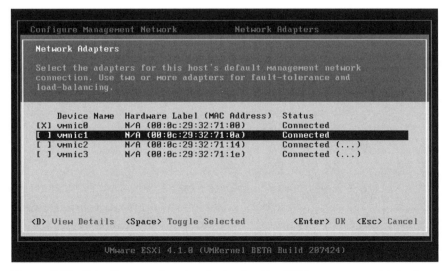

Figure 3.20 Selecting a network adapter for the ESXi management interface.

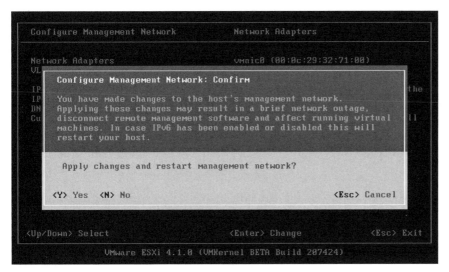

Figure 3.21 Confirming a restart of the management network.

Configure Management Network screen. At that point, you will be prompted to apply your changes and restart the management network, as shown in Figure 3.21. If you select Yes, the changes are committed and the management network is restarted, resulting in a network disconnect for any remotely running management tools. If you select No, your changes are discarded and you return to the main DCUI System Customization screen. Alternatively, you can press Esc to return to the Configure Management Network screen to make further changes.

Caution: Configuration changes made to the management network require a restart of management networking. This affects remote running management tools. VMs running on the ESXi host are not impacted unless you have made a change that might remove a vmnic from an existing VM vSwitch or your network changes IP access to an iSCSI or NFS datastore storage.

The second option on the Configure Management Network menu is the VLAN setting for the management interface. VLANs can be used to create multiple Layer 3 networks (IP subnets) on the same Layer 2 network switch. VLANs provide broadcast control and basic security tools to isolate sensitive network traffic. Chapter 7 discusses VLANs further. The default VLAN ID setting for the management interface is to use no VLAN. In the vSphere client, this is the None (0) option. You can change this to be set to any value between 1 and 4095.

Note: It is possible to configure the management VMkernel port to use VLAN ID 4095. Normally you would consider VLAN 4095 on a VM port group. In that case, you would be using Virtual Machine Guest Tagging (VGT). With VGT, the guest operating system (OS) is responsible for adding or removing the VLAN tag and not the vSwitch on the ESXi host. Using VGT is useful when the number of VLANs per VM exceeds the number of virtual NICs that are assigned to it. This requires an 802.1Q VLAN trunking driver to be running on the guest (OS), and VMware ESXi would not alter tags on packets as it would pass them from the physical switch to the guest OS and back again. In the case of using VLAN ID 4095 for the management interface, the VMkernel will be able to receive all VLAN tagged frames and be able to send on any VLAN ID.

You can use the following procedure to set the VLAN ID:

1. On the Configure Management Network screen, select the VLAN (Optional) menu choice and press Enter.

2. Enter a VLAN ID and then press Enter to save the change.

3. Press Esc to exit the Configure Management Network screen, which will prompt you to apply the change and restart the management network.

If you need to remove the VLAN ID from the management interface, select the VLAN (Optional) menu again and delete the VLAN ID that has been configured. When you press Enter to save the change, the summary for VLAN (Optional) should display Not Set. Press Esc to exit the Configure Management Network screen and apply the change to remove the prior VLAN ID.

The third option for configuring the management network is to set the IP address for the host. The default configuration choice will be set to use DHCP to assign an IP address, subnet mask, and default gateway.

To set the IP address for the host, follow these steps:

1. Select IP Configuration on the Configure Management Network screen and press Enter.

2. Use the arrow keys to select the Set Static IP Address and Network Configuration option and press the spacebar to enable it.

3. Enter the IP address, subnet mask, and default gateway and then press Enter to save the change and return to the Configure Management Network screen.

4. The IP Configuration summary should now display a setting of Manual. Press Esc to exit the network configuration screen and to apply the configuration change.

Caution: When you set a static IP address for VMware ESXi, the DCUI will not display an error message if you have selected to use an IP address that is already in use on the network.

You can also enable an IPv6 address for the management VMkernel port. The default configuration disables IPv6 support for management traffic on the host. Your host can be configured to obtain an IPv6 address automatically if you are running a DHCPv6 server or if your network supports Router Advertisement. When you select the IPv6 Configuration option, you will see the configuration screen shown in Figure 3.22. If you want to disable IPv6 for management traffic, press the spacebar to deselect the Enable IPv6 option. This requires a restart of the host to take effect. For setting IPv6 addresses on the host, you have the following options:

- Do not use automatic configuration. In this case, you will need to enter manually up to three IPv6 addresses and optionally a default gateway.

- Use DHCP stateful configuration. You can use this option if you have a DHCPv6 server. With the IPv6 stateful address configuration, the DHCPv6 server maintains a list of nodes and their state to determine the availability of each IP address in the configured DHCP range.

- Use Internet Control Message Protocol (ICMP) stateless configuration. With this option, the VMware ESXi host autoconfigures its own IPv6 addresses based on router advertisements.

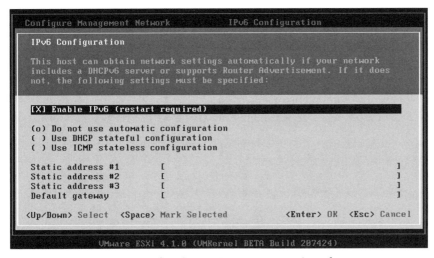

Figure 3.22 Enabling IPv6 for the ESXi management interface.

Once you have made your configuration changes, press Enter to save and exit the IPv6 Configuration screen. After you press Esc to exit Configure Management Network screen, you will be prompted to apply your change and to restart the management network.

The fifth configuration option for the management network is to set the DNS servers and host-name. The default option is to obtain DNS server addresses and a hostname automatically:

1. Select the DNS Configuration option and press Enter to make changes.

2. Select the Use the Following DNS Server Addresses and Hostname option and press the spacebar to enable it.

3. You then can enter the IP addresses of your primary and alternate DNS servers as well as the hostname. You can choose to leave the DNS server field blank.

4. Press Enter to save your changes and to exit the DNS Configuration screen.

5. Press Esc to exit the configuration screen and to apply your changes.

The last network configuration option is to set custom DNS suffixes. Select the Custom DNS Suffixes option and press Enter. You can enter multiple DNS suffixes, separating each with a comma or space. Press Enter to save your changes and then Esc to exit and apply your changes. As with the other Configure Management Network options, you will be prompted to restart the management network.

Restarting the Management Network

A restart of the management network is a required step when making a configuration change to the management VMkernel port. You may also have to perform this task should there be a problem with management network traffic to the ESXi host or if you want to renew a DHCP lease. Renewing the DHCP lease for a host may change the IP address that is assigned to that host. In such a case, any remote management tools may be unable to connect to the host. Restarting the management network may also impact the VMs running on the host.

To restart the management network, follow these steps:

1. On the DCUI System Customization screen, select Restart Management Network and press Enter.

2. Press F11 to confirm that you want to restart the management network.

3. The Restart Management Network screen displays the progress of the restart. Once it has completed, press Enter to return to the System Customization screen.

Testing the Management Network

The Test Management Network option provides the interface to perform simple network con-nectivity tests. For a default configuration ESXi, perform the following four tests:

■ Ping the VMkernel default gateway for the configured IP settings

■ Ping the primary DNS server

- Ping the alternate DNS server

- Resolve the configured hostname

If you have configured an IPv6 default gateway on your ESXi host, that IPv6 address will be used for the connectivity test instead of the alternate DNS server. You can update or remove the IP addresses or hostname as required and then press Enter to start the test. The output from the test will be similar to what is shown in Figure 3.23. Besides testing IP and DNS setup issues, this option can be useful for troubleshooting iSCSI connectivity issues. With prior versions of ESX, you would need to open a console session and then test connectivity to the iSCSI SAN with both ping and vmkping, as the former would test connectivity for the service console and the latter would test connectivity for the VMkernel. As all iSCSI network traffic is handled by the VMkernel in ESXi, the ping test run in the DCUI is sufficient to test for a network problem on your iSCSI device.

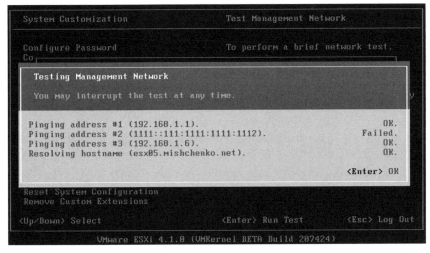

Figure 3.23   Testing management network connectivity.

Disabling the Management Network

At times you may find it necessary to isolate your VMware ESXi host from vCenter Server, perhaps to troubleshoot a problem with a High Availability (HA) or Distributed Resource Scheduler (DRS) cluster. Shutting down the host or changing the IP configuration may not be a desirable option, so the Disable Management Network option provides the opportunity to remove the ESXi host from the network without making any configuration changes. Once the management network is disabled, you will be unable to access the host via the vCenter Server or use the vSphere client or other ESXi hosts. This change will not impact running virtual machines and they will continue to run when the management network is disabled.

To disable the management network, follow these steps:

1. On the DCUI System Customization screen, select the Disable Management Network option and press Enter.

2. A dialog box appears requesting that you press F11 to disable the management network.

Once you are returned to the System Customization screen, you will notice that the Disable Management Network option is now called Enable Management Network and that the other network options have been disabled, as is shown in Figure 3.24. While the management network is disabled, no remote management tools can access the host. The VMkernel networking stack will be disabled, so if you access the Tech Support Console, you will not have network connectivity to any other hosts. The main DCUI welcome screen will no longer display the configured IP address for the management network, but will rather display that you can download tools to manage the host from http://0.0.0.0/ (STATIC). To enable the management network again, select the Enable Management Network, press Enter, and then press F11 on the confirmation screen.

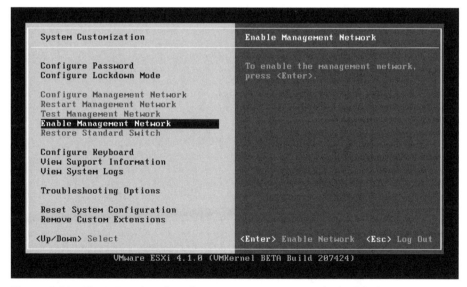

Figure 3.24 The DCUI showing the management network disabled.

Restoring the Standard vSwitch

One of the new features of vSphere 4.0 is vNetwork Distributed Switches, which allow for configuration of networking at the vCenter level rather than individually on each host connected to vCenter Server. This allows for consistent configuration of vSwitches, making it easier to migrate VMs between hosts. Should you configure vNetwork Distributed Switches on your

VMware ESXi host and you find that you then need to remove the configuration; the Restore Standard Switch option provides this functionality in the DCUI. You may need to perform this operation for the following reasons:

- The host is no longer connected to vCenter Server and most vNetwork Distributed Switch features are unavailable to your ESXi host.

- The vNetwork Distributed Switch is no longer working or needed.

- The vNetwork Distributed Switch much be removed to restore connectivity to your vCenter Server but you require the host to remain accessible.

When you restore the standard vSwitch, a new virtual adapter is created and the management VMkernel port that is connected to the vNetwork Distributed Switch is moved to the new vSwitch. If your ESXi host has a standard vSwitch, the option to restore will be grayed out. To restore the standard switch, use the following process:

1. Select the Restore Standard Switch option on the System Customization screen and press Enter.

2. Press F11 to confirm the configuration change.

Once you are returned to the System Customization screen, the Restore Standard Switch option should be grayed out.

Viewing Support Information

If you select the option View Support Information, the following information about the VMware ESXi host is displayed:

- The server's physical serial number.

- The license number that has been configured for the host.

- The SHA1 thumbprint for the Secure Sockets Layer (SSL) certificate used by the host. You can use the thumbprint to verify that you are joining the correct ESXi host to your vCenter Server as the Add Host wizard will display the SHA1 thumbprint.

If you are using ESXi Embedded or have installed a customized version of ESXi, additional support information may be shown if you press the Page Down key.

Viewing System Logs

At some point, you may find that you need to review the system logs for your VMware ESXi host to troubleshoot an issue. The View System Logs menu choice provides the opportunity to

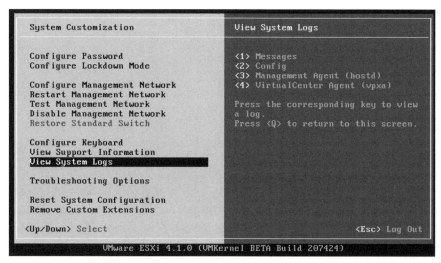

Figure 3.25   Viewing system logs in the DCUI.

view the host's logs at the DCUI. When you select this option, you will see the four following system logs to view, as shown in Figure 3.25:

- **<1> Messages.** With ESX, the `messages` file is the log for the Linux-based service console. With ESXi, `messages` is the log file for the VMkernel and is the equivalent file to `/var/log/vmkernel` and `/var/log/vmkwarnings` on ESX.

- **<2> Config.** This log file records the VMkernel initialization process. Once your VMware ESXi host has booted up, this log file is no longer written to. It will contain information about the modules and drivers being loaded, the initialization of the system filesystem, mounting of datastores, network initialization, and the starting of system agents. The `config` log file provides an extensive view of what happens to get your host from the initial loading of the VMkernel to a fully functioning host.

- **<3> Management Agent (hostd).** The `hostd` process is the agent that provides API access to the VMkernel and is used by the vSphere client and other remote management applications. This option displays the log for that agent.

- **<4> VirtualCenter Agent (vpxa).** This system log file is available only on a vCenter Server–managed host. The `vpxa` process is used to connect the host to vCenter and the log records events and errors related to vCenter communications and operations.

To view a log file, press the corresponding number key for the log. The DCUI screen will be replaced with the log file. An extensive help file can be accessed by pressing the H key. To scroll down through the log file, you can press the spacebar to move down one screen or press Enter to move down one line. You can likewise use the Page Up and Page Down keys. To perform a search of the log file, you can use the following process:

1. Press the slash (/) key.

2. Type the text you want to find. Keep in mind that the search will be case sensitive.

3. Press Enter.

If your search word is found, it will be highlighted in the log file. You can then press the N key to repeat the search. If you want to search backward through the file, you can type in ?<search term> instead of using the slash key and then press Shift+N to repeat the backward search. Another useful command for you to use when viewing log files is the F key, which will follow the log file as it is updated. This is the equivalent to using the tail -f command in the ESX console. You can press Ctrl+C to stop following the log file. Finally, you can press the Q key to exit the log file and to return to the DCUI System Customization screen.

Troubleshooting Mode Options

Troubleshooting Mode Options is a new screen with ESXi 4.1. Through this screen, you can enable access to Local Tech Support mode or Remote Tech Support mode using Secure Shell (SSH). On the screen, you can also restart the management agents for the host. This would serve the equivalent function of running services mgmt-vmware restart on a VMware ESX host. When you select the option, the screen shown in Figure 3.26 is displayed.

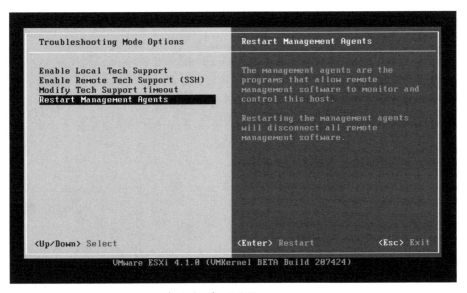

Figure 3.26 Viewing system logs in the DCUI.

With ESXi 3.5 and 4.0, to access the console, you would press Alt+F1, type in `unsupported` and then press Enter to access a login screen to the console. With ESXi 4.1, that is no longer the case. To access the console, you must enable access on the Troubleshooting Mode Options screen. Select the Enable Local Tech Support option and press Enter. The option changes to Disable Local Tech Support and when you press Alt+F1 to access the console screen, you will now see a login prompt and the following warning:

```
Tech Support Mode is not supported unless used in consultation with
   VMware Tech Support.
```

You can press Alt+F2 to return to the DCUI.

With the Enable Remote Tech Support (SSH) option, you can enable SSH sessions to your host for troubleshooting remotely without needing to access the console and modify system files. Select the option and press Enter to enable SSH access. The option will change to Disable Remote Tech Support (SSH), and as with Local Tech Support mode, you can press Enter again to disable it manually.

Caution: When you disable Remote Tech Support mode existing SSH sessions will not be automatically terminated. New session attempts will receive a `connection refused` error, but you will be able to use an existing SSH session until you close the SSH client. For a Local Tech Support session, type in the `exit` command to close your session. If you don't, your local session will remain available even after Local Tech Support mode is disabled.

To reduce the security risk of enabling Local or Remote Tech Support mode, you can enable a timeout value. When you select the Modify Tech Support timeout option and press Enter, you will be able to enter a timeout value between 0 and 1440 minutes (12 hours). If you enter 0, there will be no timeout for Local and Remote Tech Support modes and this is not a recommended setting for production systems. The default value is 10 minutes. Enter your desired timeout value and press Enter.

Note: The Troubleshooting Mode Options screen will not automatically refresh the status for Local and Remote Tech Support modes and thus the screen may show that the options need to be disabled even though they already have been. You can press the ESC key and then Enter to exit and return to the screen to refresh the enable/disable status of the support modes.

The last option on the Troubleshooting Mode Options screen is to restart the management agents. You may need to restart the agents if you are having problems accessing the ESXi host remotely. This process restarts all agents and services configured in /etc/inet.d, which includes items such as the DCUI, the hostd agent, the ntpd agent, and the sfcdb agent. If the host is a member of a High Availability cluster, the Automated Availability Manager (AAM) will also be restarted. Any remote management connection will be interrupted when you restart the management agents.

To restart the management agents on your ESXi host, use the following process:

1. Select the Restart Management Agents option and press Enter.

2. When prompted to confirm the operation, press F11.

3. The progress of the operation is displayed. You can press Enter once the process is complete.

Resetting Your System Configuration

The Reset System Configuration menu option provides a method to "reinstall" your ESXi, but in a much faster way. Within a VMware ESX environment, you would have to disconnect your SAN storage, run through the installation process, reconfigure your host, and join it to your vCenter Server again. With ESXi, you can reset the configuration and be ready to reboot your host within seconds. You don't have to make changes to any FC SAN connections, as datastores that were attached to the host are not impacted. After you have rebooted, you can reconfigure your storage and then reregister the VMs that the host was running prior to the reset.

The reset process deletes your system configuration, sets the root password to be blank, and reboots the host. If you are using ESXi Embedded, any configuration changes made by the vendor, such as a license file, will also be deleted. It is recommended to make a system configuration backup using the vCLI command vicfg-cfgbackup before resetting the system. To reset your system configuration, use this process:

1. Select the Reset System Configuraton option on the menu and press Enter.

2. Confirm the operation by pressing F11.

3. After a short period, you will be asked to reboot the host by pressing Enter.

Removing Custom Extensions

A custom VMware ESXi extension is a VMkernel driver or CIM provider that is typically provided by a third-party source. You will typically install an extension to add hardware support or to enhance monitoring of your system. An extension will typically be installed using the vCLI command vihostupdate.

Should you have a problem with an extension, the Remove Custom Extensions menu choice will allow you to remove all extensions from the system. You will not be able to remove just a single extension.

Note: If you have just installed an extension and are having problems with it, you can remove just it using the alternate boot bank. See Chapter 11, "Under the Hood with the ESXi Tech Support Mode," for a discussion of that process.

To remove all custom extensions installed on your host, use the following process:

1. On the System Customization menu, select Reset Customized Settings. Then press Enter.

2. When prompted, press F11 to confirm the process.

3. Once the process is complete, press Enter to reboot the host.

Using Third-Party Products to Manage Your Hosts

When you deploy VMware ESXi, vCenter Server is the primary tool that you use to manage your hosts. This section reviews some of the third-party products available for managing your datacenter. A rich variety of tools and products have emerged from VMware partners and third-party developers, and the products discussed in this section represent only a fraction of the options available for you to use with ESXi. These tools range from simple and free to complex and not so free.

RVTools

RVTools is a Windows .NET 2.0 application which uses the vSphere 4 software development kit (SDK) to display a wealth of information about your hosts and VM. RVTools works both with vCenter Server and standalone ESXi hosts to show information about CPU, memory, NICs, snapshots, and also every other property for your VMs and hosts. The application can be downloaded from http://www.robware.net/ and is ready for use after a very short installation process.

When you start RVTools, you enter the vCenter or ESXi host to which you are connecting, using an account that has full administrative rights. RVTools then queries the target and populates a number of tabs with information about hosts and VMs, as shown in Figure 3.27. The views are not dynamic, but you can refresh the data by selecting View > Refresh. You can select the different tabs to quickly view the information that you're looking for. vSnapshot displays a list of VMs with snapshots. With the vDatastore tab, you can quickly get a list of all the datastores and their access status, capacity, and free space. On the vTools tab, you can see the VMware Tools status for each VM and you can optionally select to install VMware Tools to those VMs that don't have it installed or have an out-of-date version.

You'll find that the most powerful feature of this product is the vHealth tab. The configuration options for the tab are shown in Figure 3.27. The Health Check Properties windows includes

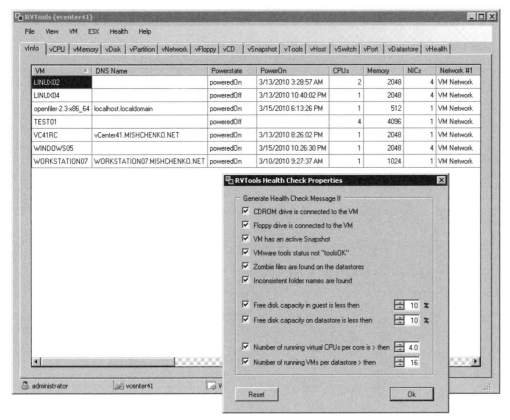

Figure 3.27   Configuring the health check options for RVTools.

options to check which VMs have snapshots, free disk capacity threshold checks for VMs and datastores, and the ability to check the number of VMs per CPU core and datastore. The vHealth tab provides a summary of the objects that have failed to meet your configured thresholds and provides you with a simple checklist of potential issues you may have to address. If you want to analyze the data provided further, you can export a specific tab or all tabs to comma-separated value (CSV) files.

Veeam FastSCP

At some point, you'll need to transfer files to your host or between your hosts. FastSCP provides a simple-to-use tool that will manage your file transfer with ESXi without requiring the enabling of the unsupported SSH service. The installation includes the GUI application for managing transfers, a built-in editor that will properly display ESXi files (unlike Notepad, which tends to bungle the formatting), and a Windows service to manage scheduled transfers. FastSCP can authenticate directly with your ESXi host or with vCenter. You can also manage files on Linux hosts.

When copying files, FastSCP uses space preallocation to ensure that the copied file is not fragmented. You can also enable e-mail reporting for scheduled jobs.

Veeam provides a number of other free tools, including Visio stencils and Veeam Monitor Free Edition, which provides real-time monitoring and alerting. Veeam's commercial products include tools for backup and replication, reporting, and monitoring and a management pack for Microsoft Systems Center Operations Manager.

Xtravirt vSphere Client RDP Plug-In

vSphere client plug-ins provide a method to extend the vSphere client by allowing you to create custom menus and tabs with vCenter that you can integrate with third-party applications. For example, vCenter Update Manager is provided as a plug-in and EMC provides the Storage Viewer plug-in to provide views of storage usage and configuration information. The Xtravirt vSphere Client RDP (Remote Desktop Protocol) Plug-in provides integration of the Windows Remote Desktop tool with the vSphere client.

The installation package for the plug-in can be downloaded from http://www.xtravirt.com and consists of a Microsoft Installer (MSI) package which you install on the same workstation where you have the vSphere client installed. The installation does require that Microsoft .NET Framework 3.5 be already installed. Once you have the plug-in installed you can start the vSphere client and connect to your vCenter Server host. Select Plug-ins > Manage Plug-ins and you should see the Xtravirt RDP plug-in installed and enabled.

If you select the Home view and then choose Solutions and Applications > Xtravirt RDP Plugin, you can configure your RDP connection information to be used for the RDP connections that you make with this plug-in. To connect to a VM with the RDP client, simply right-click on the VM and select Connect via RDP, as shown in Figure 3.28.

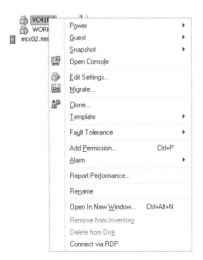

Figure 3.28   Launching an RDP session with the Xtravirt RDP plug-in.

Vizioncore vFoglight

vFoglight provides an enterprise-class solution for performance monitoring, capacity, planning and chargeback. With performance monitoring, vFoglight can detect and resolve performance and availability issues for both virtual and physical servers. Capacity planning reduces the need to overallocate infrastructure components. The chargeback features of vFoglight allow you to easily ascertain which business groups and workloads are consuming resources, which allow costs to be recovered according to actual infrastructure use.

Access to the data that vFoglight collects and analyzes is available through various Web-based dashboards. The vmExplorer dashboard provides detailed views of the datacenter, clusters, hosts, resource pools, and VMs. The dashboard view in Figure 3.29 provides a summary view of a datacenter. The page displays the overall resource usage for CPU, network, memory, and disk. A table shows the number of alerts for clusters, hosts, and VMs. The other dashboards include vmMonitor and vmAlarms. vmMonitor is responsible for performance and availability monitoring. vmAlarms provides alerts capability and is augmented with expert advice for the alerts that are generated.

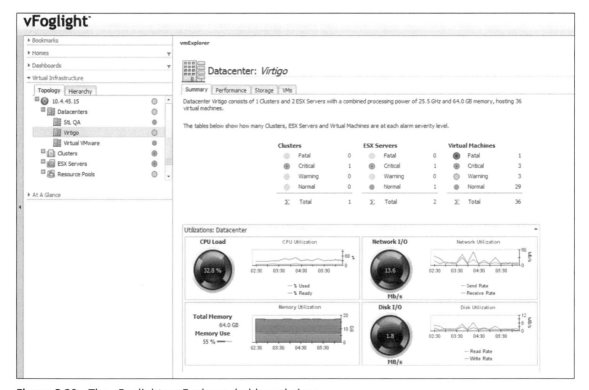

Figure 3.29   The vFoglight vmExplorer dashboard view.

ManageIQ EVM Control

EVM Control is part of ManageIQ's Enterprise Virtualization Management (EVM) suite. EVM Control provides policy-based management, security and compliance capabilities for your vCenter Server and ESXi deployment. With policy-based management of VMs, you can ensure that IT standards are enforced, improving reliability and availability.

Some of the elements of EVM Control include the following:

- **Logging and Auditing.** You can document system changes and policy updates with the ability to report on the history of changes and transactions.

- **Configurable Policy Enforcement.** vCenter Server and ESXi make the creation, migration, and cloning of VMs such an easy task that it becomes difficult to control what happens to a VM. With configuration policy, management policies can be applied at any point in the VM life cycle, including creation, cloning, migration, and even stopping and starting. EVM Control ensures that policies are enforced at all times and for all VMs.

- **Adaptive Policy Engine.** EVM Control can determine the best combination of operations, security, configuration, and business policies that are appropriate to a specific VM, host, or event.

- **Policy Actions.** A number of automated responses are available with EVM Control, including notifications, issuing warning to end users and administrators, and quarantining or disabling of noncompliant VMs.

Conclusion

There is a broad range of tools for managing VMware ESXi and vCenter Server. The vSphere client provides the ability to manage both standalone ESXi hosts and hosts that are part of a vCenter Server datacenter. VMware has introduced two great scripting options with the vCLI and PowerCLI. These scripting options can be used to reduce the load of repetitive and complex tasks. In addition to the management tools that VMware develops, there is a wide range of third-party tools, ranging from simple utilities to complete virtual machine life cycle management.

4 Installation Options

With the first release of VMware ESXi, installation options were limited to running ESXi Embedded on an original equipment manufacturer (OEM) flash device or to installing ESXi Installable from CD-ROM to a limited number of local disk options. With VMware ESXi 4.1, the installation options have been expanded to include booting from a number of different sources and using scripted installs.

In this chapter, you will learn to:

- Set up and configure VMware ESXi Embedded

- Use the various ESXi Installable media options

- Configure to boot ESXi with PXELINUX and gPXE

- Install VMware ESXi using graphical mode

- Install VMware ESXi using scripted mode

Using ESXi Embedded

As discussed in Chapter 1, "Introduction to VMware ESXi 4.1," ESXi Embedded refers to the version of VMware ESXi that comes original equipment manufacturer (OEM)-installed on a flash device in certified hardware. ESXi Embedded is available from a number of hardware venders, including Dell, Hewlett Packard (HP), and IBM. This option allows the administrator to plug the server into the network, boot up, and have the host configured within vCenter Server within a very short period of time. With ESXi Embedded, no local hard drive is required, which eliminates a point of failure, simplifies server management, and reduces power consumption and heat generation.

With ESXi Embedded, there is no install process such as that discussed in Chapter 2, "Getting Started with a Quick Install." Rather, ESXi Embedded will boot from the embedded boot device and be ready for configuration. If your network is set up with a Dynamic Host Configuration Protocol (DHCP) server, the ESXi Embedded host will obtain an IP address and be ready for network configuration and setting of the root password with the vSphere client. As previously shown, these tasks can also be accomplished with the Direct Console User Interface (DCUI) or vSphere Command-Line Interface (vCLI) commands.

To prepare your ESXi Embedded host for configuration, you should first confirm that the host is set to boot from the proper boot device:

1. While your ESXi host is powering on, press the key that will enter the host's Basic Input/Output System (BIOS) setup. Depending on the model of server, that may require pressing Del or a certain function key.

2. Edit the boot device priority to set the ESXi Embedded boot device to be the first boot device. A sample of this is shown in Figure 4.1.

3. Save the BIOS change and reboot the host.

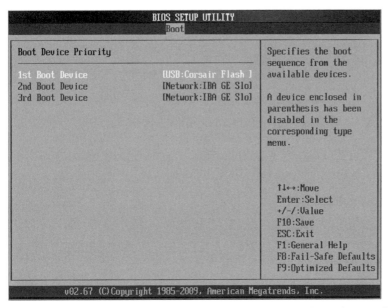

Figure 4.1 Configuring the host BIOS boot settings to boot from a flash device.

The host should boot to the VMware ESXi DCUI screen. If the host is not able to start VMware ESXi, you may need to review the BIOS settings or run the recovery process for ESXi Embedded found in Chapter 11, "Under the Hood with the ESXi Tech Support Mode."

Once the host has booted to VMware ESXi Embedded, you will be ready to configure the management port. During the autoconfiguration phase, ESXi will assign vmnic0 to vSwitch0 for management access. If there is a DHCP server available, VMware ESXi will obtain an IP address for the host. If the network interface card (NIC) assigned as vmnic0 is not on your management network, you can change this default choice by manually changing the NIC used in the DCUI. With the DCUI, you will also be able to set the IP address to be used for management traffic as well as the hostname and DNS server settings. You can access the DCUI at the console of the host or by accessing the host with a remote management card.

To configure the network adapter, follow these steps:

1. Press F2 to log in to the DCUI. If the password for the root account has not been set, log in with a blank password.

2. Select the Configure Management Network option and press Enter.

3. Select Network Adapters and press Enter.

4. The Network Adapters screen, shown in Figure 4.2, lists the network adapters that VMware ESXi recognizes in your system. Select the network adapter to use for management traffic and press the Space bar to enable the network adapter. If you do not want to use vmnic0 for management traffic, select the network adapter and press the Space bar to disable the adapter for management traffic.

5. Press Enter to close the Network Adapters screen.

6. Press Esc on the Configure Management Network screen to return to the main DCUI screen.

7. You will be prompted to confirm the change to your management network. Select Yes to apply the change and restart the management network.

If you have not set a static IP address for management traffic, you can set that with the DCUI, vSphere Client, or vCLI, as described in Chapter 2. The autoconfiguration process will have also set a blank password for the root account. The process for setting the root password is also discussed in Chapter 2.

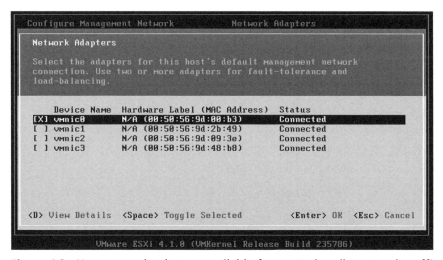

Figure 4.2 Host network adapters available for use to handle network traffic.

Changing the Management Network Adapter with the vCLI When changing the network adapter used for management traffic, you'll use three vCLI commands: `vicfg-vswitch`, `vicfg-nics`, and `vicfg-vmknic`. `vicfg-nics` can be used to list the host network adapters and also to set the speed and duplex settings for the network adapters. The following command run with the `-list` option shows the network adapters available on the server running ESXi Embedded:

```
[vi-admin@vma bin]$ vicfg-nics --server esx05.mishchenko.net --list
Name   PCI    Driver   Link Speed   Duplex MAC Address     MTU
  Description
vmnic0 02:01.0 e1000     Up  1000Mbps Full  00:0c:29:32:71:00 1500
    Intel Corporation Abstract PRO/1000 MT Single Port Adapter
vmnic1 02:04.0 e1000     Up  1000Mbps Full  00:0c:29:32:71:0a
    Intel Corporation Abstract PRO/1000 MT Single Port Adapter
vmnic2 02:05.0 e1000     Up  1000Mbps Full  00:0c:29:32:71:14
    Intel Corporation Abstract PRO/1000 MT Single Port Adapter
vmnic3 02:06.0 e1000     Up  1000Mbps Full  00:0c:29:32:71:1e
    Intel Corporation Abstract PRO/1000 MT Single Port Adapter
```

The `vicfg-vswitch` command is used to display and modify the vSwitch configuration on the host. Running the command with the `-list` option displays the setup of the host as configured by the autoconfiguration process:

```
[vi-admin@vma bin]$ vicfg-vswitch --server esx05.mishchenko.net --list
Switch Name   Num Ports    Used Ports    Configured Ports   MTU
  Uplinks
vSwitch0      128          3             128                1500
  vmnic0

    PortGroup Name           VLAN ID  Used Ports   Uplinks
    VM Network               0        0            vmnic0
    Management Network       0        1            vmnic0
```

Running the command with the `--link` option will link another network adapter to the vSwitch. In the following example, vmnic0 is linked to vSwitch0, but as the updated vSwitch listing shows, the network adapter is linked to vSwitch0 but not to the VMkernel Management Network port. The vSphere client will show vmnic1 as Active for the VM Network portgroup but unused for the Management Network port.

```
[vi-admin@vma bin]$ vicfg-vswitch --server esx05.mishchenko.net --link vmnic1
  vSwitch0
Updated uplinks: vmnic0, vmnic1
[vi-admin@vma bin]$ vicfg-vswitch --server esx05.mishchenko.net --list
Switch Name   Num Ports    Used Ports    Configured Ports   MTU
  Uplinks
```

```
vSwitch0      128         4          128           1500
   vmnic0,vmnic1
```

PortGroup Name	VLAN ID	Used Ports	Uplinks
VM Network	0	0	vmnic0,vmnic1
Management Network	0	1	vmnic0

To add vmnic1 to the Management Network VMkernel port group, it is necessary to use the --add-pg-uplink option as follows:

```
[vi-admin@vma bin]$ vicfg-vswitch --server esx05.mishchenko.net --add-
   pg-uplink
   vmnic1 --pg "Management Network" vSwitch0
Added uplink adapter successfully.
```

At this point, you'll have vmnic0 and vmnic1 configured as active network cards for the management port. Failure of either NIC port will not affect communications with the management port. If you want, you can remove vmnic0 from either the management port or the vSwitch completely. To remove the NIC port from the management port, you can use vicfg-vswitch with the --del-pg-uplink option. If you use the unlink option with the same command, you will remove the NIC port from the vSwitch completely. You should be careful with either option, as they can remove both NIC ports from the vSwitch and effectively isolate your VMware ESXi from the network. In such a case, however, you would be able to use the DCUI to reconnect one of the NIC ports to the management network.

ESXi and Virtual Networking The virtual switch (vSwitch) is the foundation for networking with VMware ESXi. vSwitches provide network connectivity for virtual machines, for management tools like vCenter Server and the vSphere client, between ESXi hosts, and for access to Internet Small Computer System Interface (iSCSI) and Network File System (NFS) storage. There are two types of vSwitches: vNetwork Standard Switches and vNetwork Distributed Switches. vNetwork Standard Switches are configured on a per-host basis. Although you can configure a number of your hosts with the same vSwitch configuration, any change you make to your standard setup must be performed on each host. With vNetwork Distributed Switches (dvSwitch), configuration is centralized within vCenter Server, and a single dvSwitch configuration is applied across multiple ESXi hosts. This reduces configuration complexity and the possibility of configuration mistakes.

vSwitches are similar to physical switches in that they function at Layer 2, support virtual local area network (VLAN) configurations, and maintain Media Access Control (MAC) address tables. vSwitches are different in that they do not support negotiation protocols such as Dynamic Trunking Protocol or Port Aggregation Protocol, are not managed independently via Telnet for example, and due to the architecture of vSwitches, they do not need to support Spanning Tree Protcol.

vSwitches rely on the following two elements: ports/port groups and uplinks. Ports and port groups provide connectivity for the VMkernel and virtual machines to a vSwitch. With ESXi, you can create a VMkernel port that is used for VMkernel network traffic such as management, network storage, and vMotion. You can also create a virtual machine port group to which you connect the virtual network cards of your virtual machines. Uplinks provide communication between the ports and port groups on your vSwitches and your physical network. For the VMkernel ports or virtual machine port groups to communicate with the rest of your network, you must link the vSwitch to one or more physical network cards in your host. Your ESXi host will list its physical network card ports as vmnic0, vmnic1, and so on. Connecting multiple network cards to a single vSwitch provides redundancy in case of the failure of a network card or the physical switch that it is connected to. You can create a vSwitch with no uplink; this is known as an *internal only vSwitch*. This type of vSwitch can be useful for isolating virtual machine network traffic as you would require when cloning production servers to a test environment.

One of the configuration tasks that you will need to take care of that is unique to ESXi Embedded is setup of a scratch partition for the VMkernel swap file. The autoconfiguration process for ESXi will attempt to create a 4GB Virtual File Allocation Table (VFAT) scratch partition on which to store the system swap file should the partition not exist on another partition. With ESXi Embedded, there is no partition space available for this, so you will need to configure the swap file to reside on one of your datastores. In prior versions of ESXi, this was a requirement to configure prior to joining the host to a High Availability (HA) cluster. This is no longer the case, but the scratch partition is used to generate a support bundle, so it remains a worthwhile option to configure. See Chapter 11 for the process to create a support bundle.

To enable the scratch partition for use by the userworld swap file, you can follow this process in the vSphere client either connected to the host directly or via vCenter Server:

1. If you are connecting via vCenter Server, select the ESXi host.

2. Click the Configuration tab and then click Advanced Settings in the Software section.

3. Select ScratchConfig to display the four scratch configuration options. ScratchConfig. CurrentScratchLocation and ScratchConfig.CurrentSwapState will display the currently configured scratch location and whether the scratch partition is enabled for you. The option will be grayed out and in this case will not be configured.

4. Select ScratchConfig.ConfiguredScratchLocation and enter a valid directory with at least 1GB of free space.

5. Check the option ScratchConfig.ConfiguredSwapState.

6. Click OK to close the Advanced Configuration window.

7. Reboot your ESXi host to apply the configuration change.

You can configure the scratch partition on either local or shared storage. While you may see the best performance with the swap file on a local disk, with ESXi Embedded this will not be an option, so you will need to use shared storage. If you plan to configure multiple hosts to use the same logical unit number (LUN) for storage of the swap file, you'll need to ensure that a unique folder is created for each host and that the ConfiguredScratchLocation path reflects that unique folder.

Configuring the Scratch Partition with the vCLI The vCLI command vicfg-advcfg is used to configure the advanced settings at Configuration > Software > Advanced Settings in the vSphere client. To check one of the options mentioned previously, you can use the get option with the command. You can configure options with the set option as shown in the following listing. Once you have made these configuration updates, you will need to reboot your ESXi host to apply the changes.

```
vicfg-advcfg --server esx05.mishchenko.net --set true
    ScratchConfig.ConfiguredSwapState
Value of ScratchConfig.ConfiguredSwapState is true
vicfg-advcfg --server esx05 --set /vmfs/volumes/datastore1/esx05_swap
    ScratchConfig.ConfiguredScratchLocation
Value of ScratchConfig.ConfiguredScratchLocation is
    /vmfs/volumes/datastore1/esx05_swap
```

ESXi Installable Media and Boot Options

With VMware ESXi 4.0 and earlier versions, ESXi Installable could be booted only from CD-ROM and installed in graphical mode as shown in Chapter 2. With VMware ESXi 4.1, a number of new methods and options have been added to better meet the diverse needs of the environments in which ESXi will be installed. The new options include selecting the storage and access of the installation media, choosing a method of booting the installer, and specifying a mode in which the installer is to run.

The default installation option is to boot VMware ESXi from a CD-ROM; then the install process uses graphical mode and the CD-ROM as the source of the installation media. You can modify this process with the following options. First, storage and access for the ESXi installation image can be via:

- CD-ROM (default)

- HTTP/HTTPS (HTTPS access via a proxy server is not supported)

- File Transfer Protocol (FTP)
- NFS

Second, the installer can now be booted from:

- CD-ROM (default)
- Preboot Execution Environment (PXE)

Third, the installer can be run in one of two modes:

- Interactive graphical (default)
- Scripted

Lastly, when run as a scripted installation, the script can be stored and accessed on:

- Within the ESXi Installer ramdisk (default)
- On the installation CD-ROM
- HTTP/HTTPS
- FTP
- NFS

Through the following sections of this chapter, you'll look at the various preceding components to understand how to set up each one. Then the components will be put together to demonstrate how you can automate your VMware ESXi install process.

Before proceeding, it is worthwhile to examine how the components will fit together for a completely automated PXE installation. This process is shown in Figure 4.3. Not all the components are strictly required for an installation. For example, you can PXE boot the ESXi installer and then run a graphical installation. Likewise, you can boot from the installation CD and then choose to run a scripted installation. An installation script is a plain text file containing commands that allow the install to proceed without intervention. Together, these components will help you create an infrastructure that enables you to install many hosts with a minimal effort.

If your installation process will use all the components discussed in this chapter, the installation will follow this process:

1. The target host is powered on.

2. The PXE client on the host obtains an IP address lease from your DHCP server. The lease contains the IP address for your Trivial File Transfer Protocol (TFTP) server and the network boot loader (PXELINUX or gPXE) to use.

3. The ESXi host downloads and executes the network boot loader. PXELINUX or gPXE loads the configuration file which enables the host to load the VMkernel and ramdisk files for the installation process.

4. The system boots the ESXi installer. If an installation script is specified in the configuration file then it is loaded and parsed by the installer.

5. The ESXi installer loads the install image from the media depot.

6. The ESXi installer copies the install image to the host's boot disk and applies the installation script. The host reboots to complete the installation.

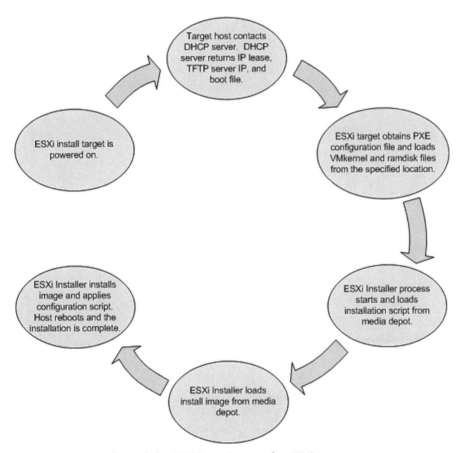

Figure 4.3 Overview of the PXE Boot Process for ESXi.

Creating a Network Media Depot for VMware ESXi

With the default media storage option, you download the ISO image from vmware.com, burn it to a CD-ROM, and then insert the CD-ROM into each host on which you want to install

VMware ESXi. This can be time intensive for a large number of hosts and difficult for remote locations.

With VMware ESXi 4.1, you can create a media depot, which is a network-accessible location that contains the ESXi installation media. This media depot can be stored on FTP, HTTP, HTTPS, or NFS.

To create a media depot on an HTTP server, you perform the following steps. In this example, Microsoft Internet Information Services (IIS) was used and a virtual directory was created to hold the media depot.

1. Create a folder on the Web server to store the VMware ESXi installation files. The files `imagedd.bz2` and `imagedd.md5` from the installation media should be copied to the destination folder as shown in Figure 4.4, in which the files were copied to `C:\Inetpub \Media Depot\ESXi_4.1_207424`.

2. Create a new virtual directory with IIS Manager. The virtual directory should point to the media depot folder created in step 1.

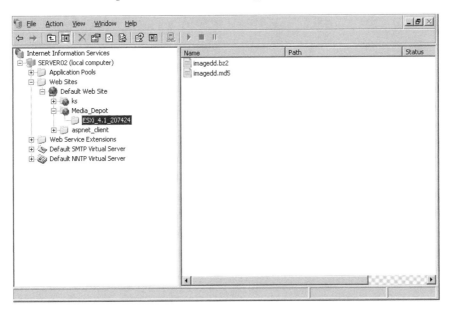

Figure 4.4 VMware ESXi installation files copied to an HTTP media depot.

Tip: When using Microsoft IIS for the media depot, you may need to edit the Multipurpose Internet Mail Extensions (MIME) types configured for the virtual directory to allow for the download of the VMware ESXi installation files. By default, IIS will not allow for the download of files that you will have copied to the media depot.

---

3. After you have configured your media depot, you can create a test script file that will use the media depot files for the installation. Scripting an ESXi installation will be covered later in this chapter, but for now you'll see a simple example of its use. You'll want to create a sample file as shown in the following listing. The default setting for the install parameter will be to use the cdrom option. In this example, that has been updated to url and the URL for the media depot has been specified. Once you have created this file, you'll want to save it on an HTTP(S), FTP, or NFS server for access during the installation process.

```
# Accept the VMware End User License Agreement
vmaccepteula
# Set the root password for the DCUI and Tech Support Mode
rootpw mypassword
# Choose the first discovered disk to install onto
autopart --firstdisk --overwritevmfs
# The installation media is in the media depot
install url http://server02.mishchenko.net/media_depot/ESXi_4.1_207424/
```

4. You'll then want to start the installation process for VMware ESXi. You can boot from the CD-ROM or a PXE source. On the VMware VMvisor Boot Menu screen, press Tab to enter additional boot options.

5. After vmkboot.gz, add the ks option and enter the URL to the script file that you created earlier, as shown in Figure 4.5. Press Enter to continue the scripted installation.

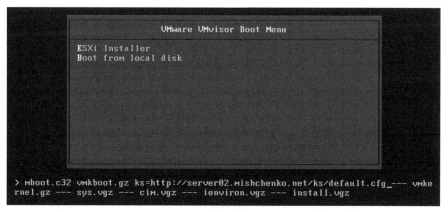

Figure 4.5   Adding the script source to the installation parameters.

Once the installation has completed, you'll be able to verify in the log files for the Web server that the install image file `imagedd.bz2` for ESXi was downloaded from the Web server for the copy-to-disk process rather than using the image file on the install CD-ROM or PXE install source.

Note: With a traditional operating system (OS) installation, the installer creates partitions on the host's storage and then copies all the required files for the OS to boot. With the ESXi installer, a `dd` image is copied to the boot device, and there is neither partitioning done for system partitions nor copying of individual boot files. `dd` is a common Unix program used for copying raw data. For ESXi, the `dd` image contains all the partition data and system files that ESXi requires to run.

If you plan to use an NFS media depot, the `install` command in the script file will need to specify the host and folder to use with the server and folder options:

```
install nfs --server=server02.mishchenko.net --dir=/media_depot/ESXi_4.1_207424/
```

PXE Booting the ESXi Installer

With VMware ESXi 4.1, it is now supported for you to use PXE to boot the ESXi Installer. PXE uses both a DHCP server and a TFTP server to bootstrap an operating system over your network. With a PXE install, you can boot and install ESXi in the same manner as you would with the installation CD-ROM without requiring installation media in either the host's physical or virtual CD-ROM device.

In the following two sections, you'll see how to set up PXE installing with both a Linux and Windows environment. Later in this chapter, you'll see how to set up an installation script to automate the install process. For both environments, you'll require the following components:

- **DHCP server.** The host on which you intend to install VMware ESXi contacts the DHCP server to obtain an IP address. The address lease also includes the DHCP options 066 Boot Server Host Name and 067 Bootfile Name. The host uses that information to access the TFTP server and request the network boot loader file.

- **TFTP server.** The TFTP server hosts two items. First the ESXi host contacts the server to download the PXELINUX or gPXE network boot image. After executing the boot image, the ESXi host downloads the files from the ESXi necessary to start and run the ESXi Installer.

- **PXELINUX/gPXE (SYSLINUX).** PXELINUX is a derivative of SYSLINUX designed to network-boot Linux.

- **Network server (FTP, HTTP, or NFS).** This is an optional component that you use to store either a script file for the installation process or the installation image. Without a network server, you are limited to interactive PXE installations.

PXE Booting in a Windows Environment

If you are working in a Windows environment, the first step to setting up PXE booting is to configure your DHCP server. You may already have that server running, so the following steps will just cover what is necessary to configure your DHCP server to point clients to the TFTP server. The following process uses the DHCP server included with Windows Server 2003 R2:

1. Open the DHCP management console and connect to the DHCP server that you will be configuring.

2. Open the DHCP scope that you will be updating.

3. Right-click on Scope Options and select Configure Options.

4. On the General tab, scroll down the list of options until you see 067 Boot Server Host Name and 068 Bootfile Name.

5. Enable the Boot Server Host Name option, and in the Data Entry field, enter either the IP address or hostname for the TFTP server.

6. Enable the Bootfile Name option and in the Data Entry field, enter `pxelinux.0`.

7. Click OK to save your changes. The scope options should now list the two new options.

Rather than configuring these options at the scope level, you may want to create a DHCP reservation for your ESXi host. In that case, you right-click on the Reservation node and select New Reservation. You will enter the name, the IP address for the reservation, the MAC address of the adapter in the ESXi host that you will use for the installation, and optionally a description. Once you have created the reservation, you right-click on it and select Configure Options. You can then follow the preceding steps to add the necessary DHCP options. When you have completed your changes, you should see the two-option setup as shown in Figure 4.6.

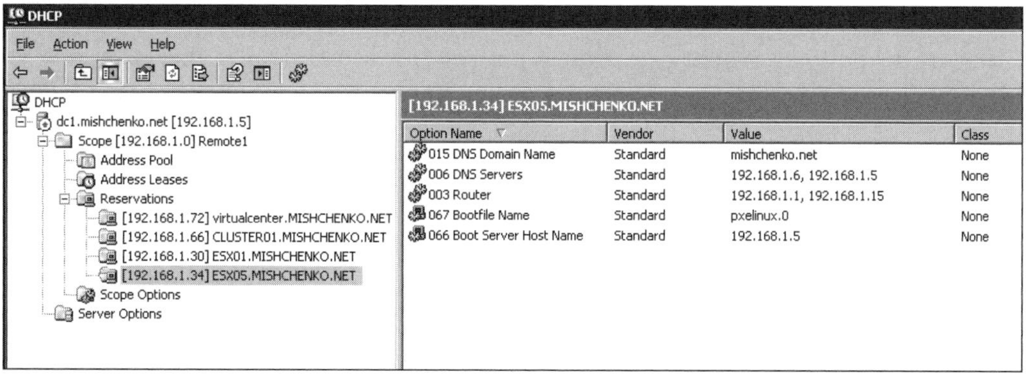

Figure 4.6 Windows DHCP server configuration for PXE booting.

What Is a TFTP Server? If you've dealt with router firmware updates or configuration back-ups in the past, you may already be familiar with a TFTP server. TFTP is a lightweight version of FTP usually used for managing firmware for network devices or booting network operating systems. TFTP runs over User Datagram Protocol (UDP) port 69 and lacks basic FTP functionality such as authentication and listing directories. TFTP essentially allows for the simple transfer of files to and from a remote server.

Most Linux distributions have a copy of the tftp-hpa server, but you can also obtain a copy from http://www.kernel.org/pub/software/network/tftp/. If you're running a network management system or using Windows Deployment Services, you may already have a TFTP server running in your network environment. In the following example, you'll see how to configure the Open Source package tftpd32 from http://tftpd32.jounin.net/.

Once you have configured your DHCP server, you are ready to set up a TFTP server. The following example uses tftpd32, but as you'll see, it is fairly easy to set up another package or modify an existing TFTP server to allow for the booting of the ESXi Installer.

1. Download the installation package for tftpd32 from http://tftpd32.jounin.net/ and start the installer.

2. The default installation choices are sufficient for your use to boot the ESXi Installer. Once the installation has completed, start the Tftpd32 shortcut that was created in the Tftpd32 program group.

3. When tftp32d starts a TFTP server, TFTP client, DHCP server, and Syslog server are started. The DHCP server will be in listening mode only. You can click on Setting and disable the services you don't want running.

4. In the Settings screen, you'll also be able to set the Base directory, which is used for storage for the TFTP server. You can optionally set the TFTP Security option to Read Only, as the ESXi PXE boot process will not be writing any data to the TFTP server.

5. On the Settings screen, check the Allow \ As virtual root option. This is required to allow the PXE boot process to access files within subfolders on the TFTP server.

6. Once you have made your changes, click OK to save them. Then close and restart tftpd32 to apply the new settings.

You can optionally test your setup to ensure that both the DHCP and TFTP server setups are correct. When you boot your ESXi host and select to boot from the network adapter, the NIC should be able to obtain an Internet Protocol (IP) address and then make a connection to the

TFTP server. The process should then generate an error as the file pxelinux.0, as you had configured for the Bootfile Name DHCP option, does not exist on the TFTP server yet. The Log Viewer tab for tftpd32 should also show a connection attempt and "file not found" error.

The next step in your setup is to add the necessary PXELINUX files to the TFTP server. You can find a link to download the latest release of PXELINUX from http://syslinux.zytor.com/ or http://www.kernel.org/pub/linux/utils/boot/syslinux/. The download includes the entire SYSLINUX package, but you'll only need the file pxelinux.o from the download.

1. Extract the SYSLINUX download and find the file /core/pxelinux.o.

2. Copy the file pxelinux.o to the folder that you are using for TFTP server data.

3. In the TFTP server data folder, create a subfolder called pxelinux.cfg. The configuration file for PXELINUX is created in this folder.

4. Within the pxelinux.cfg folder, you need to create at least a single configuration file called default. The file should have no file extension. Insert the following text into the file and save it:

```
default Local
prompt 1
timeout 30
display menu.txt
F1 help.txt

label ESXi
kernel esxi41/mboot.c32
append esxi41/vmkboot.gz --- esxi41/vmkernel.gz --- esxi41/sys.vgz
    --- esxi41/cim.vgz --- esxi41/ienviron.vgz --- esxi41/install.vgz
localboot 0x80 localboot 0x80
```

5. In the root of the TFTP server data folder, create a folder called esxi41.

6. From the ESXi installation media, copy the following files. If you are using a scripted install and media depot, you do not have to copy the files imagedd.bz2 and imagedd.md5.

   - menu.c32
   - mboot.c32
   - vmkboot.tgz
   - vmkernel.gz
   - sys.vgz
   - cim.vgz

- ienviron.vgz
- install.vgz
- imagedd.bz2
- imagedd.md5

7. In the root of the TFTP server data folder, create the files menu.txt and help.txt. Menu.txt will be used to create a boot menu showing the available options you have configured in the configuration file. Without a menu file, you will have to know the label names configured within the configuration file, which can be a problem if you start to add multiple boot options. A sample for the menu file follows. The help.txt file can contain instructions or troubleshooting information and would be accessed if you press F1.

```
VMware ESXi PXE Installation Menu
For help press <F1>
Installation options:
 ID   Description
+----+--------------------------------+
ESXi  Install VMware ESXi 4.1
Local Boot from local hard disk (default)
```

8. Once you have made your changes, click OK to save them. Then close and restart tftpd32 to apply the new settings.

At this point, you are ready to run an interactive PXE installation. Power on your ESXi host, and in the BIOS, select to boot from the system's network card. How you do so varies from system to system, but you can probably press F12 to start a network boot or press Esc to access a boot menu. If the boot menu does not show an option to boot from a network card, you may have to edit the BIOS boot options to enable this option.

Once your host has passed through the BIOS startup and initialized the host's network card ROM, the NIC attempts to obtain an IP address by broadcasting for a DHCP server. The DHCP server that you had configured earlier should respond with a DHCP lease containing the required IP information as well as the DHCP options for the TFTP server and boot file to use for a PXE boot. Your ESXi host contacts the TFTP server to download and start pxelinux.0, which will in turn load the configuration file that you created. The host's display should appear similar to Figure 4.7.

Notice that the PXE boot process attempts to load a number of configuration files prior to finding and loading the file default. PXELINUX first searches for a configuration file based on the MAC address of the NIC being used. For a MAC address of 00:0c:29:32:71:00, PXELINUX searches for a configuration file called 00-0c-29-32-71-00. If the program finds such a file, your host uses that configuration instead of searching for other files. Note that the file should

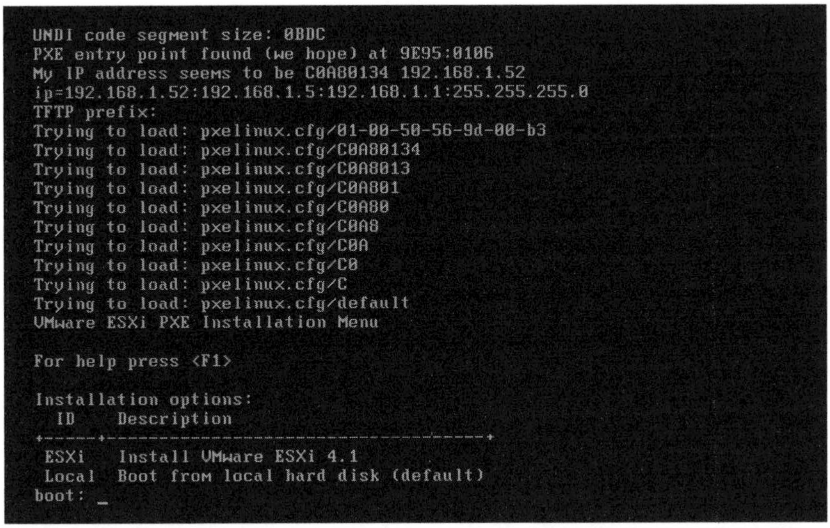

```
UNDI code segment size: 0BDC
PXE entry point found (we hope) at 9E95:0106
My IP address seems to be C0A80134 192.168.1.52
ip=192.168.1.52:192.168.1.5:192.168.1.1:255.255.255.0
TFTP prefix:
Trying to load: pxelinux.cfg/01-00-50-56-9d-00-b3
Trying to load: pxelinux.cfg/C0A80134
Trying to load: pxelinux.cfg/C0A8013
Trying to load: pxelinux.cfg/C0A801
Trying to load: pxelinux.cfg/C0A80
Trying to load: pxelinux.cfg/C0A8
Trying to load: pxelinux.cfg/C0A
Trying to load: pxelinux.cfg/C0
Trying to load: pxelinux.cfg/C
Trying to load: pxelinux.cfg/default
VMware ESXi PXE Installation Menu

For help press <F1>

Installation options:
  ID    Description
+------+--------------------------------------------------+
  ESXi   Install VMware ESXi 4.1
  Local  Boot from local hard disk (default)
boot: _
```

Figure 4.7   PXE boot configuration file enumeration and configured boot menu.

have all letters in lowercase. If a configuration file based on the host's MAC address is not found, a search is made for a configuration file based on the hexadecimal conversion of the host's IP address. In the case of Figure 4.7, the host has an IP address of 192.168.1.52. This converts to a value in hexadecimal of C0A80134. PXELINUX starts a search for that file, and if it finds no match, one hex digit is removed to see whether a further match can be found.

The PXELINUX search pattern opens the possibility for you to tailor configuration files on a per-host or subnet level. As you'll see later in this chapter, a kick start script (highlighted with boldface in this listing) can be added to the configuration file to automate the installation process. In such a case, you might create a sample configuration file such as the following and name the file to match the MAC address for the host to which it will apply:

```
default Local
prompt 1
timeout 5
label ESX05
kernel esxi41/mboot.c32
append esxi41/vmkboot.gz ks=http://server02.mishchenko.net/ks/esx05.cfg
    --- esxi41/vmkernel.gz --- esxi41/sys.vgz --- esxi41/cim.vgz
    --- esxi41/ienviron.vgz --- esxi41/install.vgz
label Locallocalboot 0x80
```

The file would be saved as 00-0c-29-32-71-00. When the ESXi host boots, no menu would be displayed, but entering ESX05 would start a scripted install process. If you press Enter or wait five seconds for the timeout to expire, the host would boot from the server's primary boot device.

Booting Memtest86+ with PXELINUX When you're deploying a new ESXi host, one of the worthwhile tasks to complete is a thorough memory check. You can use Memtest86+ from www.memtest.org to accomplish this test. As the following steps indicate, booting this utility with PXELINUX is easy:

1. Download the latest precompiled bootable binary from www.memtest.org.

2. Extract the BIN file from the download and place it in the root data folder for your TFTP server. You may want to rename the binary file `memtest86`.

3. Edit the default or other PXELINUX configuration file on the TFTP server and add the following lines:
   ```
   # memtest86+
   label memtest
   kernel memtest86
   ```

4. If you are using a menu file, you may also want to update that to show an entry to run Memtest86+.

5. Power on your ESXi host and select to boot from a network card.

6. When the PXE boot menu is shown, type in the menu choice `memtest` and press Enter to start Memtest86+.

7. Memtest86+ will continue to run until you press Esc.

PXE Booting in a Linux Environment

In the following section, you'll see how to set up a Linux host to run the DHCP and TFTP roles to allow for the running of the ESXi Installer via a PXE boot. If you're adding another DHCP server to your network, ensure that it will not conflict with an existing server. If you are planning to isolate your management network for your VMware ESXi host, you may find it a better solution to use an existing DHCP server on your main network. It is likely the case that the router providing access to the management network can be configured to provide DHCP relay, removing the need to have a dedicated DHCP server on the management network. If you plan to place your TFTP server on an open network, consider the fact that TFTP provides no security, and installation scripts, as you'll see later in this chapter, contain sensitive configuration information.

The setup in the following pages also makes use of gPXE. gPXE was formerly known as Etherboot and is an Open Source PXE bootloader. gPXE works with the built-in PXE support that your hosts will have, but extends PXE with the use of additional protocols such as HTTP, iSCSI, and ATA over Ethernet. Using gPXE to boot your ESXi Installer is significantly faster than using PXELINUX and a TFTP server for transfer of the installer files. While TFTP is simple and lightweight to implement, the protocol is not designed to be robust. When transferring large files, the

TFTP server may suffer from reliability issues, resulting in the failure of the ESXi installation process. With gPXE, only the `gpxelinux` binary file and configuration file are transferred to your ESXi host from the TFTP server. gPXE can instead use a Web server for the transfer of the kernel and ramdisk required to boot the installer. This will ensure more reliable network transfers under heavy loads.

Note: The general release of VMware ESXi 4.1 will not officially support gPXE installations. Please refer to the release notes for future updates of VMware ESXi for details regarding official support for gPXE.

There are obviously several options that you can choose for a Linux host. The following example uses an Ubuntu Server VMware image from www.thoughtpolice.co.uk, which hosts a number of VMware images that you might find useful.

Note: Ubuntu uses `sudo` rather than a root account. To execute a command that you would usually have to switch to the root account to run, you should instead prefix the command with `sudo`, as described in step 4 of the following procedure.

To set up the Linux image and configure DHCP and TFTP servers, use the following process:

1. Download the appropriate VMware image for Linux that you want to use and extract the files.

2. The download used in this example comes configured as a standalone VMware virtual machine. You can use VMware Converter (http://www.vmware.com/products/converter/) to import the VMware image to an existing VMware ESXi and then power on your new virtual machine.

3. At the console of the Ubuntu server, log in with the supplied credentials.

4. The server should be configured with a static IP address. You want to edit the network configuration by running the command `sudo vi /etc/network/interfaces`. The section for `eth0` should be replaced with something similar to the following. To save the file, press Esc, type in `:wq`, and then press Enter. You'll then want to run the command `sudo /etc/init.d/networking restart` to apply your changes.

    ```
    auto eth0
    iface eth0 inet static
    address 192.168.1.9
    netmask 255.255.255.0
    network 192.168.1.0
    ```

```
broadcast 192.168.1.255
gateway 192.168.1.1
```

5. You'll first want to install and configure a DHCP server. You can run the following command to accomplish this:

    ```
    sudo apt-get install dhcp3-server
    ```

    The install process attempts to start the DHCP server process, but this will fail until further configuration can be made.

6. You next configure several files. Run the command `sudo vi /etc/default/dhcp3-server` and find the line containing `INTERFACES=""`. Change that entry to `INTERFACES="eth0"` and then save and close the file in the same manner used to edit the interfaces file in step 4.

7. The second file you need to configure is `/etc/dhcp3/dhcpd.conf`. You should update the file to have the options shown in the following example. This example will assign IP addresses in the range of 192.168.1.75 to 192.168.1.95 and also provide a default gateway, DNS servers, and default domain name.

    ```
    default-lease-time 600;
    max-lease-time 7200;
    option subnet-mask 255.255.255.0;
    option broadcast-address 192.168.1.255;
    option routers 192.168.1.1;
    option domain-name-servers 192.168.1.5, 192.168.1.6;
    option domain-name "mischenko.net";
    subnet 192.168.1.0 netmask 255.255.255.0 {
    range 192.168.1.75 192.168.1.95;
    }
    ```

8. To start the DHCP server, run the command `sudo /etc/init.d/dhcp3-server restart`.

9. To install a TFTP server on your Linux server, you follow a similar process to setting up the DHCP server. You start with the `install` command:

    ```
    sudo apt-get install tftpd-hpa
    ```

10. You next want to edit the file `/etc/default/tftd-hpa`. Ensure that the `RUN_DAEMON` option is set to yes, as follows:

    ```
    RUN_DAEMON="yes"
    OPTIONS="-l -s /var/lib/tftpboot"
    ```

11. Restart the TFTP server by running the command `sudo /etc/initd.d/tftpd-hpa restart`.

Caution: When editing configuration files as you've seen done in the prior steps, it is always a good idea to back up the file before changing it, just in case you need to revert back to the original file. You can do that by simply running the `cp` command. To back up the TFTP configuration file, you run `sudo cp /etc/default/tftd-hpa /etc/default/tftd-hpa.backup`.

Now that your DHCP and TFTP servers are running, you're ready to configure the components to gPXE boot the ESXi Installer. As you'll have seen in the Windows section, the first step to enable this is to configure the DHCP server with the necessary information for the ESXi host to find the TFTP server.

You start this process by editing the file `/etc/dhcp3/dhcpd.conf`. As you are using gPXE, you add the following text to the file. The `next-server` option specifies the IP address or hostname for the TFTP server and filename tells the client ESXi host which file to load from the TFTP server.

```
allow booting;
allow bootp;
# gPXE options
option space gpxe;
option gpxe-encap-opts code 175 = encapsulate gpxe;
option gpxe.bus-id code 177 = string;
class "pxeclients" {
match if substring(option vendor-class-identifier, 0, 9) = "PXEClient";
next-server 192.168.1.9;
if not exists gpxe.bus-id {
filename "/gpxelinux.0";
}
}
```

After you have changed your configuration, run the command `sudo /etc/init.d/dhcp3-server restart` to restart the DHCP server. If you plan to use PXELINUX with your setup, the configuration change to `dhcpd.conf` is as follows. The rest of the setup for PXELINUX is the same as described in the Windows section, except that you place the files in the default location of `/var/lib/tftpboot/` on the Linux host.

```
allow booting;
allow bootp;
# PXELINUX options
class "pxeclients" {
match if substring(option vendor-class-identifier, 0, 9) = "PXEClient";
next-server 192.168.1.9;
```

```
filename = "pxelinux.0";
}
```

The next step in the process is to set up gPXE on the TFTP server. As mentioned earlier, only the gpxelinux.o binary and the configuration file need to be on the TFTP server. The files for the ESXi Installer can be hosted on a Web server or other server that gPXE will support.

1. Copy the file gpxelinux.o to the root of the TFTP server's data folder. The file can be found in the gpxe folder of the SYSLINUX download that was used for the Windows PXE Boot setup. In the case of the Linux server used for this setup, you would place the file in /var/lib/tftpboot.

2. In the TFTP server data folder, create a subfolder called pxelinux.cfg. The configuration file for gPXE to use will be created in this folder.

3. Within the pxelinux.cfg folder, you need to create at least a single configuration file called default. The file should have no file extension. Create a configuration file similar to the following example and then save the file:

```
default Local
prompt 1
timeout 30
display http://server02.mishchenko.net/media_depot/menu.txt
F1 http://server02.mishchenko.net/media_depot/help.txt

label ESXi
kernel http://server02.mishchenko.net/media_depot/ESXi_4.1/mboot.c32
append http://server02.mishchenko.net/media_depot/ESXi_4.1/vmkboot.gz
    --- http://server02.mishchenko.net/media_depot/ESXi_4.1/vmkernel.gz
    --- http://server02.mishchenko.net/media_depot/ESXi_4.1/sys.vgz
    --- http://server02.mishchenko.net/media_depot/ESXi_4.1/cim.vgz
    --- http://server02.mishchenko.net/media_depot/ESXi_4.1/ienviron.vgz
    --- http://server02.mishchenko.net/media_depot/ESXi_4.1/install.vgz
label Local
localboot 0x80
```

4. On your Web server, you can create a menu and help file with the same contents as discussed in the section "PXE Booting in a Windows Environment."

5. From the ESXi installation media, you need to copy the following files to your Web server. If you are using a scripted install and media depot, you need not copy over the files imagedd.bz2 and imagedd.md5.

    ■ menu.c32

    ■ mboot.c32

    ■ vmkboot.tgz

- `vmkernel.gz`
- `sys.vgz`
- `cim.vgz`
- `ienviron.vgz`
- `install.vgz`
- `imagedd.bz2`
- `imagedd.md5`

6. Check the security settings on your Web server to ensure that the download of the files you copied over will be allowed. If you are using Microsoft IIS, you must edit the MIME types to include the extensions for the files you added, as in shown in Figure 4.8.

You are now ready to test your configuration. Boot up your target ESXi host, and in the BIOS, select to boot from the system's network card. How you do so varies from system to system, but you probably will be able to press F12 to start a network boot or press Esc to access a boot menu. As was shown in the prior section, the host's NIC obtains an IP address and the necessary

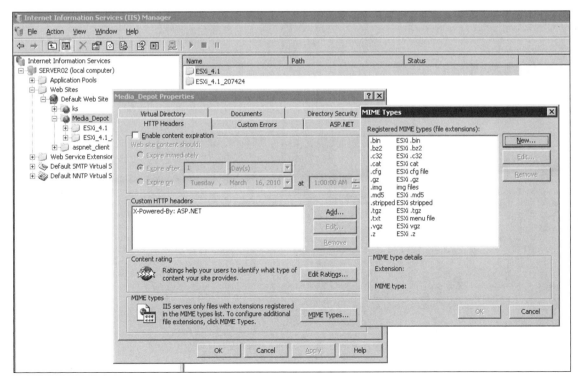

Figure 4.8   MIME types added to Microsoft IIS.

information to connect to the TFTP server. In this case, the ESXi host downloads gpxelinux.o and a configuration file to start the PXE installation process.

As shown in Figure 4.9, gPXE searches the pxelinux.cfg folder for configuration files based on the MAC address of the ESXi host and the IP address assigned to it. As discussed earlier, this provides the opportunity to configure a custom gPXE install menu for a specific host or subnet. Once you have selected the gPXE menu choice, gPXE begins to load the appropriate files. Figure 4.10 shows the files being loaded from a Web URL rather than the TFTP server, as was the case when setting up PXELINUX.

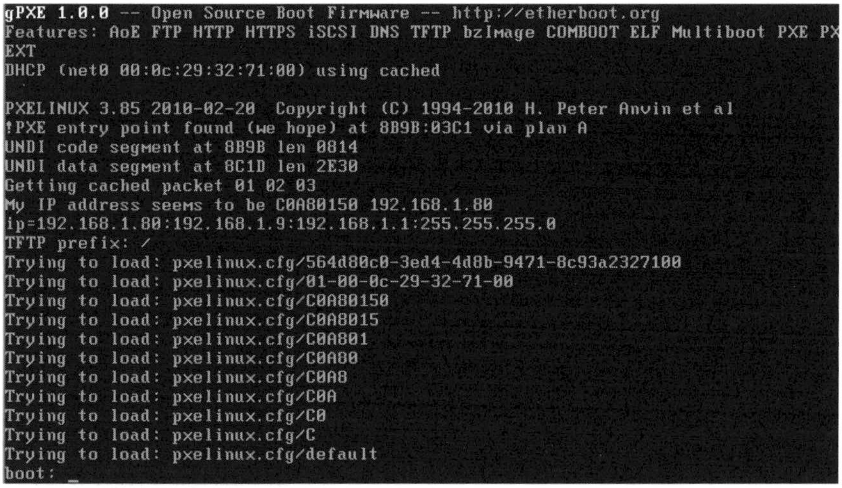

```
gPXE 1.0.0 -- Open Source Boot Firmware -- http://etherboot.org
Features: AoE FTP HTTP HTTPS iSCSI DNS TFTP bzImage COMBOOT ELF Multiboot PXE PX
EXT
DHCP (net0 00:0c:29:32:71:00) using cached

PXELINUX 3.85 2010-02-20  Copyright (C) 1994-2010 H. Peter Anvin et al
!PXE entry point found (we hope) at 8B9B:03C1 via plan A
UNDI code segment at 8B9B len 0814
UNDI data segment at 8C1D len 2E30
Getting cached packet 01 02 03
My IP address seems to be C0A80150 192.168.1.80
ip=192.168.1.80:192.168.1.9:192.168.1.1:255.255.255.0
TFTP prefix: /
Trying to load: pxelinux.cfg/564d80c0-3ed4-4d8b-9471-8c93a2327100
Trying to load: pxelinux.cfg/01-00-0c-29-32-71-00
Trying to load: pxelinux.cfg/C0A80150
Trying to load: pxelinux.cfg/C0A8015
Trying to load: pxelinux.cfg/C0A801
Trying to load: pxelinux.cfg/C0A80
Trying to load: pxelinux.cfg/C0A8
Trying to load: pxelinux.cfg/C0A
Trying to load: pxelinux.cfg/C0
Trying to load: pxelinux.cfg/C
Trying to load: pxelinux.cfg/default
boot: _
```

Figure 4.9 gPXE enumerating configuration files.

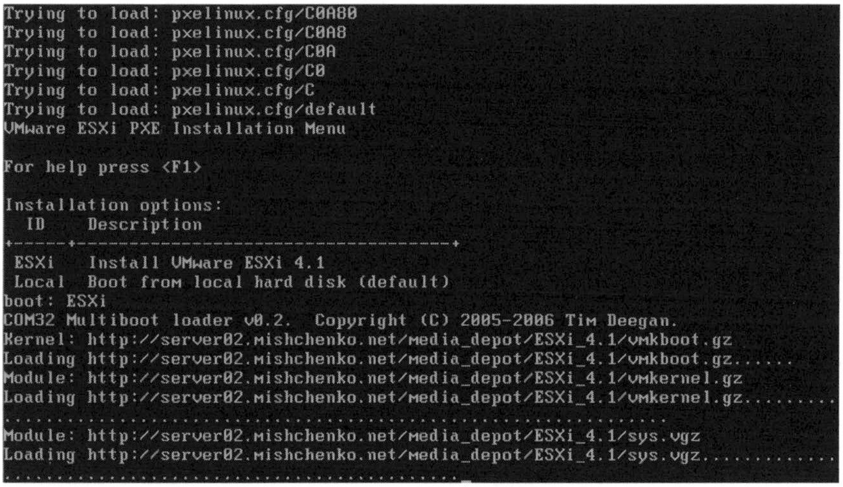

```
Trying to load: pxelinux.cfg/C0A80
Trying to load: pxelinux.cfg/C0A8
Trying to load: pxelinux.cfg/C0A
Trying to load: pxelinux.cfg/C0
Trying to load: pxelinux.cfg/C
Trying to load: pxelinux.cfg/default
VMware ESXi PXE Installation Menu

For help press <F1>

Installation options:
  ID     Description
+------+---------------------------------------------+
  ESXi    Install VMware ESXi 4.1
  Local   Boot from local hard disk (default)
boot: ESXi
COM32 Multiboot loader v0.2.  Copyright (C) 2005-2006 Tim Deegan.
Kernel: http://server02.mishchenko.net/media_depot/ESXi_4.1/vmkboot.gz
Loading http://server02.mishchenko.net/media_depot/ESXi_4.1/vmkboot.gz......
Module: http://server02.mishchenko.net/media_depot/ESXi_4.1/vmkernel.gz
Loading http://server02.mishchenko.net/media_depot/ESXi_4.1/vmkernel.gz........
.................................................................
Module: http://server02.mishchenko.net/media_depot/ESXi_4.1/sys.vgz
Loading http://server02.mishchenko.net/media_depot/ESXi_4.1/sys.vgz...........
```

Figure 4.10 gPXE loading ESXi Installer files from a Web server.

Installing ESXi with a Flash Device In most cases, you should be able to install VMware ESXi using the CD media (locally or with a remote management card) or via the PXE boot method. You can also install ESXi from a flash device; while this is not officially supported, it may provide a useful installation option for yourself:

1. Download and extract the latest version of SYSLINUX as was required for the PXE boot setup procedures.

2. Insert the flash device that you plan to use. It will require about 300MB free space for the ESXi installation files and should be formatted as FAT32. If you're using Windows, make a note of the drive letter that is assigned to the drive. With Linux, you can run `fdisk -1` to determine the device node (`/dev/sdX`).

3. For Windows, run the command `..\win32\syslinux.exe <drive letter>`, and for Linux, run `../linux/syslinux /dev/sdX`. This command alters the boot partition on the device and copies over the file `ldlinux.sys` to the root directory.

4. Extract the contents of the ESXi Installer CD to the flash device.

5. On the flash device, rename the file `isolinux.cfg` as `SYSlinux.cfg`.

The flash device is now ready to be used in a host to install ESXi. If you have problems booting the flash drive, you might want to try one of the options in Table 4.1 with the `syslinux` command in step 3.

Table 4.1 SYSLINUX Installer Options

Option	Description
s	This option causes SYSLINUX to use simpler code that boots easier on some older BIOSs.
f	This option forces the install.
m	(Windows only) This installs a bootable master boot record (MBR) sector at the beginning of the drive.
a	This marks the partitions as active (bootable).

Installing VMware ESXi 4.1 Using Graphical Mode

You have seen the installation process using graphical mode in Chapter 2, and while the install process is fairly simple, some aspects are worth further review. One of the important aspects to note is that the ESXi Installer wipes the target disk chosen for the installation of ESXi. This includes prior operating system partitions, hardware vendor partitions, previous installs of VMware ESX or ESXi, and any Virtual Machine File System (VMFS) datastores. If you're upgrading a host from VMware ESX to ESXi, you need to migrate any virtual machine data off the installation drive before you attempt to install VMware ESXi.

When installing ESXi, choose an serial attached SCSI (SAS), serial AT attachment (SATA), or small computer systems interface (SCSI) disk as an installation destination. Installing ESXi onto a Fibre Channel (FC) storage area network (SAN) device is now officially supported. It is not supported for you to install to network attached storage (NAS) or iSCSI SAN storage. You may also choose to install ESXi onto a supported flash device. If you choose to use FC SAN for the installation, be aware that each ESXi host requires a separate installation LUN. LUNs cannot be shared between hosts for the installation partitions. LUNs dedicated to VMFS datastores can be shared between hosts, just as is the case with ESX.

Prior to installing VMware ESXi, there are a few other prerequisites to be aware of:

- You should verify that the host's hardware clock is set to Coordinated Universal Time (UTC). VMware ESXi runs with the UTC time zone and there is no option to change that. The vSphere client translates the time displayed to you based on the time zone that is used on your PC. But should you export log files, be aware that the time stamps will be in UTC. This is especially important if you pass the logs on to another support group for troubleshooting purposes, as the time zone for logs that the support personnel look at may differ, resulting in them looking at the wrong part of the ESXi logs that you provide.

- You should consider disconnecting network storage. This will decrease the time that the ESXi Installer requires to enumerate installation targets and will eliminate the possibility that you will choose to install to the wrong partition. As mentioned earlier, the ESXi Installer wipes all partitions on the disk target that you select during the installation process.

- You should not have both ESXi Installable and ESXi Embedded on the same host. If you're moving to ESXi Installable, you should at least disable booting from the flash device in the BIOS, but it would be better to remove the device completely.

As seen earlier, an interactive installation of VMware ESXi is probably the easiest installation process you'll ever go through. The process is as follows.

1.   Download the VMware ESXi installation ISO image from vmware.com. You can either burn the image to a physical CD or mount it as a virtual CD-ROM with the host's remote control card.

2.   Power on the ESXi and in the BIOS set the host to boot from the CD-ROM. You may also want to check that Intel VT is enabled on an Intel server so that you will be able to run 64-bit guest operating systems and, if you plan to use VMDirectPath, that the

appropriate BIOS option is enabled for either Advanced Micro Devices (AMD) Input/Output Memory Management Unit (IOMMU) or Intel Directed I/O (VT-x).

3. When the host boots from the CD, you'll initially see the VMware VMvisor Boot Menu. This will allow you to change boot options, as you'll see shortly.

4. The boot process then continues to the Welcome screen, where you press Enter to continue.

5. The VMware End User License Agreement will appear. After you have reviewed it, press F11 to continue.

6. The ESXi Installer then enumerates the host's storage and provides a list of support installation targets. The order of display is determined by the BIOS and may not match the order you are expecting. Ensure that the target selected is where you actually intend to install ESXi. After you have selected the target disk for installation, you are required to confirm your choice.

7. Press F11 to begin the installation.

8. Once the installation has completed, the status is displayed and you are prompted to remove the installation CD and reboot the host. When the host reboots, it automatically creates the scratch partition. This is unlike the behavior for ESXi Embedded, as was discussed earlier in this chapter.

9. Once your host reboots, you can configure the host. If the host was previously running ESX, you can move the virtual machine data back to the host.

One important thing to be aware of for the installation process is how to pass an option to the VMkernel during the boot process. You'll usually configure VMkernel boot options within the vSphere client, as shown in Figure 4.11. But for the install process, your only option is to add the options to the boot statement used to load the ESXi Installer.

A list of the options that can be used is shown in Table 4.2. It is unlikely that you'll use these options without the guidance of VMware Support, but you will notice that the options correspond with what you will find in the vSphere client at Configuration > Software > Advanced Settings.

Bootstrap options are added when the VMware VMvisor Boot Menu screen appears during the install process, as shown in Figure 4.12. Press the Tab key to display the boot command and you can then add any options after vmkboot.gz. Figure 4.13 shows the options noACPI and nopowerManagement added to the VMkernel boot command.

After the VMkernel has initialized, you'll be able to verify that the options were in fact enabled. The following sample shows that both the noACPI and nopowerManagement options (highlighted with boldface in this listing) have been applied during the VMkernel initialization. Boot options can also be added when you're booting a VMware ESXi host that has already been installed. The

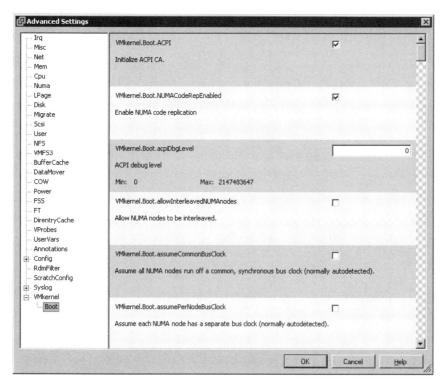

Figure 4.11 Configuring VMkernel boot options with the vSphere client.

difference in that case is that you'll need to press Shift + O on the VMware VMvisor Boot Menu screen instead of pressing the Tab key as you do during the installation. As mentioned earlier, it is unlikely that you'll need to enter any boot options unless VMware Support directs you to do so for troubleshooting purposes. The exception is when specifying the configuration script to use for an unattended installation and other installation initialization parameters, as will be discussed in the next section of this chapter.

```
May 23 04:32:10 syslogd started: BusyBox v1.9.1-VMware-visor-654
May 23 04:32:10 vmklogger: Successfully daemonized.
May 23 04:32:10 vmkernel: cpu0:0)BootConfig: 52: netNumPortsets = 128
...
May 23 04:32:10 vmkernel: TSC: 2487286550 cpu0:0)BootConfig: 115:
    powerManagement = FALSE
...
May 23 04:32:10 vmkernel: TSC: 2487481892 cpu0:0)Boot: 314: cmdline 'vmkboot.gz
    noACPI nopowerManagement bootUUID=7b74833b3e445d315642e8157483517e '
May 23 04:32:10 vmkernel: TSC: 2487494198 cpu0:0)Boot: 1102: vmk.gz : 0x21b
    - 0xa21
May 23 04:32:10 vmkernel: TSC: 20007785924 cpu0:0)Initializing chipset ...
```

May 23 04:32:10 vmkernel: TSC: 20010942868 cpu0:0)ALERT: Chipset: 219:
    using mpsIntRouting/noACPI option, make sure it is on purpose
May 23 04:32:10 vmkernel: TSC: 20011012154 cpu0:0)MPS: 209: ioapic 001 (0)
    @ fec00000 version 0x11
…

Table 4.2 VMkernel Boot Options

nouseNUMAInfo	nomeasureNUMALatency	nouseMemNodes
nosharePerNode	nompsIntRouting	noforceCRS
nocorrectBSPMTRRMasks	nomcaFindDIMMFromAddr	nomcaClearBanksOnMCE
nomcaEnableScrubber	nomcaEnableAllErrorSources	nomcaEnableCMCI
noACPI	noupdateBusIRQ	noserialUntrusted
noexecutePOST	nopageSharing	nomemCheckEveryWord
nohyperthreading	nologicalApicId	nodumpDiag
noallowInterleavedNUMAnodes	nointerleaveFakeNUMAnodes	norealNMI
nologOnScreen	nonetESX2LegacyMode	nonetPktBufUseSlab
nonetPktHeapUseHighMem	nonetPanicBadDevOpen	nonetNetqueueEnabled
nonetDVSSyncEnabled	nonoIOMMU	novga64
nosmallFontForTTY	noauditMode	norollback
nofsCheck	nousbBoot	nouwSwap
nooem	nobusSpeedMayVary	noclockMultiplierMayVary
noassumeCommonBusClock	noassumePerNodeBusClock	nobusSpeedMayVaryPerNode
notimerEnableTSC	notimerForceTSC	notimerEnableHPET
notimerEnableACPI	notimerEnableMPMC	nomemmapStressHighBitMPNs
novmkConsole	nocheckCPUIDLimit	novmkKeyboard
novmkTerminals	nodebugBreak	nofastHzEstimate
nopowerManagement	novmkLoadTPM	nouseNHCC
notestEarlyPanic	nominMemoryCheck	noskipMicrocodeCompatCheck
nocustom	noipmiEnabled	noNUMACodeRepEnabled
noNUMACodeRepStress	nodisableC1E	nodisableCFOH
nodisableTurbo	nodriverVMEnabled	nodriverVMAutoclaim
noenablePCIErrors	nocheckDMAR	noiovDisableIR

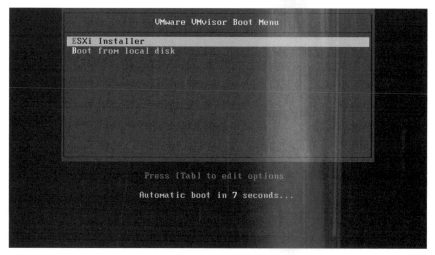

Figure 4.12 The default VMware VMvisor Boot Menu.

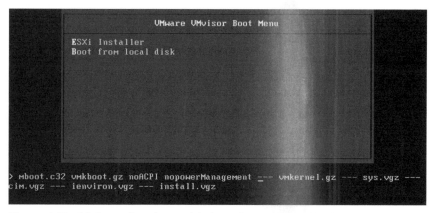

Figure 4.13 VMkernel options added on the VMware VMvisor Boot Menu.

Running ESXi on VMware Workstation 7 If you want to set up a lab or test environment, you can run ESXi as a virtual machine on VMware Workstation 7. On a host with multiple cores and 8GB RAM, you can configure two ESXi virtual machines and a third to run vCenter Server and optionally to provide iSCSI or NFS storage for the ESXi virtual machines. With such a setup, it is possible to configure and demonstrate advanced features such as vMotion and High Availability.

To run ESXi as a virtual machine, you must meet the following requirements:

- You should configure the ESXi virtual machine with at least 2GB of memory. The virtual machine should be configured with at least two virtual central processing units (CPUs), but ESXi will run with just one.

- The host running VMware Workstation must have AMD64 Family 10H or later processors with AMD-V or Intel EM64T processors with VT-x.

- You can run nested 32-bit guests only, as the only option for ESXi is to use binary translation.

Note: You can also run ESXi as a virtual machine on ESXi. You'll follow a similar process as with VMware Workstation, but you must configure the security settings on the vSwitch on the host ESXi system to allow Promiscuous Mode. You will also have to select the guest operating system as Other (64-bit).

To create an ESXi virtual machine, follow this procedure:

1. In VMware Workstation, select File > New > Virtual Machine.

2. Select the option to create a Custom configuration and click Next.

3. Set the Hardware Compatibility for your ESXi virtual machine (VM) to be Workstation 6.5–7.0 and click Next.

4. In the Guest Operating System Installation windows, select to use the Installer Disc Image File (ISO) option and browse to the ISO image that you downloaded for VMware ESXi. Click Next to continue.

5. In the Select a Guest Operation System window, VMware ESX should be the selected option. Click Next to proceed.

6. Enter a name for the virtual machine and the location to store data files. Then click the Next icon.

7. In the following screens, select the number of processors and amount of memory to use. You should select at least two virtual CPUs and 2GB of memory.

8. Select the Network Type to use that best fits with your network configuration and click Next.

9. You can use the default options in the disk setup screens. This will set up the virtual machine with a 40GB virtual SCSI disk connected to an LSI Logic virtual SCSI adapter.

10. Review the configuration for the virtual machine and then click Finish to create it. The virtual machine then powers on and the ESXi Installer will start up after a short period.

Installing VMware ESXi 4.1 Using Scripted Mode

Although the VMware ESXi installation process is a fairly simple matter and fairly quick, manually installing a large number of hosts is still a time-consuming task. You'll find the option to an unattended installation script a welcome addition to ESXi 4.1, especially if you've been using kickstart scripts for your vSphere ESX installations.

You can start looking at installation scripts by running the script that comes on the installation media. At the VMware VMvisor Boot Menu, you will need to press the Tab key as discussed in the previous section to add the script option as shown in Figure 4.14. The default script is located at /etc/vmware/weasel/ks.cfg. Note that the ks option does require a double slash when using the file location so the syntax used in Figure 4.14 is correct.

After the VMkernel initializes and has loaded all required modules, the Welcome screen usually appears for an interactive install. With a scripted install, the installation script is parsed as shown in Figure 4.15. If there are any problems with the script, you will have the option to continue if a warning is displayed or you will have to abort the install should an error in the script be detected.

If the installation script is parsed with no errors, the ESXi Installer continues the installation process by writing the install image to disk as shown in Figure 4.16.

Once the installation image has been copied to disk, the ESXi Installer applies further configuration changes from the installation script. Figure 4.17 shows the networking options applying to the ESXi installation. If the installation completes successfully, you are prompted to reboot

Figure 4.14 Running the default installation script.

Figure 4.15   The ESXi Installer parsing an installation script.

Figure 4.16   The ESXi Installer writing the installation image to disk.

your host. If you're booting from CD, you may need to update the BIOS boot order to boot from your new ESXi installation.

The default installation script contains the following commands. The first four options in the script are required. The script must accept the End User License Agreement (EULA), set a root password, choose the installation disk target with the `autopart` command, and select the installation media. The password can be encrypted, as you'll see later in this section, but in this case the password for the root account is plain text and the script sets this to `mypassword`. The

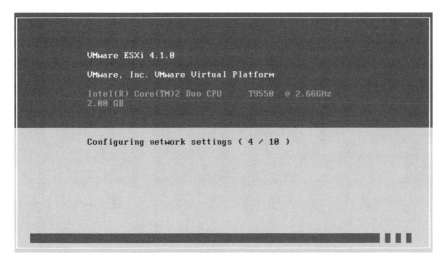

Figure 4.17 The ESXi Installer applying an installation script.

autopart command instructs the installer to choose the non-USB disk found and to overwrite any existing VMFS datastores on that disk. The install command selects the CD-ROM being used as the source for the installation image.

The network command is optional and in this case sets the management port for the ESXi host to use DHCP and to be linked to the NIC detected as vmnic0. The %post section of the default script highlights the unsupported abilities of an installation script. In this case, a python script is run to create the file /finshed.stamp with the time that the installation completed. If you're planning to use the %post section in a script, you should be aware that the root folder will be a ramdisk initialized by the ESXi Installer and thus any files written to /, /tmp, or /var will be lost after the host is rebooted. If, for example, you want to save the installation file for review, the %post script could be written to mount an NFS share and copy the install log file to that share or to the VMFS datastore created during the installation.

```
# Accept the VMware End User License Agreement
vmaccepteula
# Set the root password for the DCUI and Tech Support Mode
rootpw mypassword
# Choose the first discovered disk to install onto
autopart --firstdisk --overwritevmfs
# The installation media is in the CD-ROM drive
install cdrom
# Set the network to DHCP on the first network adapter
network -- bootproto=dhcp --device=vmnic0
# A sample post-install script
```

```
%post -- unsupported-- interpreter=python -- ignorefailure=true
import time
stampFile = file('/finished.stamp', mode='w'
stampFile.write( time.asctime() )
```

Considerations for Scripting ESXi Installations

If you've been running installation scripts for vSphere ESX, you'll likely already have a set strategy for running installation scripts. With little difficulty, you'll be able to modify those scripts to run on ESXi. If you're new to scripted installations for vSphere, you'll need to give some thought to whether to run a single install script for all your ESXi hosts or to manage individual scripts for each host.

If you create individual scripts, you will be able to set a static IP address for each ESXi host you'll install this way. In the section "PXE Booting the ESXi Installer" in this chapter, you learned how you can configure PXE booting to use a specific PXELINUX or gPXE configuration file for each host you have.

If you choose to use a custom script for each host, you can then configure PXELINUX or gPXE to use a specific ESXi installation script for each host. Should you choose to maintain a single script, you'll need to use DHCP for the management network and then change that to a static IP address after the installation. VMware recommends the use of static IP addresses for your ESXi hosts. You could use a static IP address in a single script for all your host installations, but if you were to fail to change the IP address of a host after an installation, this could lead to a duplicate IP address between two of your hosts and you would not be able to manage the one host over the network.

You will also have to decide where you will store your installation scripts. You'll be able to use the following storage options:

- Within the ESXi Installer ramdisk (the default option)
- On the installation CD-ROM
- Using HTTP/HTTPS
- Using FTP
- Using NFS

If you plan to use NFS, the ESXi Installer attempts to connect to the share with the login of root and a blank password.

Tip: At the time of the writing of this book, storing the installation script on a USB device is not an available option. This may change with the Generally Available (GA) release of VMware ESXi 4.1.

Table 4.3 Installation Script Storage Options

ks= Option	Description
ks=cdrom:/ks.cfg	The installation script is located on the CD-ROM drive attached to the machine.
ks=file://<path>/ks.cfg	The installation script is at file <path>, which exists inside the ESXi Installer ramdisk image. Note that the option requires a double slash at the start of the file path.
ks=ftp://<server>/<path>/ks.cfg	The installation script is located at the specified FTP server URL.
ks=http://<server>/<path>/ks.cfg	The Installation script is located at the specified Web server URL.
ks=nfs://<server>/<path>/ks.cfg	The installation script is located at <path> on the specified NFS server.

The storage option you choose for your installation script determines the syntax of the ks command that you enter on the VMware VMvisor Boot Menu screen. Table 4.3 lists the available options.

To enter the ks command, you'll follow the process used for the default installation script shown earlier in this section, updating the URL and storage type to match where you have stored your script.

Along with configuring the ks bootstrap command, you'll also be able to configure the networking setup used for your ESXi installation process. These additional options are summarized in Table 4.4.

With the additional bootstrap commands, you can either edit the PXELINUX or gPXE configuration files you use for your installations or add them manually at the VMware VMvisor Boot Menu, as shown in Figure 4.18.

Installation Script Commands

If you've written kickstart scripts for vSphere ESX, the command options in the following section will be familiar. But you should be aware that the partitioning commands autopart, clearpart, and part are different from what you would use with kickstart scripts. If your current ESX scripts set specific sizes for the system partition, you will need to change that. As there is no Service Console to configure with ESXi, the ESXi Installer will size all the system partitions.

Table 4.4 Additional Bootstrap Commands for the ESXi Installer

Command	Description
BOOTIF=<hwtype>-<MAC address>	Accepts the format for the boot network adapter as supplied by PXELINUX.
ip=<ip address>	Sets a static IP address to be used for downloading the script and the installation media. The IPAPPEND option is also supported if you PXE-boot the installer.
netmask=<subnet mask>	Sets the subnet mask for the network interface.
gateway=<ip address>	Sets the default gateway for the installation.
vlanid=<vlanid>	Configures the VLAN for the VMkernel network interface.
netdevice=<device>	Tries to use a network adapter <device> for network operations during the installation. You can specify a MAC address in the format of 00:0c:29:32:71:00 or you can use the vmnic name. If you do not specify this address, the ESXi Installer uses vmnic0, which will be the first NIC that it detects.
nameserver=<ip address>	Specifies a DNS server to be used during the installation.

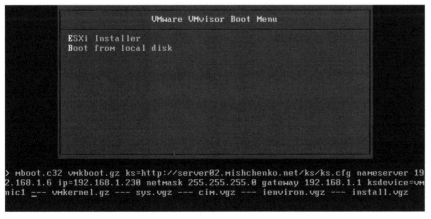

Figure 4.18 The ESXi Installer applying an installation script.

If you're creating a new script, you will have to include the following four commands, as they are considered required. If one of these options is missing or incorrectly formatted, your automated installation will generate an error and will not be able to proceed.

accepteula or vmaccepteula. Your script should either include the command `accepteula` or `vmaccepteula`. These commands require no options and, as implied, allow the installation script to accept the End User License Agreement for the installation process.

autopart. The `autopart` command specifies the disk that is used as the target for the ESXi Installer. The installer clears all existing partitions on this disk, copies over the system disk image, and then partitions the remaining space as a VMFS datastore. Unlike with an ESX install script, you do not specify any system partitions, as ESXi uses a default partition schema and thus you do not need to configure the `/tmp` or `/var` partitions, for example, as you would with an ESX script.

Table 4.5 lists the options accepted by the command.

Within your installation script, this command appears similar to the following:

```
autopart --firstdisk=local,remote --overwritevmfs
```

Table 4.5 autopart Command Options

Command	Description
`--drive=` or `--disk=`	This specifies the disk to partition. See Table 4.6 for a list of acceptable disk device names.
`--firstdisk=` `<disk-type1>,[<disk-type2>,…]`	You can use this option flag to direct the installer to use a specific order for the target disk. The acceptable disk-type options are `local`, `remote`, and the VMkernel device driver name. To have the installer first use a local disk and then remote as the target for the ESXi installation image, you would use `--firstdisk=local,remote`. To have the installer prefer a disk attached to a specific controller, you could use `--firstdisk=mptspi,local`, which gives preference to disks with that device driver over any other local disks.
`--overwritevmfs`	This flag is required to overwrite any VMFS partition on the disk targeted for the installation of the ESXi system partitions. It is required if you plan to install over an existing ESXi or ESX installation.

Table 4.6 Disk Device Names

Format	Examples
VML	`mpx.vmhba0:C0:T0:L0`
`/dev/.+`	`/dev/sda, /dev/cciss/c0d0`
`sdX, cciss/cNdN`	`sda, cciss/c0d0`

Table 4.7 install Command Options

Command	Description
`<cdrom|nfs|url>`	Specifies the media source to use for the installation media.
`--server=`	Used with the `nfs` option to specify the IP address or hostname of the NFS server to use.
`--dir=`	Specifies the directory on the NFS server to mount for the installation media.
`<url>`	Defines the location of the installation media and has a type of `http`, `https`, `ftp`, or `nfs`.

install. The `install` command specifies that your script is to run a fresh install, which is the only option for a scripted installation. Table 4.7 lists the command's options.

The default installation script specifies that the installation should be made from the CD being used to boot the installer, so the command in the script is `install cdrom`. If you plan to use another media option, you would update the entry to something like the following:

```
install url http://server02.mishchenko.net/Media_depot/ESXi_4.1/
```

rootpw. This command sets the password for the root account. The password can be between 6 and 64 characters and should conform to the password requirements discussed in Chapter 2. Table 4.8 lists the command's options.

Ideally you will have the password in encrypted form. To generate the encrypted password on a Linux machine, you can run the command `grub-md5-crypt`, as shown in the following example. If you're using Windows, you can search online for an MD5 calculator, which you can use to generate an MD5 hash for your password.

Table 4.8 rootpw Command Options

Command	Description
--iscrypted	This optional flag specifies that the password has been encrypted.
<password>	The password for the root account must be included either in clear text or encrypted form.

```
sudo grub-md5-crypt
Password: ********
Retype password:  ********
$1$E4XdT/$xYUqVgsVElgEeyTqLazX41
```

The remaining commands that will be discussed are optional.

clearpart. The clearpart command can be used to remove partitions from the system before creating new ones. Table 4.9 lists the command's options.

dryrun. If you include the dryrun command, the installation script is parsed and checked, but the ESXi Installer does not actually perform the installation. You can see the troubleshooting section later in this chapter for information on accessing the installation log.

keyboard. This command sets the keyboard type to be used in the DCUI. Table 4.10 lists the command's options.

serialnum or vmserialnum. These commands set the license string for the host. If the option is not included, the host is set to run in evaluation mode for 60 days. In this mode, the host is licensed at the vSphere Enterprise Plus edition. Table 4.11 lists the commands' options.

network. The network command configures the VMkernel management port to which you'll connect with the vSphere client or vCenter Server. You can set the host to use a static IP address or DHCP. VMware recommends using a static IP address. Table 4.12 lists the network command's options.

paranoid. The default behavior of the installation script process is to continue if warnings are encountered, but to halt on errors. If your script were missing the install command, this would generate an error and the installation process would terminate. But if the script were to set a static IP address but did not include the nameserver flag, it would generate a warning and you would be able to proceed with the installation, as shown in Figure 4.19. If you include the paranoid command, the script terminates when it encounters any error or warning.

Table 4.9 clearpart Command Options

Command	Description
`--drives=`	This specifies the disk to partition. See Table 4.6 for a list of acceptable disk device names.
`--alldrives`	This flag causes your script to ignore the drives flag and instructs the installer to clear all partitions on all disks visible to the installer.
`--ignoredrives=`	Your script will require this flag if the options `drives` or `alldrives` are not used. In this case, all partitions will be deleted except for those on the disk that you specify. See Table 4.6 for a list of acceptable disk device names.
`--initlabel`	This flag causes the installer to initialize the disk label to the default for your architecture.
`--firstdisk=`<disk-type1>, [<disk-type2>,…]	You can use this option flag to direct the installer to use a specific order for the target disk. The acceptable disk-type options are `local`, `remote`, and the VMkernel device driver name. To have the installer first use a `local` disk and then `remote` as the target for the ESXi install image, you would use `--firstdisk=local,remote`. To have the installer prefer a disk attached to a specific controller, you could use `--firstdisk=mptspi,local`, which would give disks with that device driver preference over any other local disks.
`--overwritevmfs`	This flag is required to overwrite any VMFS partition on the disk targeted for the installation of the ESXi system partitions. It is required if you plan to install over an existing ESXi or ESX installation.

Table 4.10 keyboard Command Options

Command	Description
`<keyboardType>`	You can set the keyboard type to one of the following options: `Default`, `French`, `German`, `Japanese`, or `Russian`.

Table 4.11 serialnum Command Options

Command	Description
--esx=<license-key>	This flag specifies the vSphere license key to use for the host. The key should be formatted in five five-character groups, as in the following example: serialnum --esx=103JP-14HU5-N9J08-0OBH2-83B4J

Table 4.12 network Command Options

Command	Description
--bootproto=[dhcp|static]	This flag sets the management port to use either a static IP address or DHCP.
--device=	This flag specifies which network port is linked to the default vSwitch. You can specify either the MAC address of the network card or the vmnic device name.
--ip=	This sets an IP address for the management port and is required with the --bootproto=static option.
--netmask=	This flag sets the subnet mask for the management port and is used with the --bootproto=static option. If you don't include this option, the standard subnet mask will be used based on the static IP address you have chosen.
--gateway=	This sets the default gateway for the management port and is required with the --bootproto=static option.
--nameserver=	This designates the primary and optionally secondary DNS server for the management port. It is used with the --bootproto=static option. If you plan to use DHCP, you can omit this option. The --nameserver option can accept up to two IP addresses. For example: --nameserver="192.168.1.5,192.168.1.6".
--hostname=	This specifies the hostname to be used for the system. This only works with --bootproto=static.
--vlanid=<vlanid>	This specifies a VLAN to use for the management port and can be set to an integer between 0 and 4095.
--addvmportgroup=(0|1)	This flag instructs the installer whether to create the default VM Network port group. The default value is 1, which does create the port group.

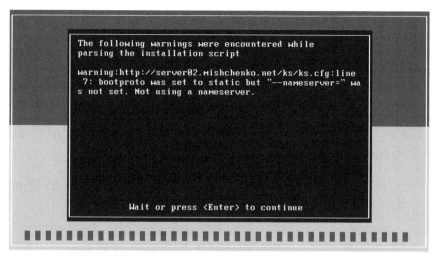

The following warnings were encountered while parsing the installation script

warning:http://server02.mishchenko.net/ks/ks.cfg:line 7: bootproto was set to static but "--nameserver=" was not set. Not using a nameserver.

Wait or press <Enter> to continue

Figure 4.19 An ESXi installation script warning.

part or partition. The part or partition commands allow your script to create addition datastores on your host. Only a single datastore per disk can be created. You cannot use the part command on the same disk used for the ESXi system partition as specified by the autopart command, as the installer automatically creates a VMFS datastore with the remaining space on that disk after the system partitions are created. Table 4.13 lists the available options.

%include or include. When you select this option, you can include an additional script to be parsed and run by the ESXi Installer. You can have multiple include commands within your script. The include command is followed by the name of the script that you want to include, as shown in the following example:

```
%include partition.cfg
```

%pre. You can use this option to specify a script to be run before the kickstart installation script is evaluated. Table 4.14 lists the available options.

In the following example, the %pre script is used to generate a partition script that is then included in the configuration script:

```
%pre --intepreter=busybox --unsupported
cat > /tmp/part.cfg ≪EOF
part datastore2 --fstype=vmfs3 --size=200000 --onfirstdisk="remote"
part datastore3 --fstype=vmfs3 --size=100000 --grow
   --ondisk="mpx.vmhba1:C0:T0:L0"
EOF

# Disk Partitioning
%include partition.cfg
```

Table 4.13 part Command Options

Command	Description
`<datastore name>`	This specifies the name for the datastore.
`--size=`	This sets the minimum partition size in megabytes.
`--grow`	If you include this flag, this allows the datastore to grow to use all available space on the disk or up to the limit set by the `--maxsize` option.
`--maxsize=`	This sets the maximum size for a partition to grow in megabytes.
`--ondrive=` or `--ondisk=`	This specifies the disk to partition. See Table 4.6 for a list of acceptable disk device names.
`--onfirstdisk=<disk-type1>,[<disk-type2>,…]`	You can use this option flag to direct the installer to use a specific order for the target disk. The acceptable disk-type options are `local`, `remote`, and the VMkernel device driver name. To have the installer first use a `local` disk and then `remote` as the target for the ESXi install image, you would use `--firstdisk=local,remote`. To have the installer prefer a disk attached to a specific controller, you could use `--firstdisk=mptspi,local`, which specifies that disks with that device driver are preferred over any other local disks.
`--fstype`	This option sets the file system type for the partition and can be set only to `VMFS3`.

Table 4.14 %pre Command Options

Command	Description
`--interpreter=[python | busybox]`	This flag specifies the interpreter to use. The default is `busybox`.
`--unsupported`	This argument is required to acknowledge that use of the command is unsupported.

Table 4.15 %post Command Options

Command	Description
`--interpreter=[python | busybox]`	This flag specifies the interpreter to use. The default is `busybox`.
`--unsupported`	This argument is required to acknowledge that use of the command is unsupported.
`--timeout=secs`	You can specify the timeout for executing the script. If the script has not completed before the timeout has expired, it will be forcibly terminated.
`--ignorefailure=[true | false]`	If this option is set to `true`, the installation will be considered a success even if the `%post` script encounters an error.

%post. You can use the `%post` command to include a script that will be executed after the installation process has been completed. If you specify multiple `%post` commands in the script, they will be executed in the order in which they appear in the script. Table 4.15 lists the available options.

The default installation script discussed earlier contains a sample of the `%post` command, and in that instance the command is used to generate a timestamp file marking the completion of the installation process.

%firstboot. As with the `%pre` and `%post` commands, the `%firstboot` command is not supported. This command creates an init script that will be executed the first time the host boots after the installation process. You can specify multiple `%firstboot` sections and assign an order of execution with the `--level` argument. The default level will be 999, and if you examine `/etc/vmware/init/init.d`, you will see that various system init scripts have a level of 0 to 199 assigned to them, so you should typically assign a level higher than 200. Table 4.16 describes the command's options.

The `%firstboot` command offers some significant capabilities to customize your ESXi installations. Most of the `esxcfg` commands that you'll have dealt with in the ESX Service Console will also be available in the ESXi console and you'll be able also run python scripts. You should be aware that the script is not checked during the installation, so you will not know how it runs until the host has booted for the first time after the installation. Any syntax errors are detected when it runs; see the troubleshooting section later in this chapter to learn how you can obtain log data for the `%firstboot` commands.

Table 4.16 %firstboot Command Options

Command	Description
`--interpreter=[python	busybox]`	This flag specifies the interpreter to use. The default is `busybox`.
`--unsupported`	This argument is required to acknowledge that use of the command is unsupported.
`--level=level`	The level that you assign to the script determines the order in which the init script will be executed. The default value is 999.

A Sample Installation Script

The following sample script makes use of the commands found in the previous section to automate the installation of VMware ESXi. The required commands of vmaccepteula, rootpw, install, and autopart are included. In this case, the root password has been encrypted. The install command is set to use an HTTP media depot for the installation disk image. The autopart command tells the installer to use the first disk found and to overwrite any existing VMFS datastore.

A number of optional commands are also included. The keyboard command is set to be Russian and a serial number is set for the host. The serial number is validated by the installer, so if you use an invalid serial number, such as the one in the sample, or have not properly formatted the serial number, an error will be generated when the script is initially parsed at the start of the automated installation process. The script also uses the paranoid command, which ensures that the script is parsed without any warning; otherwise, the installation will be aborted.

The network command is used to set a static IP address for the host, the hostname, and DNS servers to use. The vmnic to use for the management port is not specified, so vmnic0 defaults to this purpose. The commands clearpart and part are used to clear the partitions on two other disks in the ESXi host and then create new VMFS datastores on them. The size for the datastores is set to 1200MB, which is the minimum value that you can use, but the --grow flag instructs the installer to use all available space on those disks.

The last part of the script uses the %firstboot command to execute a script during the initial boot of the new ESXi installation. As mentioned earlier, this portion of the script is not checked during the installation process, so you won't know of any errors until after the first time the host has booted up. The %firstboot command is used to include console commands that will create a new vSwitch with vmnic2 and vmnic3 and then add a virtual machine port group called DMZ on VLAN 200. The script then mounts an NFS datastore and finally takes a configuration backup with the installer stores on the NFS share.

```
# Accept the VMware End User License Agreement
vmaccepteula

# Set the root password for the DCUI and Tech Support Mode
rootpw --iscrypted $1$vFXeT/$oqg2GUIgz9ucneF4YsKq9.

# Install from media depot
install url http://server02.mishchenko.net/Media_Depot/ESXi_4.1/

# partitioning command
autopart --firstdisk --overwritevmfs

# set keyboard type
keyboard Russian

# set serial number
serialnum --esx=10ADP-140E5-NZ008-00DH2-821KJ

# abort script if any warnings are generated
paranoid

# Network settings for the management port
network --bootproto=static --ip=192.168.1.34 --gateway=192.168.1.1
   --netmask=255.255.255.0 --hostname=esx05.mishchenko.net
   --nameserver="192.168.1.5,192.168.1.6"

# formatting of other datasources to maximum of LUN size
part datastore2 --fstype=vmfs3 --size=1200 --grow --ondisk=mpx.vmhba1:C0:T1:L0
part datastore3 --fstype=vmfs3 --size=1200 --grow --ondisk=mpx.vmhba1:C0:T2:L0

# initial configuration after install process
%firstboot --unsupported --interpreter=busybox
esxcfg-vswitch --add vSwitch1
esxcfg-vswitch --link=vmnic2 vSwitch1
esxcfg-vswitch --link=vmnic3 vSwitch1
esxcfg-vswitch --add-pg=DMZ vSwitch1
esxcfg-vswitch --pg=DMZ vSwitch1 --vlan=200
esxcfg-nas --add --host 192.168.1.100 --share /NFS2  NFS2
sleep 60
cd /vmfs/volumes/NFS2/
mkdir ESX05
backup.sh 0 /vmfs/volumes/NFS2/ESX05
```

Troubleshooting Installation Scripts

If there is a problem in your script, a warning or error message will be displayed after the ESXi Installer has parsed the configuration script. A sample of a warning is shown in Figure 4.20. In this case, the network command was not found in the script, but the installation process would be able to continue after a timeout had expired or you had pressed the Enter key to continue. If you had used the paranoid command in the script, the installation process would have terminated and prompted you to reboot the host. If your script has an error, such as missing the install command, you would be informed of the error and only be able to reboot the host.

In most cases, such as the error in Figure 4.20, the error or warning message will be self-explanatory and you'll be able to correct your script based on the information provided. That may not always be the case; at the conclusion of the script, you may be informed that a warning was generated and that you should review the log file for more information.

To begin gathering information about the script problem, you can access the VMkernel log file. At the console of the host or in your remote control session, press Alt+F12. The display will change from the installation DCUI screen to display the VMkernel log, as shown in Figure 4.21. The file displayed on this screen corresponds with the file /var/log/messages on the host. You can scroll back and forth through the log file to see the commands run by the installation script and any warnings or errors that were generated. You can press the H key to access a help menu and then Alt+F2 to return to the main installation screen.

You may also want to access the console to open the installation log file. In some cases, the installation may complete, but the program will inform you that there were warning messages

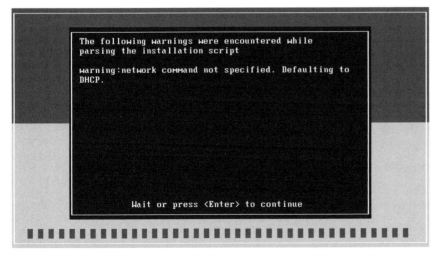

Figure 4.20 A warning message during an automated ESXi installation.

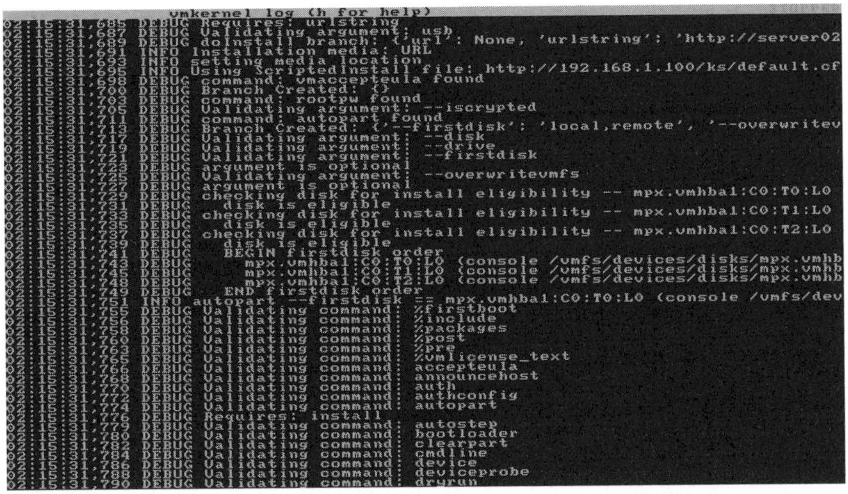

Figure 4.21   Accessing the VMkernel log file during an installation.

and that you should check the log file. To get to the log file, press Alt+F1 to access the console. You will be prompted for a login and you can enter root. The password will be blank. Once you have logged in, you will have access to the console, as shown in Figure 4.22.

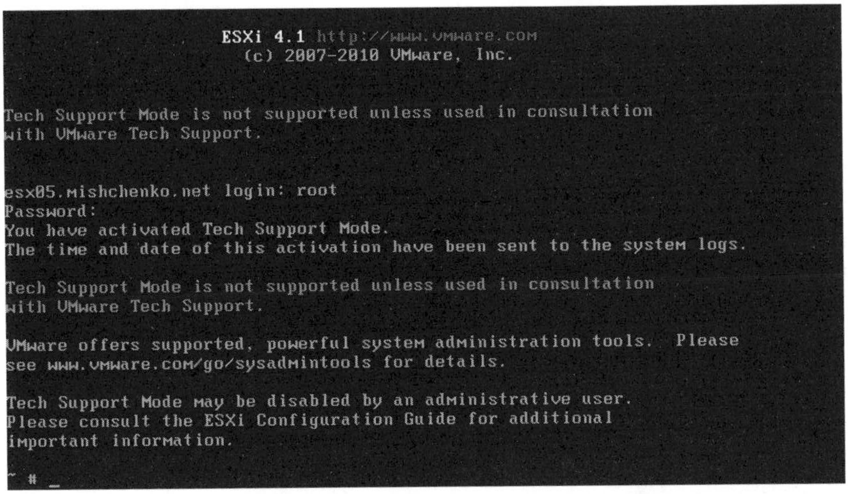

Figure 4.22   Accessing the ESXi Installer console during an installation.

You'll find the log files in the folder /var/log. The messages file will be the VMkernel log file that you can access by pressing Alt+F12. You will also see the file esxi_install.log, which is a symlink to the install log file weasel.log. You can view the contents of those files with the command cat or the vi editor. As the ESXi Installer will have initialized a network connection, you could optionally copy the log files to another host with the scp command. Alternatively, you could enable Secure Shell (SSH) on the host by following these steps:

1. Run the command vi /etc/initd.conf.

2. Edit inetd.conf to remove the # from in front of the first line with #ssh.

3. Press Esc and then enter :wq to save the file and quit vi.

4. Run the command ps|grep inetd to identify the process ID for inetd.

5. Restart the inetd process with the command kill <process id> -HUP, where <process ID> is the same ID from step 4.

Note: The method shown to enable SSH during the installation process should not be used on your ESXi host once the installation is complete. Refer to Chapter 3, "Management Tools," for the method to enable Remote Tech Support Mode for SSH access to your host.

Once you've completed these steps, you'll be able to connect with your preferred SSH client and download the log files that you need to troubleshoot your issue. If you're having problems with disk formatting, you could run the command fdisk -l to identify the device names corresponding to the formats provided in Table 4.6.

If you're troubleshooting a problem with the %firstboot portion of the script, you'll have to wait until after the first reboot to access the log files. After the reboot, you can enable Tech Support Mode to access either the local console or SSH, as described in Chapter 3. Once you have access, you can check the install log file /var/log/esxi_install.log. As you'll see later, /var/log is part of the ESXi ramdisk and files within that folder are not preserved across a server restart. In this case, however, the installer bundles the log file into the file onetime. tgz and stores that file on the system partition that will be mounted as /bootbank when the host next reboots. The bootstrap command to start the VMkernel on /bootbank includes a link to this file, so the log file will be accessible after the first reboot following installation. The esxi_install.log file contains elements such as the following.

- Installation script name and URL

- List of disk LUNs detected by the VMkernel.

- Media depot source as configured by the install command

- Parsing and validation of the installation script

- Download status of the installation media

- Partitioning and formatting of datastores

- Application of commands in the configuration script

- Creation of the `onetime.tgz` archive for ESXi configuration files and command scripts that will be run after installation

The `onetime.tgz` file also contains the file `/etc/vmware/init/init.d/999.firstboot_001`. If you used the `--level` flag with the `%firstboot` command, you will see that reflected in the filename. If you have used the scripting command `keyboard`, you will also see `999.firstboot.keyboard`, `999.firstboot_license` for the `license` command, and, as a required command, `999.firstboot_password` for the `password` command. There is also a file called `999.firstboot_remove`.

If you've used busybox as the interpreter for your `%firstboot` script, you'll be able to open the file and review the syntax of your commands. The keyboard and license files contain scripts that manipulate configuration data within the `/etc` folder. The `999.firstboot_password` file executes the python script `/var/lib/firstboot/999.firstboot_password.py`. This script in turn edits `/etc/shadow` to insert the MD5 hash for the password you used in the installation script.

The `999.firstboot_remove` script cleans up your `%firstboot` script and other scripts for commands, such as the `keyboard` and `password` commands, which are run after the install process. The script starts the python script `/var/lib/firstboot/999.firstboot_remove.py`, which edits `/bootbank/boot.cfg` to remove the bootstrap entry to the `onetime.tgz` file and also deletes the `onetime.tgz` file.

Conclusion

With the initial release of VMware ESXi 3.5, two editions were available: Embedded and Installable. Although both were fast to install and easy to configure initially, the manual installation steps for both did not lend the release well to mass installations.

VMware ESXi 4.1 has overcome those limitations by officially supporting PXE boot installations and the introduction of scripted installations. If you're using scripts for your ESX installations, you'll be able to update those to run with ESXi, and with the configuration options for PXELINUX or gPXE, you'll find it easy to create a configuration file that passes a specific installation script for each of your hosts.

5 Migrating from ESX

Migrating from VMware ESX and Virtual Center 2.5 or vCenter Server 4.0 to VMware ESXi and vCenter Server 4.1 requires careful planning and consideration of a number of factors. Your move to ESXi may open the opportunity to reimplement vCenter Server to meet changing business, management, or security requirements. You may consider redesigning your network configuration, implementing a different security model, or fine-tuning other factors that make starting with a fresh installation worthwhile. Or you may desire to keep your existing vCenter Server configuration and just upgrade the server directly to vCenter Server 4.1.

This chapter examines the following items:

- Understanding the prerequisites for installing vCenter Server 4.1

- Preparing for the upgrade to vCenter Server 4.1

- Upgrading to vCenter Server 4.1

- Migrating virtual machines to ESXi 4.1

- Upgrading virtual machines

Prerequisites

Upgrading your datacenter to vSphere 4.1 is a multistep process involving all components of your deployment, including vCenter Server, ESXi hosts, and virtual machines. The upgrade requires a specific order to upgrade components, beginning with vCenter Server and ending with virtual machines. Upgrading to ESXi 4.1 before vCenter Server has been updated to version 4.1 will result in a loss of connectivity between vCenter Server and the ESXi hosts. For the most part, the upgrade process involves steps that are not reversible. Should you encounter a problem with vCenter Server after the upgrade, you can only revert to the prior version using a backup of the vCenter Server host and a vCenter Server database backup. With that in mind, it may be worthwhile to include stabilization periods among the major components of your upgrade to minimize the impact of a potential rollback. For example, if you are migrating from ESX 3.5 to ESXi 4.1, you can upgrade the virtual machine's hardware version to 7 after it has been migrated to the ESXi 4.1 hosts. However, once you have upgraded the hardware version, you will no longer be able to migrate those virtual machines back to ESX 3.5 should you have to revert the upgrade process for any reason. Thus you would require prior backups of those virtual machines to reverse the hardware version change to be able to run the virtual machines on ESX 3.5 again.

With a migration to vSphere 4.1, one of the significant requirements is the need for a 64-bit host operating system (OS) for vCenter Server. If you are currently running vCenter Server on a 32-bit OS, you need to provide a new host running a 64-bit OS. Any database drivers that you install to support vCenter Server's database connection need to be 64-bit as well. For a list of supported OSs for vCenter Server 4.1, you can consult the Compatibility Matrix at http://www.vmware.com/pdf/vsphere4/r40/vsp_compatibility_matrix.pdf. To aid with the migration of vCenter Server to a 64-bit host, VMware has developed the vCenter Server data migration tool to assist with copying of your vCenter Server configuration between hosts. This tool is discussed later in this chapter. vCenter Server no longer supports Microsoft SQL Server 2000 or Oracle 9i, so a database migration may be required prior to upgrading vCenter Server.

Another critical prerequisite is to verify compatibility of the various components that host your virtual infrastructure as well as interact with it. The hardware requirements for your ESXi host can be found in the Upgrade Guide, which you can download from http://www.vmware.com/pdf/vsphere4/r41/vsp_41_upgrade_guide.pdf. It is also worthwhile to check the Hardware Compatibility List (HCL) at http://www.vmware.com/go/hcl to ensure that the hardware you plan to use is compatible with ESXi. This is especially the case if you plan to reuse the hardware that is currently running ESX 3.5. You should also verify that all your input/output (I/O) devices and storage devices also appear on the HCL.

If you are employing any the following VMware products within your virtual infrastructure, you should ensure that they are compatible with vSphere 4.1:

- VMware Lab Manager
- VMware Site Recovery Manager
- VMware View

It is often the case that the preceding products require a version update before they are supported with a new release such as vSphere 4.1. If you are using any third-party products for backup, management, monitoring, or other purposes, you should ensure that the version you have deployed supports vSphere 4.1 and especially that the products are able to operate properly with ESXi.

If your vCenter Server 4.1 instance will manage ESX 3.5 hosts, you need to install a license server to support those hosts. The vCenter Server data migration tool does not migrate the license configuration from the source vCenter Server. In such a case, you need to install the license server manually and then copy the license file from the source server when you perform the vCenter Server upgrade. After you have decommissioned all ESX 3.5 hosts, you can uninstall the license server, as licensing for ESXi 4.1 is configured and managed within vCenter Server using the vSphere client.

Throughout this book, a number of new vSphere features are discussed, and those features often have specific requirements. For example, some of the requirements for using Fault Tolerance include the following:

- ESXi servers must be used with specific processor models.

- Hardware Virtualization (HV) must be enabled in the Basic Input/Output System (BIOS) of the ESXi hosts.

- Only certain guest operating systems are supported.

- Host certificate checking must be enabled in vCenter Server.

- Only single virtual CPU (vCPU) machines are supported.

VMware has compiled a prerequisites checklist that describes the requirements, optional requirements, and recommendations to migrate from VMware Infrastructure 3 to vSphere 4. That document is available at the following link: http://www.vmware.com/files/pdf/vsphere-migration-prerequisites-checklist.pdf.

Upgrading to vCenter Server 4.1

The first step to moving your environment to ESXi 4.1 is to upgrade to vCenter Server 4.1. The exact process to upgrade depends on your environment. As mentioned earlier, you may choose to reimplement vCenter Server, in which case you start with a fresh install of vCenter Server and add ESXi hosts as required.

One of the simpler scenarios may involve upgrading from vCenter Server 4.0. If the vCenter Server host is running a 64-bit OS and the database server is running a version compatible with vSphere 4.1, then you just have to run the installation wizard to upgrade vCenter Server. This process requires downtime for vCenter Server during the upgrade, but virtual machines can continue to operate without interruption. The upgrade process does not include a rollback process, so you should ensure that you have an adequate backup of both the vCenter Server host and database before proceeding.

To upgrade from vCenter Server 4.0 to 4.1 on the same host, use the following procedure:

1. Log in to the vCenter Server with an account that has administrative rights. If you are connecting to SQL Server with Windows NT Authentication, log in with the account that has been given database owner (DBO) rights to the database and that owns the vCenter Server tables within the database.

2. Open the vCenter Server installation media and start `autorun.exe`.

3. On the vCenter Server Installer page, choose vCenter Server. The vCenter Server installer begins, detects the existing installation, and informs you that an upgrade will be performed.

4. Click Next on the license and patent agreement pages.

5. Select the data source name (DSN) to use to connect to the vCenter Server database. This DSN must be 64-bit and should exist before you run the vCenter Server installer.

6. On the Database Options screen, verify that the correct database is displayed. If you are not using Windows NT Authentication for the database connection, then enter the correct password that corresponds to the username that the installer displays.

7. On the Database Upgrade Warning screen, check the options Upgrade Existing vCenter Server Database and I Have Taken a Backup of the Existing vCenter Server Database and SSL Certificates. Click Next to continue.

8. The upgrade to vCenter Server 4.1 requires an upgrade of the vCenter Agent on all hosts. On the vCenter Agent Upgrade screen, shown in Figure 5.1, you can select between an Automatic or Manual upgrade. With an Automatic upgrade, the vCenter Agent is upgraded seamlessly on all hosts in the vCenter Server inventory. For a Manual upgrade, all hosts are disconnected when you connect to vCenter Server after the upgrade. To upgrade the vCenter Agent, you must reconnect to each host. If you select a manual upgrade, VMware High Availability and Fault Tolerance continue to work while the hosts are disconnected from the vCenter Server.

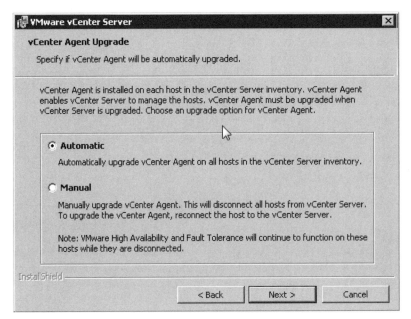

Figure 5.1 The vCenter Server Agent Upgrade screen.

9. Specify the service account to use for vCenter Server on the vCenter Server Service screen. You can select between using the SYSTEM account or entering a Windows login and password. If you are using Windows NT Authentication to connect to SQL Server, then you should specify the account setup for the database.

10. On the Configure Ports screen, you can accept the default ports that vCenter Server is to use for communication or change the settings to match your environment. The installer displays any changes that were made for the previously installed vCenter Server installation.

11. Choose the amount of memory to allocate to the vCenter Server Web service and click Next.

12. Click Install on the Ready to Install the Program screen to proceed with the upgrade.

Once the upgrade has completed, you can connect to the vCenter Server to verify that the upgrade has completed successfully. If you have other vCenter components installed, such as Update Manager, you should upgrade those as well. You require version 4.1 of the vSphere client to connect to the upgraded vCenter server instance. You can install that version from the vCenter Server installation media or open a Web browser and connect to your vCenter Server host for a download link. After you have connected, you can add new ESXi hosts and prepare to migrate the virtual machines running on ESX 3.5 and 4.0 to ESXi.

If your upgrade scenario involves VirtualCenter Server 2.5, a 32-bit host OS, and a database server unsupported for vSphere 4.1, such as Microsoft SQL Server 2000, the upgrade process is more complicated. Such a scenario involves the following steps:

1. Back up the VirtualCenter Server and database.

2. Migrate the database to a supported database server.

3. Prepare a new vCenter Server host running a 64-bit OS.

4. Export configuration data from VirtualCenter with the data migration tool.

5. Restore the data collected with the data migration tool.

6. Install vCenter Server on the new host.

7. Migrate the licensing server to the new host to support ESX 3.5 hosts.

As the upgrade process to vCenter Server 4.1 is a one-way process, you should ensure that you have adequate backups before proceeding with your upgrade. At a minimum, the following items should be included:

- A full database backup of the VirtualCenter database.

- A backup of the VirtualCenter SSL certificates. These are found either in %ALLUSERSPROFILE%\Application Data\VMware\VMware VirtualCenter or %ALLUSERSPROFILE%\VMware\VMware VirtualCenter\.

- Notes on the existing VirtualCenter configuration. These notes should include information such as the Internet Protocol (IP) address, the database DSN, assigned ports, and the SQL login and password.

- A backup of the VirtualCenter configuration file vpxd.cfg.

Migrating the VirtualCenter Database to a Supported Version

The first step to migrating to vCenter Server 4.1 in this scenario is to migrate the database to a database server supported by vSphere 4.1. In the following example, the database is migrated from SQL Server 2000 to SQL Server 2008:

1. On the VirtualCenter host, stop the VirtualCenter Windows service.

2. Open SQL Enterprise Manager and connect to the SQL Server 2000 database server. As an extra precaution, make a full database backup. Also make a note of the SQL login that is set up for this database.

3. Right-click on the database and select Tasks > Detach.

4. After detach is complete, copy the database files to the host running SQL Server 2008.

5. Start SQL Management Studio and connect to the SQL Server 2008 instance.

6. Create the same SQL login used to connect to the database on the source database server.

7. Right-click on the Databases folder and select Attach.

8. On the Attach Database screen, click Add, browse to the data file (.mdf) for the database, and then click OK. Click OK again to attach the database.

9. Right-click on the database, choose Properties, and then select the Options page. Change the Compatibility Level to SQL Server 2008 (100).

10. Ensure that the Recovery Model is set to an appropriate setting for your backup strategy. This setting is also found on the Options page.

11. Click OK to close the Database Properties windows and exit SQL Management Studio.

Once you have migrated the database, you should verify connectivity to the database. If your new vCenter Server host has been set up, create a new DSN to the database. The DSN should use the SQL Server Native Client. This should also be a 64-bit DSN, which you can create by selecting Control Panel > Administrative Tools > Data Sources (ODBC). You should also ensure that the database has been added to a maintenance and backup plan appropriate for your data recovery requirements. Regular index rebuilds are required to maintain optimal performance, especially if you gather a large amount of performance data. If you want to migrate the database using a backup and restore method, or if you are hosting the database on Oracle, you can consult the vSphere 4.1 Upgrade Guide for the appropriate procedure. You are now ready to back up the VirtualCenter configuration with the data migration tool.

Tip: For vSphere 4.1, Update Manager remains a 32-bit product. If you are hosting this component on your vCenter Server host, then you need to create a 32-bit DSN for it.

Backing Up vCenter Server Configuration Data with the Data Migration Tool

The data migration tool is included with vCenter Server 4.1 to migrate your configuration from your 32-bit VirtualCenter or vCenter Server host to your new 64-bit vCenter Server host. The data migration tool backs up the following configuration items:

- Port settings for HTTP, HTTPS, heartbeat, Web services, Lightweight Directory Access Protocol (LDAP), and LDAP Secure Sockets Layer (SSL).

- SSL certificates.

- LDAP data.

- Licensing configuration.

- If you are using SQL Server Express locally on the 32-bit host to store the database, the data migration tool backs this up as well.

The data migration tool also backs up and restores data for other vCenter products. The tool can back up vCenter Orchestrator data, but not the database if it is hosted on the source host. The tool can also migrate Update Manager settings and the database if you are using SQL Server Express. The data migration tool does not back up patch binaries.

To back up configuration data on your VirtualCenter 2.5 or vCenter Server 4.0 host, use the following procedure:

1. Log in to the source host with an administrative account.

2. Stop the VMware VirtualCenter Server service.

3. Access the installation media for vCenter Server 4.1 and copy the file \datamigration \datamigration.zip to a temporary folder on the host.

4. Extract the contents of datamigration.zip.

5. Open a command prompt, change to the folder where you extracted the ZIP file, and execute `backup.bat`.

6. If Update Manager does not exist on the host, the error shown in the following sample output is displayed. Enter y and press Enter to continue the backup process.

```
[INFO] Starting vSphere configuration backup script...
[INFO] Checking prerequisites...
[INFO] Checking vCenter Server version...
[INFO] vCenter Server installation version 2.5.0.64217
[INFO] Checking for DB type
[INFO] DB is not bundled
[INFO] Checking for DSN
[INFO] VMware vCenter Server DSN: SQL04
[INFO] VMware vCenter DB Server name: None
[ERROR] VMware vCenter DB Server name is not found
[INFO] vCenter Server installation satisfies migration prerequisite
[INFO] Checking VMware vCenter Update Manager version...
[WARNING] VMware vCenter Update Manager is not installed or its version cannot
  be determined.
[WARNING] VMware Update Manager does not satisfy migration prerequisite
  Do you want to continue backup...? y|n:
```

7. Once the backup process has completed, check the file `log\backup.log` for any errors. If there are any errors, correct the source of the problem and rerun `backup.bat`. A successful backup may contain warnings that can be ignored, as shown in this sample:

```
[INFO] Successfully backed up vCenter Server installed data information
[INFO] Backing up vCenter Server DB...
[INFO] Checking vCenter Server DB configuration...
[INFO] Only SQL Server Express is supported for DB backup
[INFO] Skipping DB backup...
[WARNING] Could not back up VMware vCenter Update Manager data.
[WARNING] Could not back up vCO data.

[INFO] vSphere configuration backup script completed successfully
```

Tip: If you need to run the data migration tool more than once, you should first rename or delete the `data` folder that is created by the data migration tool. If that folder exists when `backup.bat` is run, the process terminates with an error.

Restoring the vCenter Server Configuration Data and Installing vCenter Server 4.1

Once you have completed the backup process on the source host, you can copy the data migration tool folder to the destination host to start the restore process and to install vCenter Server 4.1. If your source host was hosting the vCenter Server database on SQL Server Express, then the restore process copies this database to the new host as well.

Tip: To ease the restore process and post restore configuration, it is worthwhile to configure the new host with the same network name and IP address as the source host.

Prior to beginning the restore process, you should ensure that the new vCenter Server host has access to all dependent hosts such as Active Directory domain controllers, the database server, and the license server. Use the following procedure to restore the configuration data and install vCenter Server 4.1:

1. Copy the `datamigration` folder from the source host to the destination host. This may require a multicopy process if you plan to configure the destination host with the same network name and IP address.

2. Ensure that the installation media for vCenter Server 4.1 is available on the destination host. You can insert the DVD into the host's DVD-ROM drive or copy the contents of the installation media to a folder on the new host.

3. Verify that a DSN has been created to connect to the vCenter Server database. This should be a 64-bit database client. For SQL Server, you must use the SQL Server Native Client.

4. Open a command prompt, change to the `datamigration` folder, and execute the `install.bat` batch file.

5. If the network name of the new host does not match the source host, press y to continue the restore process.

6. Enter the path to the vCenter Server installation path as shown in the following example. The path you enter should point to the root of the installation media where `autorun.exe` is located.

   ```
   [INFO] Starting vSphere 4.1 migration installer script...
   [INFO] Checking prerequisites...
   [INFO]  Migration data directory: C:\tmp\data\data
   [INFO] Checking vCenter Server migration data...
   [INFO] vCenter Server DB migration data not present: no inventory data will be
      migrated
   ```

```
Enter path to vCenter Server 4.1 install media: C:\tmp\vc41
[INFO] vCenter Server install media found
[INFO]  vCenter Server migration data successfully verified

[INFO] Checking VMware vCenter Update Manager migration data...
[WARNING] VMware vCenter Update Manager migration configuration data is missing.
[WARNING]  VMware Update Manager backup data or system does not meet prerequisite

[INFO] Checking vCenter Orchestrator prerequisites...
[WARNING] vCenter Orchestrator migration data not present
[WARNING]  vCenter Orchestrator backup data or system does not meet prerequisite

[INFO] Installing vCenter...
[INFO] vCenter Server HTTP port: 80
[INFO] vCenter Server HTTPS port: 443
[INFO] vCenter Server heartbeat port: 902
[INFO] vCenter Server Tomcat HTTP port: 8086
[INFO] vCenter Server DB Server type: Custom
[INFO] vCenter Server License path: 27000@localhost
[INFO] vCenter Server License edition: vcExpress
[INFO] Launching installer with backed up install data configuration
```

7. The batch file restores configuration data such as the SSL certificates and then launches the installer for vCenter Server 4.1.

8. Select an installation language and then click OK.

9. Click Next on the initial Welcome and license agreement screens.

10. If you backed up a vCenter Server database that was hosted with SQL Server Express, select the option Install a Microsoft SQL Server 2005 Express Instance and click Next. Otherwise, select Use an Existing Supported Database and then select the DSN that you created earlier. For this example, the database is hosted on another server, so the second option is chosen.

11. On the Database Options screen, verify that the database username is correct and enter the database password. Click Next to continue.

12. The Database Upgrade Warning screen is displayed next. Select the option Upgrade Existing vCenter Server Database and check the box to confirm that you have made a backup of the SSL certificates, as shown in Figure 5.2.

13. On the vCenter Agent Upgrade screen, choose either an Automatic and Manual upgrade for the vCenter Agent running on the hosts in the vCenter Server's inventory. These choices are shown in Figure 5.1 and an explanation of the options are described earlier in the section "Upgrading to vCenter Server 4.1."

Figure 5.2   The vCenter Server Database Upgrade Warning screen.

14.   Select an account to use for the vCenter Server service. This can be the SYSTEM account; however, if you are using Windows NT Authentication to connect to the database on SQL Server, it should be the account setup with access to the database.

15.   Select the installation folder and click Next.

Tip: The installation of vCenter Server 4.1 requires Microsoft Active Directory Application Mode (ADAM), which is an implementation of LDAP. ADAM is used primarily to support a new vSphere feature called Linked Mode, but it is also required for single instance installations of vCenter Server. Linked Mode allows a single instance of the vSphere client to access inventory and configuration information across multiple vCenter Servers. In Linked Mode, ADAM is used to store and synchronize data across multiple vCenter Server instances. The installation path you choose for vCenter Server should be compatible with ADAM; for example, the path cannot contain any periods or commas.

---

16.   On the Configure Ports screen, review the various ports that vCenter Server will use for communication. These settings have been imported from the configuration backup. Click Next to continue.

17.   Select the amount of memory to use for the vCenter Server Web service and click Next.

18. Click Install to begin the installation of vCenter Server and the upgrade of the database. If the Microsoft .NET Framework is not installed, the vCenter Server installs that component. This may require a reboot of the host after the installation process has completed.

19. When the installation has completed, click Finish to close the vCenter Server installation program.

20. Review the `file log\restore.log` in the `datamigration` for errors.

Caution: If you are upgrading vCenter Server and hosting the database on Microsoft SQL Server, you need to grant DBO rights to the MSDB database for the login that is used to connect to the vCenter Server database prior to starting the upgrade. Several scheduled jobs that manage performance data are created in the MSDB database. After the upgrade has been completed, you can remove the DBO role to the MSDB from the vCenter Server SQL login. If your organization's security policies do not permit access to the MSDB database, the scheduled jobs can be created after the upgrade. Your database administrators can follow the procedure documented in the following Knowledge Base article to create the maintenance jobs manually: http://kb.vmware.com/kb/1004382.

If the data migration tool was used to back up Update Manager or vCenter Orchestrator data, then the installation wizards for those products are also started. Once the upgrade has completed, you can upgrade the vSphere client to version 4.1 and then connect to your vCenter Server host. If the network name for the new vCenter Server host did not match the old host's network name, you may receive errors for any plug-ins that were registered with vCenter Server. To correct that, you can follow these steps:

1. Each plug-in has an extension file stored within a subfolder of `C:\Program Files \VMware\Infrastructure\VirtualCenter Server\extensions`. Open each instance of `extensions.xml` with a text editor.

2. Edit the contents of the `<url>` tag to update the listed vCenter Server hostname.

3. Save the file after you have updated the hostname.

4. Reregister the extension with vCenter Server.

Once you have connected to vCenter Server 4.1, you can verify that the upgrade has completed successfully. If you chose to update the vCenter Agent on your ESX hosts manually, you may see tasks in progress related to that. If you chose to upgrade the vCenter Agent manually, then all your hosts will show a status of disconnected. Right-click on each host and select Connect to reconnect to those hosts and to upgrade the vCenter Agent.

Running the vCenter Agent Pre-Upgrade Check Tool The vCenter Agent Pre-Upgrade Check tool is included with vCenter Server 4.1 to provide a report showing known issues that might prevent a successful upgrade of the vCenter Agent on your ESX hosts. If the tool reports any issues, you may correct these before proceeding with the upgrade of vCenter Server and the subsequent upgrade of the vCenter Agent on your hosts. If the upgrade of the vCenter Agent fails on any of your hosts, you will not be able to manage these hosts with vCenter Server until you have corrected the problem.

Before you can run the vCenter Agent Pre-Upgrade Check tool, there are a number of prerequisites, which are documented in the vSphere Upgrade Guide. The tool checks the hosts only for specific issues, such as network connectivity, disk space, required patches, and whether the file system is intact. The tool does not fix any problems that are reported.

To begin the processes of checking your hosts, use the following steps:

1. On the VirtualCenter 2.5 or later system, insert the vCenter Server 4.1 installation media or copy the contents to a local drive.

2. Open the installation media and start `autorun.exe`. Select the Agent Pre-Upgrade Check option from the Utility list.

3. The Pre-Upgrade application will launch. Click Next on the Welcome screen to continue.

4. On the Database Connect screen, select the vCenter database DSN and enter the username and password used to connect to the database.

5. On the Select Mode screen, you can choose between Standard Mode, which scans all your hosts, and Custom Mode, which allows you to select which hosts to check.

6. On the Run Tests screen, click Run Precheck to start the check process. Each host requires about 30 to 40 seconds to be scanned.

7. Once the scans have completed, click Next to continue to the Pre-Check screen. On this screen, you can review the status of all the hosts that were scanned. You can click View Report to view a summary report for all hosts or click the Last Checked Status link for an individual host to review the status of that host.

The reports link to VMware Knowledge Base articles that address the issues detected by the vCenter Agent Pre-Upgrade Check tool. Once you have resolved the reported problems, you can rerun the tool until all hosts report a status of Pass. At that point, you can then proceed with your upgrade to vCenter Server 4.1.

Installing the License Service on the New vCenter Server Host

With vSphere, licensing for vCenter Server and your hosts is embedded within vCenter Server and you no longer have to use a separate licensing service for your vSphere hosts. However, if you plan to support ESX 3.5 hosts as part of your migration plan, you need to maintain a licensing service for those hosts. If the licensing server was installed on your vCenter Server host, then you'll need to install the service on the new host. To configure the licensing service, you can follow these steps:

1. Download the license service installation package from vmware.com. This download can be found in the Drivers and Tools section of the downloads for VMware Infrastructure 3.

2. Start the installation program to install the license service.

3. The program prompts you for the path to your VMware license file. Find the file and click Next to continue.

4. After the installation has completed, you can verify that the license file has been imported correctly by running the VMware License Server Tools application and performing a status enquiry.

5. If the hostname for the licensing server has changed since the upgrade, you should also update the licensing settings within vCenter Server. Connect to vCenter Server with the vSphere client and select Home > vCenter Server Settings. Then select the Licensing view and update the License Server configuration to match the new hostname and check the option Reconfigure ESX 3 Hosts Using License Server to Use This Server. Click OK to save your changes.

At this point in the upgrade process, your vCenter Server host is running version 4.1 and all your hosts should be connected. Your configuration of hosts and clusters should be the same as before the upgrade began, but it would be worthwhile to look around to ensure that no changes have been missed and that all your options and features are working as expected. Before discussing the migration of virtual machines to ESXi, it would be worthwhile to review the changes made in vSphere to permissions for datastores and networks.

Adding ESXi Hosts Securely to vCenter Server Once you have vCenter Server 4.1 installed, you can begin to add your ESXi hosts to it. The process to add an ESXi host is similar to the process of adding an ESX host. There are two items to note about the process. First, vCenter Server attempts to verify the authenticity of the ESXi host by checking the SSL certificate in use on the host. If the certificate can't be verified, a security alert is displayed, as shown in Figure 5.3. The SHA1 thumbprint that is displayed can be verified in the Direct Console User Interface (DCUI) for the host you are adding. This and enabling certificate checking is discussed further in Chapter 7, "Securing ESXi," in the section titled "Enabling Certificate Checking and Verifying Host Thumbprints." The second item to note is that the ESXi host can be placed in Lockdown Mode when a host is added to vCenter Server. Lockdown Mode is also discussed further in Chapter 7.

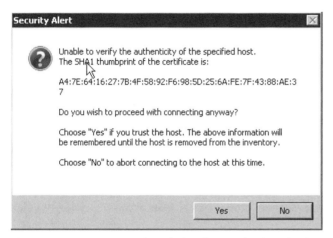

Figure 5.3   A Security Alert dialog box is displayed when adding an ESXi host with an untrusted SSL certificate.

Upgrading Datastore and Network Permissions

One of the new features with vSphere is the ability to assign role-based permissions to datastores and networks. With VirtualCenter Server, permissions for these objects were inherited from the datacenter object. After the upgrade to vCenter Server 4.1, users who did not have Administrator permissions on the datacenter object may be granted the role Datastore/Network Access (Upgrade), which has limited permissions for datastores and networks.

During the upgrade process, all existing permissions are upgraded without changes. For new managed objects in vCenter Server 4.1, users are initially granted the No Access role, which applies to datastores and networks. Without permission to a datastore, a user cannot perform a simple operation such as Browse Datastore. During the upgrade process, the Read-Only privilege on the datacenter objects determines what permissions are assigned to any datastores or networks in that datacenter. If the Read-Only privilege is nonpropagating and thus the permission is not applied to child objects, the upgrade process does not assign permissions to any datastores or networks. Users with full administrative rights on a virtual machine cannot make datastore or network-related changes until they have been assigned the appropriate privileges. If the Read-Only privilege is propagating, then the upgrade process assigns the Datastore/Network Access (Upgrade) role to the user. The role includes the privilege Allocate Space for datastores and Assign Network for networks, which allows the user to perform basic administrative operations.

Tip: The new datastore and network privileges provide an extra layer of security in your vSphere environment; when properly set, these privileges can prevent security breaches due to accidental or deliberate misconfiguration of your virtual machines. It is important to note that these permissions are managed by vCenter Server and not applied directly to the datastore or network. A user accessing the ESXi host directly with the vSphere client would not be affected by any restrictions enabled for them in vCenter Server. You can consider enabling Lockdown Mode to ensure that all client connections are made through vCenter Server.

If a user needs to perform operations on a datastore, then you have to assign a role with appropriate permissions. The vCenter Server upgrade creates the role Datastore Consumer (Sample). Like the Datastore/Network Access (Upgrade) role, Datastore Consumer (Sample) includes the Allocate Space privilege, which enables a user to allocate space on a datastore for virtual machines, snapshots, or clones. If a user needs to perform additional datastore maintenance tasks such as deleting files or datastores, then you need to assign those privileges. Table 5.1 lists the datastore privileges that you can assign to a role.

Table 5.1 vSphere Datastore Privileges

Privilege Name	Actions Granted
Allocate Space	This allocates space on a datastore for virtual machine files, snapshots, or clones.
Browse Datastore	This privilege allows the user to browse files on the datastore. This is required when accessing files for a virtual machine's virtual CD-ROM or floppy drive devices. The privilege also enables a user to add existing disks to a datastore.
Delete Datastore	This removes a datastore.
Delete Datastore File	With this privilege, a user can delete a file in the datastore.
File Management	This privilege enables a user to carry out file management tasks such as copying or moving files.
Move Datastore	This enables a user to move the datastore to another folder in the vCenter datastore inventory structure.
Rename Datastore	This enables the user to rename a datastore.

For network permissions, the vCenter Server upgrade process creates a sample role called Network Consumer (Sample). This role has the Assign Network privilege, which is required for a user to assign a virtual machine to a specific network. Should your users need additional

Table 5.2 vSphere Network Privileges

Privilege Name	Actions Granted
Assign Network	Set a virtual network interface card (NIC) to be connected to the network.
Configure Network	Make configuration changes to the network.
Delete Network	Remove a network.
Move Network	Move a network within the vCenter inventory folders for networks.

privileges, you can create a role that contains the privileges shown in Table 5.2. Careful planning of network permissions can be helpful if your hosts are connected to numerous networks with different security sensitivities. An example is a host that is connected to both internal and demilitarized zone (DMZ) networks. Improper network configuration could result in sensitive networks being accessible from the Internet, which could put your infrastructure at risk. By restricting permissions to the DMZ virtual switch, you can ensure that a general virtual machine administrator does not mistakenly plan an internal virtual machine in the DMZ.

Once you have completed your vCenter Server upgrade, you are ready to assign permissions to your datastores and networks. You may need to create custom roles to tailor the permissions to your environment. Use the following procedure to assign permissions to your datastores:

1. Start the vSphere client and connect to vCenter Server.

2. On the Home page, select Datastores to display the datastores on your vSphere hosts.

3. Select a datastore or folder and click the Permission tab.

4. Right-click on the Permissions tab and select Add Permission.

5. In the Assigned Role pane, select an appropriate role that you want to grant to the user or group. If you grant the Read-Only role, a user will be able to browse a datastore but will not be able to perform any further functions. This can be useful if a user just needs to access CD or DVD ISO images stored on the datastore.

6. If you are setting permission on a folder, check the option Propagate to Child Objects.

7. In the Users and Groups pane, click Add and then select the users or groups that are to be assigned to the chosen role.

8. Click OK to apply your change and to close the Assign Permissions window.

To change permissions for your virtual machine networks, you can follow the same process as you did with datastores, except that you need to select Networks from the Home screen. With both datastores and networks, you can create a folder structure that best matches your management needs. These folder structures are independent of the ones that exist for host and virtual machines. If you create a new network or datastore, it is located under the datacenter object, as is the case with the DMZ network object in Figure 5.4. You should ensure that the permissions set at the datacenter are appropriate for any new networks or datastores and that permissions are set to propagate to child objects. Otherwise, you should directly assign permissions to new datastores or networks or move those new objects to a folder where appropriate permissions are

Figure 5.4   When a new network is created, the object is located under the datacenter object.

set with propagation enabled.

Joining a Linked Mode Group after the vCenter Sever Upgrade   Linked Mode is a new feature to vSphere that allows you to join multiple instances of vCenter into a single view within the vSphere client. This can be helpful if you have deployed multiple vCenter Servers for different location or branch offices or if you need to manage your production and disaster recovery servers within a single view. As mentioned earlier, Linked Mode used Microsoft ADAM to replicate configuration data, which includes items such as the following:

- Connection information (IP ports and addresses)
- Certificates and host thumbprints
- License information
- User roles

Before you attempt to join your vCenter Server host to another host, you should ensure that the following prerequisites are met:

- The DNS must be functional and able to resolve the IP address of the target host to its fully qualified domain name.
- The two vCenter hosts can be in different domains, but if so, a two-way trust must exist between the domains.

- When you start the installation program to join a vCenter Server instance to a Link Mode group, you must be logged in with an account that has administrative rights on both vCenter Server hosts.

- You must enable time synchronization on all vCenter Server hosts and they must be no more than five minutes apart.

Once you have met the prerequisites, you can start the wizard to configure Linked Mode:

1. Log in to one of the vCenter hosts with an account that has administrative rights on both hosts.

2. From the Start menu, select All Programs > VMware > vCenter Server Linked Mode Configuration.

3. Select the Modify Linked Mode Configuration option and click Next.

4. Check the Join vCenter Server Instance to an Existing Linked Mode Group or Another Instance and click Next.

5. On the Connect to a vCenter Server Instance screen, enter the IP address or hostname for the remote vCenter Server and the LDAP port number that is configured on that host.

6. On the Linked Modes Conflicts Resolution screen, you are asked to choose the method to use for resolving role conflicts. With the option Yes, Let VMware vCenter Server Resolve the Conflicts for Me, as shown in Figure 5.5, the Linked Mode

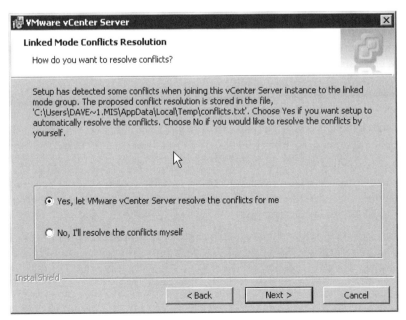

Figure 5.5 Conflict resolution options for the Linked Mode setup.

installation wizard renames any conflicting roles. Otherwise, you must manually log in to the vCenter hosts, rename the roles, and then click Back and Next on the Linked Mode installation program to continue.

7.   Once the installation has completed, click Finish to close the installer.

The vCenter Server hosts are now part of a Linked Mode group. After several minutes, data between the hosts will replicate. When you log in to either vCenter Server instance, you can now view and configure the inventories of both hosts. For more information about Linked Mode, you can consult the vSphere Datacenter Administration Guide.

Migrating ESX Hosts

Once you have vCenter Server 4.1 deployed, you are ready to begin installing ESXi 4.1. There is no installation upgrade path from ESX to ESXi, so moving to ESXi involves some sort of migration scenario. This means that you are not able to use Update Manager to upgrade your hosts from ESX to ESXi. You can use Update Manager to upgrade VMware Tools and the virtual machine hardware version for the virtual machines that you migrate to ESXi. That process is described later in this chapter. The exact path that you take depends on your infrastructure. The following section examines some of the options and shows you how you can use PowerCLI to automate the migration of virtual machines. Figure 5.6 shows the process flow for a typical migration from ESX to ESXi. By utilizing your current cluster and vMotion configuration, you can minimize the downtime for virtual machines during your migration process.

In the first scenario, the ESX hosts are part of a cluster. After the upgrade to vCenter Server 4.1, the hosts can be reconnected to vCenter Server either automatically or manually, as previously discussed, and your High Availability (HA) and Distributed Resource Scheduler (DRS) clusters are automatically reconfigured to function with vCenter Server 4.1.

After your cluster proves to be stable and free of upgrade issues, you can begin to introduce ESXi hosts into your cluster. ESXi 4.1 can operate with your ESX 3.5 and 4.0 hosts without any problem. Thus, there is no need to upgrade your current hosts to ESX 4.1 before migrating your virtual machines to your new ESXi hosts. Given the age of your existing hardware, you may be introducing new hardware that can support ESXi. Otherwise, you may choose to restage existing hardware with ESXi. In the case of reusing hardware, you need to migrate virtual machines from the host that is to be restaged before it can be shut down. If DRS is set to be fully automated, then you can place the host in maintenance mode and migrate your virtual machines using vMotion to other hosts. In the case of a partially automated DRS cluster, you must review the migration recommendations and accept them before the virtual machines can begin to be migrated.

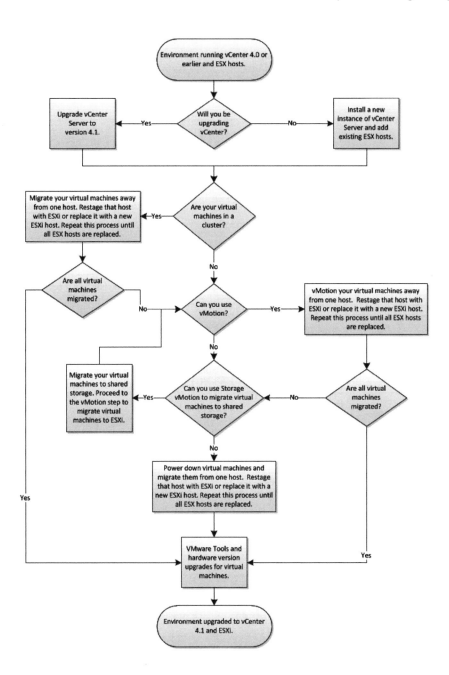

Figure 5.6   Process flow for migrating from ESX to ESXi.

As long as there are no DRS affinity rules or HA constraints that are violated by putting your host in maintenance mode, your virtual machines are migrated to other hosts in the cluster. You can then shut down the host and remove it from the cluster. After the host has been restaged with ESXi, it can be added to the cluster again, and the process is repeated until all hosts are running ESXi. You are then ready to proceed to the next section dealing with virtual machine upgrades.

One circumstance that can prevent migration of a virtual machine is to have a virtual CD-ROM device connected to a datastore ISO image or to the host's physical CD-ROM device. The following PowerCLI script sets the CD-ROM of all virtual machines to a state of disconnected. If you're migrating hundreds of virtual machines, such a small PowerCLI script can be quite a time-saver. You can encapsulate this within a general script that checks the connected status of virtual machine CD-ROM devices, migrates the virtual machines to another host, and then puts the host into maintenance mode.

```
Get-VMHost esx01.mishchenko.net | Get-VM | Get-CDDrive | Set-CDDrive -Connected
    $false -Confirm:$false
```

In the case of adding a new server running ESXi to your cluster, you may need to review the cluster settings for Enhanced vMotion Compatibility (EVC). EVC was introduced with ESX(i) 3.5 Update 2 to enable the migration of virtual machines between different generations of CPUs. This allows for the mixing of older and new servers within the same cluster. When EVC is enabled, all hosts in the cluster are configured to present the central processing unit (CPU) features of the user-selected CPU type to all virtual machines in the cluster. This allows vMotion to proceed even if the hosts' CPUs are from different generations. Enabling EVC on a cluster may require that virtual machines be powered off, so you may need to plan an appropriate maintenance window if you require EVC as part of your migration to ESXi. If your migration to ESXi includes new hardware, you might consider raising the EVC mode after the older hosts running ESX have been removed from the host. You can use the Change EVC Mode dialog box to determine the EVC modes currently available to your cluster.

In the second migration scenario, your hosts are not part of a cluster. Rather, you have a number of hosts that are managed by vCenter Server that may be using some form of shared storage. As was the case with the prior scenario, you may be restaging your existing hosts with ESXi or including a hardware refresh as part of your migration to ESXi. If you plan to restage a host, the first step is to migrate the virtual machines to another host. The ideal mechanism to use is vMotion, as no downtime is required for the virtual machines. You can initiate vMotion for each virtual machine using the vSphere client, or you can automate the process with PowerCLI. PowerCLI includes the Move-VM cmdlet, which can be used to automate the migration of a virtual machine to another host. Move-VM can be used to change a virtual machine's folder, cluster, host, resource pool, or datastore. With the following single line of code, you can migrate all virtual machines with vMotion from one host to another:

```
Get-VMHost esx01 | Get-VM | Move-VM -Destination (Get-VMHost esx02) -RunAsync
```

You can also use `Move-VM` to perform a storage vMotion migration. If you have to migrate the virtual machine to a shared datastore, you can use the following script to change the datastore before you vMotion the virtual machine to another host. With the `RunAsync` option, the cmdlet returns immediately to the command line rather than waiting for the task to complete, as shown in the following example:

```
Move-VM -VM windows01 -Datastore ISCSI2 -Destination esx01.mishchenko.net
    -RunAsync
Id                       :
IsCancelable             : False
Result                   :
Name                     : RelocateVM_Task
Description              : Relocate virtual machine
State                    : Running
PercentComplete          : 0
StartTime                : 8/5/2010 12:57:16 AM
FinishTime               :
ObjectId                 :
Uid                      : /Local=/ClientSideTask=3b19de69-0d9f-497c-b756827bc47/
NonTerminatingErrorList  : {}
TerminatingError         :
```

To determine the status of the task, you can run the `Get-Task` cmdlet as shown in the following example:

```
Get-Task

Name                     State      % Complete    Start Time      Finish Time
----                     -----      ----------    ----------      -----------
RemoveAllSnapshots_Task  Success    100           12:50:02 AM     12:54:00 AM
RelocateVM_Task          Running    23            12:57:16 AM
```

After your virtual machines have been migrated, you can remove the host from vCenter Server and restage it with ESXi. You can then manually migrate the virtual machines back to the ESXi host or use PowerCLI to automate the move to the new ESXi host.

The third upgrade scenario that you may encounter involves a standalone host that may not be managed by vCenter Server. Such a server might be located at a branch office, and there may not be any form of shared storage that would allow for the easy migration of virtual machines, as was the case in the first two scenarios. If the migration involves a hardware refresh, then you can simply stage the new ESXi alongside the ESX host and then use a tool such as VMware Converter to migrate the virtual machines from the ESX host to ESXi.

If you have to restage the standalone with ESXi, then you have a few options. If the host has a single storage array, then the ESXi installer will wipe out all data on the partition, resulting in the loss of your virtual machines. You must first back up any virtual machines on the ESX host, then install ESXi, and lastly restore the virtual machines. Optionally, you could add a flash device or another boot device and install ESXi on it. The old ESX datastore would be visible to the ESXi host and you could reregister the virtual machines on it.

Lastly, you may choose to perform a new installation of vCenter Server and add ESXi hosts to it. In that case, you could join the ESX hosts to the new vCenter Server and then migrate the virtual machines to ESXi as was described earlier. Otherwise, you could just remove the shared storage from the ESX hosts and present the logical unit numbers (LUNs) to the ESXi hosts. The hosts would recognize the existing datastores and be able to mount them without formatting them. Then you would just need to register the virtual machines by browsing the datastores and registering the vmx files.

With any of these scenarios, you may find that you need to upgrade the configuration of your virtual machines or other components. PowerCLI may provide the tools necessary to make the updates quickly. An example would be the need to change the virtual machine port group after a migration, which normally would involve manually editing each virtual machine. With the following script, any number of virtual machines can be quickly updated, saving time and reducing the risk of making errors. The following example changes the virtual machine port group from DMZ1 to DMZ2 for all virtual machines running on the specified host:

```
Get-VMHost esx01 | Get-VM | Get-NetworkAdapter |
   Where {$_.NetworkName -eq "DMZ1" } | Set-NetworkAdapter -NetworkName "DMZ2"
   -Confirm:$false
```

Preserving Performance Data When you're viewing performance data, you can obtain real-time data from the vSphere hosts, whereas you must obtain historical data from the vCenter database. Within the database, vCenter stores data using a unique ID for each vCenter object, such as hosts, clusters, datastores, and virtual machines, rather than using the name that appears in the vSphere client. If you delete a virtual machine and then create a new one with the same name, the historical data for the deleted virtual machine is not displayed, because each virtual machine has a unique ID in the vCenter database.

This presents a problem when migrating to ESXi. Virtual machine historical data can be preserved because virtual machines are typically migrated to new hosts; thus, the vCenter database object ID does not change. If you use cloning as part of your migration plan, the new copy of the virtual machine is given a new database object ID and thus does not retain performance data from the source virtual machine. If you are restaging your existing hosts with ESXi, you can potentially lose that data because the new ESXi host will be seen as a unique host even if you install ESXi onto your existing hardware.

The vCenter Server database assigns a unique ID to each host and then identifies that host by the SHA1 thumbprint of its SSL certificate. If you disconnect and then reconnect an existing host, the object ID for that host is not changed, and historical data is preserved. If you remove a host from vCenter Server, the object ID is deleted from the database and a new object ID is assigned to the host if it is joined to vCenter Server again. Historical performance data is not assigned to the new host. Therefore, if you need to preserve historical data for your hosts, it is critical that you do not remove the hosts from vCenter Server. Rather, you should select to disconnect the host. When a host is disconnected, you can still access historical performance data. If you don't plan to reuse your existing hardware, you can simply leave the ESX host in vCenter for as long as you need to access that data. If you need to restage ESXi onto your existing hardware or need to reuse the host network name, you can use the following process to preserve historical performance data for the host:

1. Select the existing host in vCenter Server; then right-click and select Disconnect. You should perform this after you have migrated any virtual machines on that host to other hosts.

2. If you are using custom SSL certificates on your hosts, copy the `rui.crt` and `rui.key` files from the ESX host. These files are located in `/etc/vmware/ssl/`.

3. Restage the server with ESXi. Assign the same hostname and IP address to the new host. If you are using custom SSL certificates, copy those files to the restaged host. That process is described in Chapter 7.

4. In vCenter Server, select to connect the host. If you are reusing an SSL certificate, the error message `Cannot Complete Login Due To An Incorrect User Name Or Password` is displayed. Click OK, and the Add Host wizard is started to allow you to reconnect the host. The wizard is launched because vCenter Server cannot connect to the ESXi host with the `vpxuser` account. This account is discussed further in Chapter 7. If you use a new certificate or just leave ESXi with the self-generated certificate, you will see the error `Authenticity of the Host's SSL Certificate Is Not Verified` when you reconnect the host. After you dismiss the error message, the Add Host wizard begins.

After the host has been reconnected, verify that you are able to view historical performance data for the host. If it is critical to maintain your performance data, you should back up the vCenter database before going through this process.

Upgrading Virtual Machines

The last steps in the process of migrating from VMware ESX 3.5 or 4.0 to ESXi 4.1 are to upgrade VMware Tools and upgrade the virtual machine hardware. If any of your virtual machines do not have VMware Tools installed, you can use the upgrade procedure described in this section to install them. These steps can be performed using the vSphere client, vCenter Update Manager (VUM), or PowerCLI. With the vSphere client, you typically upgrade a virtual machine one step at a time. With VUM, you can automate the process of updating VMware Tools and the virtual machine hardware. PowerCLI includes cmdlets that allow for the scripting of the processes that you would follow both in the vSphere client and with VUM.

VMware Tools is a suite of utilities that enhances the performance and manageability of the guest OS running within your virtual machines. While it is not a requirement to run VMware Tools, you lose convenience and potentially decrease performance. Without VMware Tools, you can only power off a virtual machine, which results in an abrupt stop of the guest OS. With VMware Tools, ESXi can issue a command directly to the guest OS to shut it down properly.

VMware Tools includes a number of drivers that optimize the network, disk, and video performance within your virtual machines. VMware Tools also includes the memory balloon driver (vmmemctl), which the ESXi host can use to force the guest OS to swap unused memory in the virtual machine to the guest OS page file if the host needs to reclaim memory from virtual machines.

VMware Tools is provided in ISO images for Linux, Windows, Solaris, and NetWare; these images are stored on an ESXi system partition. When the process to install VMware Tools is initiated, the ISO image for the appropriate guest OS is mounted to the virtual CD-ROM in the virtual machine and the installation process proceeds. The contents of the ISO images can be extracted should you wish to employ another software deployment tool to manage your VMware Tools installations. When upgrading VMware Tools, the installation process uninstalls the prior version and then installs the new versions. This may result in a momentary network disruption for the guest OS, but connectivity is restored by the end of the upgrade process.

The virtual machine hardware version dictates the capabilities of the virtual hardware that the guest OS can recognize and use. This includes the maximum number of virtual CPUs and Peripheral Component Interconnect (PCI) slots and amount of memory. The native hardware version for VMware ESX(i) 3.5 is version 4. This hardware version has the limits shown in Table 5.3. VMware ESXi 4.x supports hardware version 7. As shown in the table, there are a number of improvements in the capabilities of the virtual hardware for version 7.

The change in hardware version with VMware vSphere also introduces new virtual machine capabilities. A number of these new capabilities are summarized in the following list:

- Virtual Machine Hot Add Support. With hardware version 7, it is possible to increase CPU and memory resources in virtual machines running a supported guest OS.

Table 5.3 Comparing Hardware Version 4 and 7 Configuration Maximums

Resource	Hardware Version 4	Hardware Version 7
CPUs	4	8
Memory	64GB	256GB
SCSI Adapters	4	4
Virtual SCSI Disks	60	60
Virtual IDE Disks	0	4
Virtual NICs	4	10
Virtual PCI Devices (Video Card, NICs, SCSI Controllers)	6	14
VMDirectPath Devices	0	2
Remote Console Connections	10	40

- New Storage Virtual Devices. Virtual machines can be created with serial attached SCSI (SAS) controllers, which support Windows Server 2008 failover clusters. Also supported are IDE virtual disks, which enable the virtualization of older OSs that may not have small computer systems interface (SCSI) adapters that work within a VMware virtual machine.

- VMXNET Generation 3. The third-generation paravirtualized NIC device from VMware includes a number of performance enhancements.

- VMware Paravirtualized SCSI (PVSCSI). This new virtual storage adapter lowers CPU load and increases disk I/O throughput for virtual machines.

- VMDirectPath. VMDirectPath I/O enables a virtual machine to access a PCI device directly, decreasing CPU load and improving performance. A number of network and storage adapters are supported, but other hardware may function properly, allowing for the virtualization of servers that were previously excluded due to special hardware requirements.

- Virtual Machine Communication Interface (VMCI). The VMCI is an application programming interface (API) that enables high-speed communication between a virtual machine and its host or other virtual machines. This communication is not dependent on the networking capabilities of the guest OS. The VMCI is used by VMsafe, which is a vSphere feature designed to protect virtual machines.

When you create virtual machines on ESXi 4.1, the default hardware version is version 7. A virtual machine created with this version cannot be run on ESX 3.5. A virtual machine can be migrated from ESX 3.5 to ESXi 4.1 and back again if required. However, the virtual machine must remain at version 4, which is the default for new ESX 3.5 virtual machines. After a virtual machine is upgraded to version 7, it cannot run on an ESX 3.5 host. If you take a snapshot of the virtual machine before upgrading the hardware version, the change can be reversed. Or you can make a copy of the virtual machine with a tool such as VMware Converter to create a virtual machine that could be run on ESX 3.5 should you need to reverse the hardware version change.

Note: As you examine the new features available with hardware version 7, it is important to understand the dependencies and interactions of these features with other components of vSphere. If you enable VMDirectPath for a virtual machine, you disable the machine from using vMotion to move to another host. Configuring a virtual machine for Fault Tolerance disables VMCI for that virtual machine and disables it from being accessed through the VMsafe API.

As you've seen in the prior sections of this chapter, it is possible to upgrade your environment to ESXi 4.1 without imposing downtime on your virtual machines. vMotion and Storage vMotion can be used to migrate virtual machines to your ESXi host, preventing a service outage. However, the upgrade of VMware Tools and virtual hardware requires some downtime. Regardless of the guest OS, you must shut down the virtual machine to upgrade the virtual hardware. With a Windows guest, at least one restart of the virtual machine is required during an upgrade, and for any guest OS, there may be a temporary network outage while the VMware Tools installation package upgrades the virtual machine.

Performing an Interactive Upgrade of VMware Tools with the vSphere Client

Using the vSphere client, you can upgrade VMware Tools for a single virtual machine. As the process of upgrading VMware Tools does represent a significant change to the virtual machine, you should ensure that a backup or snapshot has been taken prior to performing the change. Use the following process to upgrade VMware Tools for a Windows guest OS:

1. Start the vSphere client and connect to vCenter Server or directly to the ESXi host.

2. Ensure that the Windows virtual machine is powered on and then select the Summary tab for the virtual machine. The VMware Tools label indicates whether VMware Tools is installed and current, installed and not current, or not installed.

3. Right-click on the Windows virtual machine and select Guest > Install/Upgrade VMware Tools.

4. Select Interactive Tools Upgrade as shown in Figure 5.7 and click OK. The host will mount the VMware Tools ISO for Windows.

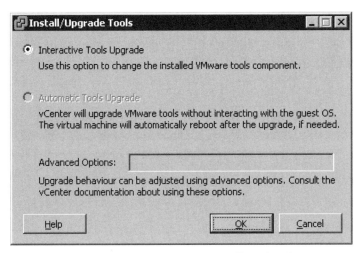

Figure 5.7   Enabling the interactive install option for VMware Tools.

5. Access the console for the virtual machine and log in if necessary.

6. If Autorun is enabled, click OK to confirm that you wish to run `setup.exe` to install VMware Tools. Otherwise, open the virtual CD-ROM device and start `setup.exe`.

7. Follow the installation wizard through the install process. A typical installation of VMware Tools is the best choice for virtual machines hosted on ESXi.

8. Reboot the virtual machine if prompted to do so at the end of the installation process.

After the installation process has completed, the VMware Tools label on the Summary tab for the virtual machine should display a status of OK. The process to update VMware Tools on a Linux virtual machine is similar to the preceding process. You can follow these steps to upgrade a Linux guest with the RPM Package Manager (RPM) installer.

1. Start the vSphere client and connect to vCenter Server or directly to the ESXi host.

2. Ensure that the Linux virtual machine is powered on and then select the Summary tab for the virtual machine. The VMware Tools label indicates whether VMware Tools is installed and current, installed and not current, or not installed.

3. Right-click on the Windows virtual machine and select Guest > Install/Upgrade VMware Tools.

4. Select Interactive Tools Upgrade as shown in Figure 5.7 and click OK. The host will mount the VMware Tools ISO for the appropriate OS.

5. At the console of the virtual machine, log in with the root account.

6.   If the folder /mnt/cdrom does not exist, create it with the command mkdir /mnt/cdrom.

7.   If your Linux distribution doesn't automatically mount CD-ROMs, you can run the mount command with a similar format: /dev/cdrom /mnt/cdrom.

8.   Change to a working directory with the command cd/tmp.

9.   Extract the RPM installer with a command such as rpm -Uhv /mount/cdrom/ VMwareTools-4.0.0-<xxxxxx>.i386.rpm. <xxxxxx>. This command's syntax reflects the build number for the VMware Tools package.

10.   Double-click on the RPM installation file to begin the upgrade.

11.   When the installation is complete, run the command ./usr/bin/vmware-config-tools .pl to configure VMware Tools.

12.   After the configuration of VMware Tools is complete, run the following commands to restore the network:

```
/etc/init.d/network stop
rmmod vmxnet
modprode vmxnet
/etc/init.d/network start
```

13.   Unmount the CD-ROM image with the command umount /dev/cdrom.

14.   Log out of the virtual machine and close the console session.

You can now verify that the VMware Tools label on the Summary tab has a status of OK. You can also manually install VMware Tools in an X Terminal session or by using the TAR installer. Those procedures can be found in the vSphere Upgrade Guide along with the procedures for upgrading Solaris and NetWare virtual machines.

Automating the Upgrade of VMware Tools with the vSphere Client

When selecting to perform an option to upgrade VMware Tools, you can select an Automatic Upgrade. Such an upgrade does not require you to perform any actions within the guest OS. The automated process uninstalls and then installs the latest version that is available on the ESXi running the virtual machine. If the process requires a reboot of the guest OS, this is performed automatically. The Automatic Upgrade option is not available for NetWare or Solaris virtual machines.

Prior to running an automated upgrade, you must first enable the virtual machine option Check and Upgrade Tools during Power Cycles. As this option's name implies, an attempt is made to update the guest to the latest VMware Tools revision each time a power cycle operation is performed on the virtual machine. Without this option enabled, the Automatic Tools Upgrade option is disabled, as shown in Figure 5.7. To enable this option, take the following steps:

1. Start the vSphere client and connect to vCenter Server.

2. Right-click on the virtual machine and select Edit Settings.

3. Select the Option tab and then the VMware Tools settings.

4. Enable the option Check and Upgrade Tools during Power Cycling as shown in Figure 5.8.

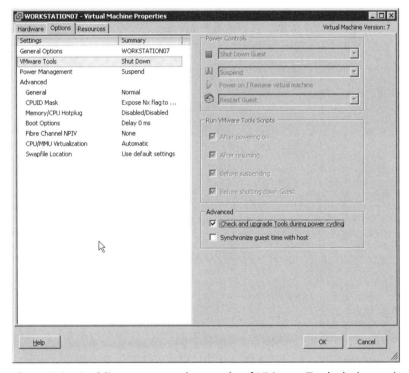

Figure 5.8 Enabling automated upgrade of VMware Tools during a virtual machine's power cycles.

5. Click OK to save your change.

6. Restart the virtual machine to enable the new setting.

After the option has been enabled, the host checks the version of VMware Tools installed when the virtual machine guest OS is started and attempts an upgrade if a newer version exists on the ESXi host. If you enable this option, you should be aware of how a VMware Tools upgrade may behave on your virtual machines. The sample upgrade shown in Figure 5.9 has paused midway through the upgrade due to a dialog box that required a response and which is visible only in the console of the virtual machine. You should also be aware that a reboot might be required after the automatic upgrade of VMware Tools, which occurs immediately after the process has completed.

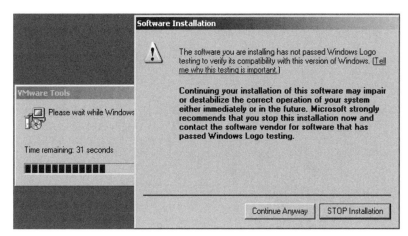

Figure 5.9 A dialog box preventing an automatic upgrade of VMware Tools at the console of a Windows virtual machine.

To perform an automatic upgrade of VMware Tools, you can follow these steps:

1. Start the vSphere client and connect to vCenter Server or directly to the ESXi host.

2. Ensure that the virtual machine is powered on.

3. Right-click on the virtual machine and select Guest > Install/Upgrade VMware Tools.

4. Select the Automatic Tools Upgrade option on the Install/Upgrade Tools dialog box.

5. For a Windows guest, you can specify installation switches in the Advanced Options field. Entering the options /s /v /"qn" /l <filename.log> performs a silent upgrade of VMware Tools and creates a log file for the process.

6. Click OK to start the upgrade process.

7. For a Linux virtual machine, run the following commands to restore networking:

    ```
    /etc/init.d/network stop
    rmmod vmxnet
    modprobe vmxnet
    /etc/init.d/network start
    ```

8. After the upgrade has completed, the VMware Tools label on the Summary tab should display a status of OK.

The preceding methods have focused on upgrading a single virtual machine at a time. With the vSphere client, it is also possible to upgrade many virtual machines at the same time. After you have selected a host or cluster, choose the virtual machines to upgrade on the Virtual Machines tab. Right-click on your selection list and select Guest > Install/Upgrade VMware Tools.

Upgrading Virtual Hardware

Once you have migrated your virtual machines to ESXi 4.1 and have no plans to migrate them back to ESX 3.5, you are ready to upgrade the virtual hardware version. Prior to upgrading the hardware version, you should ensure that a backup or snapshot exists for the virtual machine. You should also upgrade VMware Tools prior to this operation, as Windows virtual machines in particular can lose network settings if you upgrade the virtual hardware version before upgrading VMware Tools.

To upgrade a single virtual machine, you can follow this procedure:

1. Start the vSphere client and connect to your vCenter Server or ESXi host.

2. Power down the virtual machine.

3. Select an inventory view that shows the virtual machine. Right-click on the virtual machine and select Upgrade Virtual Hardware. This option is not available if the hardware version is already upgraded.

4. Power on the virtual machine.

5. For a Windows guest, log in and confirm that all new devices have been configured automatically. You may be prompted to restart the OS.

The Summary tab for the virtual machine should now show that the hardware version is 7. You can also upgrade the hardware version for multiple virtual machines concurrently. Select a host or cluster to update, and then click the Virtual Machines tab for that object. Follow the preceding steps that were used to update a single virtual machine, this time selecting any number of virtual machines.

Using PowerCLI to Upgrade VMware Tools and the Hardware Version

PowerCLI includes a number of cmdlets that you can use to automate the upgrading of VMware Tools and the hardware version for a virtual machine. In the following example, the ISO image for VMware Tools is first mounted to a virtual machine called SQL01. The upgrade of VMware Tools is started with the cmdlet Update-Tools. After the upgrade has completed, VMware Tools is removed. Lastly, the virtual machine hardware version is updated.

```
Mount-Tools SQL01
Update-Tools SQL01
Dismount-Tools SQL01
Get-VM SQL01 | Get-View | % { $_.UpgradeVM($null) }
```

Using vCenter Update Manager to Upgrade VMware Tools and the Hardware Version

The last option for upgrading VMware Tools and the hardware version of your virtual machines is to use vCenter Update Manager. Installation and configuration of Update Manager is discussed further in Chapter 10, "Patching and Updating ESXi." The following section demonstrates the steps required to use Update Manager to perform these two tasks. As is the case with the other methods, updating the hardware version for a virtual machine requires that you briefly power off and on the virtual machine.

1. Start the vSphere client and connect to your vCenter Server host.

2. On the Home screen, select the Update Manager icon.

3. Select the Baselines and Groups tab and then click the link to View Baselines for VMs/VAs. You should see the predefined baselines VMware Tools Upgrade to Match Host and VM Hardware Upgrade to Match Host.

4. In the Baselines Groups view, click Create to start the New Baseline Group wizard.

5. On the Name and Type screen, enter a name for the baseline group and click Next.

6. On the Upgrades screen, check the baselines VMware Tools Upgrade to Match Host and VM Hardware Upgrade to Match Host. Click Next to proceed.

7. Click Next on the Patches screen without selecting any defined baselines.

8. Click Finish on the Ready to Complete screen to finish creating the new baseline group.

9. Return to the Home screen, and then select VMs and Templates.

10. Select the vCenter Server object to which you want to apply the new baseline group. This may a datacenter, resource pool, or virtual machine folder.

11. Select the Update Manager tab and click Attach.

12. Check the baseline group that you created and click Attach.

13. Click Scan, and on the Confirm Scan dialog box, check only the VM Hardware Upgrades and VMware Tools Upgrades options. Click Scan on the dialog box to begin the process.

14. After the scan has completed, the Update Manager tab updates to display the compliance status for the baseline group.

15. To update virtual machines that are not compliant, click Remediate.

16. When the Remediate wizard begins, select the baseline group that you created and click Next.

17.   On the Schedule screen, enter a task name. You can update all virtual machines imme-diately, or you can schedule a suitable time for virtual machines that are powered on, powered off, and suspended, as shown in Figure 5.10. Click Next to continue.

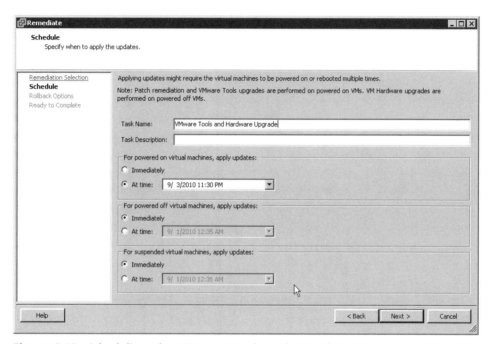

Figure 5.10   Scheduling the VMware Tools and virtual hardware upgrade with Update Manager.

18.   On the Rollback Options screen, configure the snapshot options for the upgrade. Tak-ing a snapshot enables you to roll back the change should a problem arise from the upgrade. Click Next to continue.

19.   Click Finish to complete the wizard and start the upgrade tasks.

When the tasks begin, any virtual machines that are powered off or suspended are powered on for the process. Any tasks that you schedule to happen in the future will appear in the scheduled tasks list for your vCenter Server host. Once the tasks have completed, you can click Scan on the Update Manager tab again to check the virtual machines for compliance, as described in step 13.

Conclusion

vSphere 4.1 represents a significant step forward, with many new features that enable easier management of your virtual infrastructure. Because ESXi and ESX share feature equality, you can easily incorporate ESXi hosts into your datacenter without making significant changes.

In this chapter, you have seen that the first step to migrating to ESXi 4.1 involves upgrading vCenter Server. Once that step is complete, you can begin to plan how you can migrate your virtual machines from ESX to ESXi. With vMotion, you can migrate to ESXi without imposing downtime on your virtual machines. After you have migrated to ESXi 4.1, you can upgrade your virtual machines to take advantage of the new features in vSphere such as Fault Tolerance and VMDirectPath. As you have seen, PowerCLI can be leveraged to automate a number of tasks that will be a part of your migration to ESXi.

6 System Monitoring and Management

As you have seen in the preceding chapters, VMware provides a number of tools and features to manage your ESXi environment. As your environment grows, you will likely find that you need to integrate your vSphere deployment with the other systems that exist on your network. This chapter examines a number of features and tools that help integrate ESXi and vCenter Server with the rest of your network.

This chapter examines the following items:

- Using Active Directory Integration to eliminate the need for using local accounts when managing an ESXi host directly

- Synchronizing the time on your hosts with Network Time Protocol (NTP)

- Configuring ESXi to forward log data to a centralized syslog servers

- Monitoring your host with vCenter alarms, performance charts, and storage views

- Managing the hardware health for your ESXi hosts

- Integrating your hosts with systems management software

- Backing up ESXi configurations and virtual machine data

Configuring Active Directory Integration

Past versions of ESX have included the ability to integrate authentication with Active Directory (AD), but the setup could be difficult and required access to the service console. With vSphere 4.1, AD integration is now configurable within the vSphere client and support now extends to ESXi. It is also possible to configure AD integration with the vCLI or Host Profiles. In the same manner as with vCenter Server, it is possible to assign AD users to either the predefined or custom roles on an ESXi host to grant those users specific permissions that they may require to manage the host. ESXi AD integration can also eliminate the need to share the root login to the host and instead vSphere administrators can rely on their AD credentials for running vCLI scripts or for accessing local and remote Secure Shell (SSH) technical support.

AD Integration Prerequisites

A number of prerequisites need to be met to ensure that the ESXi host is able to join the AD domain:

- Ensure that the account that will be used to join the ESXi host to the domain has the required privileges to join a computer to the domain.

- Ensure that the ESXi host is using the same time source as the AD controllers. The NTP configuration settings for the host can be set in the vSphere client on the Configuration \ Time Configuration screen or with the command esxcfg-ntp from the vCLI.

- Configure the ESXi host to use the AD domain's domain name service (DNS) server(s) and to have the same DNS suffix. DNS settings can be configured in the vSphere client on the Configuration \ DNS and Routing screen. With the vCLI, the esxcfg-dns command can be used to set both the DNS suffix for the host and the DNS server(s) that will be used by the host.

Caution: When an ESXi host is joining a domain, if the group ESX Admins exists within AD, that group is granted the built-in Administrator role to the host. This is shown in Figure 6.1.

Summary	Virtual Machines	Resource Allocation	Performance	Configuration	Local Users & Groups	Events	Permissions

User/Group	Role	Defined in	
root	Administrator	This object	
vpxuser	Administrator	This object	
dcui	Administrator	This object	
MISHCHENKO\esx^admins	Administrator	This object	

Figure 6.1 The AD group ESX Admins is automatically granted the Administrator role at the host level.

Configuring AD Integration with the vSphere Client

After the prerequisites are in place, the ESXi host can be joined to the AD domain using the Configuration > Authentication Services screen:

1. On the Authentication Services screen, click Properties.

2. For the User Directory Service option, change the type from Local Directory (default) to Active Directory.

3. Enter the AD domain to join and click Join Domain. The Join Domain screen then appears, as shown in Figure 6.2. After the appropriate AD credentials are entered and you click Join Domain, the task pane displays the Join Windows Domain task.

4. After the task has completed, click OK to close the configuration screen.

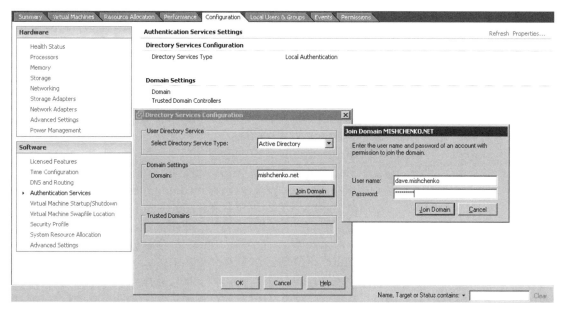

Figure 6.2   Enabling AD Integration on ESXi.

If the task has completed successfully, the Authentication Services screen should display Active Directory as the Directory Services Type. The Domain Setting section will show the AD domain that was joined and should the domain trust other domains, those will be listed in the Trusted Domain Controllers section. A computer account will have also been created in the default Organizational Unit for computer objects. Should the ESXi fail to join the domain, an error will be displayed and further troubleshooting information may be logged to the system log (/var/log /messages).

You may encounter the error The specified domain either does not exist or could not be contacted. Within /var/log/messages, you would also see the following error. If this is your case, you should check the NTP setup for the host and also ensure that previously specified DNS requirements have been met.

```
Mar 22 04:08:21 Hostd: [2010-03-22 04:08:21.343 49D81B90 error 'ActiveDirectory
Authentication' opID=D697C122-00000091] vmwauth NoSuchDomainException: Exception
0x0000054b: The specified domain either does not exist or could not be contacted.
```

If you need to remove a host from a domain, you can use the Configuration > Authentication Services screen. Once you have completed the following process, the Authentication Services screen should display a Directory Services Type of Local Authentication.

1.   On the Authentication Services screen, click on the Properties link.

2.   The Directory Services Configuration screen appears. Click Leave Domain.

3. You will be prompted with the Leave Domain Warning screen. This screen informs you that leaving the domain will remove all domain-related permissions that have been configured for this host. Click OK to continue.

4. The Leave Windows Domain task begins and is shown in the Recent Tasks view. Click OK to close the Directory Services Configuration screen.

Configuring AD Integration with Host Profiles

The second option to configure AD Integration is with Host Profiles. Chapter 3, "Management Tools," reviewed the process of creating and applying a host profile. You can configure one of your hosts and then create a host profile with the process provided to apply that change to your other hosts. If the host being used for the Host Profile has already been joined to the domain, you can refresh the Host Profile to import the AD Integration settings configured on the host. With the vSphere client connected to vCenter Server, go to the Home view and then select Host Profiles. Right-click on the Host Profile you want to update, and select Update Profile from Reference Host. Once the Update Host Profile task has completed, you can edit the profile to review the changes. The username and password used to join the domain will not be stored in the Host Profile. The following process configures an existing profile to join your ESXi hosts to your domain:

1. Start the vSphere client and connect to vCenter Server.

2. Select the Home view and then click the Host Profiles icon.

3. Choose the profile to update and click Edit Profile.

4. Browse to the Active Directory Configuration node to configure the options shown in Figure 6.3.

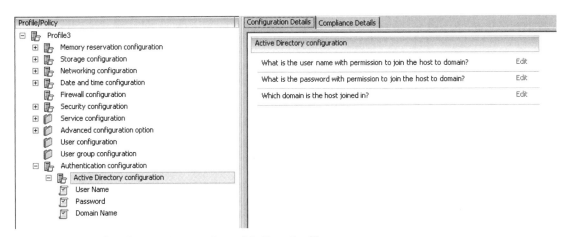

Figure 6.3 Configuring AD Integration with Host Profiles.

5.   For the User Name and Password options, the only available choice with this release is to be prompted during the application of the profile for appropriate user credentials. For the Domain Name option, select the option Configure a Fixed Domain Name and specify the domain that your ESXi host will join.

6.   Select the Compliance Details tab for the Domain Name policy and ensure that the option Validate That the Host Is Not Joined in Any Domain is checked. This ensures that the policy will not attempt to join the ESXi host to the domain repeatedly.

7.   Click OK to save your changes and close the Edit Profile window.

Once you have updated or created a profile that includes the Active Directory Configuration policy, you are ready to apply the profile to a cluster or host. The process for applying a profile to a cluster was discussed in Chapter 3. The following process applies the policy to an individual host.

1.   To apply the profile to a host, first select the Inventory > Hosts and Clusters view.

2.   Right-click on the ESXi host and select Host Profile > Manage Profile. If no profile has been set for this host, you can select the profile that was updated earlier in this process. Otherwise, you can click Change to switch the profile used or Cancel if the correct profile is being used.

3.   Right-click on the host and select Host Profile > Check Compliance. Once the Check Compliance task has completed, the Summary tab displays a message if the host is not compliant.

4.   Before the policy can be applied, the host must be in maintenance mode. Right-click on the host and select Enter Maintenance Mode.

5.   To apply the policy, right-click on the host and select Host Profile > Apply Policy.

6.   In the Apply Profile wizard, you will be prompted to enter a User Name and Password that will be used to join the host to the domain. After you enter the appropriate credentials, click Join Domain.

7.   The Apply Profile wizard displays a summary of changes to be made to the host. A task to join the host to your domain should be listed. Click Finish to apply the changes listed.

Configuring AD Integration with the vCLI

The third option for configuring your host for AD Integration is the `vicfg-authconfig` command from the vCLI. With this command, you can add your host to a domain, check the current setup, or remove the host from a domain. The following section demonstrates the basic usage for the command.

The `--getremoteauthstore | -a` option is used to query the ESXi host for the current authentication mechanism. The following example shows a host that has not been configured for AD Integration. A configured host would show `Active Directory` as the configured mechanism.

```
vicfg-authconfig.pl --server esx05 --getremoteauthstore
Currently active authentication schemes:
============================================ =================
Local Authentication
```

The `--joindomain | -j <domain_FQDN>` option is used to join a host to your domain. The `--authscheme` option is required with the AD argument. You can also specify the `--adusername` and `--adpassword` options, but if you do not, you are prompted for credentials to join a server to the domain as follows:

```
vicfg-authconfig.pl --server esx05 --joindomain mishchenko.net --authscheme AD
Enter AD username: dave.mishchenko
Enter AD password:
Successfully joined mishchenko.net
```

The `--currentdomain` option can be used to query the currently joined domain. You must include the `--authscheme` option.

```
vicfg-authconfig.pl --server esx05 --currentdomain --authscheme AD
Current Domain: MISHCHENKO.NET
```

Lastly, if you want to remove your host from the domain, you use the `--leavecurrentdomain | -L` option. You must also specify the `--authscheme` option. If you have assigned permissions to AD users and run this command, you get the error shown in the first example that follows. To overcome this situation, use the `--force` option to delete all AD-assigned permissions and remove the host from the domain.

```
vicfg-authconfig.pl --server esx05 --leavecurrentdomain --authscheme AD
Could not part with the current domain: The operation is not allowed in the current state.
```

```
vicfg-authconfig.pl --server esx05 --leavecurrentdomain --authscheme AD --force
Successfully parted with the current domain.
```

Assigning AD Permissions on VMware ESXi

Once you have joined your ESXi host to your domain, you'll be ready to assign permissions to AD users and groups. Permissions and roles are discussed further in Chapter 7, "Securing ESXi," but for now you will see how to briefly assign a role to your AD user or group. If you plan to assign permissions manually with the vSphere client, you must connect directly to the ESXi host. If the vSphere client is connected to vCenter Server, the permissions will be granted in vCenter but not specifically on the host for direct client connections. You may also use Host Profiles to assign permissions at the host level.

To assign permissions with the vSphere client, you will follow this process:

1. Start the vSphere client and log in directly to the VMware ESXi host.

2. Select the Permissions tab for the object to which you want to add a new role for an AD user or group.

3. Right-click on a blank space on the Permissions tab and select Add Permission or select File > New > Add Permission.

4. Click the Add icon on the Assign Permissions screen to access the Select Users and Groups window as shown in Figure 6.4.

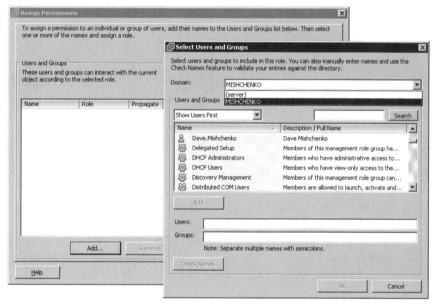

Figure 6.4   Assigning AD permissions for VMware ESXi.

5. Select the domain to use as the source for the user and group listing. You can choose among (Server), which refers to the security entities defined locally on ESXi, the domain to which you joined your ESXi host, or any trusted domains.

6. Select the user of group to which you want to assign a role on the ESXi host, and then click OK.

7. Choose a role to grant to the user or group account and click OK on the Assign Permissions screen to complete your change.

Tip: If you manually enter a user or group and then use the Check Names button on the Select Users and Groups screen, a case-sensitive search is performed. Searching for `MISHCHENKO\Domain Users` will result in success, whereas searching for `mishchenko \domain users` will not.

You can also assign roles to AD users and groups at the host level with Host Profiles. If the host being used for the Host Profile has already been configured, you can refresh the Host Profile to import the settings configured on the host. With the vSphere client connected to vCenter Server, go to the Home view and then select Host Profiles. Right-click on the Host Profile you want to update, and select Update Profile from Reference Host. Once the Update Host Profile task has completed, you can edit the profile to review the changes. Use the following process to accomplish that:

1. Start the vSphere client and connect to vCenter Server.

2. Select the Home view and then click on the Host Profiles icon.

3. Choose the profile to update, and then click Edit Profile.

4. Open the Security Configuration policy, right-click on Permission Rules, and select Add Profile.

5. Select the new policy and then click on the Edit link to configure a new permission.

6. Change the policy to use the Require a Permission Rule option.

7. Enter the User or Group Name and check the Name Refers to a Group of Users option if applicable, as shown in Figure 6.5.

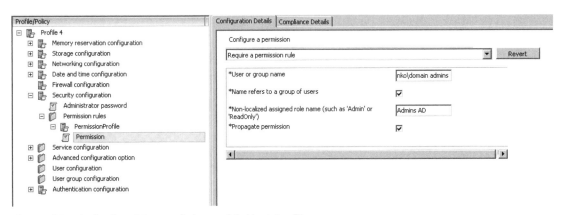

Figure 6.5 Assigning AD permissions with Host Profiles.

8. Enter the Role Name to be assigned to the AD user or group. This will be a local role on the ESXi host and can be either one of the built-in roles or a role that you have created. If you are using one of the three built-in roles of Administrator, Read-Only, or No Access, you should enter the role as Admin, ReadOnly, or NoAccess.

9. If applicable, check the Propogate Permission option.

10. Click OK to save the profile. You are now ready to apply the profile as has been previously shown.

Enabling Time Synchronization and NTP

Time synchronization will play an important role on your hosts. As noted earlier, the time on your ESXi hosts must be in sync with your domain controllers for AD Integration to function properly. Accurate time keeping for the host will also ensure that log files accurately reflect the real time when troubleshooting any problem events. For virtual machines, you may configure the guest operating systems to use the Windows Time Service or NTP to manage time, but certain events for the virtual machine will still depend on the time kept on your VMware ESXi host. These events include starting up VMware Tools, taking a snapshot, resuming from a snapshot or suspension, and using vMotion of the virtual machine. In these cases, the guest operating system is synced with the host's clock even if VMware Tools periodic time sync is disabled. Thus it is critical to ensure that the host's clock is kept in sync with a reliable time source.

To read more about timekeeping in virtual machines, you can consult the following resources.

- Timekeeping for Linux guests: http://kb.vmware.com/kb/1006427

- Timekeeping for Windows guests: http://kb.vmware.com/kb/1318

- Timekeeping in VMware Virtual Machines: http://www.vmware.com/resources/techresources/238

Configuring NTP with the vSphere Client

You can configure the NTP client settings for your host on the Configuration > Time Configuration screen. This screen displays the current time, the status of the NTP client, and currently configured NTP servers, as shown in Figure 6.6. Note that the host will be running in the Coordinated Universal Time (UTC) time zone and that the time displayed is translated to match the time zone on the workstation running the vSphere client.

Click on the Properties link to edit the time and date on the Time Configuration screen. You should avoid manually changing the time if possible, as it is ideal to allow the NTP client on ESXi to synchronize your host's time. You can click Options to configure the NTP client. The NTP Daemon (ntpd) Options screen consists of the following configuration options: General and NTP Settings. The General tab, which is shown in Figure 6.6, displays the current service status as well as the Startup Policy for the service. The policy should be set to either Start

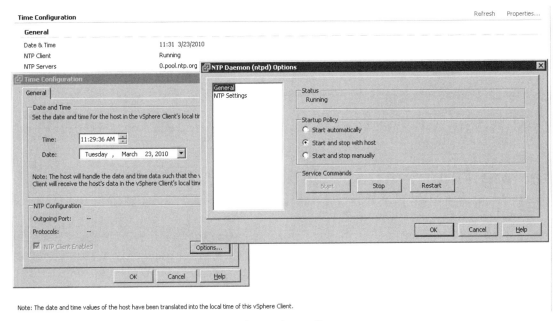

Figure 6.6 Configuring NTP settings with the vSphere client.

Automatically or Start and Stop with Host. Lastly, on the General tab, you can control the service with the Start, Stop, and Restart buttons.

Tip: If you need to restart the NTP service, you can also do this on the Configuration > Security Profile screen. When you click Options for the NTP Daemon, you will be presented with the same NTP Daemon screen as described previously. If you are at the console of your ESXi host, you can use the Restart Management Agents to restart the NTP service along with other system services.

On the NTP Settings tab, you can configure the NTP servers that the ESXi host will use. You can use the Add, Edit, or Remove buttons to manage the list of servers that you want to use. The NTP servers can be entered as a hostname, an Internet Protocol (IP) address, or an IPv6 address. If you make changes to the server list, you can check the Restart NTP Service to Apply Changes option to restart the NTP service on ESXi when you click OK to save your changes.

Configuring NTP with Host Profiles

If you have updated your reference host with your required NTP configuration using the vSphere client, you are ready to update your Host Profile. With the vSphere client connected to vCenter Server, go to the Home view and then select Host Profiles. Right-click on the Host Profile you want to update and select Update Profile from Reference Host. Once the Update Host Profile task has completed, you can edit the profile to review the changes.

You can also manually edit the profile to configure NTP settings by following these steps:

1.   Start the vSphere client and connect to vCenter Server.

2.   Select the Home view and then click on the Host Profiles icon.

3.   Choose the profile to update and click Edit Profile.

4.   Open the Date and Time Configuration policy and select Time Settings. You will note that there is a Time Zone policy but you cannot apply this policy to ESXi hosts.

5.   For the Time Settings policy, change the setting to Configure a Fixed NTP Configuration. Enter a list of NTP servers by hostname or IP address. Separate multiple hosts with a comma, as shown in Figure 6.7. If you have configured your host to use IPv6, you can enter an IPv6 address.

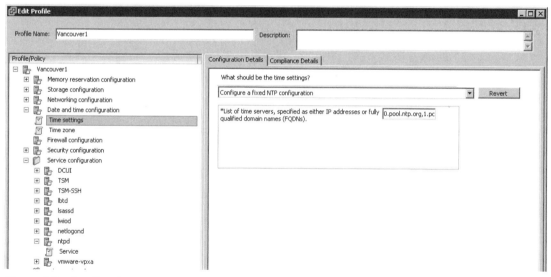

Figure 6.7 Configuring NTP settings with Host Profiles.

6.   Open Service Configuration > Ntpd and select the service policy. Choose the Establish a Fixed Service Configuration and set the service policy to `automatic` or `on`.

7.   Click OK to save and close the policy. Then use the procedures described earlier to apply the policy to your hosts.

Configuring NTP with PowerCLI

The vCLI contains the command vicfg-ntp, which you use to manage the configured NTP servers for a host as well as to stop and start the NTP service. While the command is adequate for running on a single host as part of a configuration script, if you want to update a number of hosts, the advantages of PowerCLI become evident. PowerCLI includes the cmdlets Add-VMHostNtpServer, Get-VMHostNtpServer, and Remove-VMHostNtpServer to configure the NTP settings for your host. You will also use Get-VMHostService and Restart-VMHostService to restart the NTP server after making your changes.

If you run Get-VMHostNtpServer against a single host, the command simply returns the list of configured NTP servers just as the vicfg-ntp command would do:

```
get-vmhostntpserver
0.pool.ntp.org
```

If you utilize Get_VMHost, you can obtain a list of all your ESXi hosts in vCenter Server. That output can then be used to query for the NTP server for each host as well as to check the status of the NTP service on each host:

```
Get-VMHost |Sort Name|Select Name, @{N="NTP Server(s)";E={$_
    |Get-VMHostNtpServer}}, @{N="Service Status";E={(Get-VmHostService
    -VMHost $_ |Where-Object {$_.key-eq "ntpd"}).Running}}
```

Name	NTP Server(s)	Service Status
esx01.mishchenko.net	0.pool.ntp.org	True
esx02.mishchenko.net	{0.pool.ntp.org, 1.pool...	False
esx05.mishchenko.net	0.pool.ntp.org	True

The following script generates a list of ESXi hosts connected to vCenter Server. For each host, the script creates a list of currently configured NTP server and then removes those items. It then adds a new NTP server to the host and restarts the NTP service so that your ESXi hosts can begin to use the new NTP server.

```
$Hosts = Get-VMHost
ForEach ($Hostname in $Hosts)
{
$Current_NTP = Get-VMHostNtpServer -VMHost $Hostname
    ForEach ($NtpServer in $Current_NTP)
    {
    Remove-VMHostNtpServer -NtpServer $NtpServer -VMHost $Hostname
    }
Add-VmHostNtpServer -NtpServer "2.pool.ntp.org" -VMHost $Hostname | Out-Null
Get-VmHostService -VMHost $Hostname | Where-Object {$_.key -eq "ntpd"} |
    Restart-VMHostService -Confirm:$false | Out-Null
```

```
write "NTP Server was changed on $Hostname"
}


Remove NtpServer '0.pool.ntp.org' from VM host 'esx01.mishchenko.net'?
[Y] Yes [A] Yes to All [N] No [L] No to All [S] Suspend [?] Help
(default is "Y"):
NTP Server was changed on esx01.mishchenko.net
Remove NtpServer '0.pool.ntp.org' from VM host 'esx02.mishchenko.net'?
[Y] Yes [A] Yes to All [N] No [L] No to All [S] Suspend [?] Help
(default is "Y"):
NTP Server was changed on esx02.mishchenko.net
```

Tip: As you begin to create complex PowerCLI scripts, you will have to start spending time on troubleshooting and coding for error conditions in your scripts. The preceding script assumes that each host has at least one NTP server configured and that the NTP service is running. For a host that does not have the service running, an error is generated as shown in the following script, but the script continues to run. Since the script is executed against vCenter Server, you can track the progress in the Recent Tasks pane or on the Tasks & Events tab for each host. In the case of this script, two Update Configuration tasks are created for each host followed by a Restart Service task for each host as well.

```
Restart-VMHostService : 3/23/2010 9:18:24 PM   Restart-VMHostService
    06BB6C44-57D2-400C-825B-46F84BB0487E   The operation is not allowed in
    the current state.
```

Redirecting ESXi Logs to a Remote Syslog Server

The syslog protocol was developed in the 1980s as a method to separate the application that was generating log data from the system that would store the logging data. Syslog has been the standard logging solution for Unix and Linux systems for some time and is generally used to send system management and security auditing data to a central syslog receiver. Syslog messages can be sent via User Datagram Protocol (UDP) or Transmission Control Protocol (TCP) and uses a default port of 514.

As the ramdisk file system does not persist when the host is restarted, the log files for ESXi do not survive a reboot. Enabling the syslog service on ESXi enables you to forward all log information to a central server. VMware ESXi will use UDP to transmit data to the syslog receiver.

Configuration of the syslog settings on ESXi is done on the Configuration > Advanced Settings (Hardware) screen. The following options are available for configuration (see Figure 6.8):

- **Syslog.Local.DatastorePath.** This is a local path to which the syslog files will be written. This can be a location within the ramdisk or a datastore location.

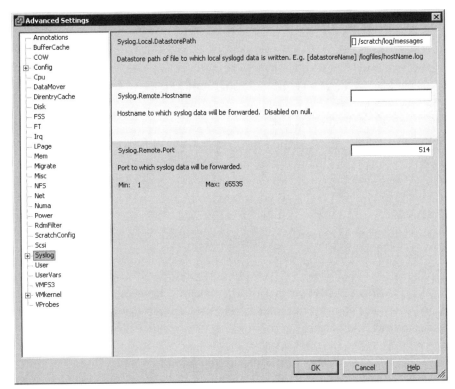

Figure 6.8 VMware ESXi syslog settings.

- **Syslog.Remote.Hostname.** This is the remote host to which syslog data will be forwarded. If this setting is left empty, remote syslog forwarding will be disabled.

- **Syslog.Remote.Port.** This is the destination port to which syslog data will be forwarded.

Note: The default setting for Syslog.Local.DatastorePath has changed with VMware ESXi 4.1. With ESXi 4.0 and earlier versions, the setting was not defined and thus the syslog service would use the default location of /var/log/messages. Files in this location were not preserved over a restart of the host. With ESXi 4.1, the default location is now /scratch/log/messages. With that new setting, syslog files will survive a reboot, but you need to access the Tech Support Console to gain access to the files.

Configuring Syslog Settings with the vSphere Client

You can use the following process to configure syslog for an ESXi host. The vSphere client can be connected directly to the host or to vCenter Server.

1. Select the host in the vSphere client inventory.

2. Select the Configuration tab and then click on Advanced Settings (Hardware).

3. Select Syslog in the tree control as shown in Figure 6.8.

4. Enter a valid datastore for Syslog.Local.Datastore. The path format is [<datastore-name>] </path/file>, but you can also enter /vmfs/volumes/<datastorename>/ <path>/<file> and the path will be stored in the preferred format.

5. In the Syslog.Remote.Hostname box, you can enter the hostname or IP address for the server to which syslog data will be forwarded. If no value is entered, forwarding is disabled.

6. In the Syslog.Remote.Port box, enter the port on which the syslog receiver will be listening. The default value is port 514. This setting is ignored if Syslog.Remote.Hostname is not configured.

7. Click OK to close the Advanced Settings window.

Any changes you make immediately take effect. There is no need to restart the host or any services after configuring syslog settings.

Note: If you have configured syslog with ESX, you'll have become familiar with the process of editing /etc/syslog.conf, opening the Service Console firewall to allow syslog traffic, and restarting the management services to complete the configuration. With ESXi, you can use the vSphere client, vicfg-syslog from the vCLI, or PowerCLI commands to configure your hosts. You should also note that with ESXi you can configure only a single syslog receiver. If you need to send data to multiple syslog hosts, you'll need to send the host's syslog data to a host that is configured to forward the data to other syslog receivers. Lastly, with ESXi, you cannot configure the level of errors that are forwarded. All events in the system logs will be forwarded; this is unlike ESX, which you can configure, for example, to send log items at a level of critical or higher to the syslog receiver.

Configuring Syslog Settings with PowerCLI

PowerCLI includes two cmdlets that may be used to query and set syslog receiver on your ESXi hosts. These are get-VMHostSysLogServer and set-VMHostSysLogServer. As with vicfg-syslog from the vCLI, these cmdlets can be used to set and query the remote syslog server settings on a host as shown in the following listing. When setting the syslog server, you can specify either the IP address, hostname, or IPv6 address.

```
get-VMHostSysLogServer -VMHost esx02
Host                          Port
-----                         -----
vcenter41                     514


Set-VMHostSysLogServer -SysLogServerPort 514 -SysLogServer 192.168.1.52
Host                          Port
-----                         -----
192.168.1.52                  514
```

If you need to check or update a number of hosts, you can use the following simple script. For configured hosts, a syslog server and port are displayed. Unconfigured hosts will not show a syslog server or port.

```
Get-VMHost |Sort Name|Select Name, @{N="Syslog Server";E={$_ |
   Get-VMHostSyslogServer}}
Name                          Syslog Server
-----                         -------------
esx01.mishchenko.net          192.168.1.52:514
esx02.mishchenko.net          192.168.1.52:514
esx05.mishchenko.net
```

The following script updates all hosts connected to your vCenter Server host with the specified syslog server IP address and port number:

```
$Hosts = Get-VMHost
ForEach ($Hostname in $Hosts)
{
Set-VMHostSysLogServer -SysLogServerPort 514 -SysLogServer 192.168.1.52
   -VMHost $Hostname
write "Syslog Server was changed on $Hostname"
}
Host                          Port
-----                         -----
192.168.1.52                  514
Syslog Server was changed on esx05.mishchenko.net
192.168.1.52                  514
Syslog Server was changed on esx01.mishchenko.net
192.168.1.52                  514
Syslog Server was changed on esx02.mishchenko.net
```

> **Note:** The `Get-VMHostSysLogServer` and `Set-VMHostSysLogServer` cmdlets work only with VMware ESXi. If you run the cmdlets on VMware ESX, you will receive an error that the host is not supported.

Managing ESXi Syslog Data

Now that you know how to configure your hosts to forward log data to a syslog server, it is worthwhile to see what it will be like to manage that data. Use of a syslog server provides an easy way to create a central repository of your log data. This repository of data is beneficial to provide an untouched set of logs for review should you experience an intrusion or other problem that requires careful examination of log data. As mentioned earlier, ESXi stores log files in a ramdisk for a limited period so that log files will not be permanently available.

The following sample uses Splunk, which is available from www.splunk.com. After the product is installed, the first step is to set up Splunk to receive syslog data. The following setup was done with Splunk 4.1 running on Windows 2008. If you have a firewall enabled on your syslog receiver, ensure that it is configured to allow inbound syslog data.

You can use the following process to enable Splunk to receive syslog data:

1. Log in to the Splunk administration Web site. The login after a new installation is `admin` and the password is `changeme`.

2. Click the Add Data link to create a new Data Input.

3. On the Data Inputs page, click the Add New link for the data type of UDP.

4. On the Add New page, enter a UDP port of 514. You may also change the Host setting to DNS to have Splunk log data with the DNS hostname for your ESXi hosts instead of their IP addresses.

5. Click Save on the Add New page to save your new syslog data input.

If you have previously configured your ESXi hosts to forward syslog data, Splunk immediately begins to collect that data. As the syslog data is an exact duplicate of the log data that ESXi is generating internally, the number of events sent to your Splunk server can be significant. To view the raw data, return to the home page for your Splunk server and select the Search link. The Search page displays the links for all the syslog data that has been captured and links to access syslog data for specific hosts, as shown in Figure 6.9.

If you select to view syslog data for a specific host, Splunk provides that data as shown in Figure 6.10. Note that each event contains two time stamps. The first reflects the time that the Splunk server received the data and the second is the time that the event was generated on the ESXi host. The seven-hour difference is caused by the ESXi host running in the UTC time

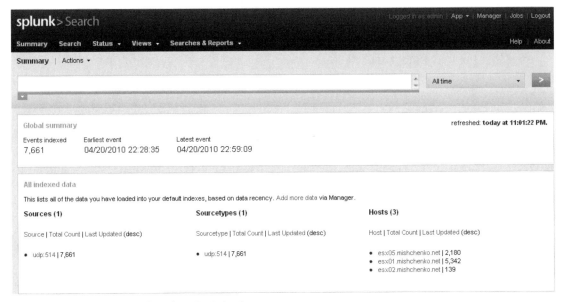

Figure 6.9   Accessing syslog data in Splunk.

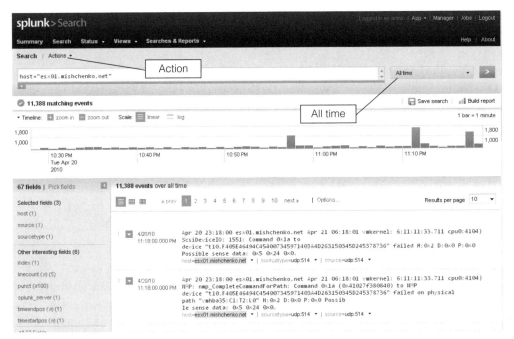

Figure 6.10   Viewing syslog data for a specific host.

zone. You can change the settings for Splunk to have the second time stamp match the time zone in which your ESXi hosts are located, using the procedure outlined at this link: http://www.splunk.com/wiki/Community:VMwareESXSyslog.

The default Search view for a specific host displays all data collected for the data. If you want to view data only for a specific period, select the All Time drop-down menu as shown in Figure 6.10 and select a more appropriate time period. The time ranges shown are based on the time zone for the Splunk host, so you may need to adjust your time period to reflect the correct time period that you want to examine for your host. If you want to use the data in another application, select the Actions drop-down menu and choose Export Results. You can export to a number of formats, including Comma Separated Values and Raw Events.

You may also find it valuable to configure your syslog server to alert you based on certain events that are found. For example, you could use your syslog receiver to alert you to a certain event that is being logged but not generating alerts in your other monitoring tools. The following example configures Splunk to send an alert should a syslog entry contain the text "failed on physical path":

1. On the Search screen, create a search that will find the events for which you want to receive an alert. For this example, the search is `sourcetype="udp:514" startminu-tesago::5 "failed on physical path"`, which will include syslog data coming from all ESXi hosts. The `startminutesago::5` option limits the search to the last five minutes of syslog data.

2. Select the Action drop-down menu, as shown in Figure 6.10, and choose Save Search.

3. On the Save Search dialog box, specify a Name and optionally a Description.

4. Check the Schedule This Search option and then enter an appropriate frequency in the Run Every drop-down menu, as shown in Figure 6.11.

5. Change the Alert Conditions to generate an alert if the number of events is greater than zero.

6. Choose your desired alert Action. Splunk is able to send an e-mail, create an RSS feed, or run a shell script. In this example, the e-mail option is chosen, but you could use the script option to run a PowerCLI or vCLI script.

7. Click Save to close the dialog box.

To receive e-mail alerts, you must specify a mail host to be used to relay e-mail. You can set this in Manager > System settings > Email alert settings. With the option to run a shell script, you could even create a script that could generate an alert within another monitoring system. Splunk can also be configured to forward data to other syslog receivers, which can overcome the limit on ESXi of being able to set only a single syslog server.

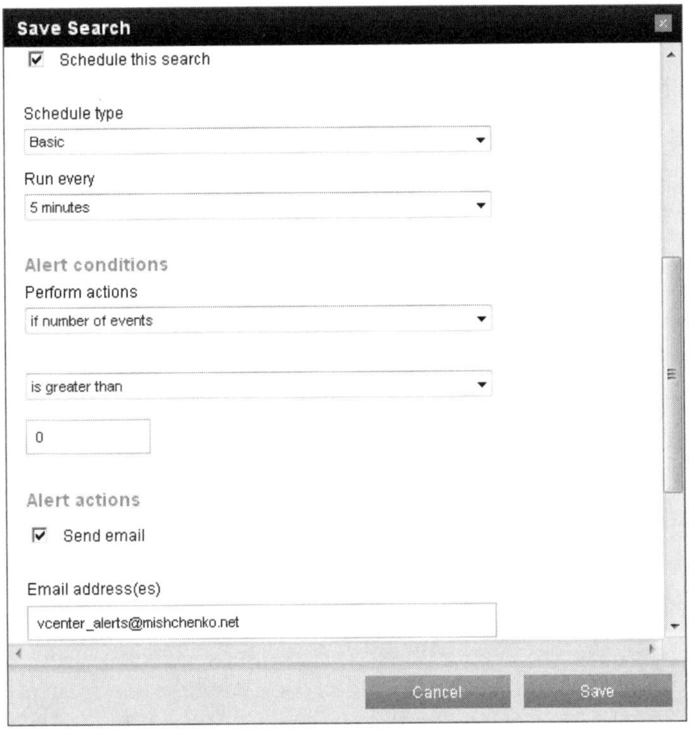

Figure 6.11   Scheduling an alert in Splunk based on a specific event.

Monitoring ESXi and vCenter Server with SNMP

Simple Network Management Procotol (SNMP) is a UDP-based protocol developed in the 1980s to manage network devices. An SNMP deployment consists of the managed devices, the SNMP agents running on the devices, and a network management server that receives and retrieves data from the agents. The SNMP agents running on the devices expose data such as the host hardware model, memory use, and network configuration. The management system is able to acquire this data with one of the following methods. The management system can use an SNMP GET operation, in which it sends a specific request for data to the SNMP agent. The SNMP agent can also send a trap to the management server to notify it of a certain condition or event. SNMP typically uses UDP port 161 for the agent and port 162 for the management server. The configuration of SNMP also uses the concept of communities. Communities are used to group devices and management stations. A device running an SNMP agent can belong to multiple communities.

If you plan to integrate vCenter Server and VMware ESXi into your SNMP deployment, it is important to understand that both products support only SNMP traps. The vCenter and ESXi SNMP agents do not support other SNMP operations such as GET.

Configuring SNMP on ESXi and vCenter Server

To configure SNMP to monitor your vSphere datacenter, you need to enable SNMP on your ESXi hosts and vCenter Server. To configure SNMP on vCenter Server, use the following process:

1. Start the vSphere client and connect to vCenter Server.

2. Select Administration > vCenter Server Settings.

3. Click SNMP on the navigation list.

4. Change the Receiver uniform resource locator (URL) for the Primary Receiver from localhost to the hostname or IP address for your SNMP management server.

5. If required, you can also change the Port and Community String for the Primary Receiver.

6. Click OK to save your changes.

On the vCenter Server Settings dialog box, notice that you can enable up to four SNMP receivers. These could be different management servers or different communities on the same server.

To configure VMware ESXi to enable SNMP, you use the vCLI command `vicfg-snmp`. The command has the options found in Table 6.1.

Table 6.1 Options for the vCLI Command vicfg-snmp

Option	Description
`--communities	-c <comm1>` `[,...]`	Specifies the SNMP communities to which the host will belong. When you use this option, any prior settings are overwritten.
`--disable	-D`	Stops the SNMP service on your host.
`--enable	-E`	Starts the SNMP service on your host.
`--port	-p <port_number>`	Sets the port to be used by the SNMP agent. The default is UDP 161.
`--reset	-r`	Clears the currently configured communities and targets on the host.
`--show	-s`	Displays the current SNMP configuration.
`--targets	-t <hostname[@port]` `> </community>[,...]`	Sets the destination for SNMP traps. For vSphere 4.0 and later versions, you can use IPv6.
`--test	-T`	Sends a test notification to the configured target or targets.

The following process can be used to configure your ESXi host for SNMP. The `--show` option can be used to display the current configuration on the host. By default, there is no configuration for targets and communities and the value of 0 for the Enabled parameter indicates that the agent is not running.

```
vicfg-snmp --server esx01 --show

Current SNMP agent settings:
Enabled  : 0
UDP port : 161
Communities :
Notification targets :
```

Before you can enable the SNMP agent on ESXi, you must configure at least one community. Your host can be a member of multiple communities, but it will be able to share SNMP data only with management servers that belong to the same community group. The following command sets the communities for the host to `public` and `vsphere`. If you set multiple communities, you have to set them with one command. Running the `vicfg-snmp` command again to set a second community overwrites the previous community configuration.

```
vicfg-snmp --server esx01 --communities public,vsphere
Changing community list to: public,vsphere...
Complete.
```

The next step to set up your host for SNMP is to specify your SNMP management server. The `--target` option is used to specify the target (SNMP receiver) address, community, and optionally the UDP port to use. The following command sets two target servers:

```
vicfg-snmp.pl --server esx01 -targets
   192.168.1.52@162/public,192.168.1.53@162/vsphere

Changing notification(trap) targets list to:
   192.168.1.52@162/public,192.168.1.53@162/vsphere...
Complete.
```

Once you have configured the appropriate community and target, you can use the `--enable` option to start the SNMP agent on your host, as shown in the following command:

```
vicfg-snmp --server esx01 --enable

Enabling agent...
Complete.
```

If you want to review the configuration of your host, you can use the `--show` option:

```
vicfg-snmp --server esx01 --show
```

```
Current SNMP agent settings:
Enabled : 1
UDP port : 161
Communities :
public
vsphere
Notification targets :
192.168.1.53@162/vsphere
192.168.1.52@162/public
```

If you are having any problems with your SNMP configuration, you can run `vicfg-snmp` with the `--test` option to send an SNMP trap to your configured management servers:

```
vicfg-snmp --server esx01 --test
```

```
Sending test nofication(trap) to all configured targets...
Complete. Check with each target to see if trap was received.
```

Configuring Your SNMP Management Server

After you have configured your ESXi hosts and vCenter Server to send SNMP traps to your SNMP management server, you must configure the management server to accept those traps and to have the necessary information to interpret the traps. Interpretation of the SNMP trap data is handled by Management Information Base (MIB) files. The VMware MIB files define the structure of the management data sent by the monitored device using a hierarchical namespace containing object identifiers (OIDs). Each OID identifies a variable that can be set or read with SNMP.

Caution: Both vCenter Server and VMware ESXi use SNMP version 1 to send trap data. The SNMP agent sends the community strings as clear text data, and anyone with a packet sniffer can capture and view this data. Further, as the data is sent via UDP, it is possible to spoof the IP address of one of your hosts to send fraudulent or corrupted data to your SNMP management server. If you use SNMP to monitor your ESXi host and vCenter Server, it is best to ensure that the SNMP traffic remains on a secured management network.

To configure your host to accept SNMP traps from your ESXi hosts and vCenter Server, use the following process:

1. Access your SNMP management software and ensure that your ESXi hosts and vCenter Server are listed as SNMP managed devices.

2. Add the same community names to your SNMP software as you used to configure your ESXi hosts and vCenter Server.

3.   If you have configured your hosts to send SNMP traps to a port other than UDP 162, update your management software to use the same port.

4.   Download the latest VMware MIB files from http://communities.vmware.com/community/developer/managementapi.

5.   Load the VMware MIB files into your management software to ensure that the management software is able to display the appropriate names for the variables that will be sent in the SNMP traps.

Table 6.2 provides a list of VMware MIB files that are available for use with VMware ESXi and vCenter Server along with a description of the information that each file provides.

Table 6.2 VMware MIB Files

MIB File	Description
VMWARE-ROOT-MIB.mib	Contains VMware's enterprise OID and top-level OID assignments.
VMWARE-TC-MIB.mib	Contains common textual conventions used by all VMware MIB files.
VMWARE-PRODUCTS-MIB.mib	Defines OIDs to identify each SNMP agent for each VMware platform by name, version, and build platform.
VMWARE-ENV-MIB.mib	Defines trap types and variables used to report on the state of physical hardware of the host computer.
VMWARE-RESOURCES-MIB.mib	Defines variables used to report information on resource usage of the VMkernel.
VMWARE-VC-EVENTS-MIB.mib	Contains trap definitions sent by vCenter Server.
VMWARE-AGENTCAP-MIB.mib	Defines the capabilities of the VMware agents by the various product versions.
VMWARE-VMINFO-MIB.mib	Contains the variables used to report information about virtual machines.
VMWARE-OBSOLETE-MIB.mib	Defines OIDs that have been made obsolete to maintain backward compatibility with earlier versions of VMware ESXi. These variables were previously defined in the obsolete files VMWARE-TRAPS-MIB.mib and VMWARE-VMKERNEL-MIB.mib.

Monitoring Your Hosts with vCenter Server

One of the critical aspects of managing your VMware ESXi deployment is monitoring the performance and health of your hosts to ensure that you have sufficient capacity and that performance issues are not adversely impacting your end users. VMware ESXi and vCenter Server provide a number of tools that you will use to monitor the performance of your hosts.

The Resources pane is available on host and virtual machine objects. On a host object, the Resources pane provides a summary of central processing unit (CPU) usage, memory usage, a summary of accessible datastores, and a list of available virtual machine networks. The Resources pane for a virtual machine shows the same items, but for memory displays both the amount of host memory consumed as well as the quantity of memory being actively used by the virtual machine. The pane also displays both the amount of storage being used and the quantity of storage provisioned. These values can be useful to determine whether you are using snapshots or thin provisioned disks. While the Resource pane does not provide comprehensive performance data, it can be used to get a quick view of the performance of a host or virtual machine and potentially point in the direction of a resource bottleneck or constraint.

Another tool to gather a performance overview quickly is the Virtual Machines tab. This tab is available at a number of vCenter Server objects and displays the data shown in Table 6.3. This information can be used to isolate a virtual machine that may be consuming an excessive quantity of resources. Similar to the Virtual Machines tab is the Hosts tab. The Hosts tab is available on the vCenter Server, folder, datacenter, and cluster objects. As with the Virtual Machines tab, the Hosts tab provides a high-level overview of performance, which may, for example, isolate a problem host within a cluster.

vCenter Server provides the ability to create alarms for events, conditions, and states that occur with objects in your vSphere datacenter. A number of predefined alarms are available that monitor clusters, hosts, virtual machines, and other objects. You may also create custom alarms for conditions, states, and events that are not covered by the predefined alarms. Creating and managing alarms are covered in the following section.

Another of the tools in vCenter Server for monitoring the performance of your ESXi hosts is the Performance tab. ESXi collects a large number of performance statistics for various objects and these are stored in the vCenter database for long-term analysis. With vSphere 4.1, a number of new counters are now included in the following categories: Datastore, Power, Storage Adapter, and Storage Path. Use of the Performance tab is covered further in the section "Working with Performance Charts."

The last vCenter tool that will be highlighted in the following sections is the Report view on the Storage Views tab. The Reports view can quickly show information about items such as storage allocation and utilization, summarized storage use by individual virtual machines, and multipathing status.

Table 6.3 Virtual Machines Tab Column Information

Label	Description
Name	The name of the virtual machine
State	The virtual machine state, such as powered on, powered off, or suspended
Status	The condition of the virtual machine
Provisioned Space	The maximum potential datastore space required to run the virtual machine
Used Space	The datastore space currently used by the virtual machine, including snapshot data
Host	The vSphere host that is currently running the virtual machine
Host CPU – MHz	The processor usage of the virtual machine
Host Mem – MB	The amount of host memory being used to run the virtual machine
Guest Mem - %	The percentage of memory assigned that is actively being used by the guest operating system
Guest OS	The guest operating system for the virtual machine
VM Version	The virtual machine hardware version
Memory Size	The amount of memory allocated to the virtual machine
CPU Count	The number of virtual CPUs assigned to the virtual machine
NIC Count	The number of virtual NICs assigned to the virtual machine
Uptime	The amount of time that the virtual machine has been powered on
IP Address	The IP address of the guest operating system as detected by VMware Tools
VMware Tools Status	The status of VMware Tools, which may be OK, Not Installed, Out of Date, or Unmanaged
DNS Name	The DNS name for the guest operating system as detected by VMware Tools
EVC Mode	The Enhanced vMotion Compatability mode under which the virtual machine is operating
UUID	The Universally Unique Identifier for the virtual machines
Notes	Note data entered for the virtual machine
Alarm Actions	The status of alarms, which can be set to Enabled or Disabled for each virtual machine

Working with Alarms

vCenter Server alarms are not a new feature with vSphere 4.1, but each new release increases the number and scope of triggers that are available to generate new alerts about potential problems with your vSphere environment. For example, with vSphere 4.1, there are two new host alarms. With one of the alarms, you can monitor the status of your host's Baseboard Management Controller. With the other, you can monitor the fullness of the host's IPMI System Event Log.

vCenter Server comes with a number of predefined alarms on the vCenter Server objects. These include alarms for host errors, virtual machine issues, and storage problems, among others. To view these alarms, select your vCenter Server host, and then select the Alarms tab and click Definitions. When you create an alert on a vCenter object, it applies to all child objects, such as folders, datacenters, clusters, network, datastores, hosts, and virtual machines. So the alarms that come predefined on the vCenter Server object will be applied to all objects within your datacenter. If you select the Alarms tab on a child object, the list will be filtered to show only applicable alarms. The Alarms tab for a host will show alarms related to host hardware, licensing, and networking, but none for virtual machines. Likewise, the Alarms tab for a virtual machine will display only alarms that apply to virtual machines.

You can create alarms at any level within vCenter. In some cases, you may find it best to define your alarms at the vCenter Server object so that it will apply to your entire vSphere infrastructure. However, sometimes you may want to create an alarm for a specific cluster should you have specific alerting requirements for it that do not apply to the other clusters in your datacenter.

Creating Alarms

When you create an alarm, you must define a trigger that generates a warning or alerts for a specific criteria being met. Triggers can either be event triggers or condition and state triggers. With an event trigger, a specific event will have occurred for a vCenter Server object. This can include a host being found to be noncompliant with the host profile assigned to it or an account being created on the host. Condition and state triggers monitor the current condition and state of vCenter Server objects, such as hosts and virtual machines. Common examples of these triggers include the CPU usage for a host or the power state for a virtual machine.

When you've decided which level to create a new alarm at, the following process can be used to create a new alarm. This example creates an alarm that monitors for datastore overallocation. With the support in vSphere for Thin Provisioning, it is possible to allocate more disk space to virtual machine disk files than is actually available in the datastore, so it is important to monitor available space on your datastores. There is a predefined alarm that will monitor the actual space being used on the datastore, but the disk overallocation trigger will help you find datastores that may experience future space constraints.

1. In the inventory view, select the vCenter object on which you will create the alarm.

2. Select the Alarms tab and then click Definitions. You will see a list of alarms that have been defined for the object.

3. Right-click on a blank space around the predefined alarms and select New Alarm.

4. Enter an Alarm Name and Description on the General tab of the Alarm Settings dialog box.

5. In the Monitor drop-down list, select Datastores. If the Datastores option is not available, you need to create the alarm on a vCenter object that supports Datastore alarms. For example, if you try to create a new alarm on a cluster object, you have only the Monitor options of Virtual Machines, Hosts, and Clusters.

6. Select the radio button Monitor for Specific Conditions or State.

7. Select the Triggers tab and then click Add to create a new trigger. In this example, a single trigger is used, but you can add multiple triggers and also specify whether the alert should trigger if any or all conditions are met.

8. Change the Trigger Type to Datastore Disk Overallocation (%) as shown in Figure 6.12. As a condition trigger, the Condition state is set to issue a warning or error when the condition is above a certain measurement. You can change the default values of 100 and 200 that are used to determine when to send a warning or alert.

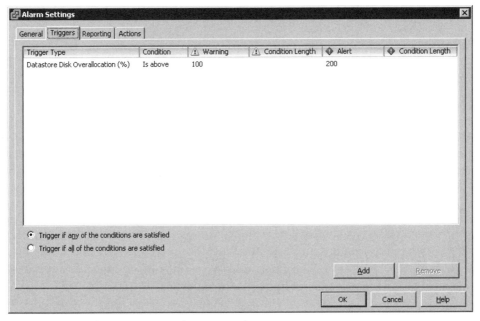

Figure 6.12 Defining a trigger for a new alarm.

9. On the Reporting tab, no change to the Range and Frequency setting is required.

10. Select the Actions tab and click Add. For a datastore alert, you may select among the actions of Send a Notification Email, Send a Notification Trap, or Run a

Command. You can have multiple actions and you can also specify to which change-level notification an action will apply. Select the default Action of Send a Notification Email, and then click the Configuration field. Enter an e-mail address to which the alert will be sent. If you enter multiple e-mail addresses, separate them with commas.

11.   Click OK to complete the process of creating an alarm.

General Tips for Using Alarms vCenter Server provides a wide range of alarms to monitor both the condition and performance of your ESXi hosts. The predefined alarms cover a number of error conditions and potential performance issues that you should be aware of, but it is likely that you will create new alarms to meet the requirements of your environments. The following list includes some tips for creating alarms and other items that you should be aware of:

■   You must be connected to the vCenter Server to create and manage alarms. The Alarm tab is not available when you are connected directly to your ESXi host, even if it is being managed by vCenter Server.

■   The predefined alerts within vCenter are configured either to send an SNMP trap or have no action defined. By default, vCenter Server is configured to send SNMP traps to the localhost, so the alerts that are predefined will not alert any systems outside of vCenter Server without further configuration.

■   It is best not to modify the predefined alarms. Rather, you can right-click on the alarm, select Edit Setting, and then uncheck Enable This Alarm. You can then create a new alarm that meets your specific requirements.

■   Alarms can be edited only when you have selected the vCenter object on which the alarm was created. Otherwise, you will only be able to right-click and select View Settings. The Edit Settings option will not be available and the options to Remove or Rename the alert will be grayed out.

■   You can right-click on any vCenter object and select Alarms > Add Alarms to create a new alarm. It is worthwhile to select the Alarms tab and then click Definitions to verify whether any preexisting alarms will meet your needs.

■   All alerts have the default actions of Send a Notification Email, Send a Notification Trap, and Run a Command. To use e-mail and SNMP traps, you need to set up vCenter Server with the appropriate information. You can configure settings for e-mail and SNMP by accessing the vCenter Server Settings window; to do so, select Administration > vCenter Server Settings within the vSphere client. You can set up which SMTP mail server to use and up to four SNMP receivers. In Chapter 9,

"Scripting and Automation with PowerCLI," you will see how to use the Run a Command option to execute a PowerCLI script.

- For most of the Monitor types, such as Virtual Machines and Host, other actions exist in addition to the three aforementioned ones. For a host that is configured as part of a VMware Distributed Resource Scheduler (DRS) cluster, you can create an alarm that will respond to a host hardware failure. The actions for the alarm can be set to send a notification and then to place the host in maintenance mode. Within a DRS cluster, this results in the migration of virtual machines to other hosts in the cluster and eliminates the risk of a service outage should the host's hardware fault unexpectedly take the server offline.

- When you create an alarm, you can use the Reporting tab to reduce the frequency at which an alarm is triggered. You can set the tolerance range to a percentage above or below a configured threshold after which an alarm will trigger or clear. With a Host CPU threshold set to 75 percent, an alarm will trigger or clear as the host's CPU crosses that threshold. With a 5 percent tolerance range, the alarm will not trigger until the host's CPU crosses 80 percent or clear until CPU usage falls below 70 percent. With the trigger frequency setting, you can set the time period for which an alarm action is not reported again. The default setting is five minutes and increasing that frequency can reduce the number of alerts generated due to insignificant alarm transitions.

One of the improvements to alarms that was introduced in vSphere was the ability to create triggers based on events. This allows for the monitoring of a wide range of events for virtual machines, hosts, clusters, and other vCenter objects. Event triggers can be created on any event that is available within the vSphere application programming interface (API). The API reference for vSphere 4.1 can be found at the following link: http://www.vmware.com/support/developer/vc-sdk/visdk41pubs/ApiReference/index.html. The API Reference documentation does not include a specific list of event triggers, but the VMware Communities document "vSphere Alarm Triggers" found at http://communities.vmware.com/docs/DOC-12145 includes a number of PowerCLI scripts to generate a list of event triggers.

The first example will create an alarm that triggers should the host loose network connectivity.

1. In the inventory view, select the vCenter object on which you will create the alarm.

2. Select the Alarms tab and then click Definitions. You will see a list of alarms that have been defined for the object.

3. Right-click on a blank space around the predefined alarms and select New Alarm.

4. Enter an alarm name and description on the General tab of the Alarm Settings dialog box.

5. Select Hosts for the Monitor type, and check the option Monitor for Specific Events Occurring on This Object.

6. Select the Triggers tab; then click Add to add a new event.

7. Change the event to Lost Network Connectivity. The status should be changed to Unset.

8. You can then configure any desired actions to be taken should the aarm be triggered.

9. Click OK to save the new alarm.

With the proceeding example, no advanced conditions were set for the event trigger. The trigger of Lost Network Connectivity will either be true or false, so no further conditions need to be configured. The following example looks at the host's power status. In this case, the trigger has a status of Normal, Warning, or Alert. When you're examining the API documentation or the output of the PowerCLI scripts from the "vSphere Alarm Triggers" document, you'll find that the Power status of a host is a condition of the Hardware Health Changed event trigger. To enable an alarm based on the power status of the host, you have to configure advanced conditions, as shown in this example.

1. In the inventory view, select the vCenter object on which you will create the alarm.

2. Select the Alarms tab, and then click Definitions. You see a list of alarms that have been defined for the object.

3. Right-click on a blank space around the predefined alarms, and select New Alarm.

4. Enter an alarm name and description on the General tab of the Alarm Settings dialog box.

5. Select Hosts for the Monitor type, and check the option Monitor for Specific Events Occurring on This Object.

6. Select the Triggers tab; then click Add to add a new event.

7. Change the event to Hardware Health Changed. Set the status to Normal; then click the Advanced link in the Conditions column.

8. Create two arguments. The first will have an argument type of Group with an operator of Equal To and a value of Power. The second argument should be set to a type of NewState with an operator of Equal To and a value of Green. Click OK to close the Trigger Conditions window.

9.   Repeat steps 6 to 8 to add events with a status of Warning and Alert. The Warning event will be set to have a NewState of Yellow, and the Alert event will have a NewState of Red.

10.   Once you have added the three event triggers, add your desired Actions. Then click OK to save the new alarm.

Managing Alarms

In the previous section of this chapter, you learned how to create alarms with vCenter Server. You create and edit alarm definitions by selecting the Alarms tab and then choosing the Definitions view. To view triggered alarms, you select the Triggered Alarms view as shown in Figure 6.13. The Triggered Alarms view shows any warning or alerts that have been triggered for the vCenter object that you have selected or any child objects. The sample in Figure 6.13 has the vCenter Server object selected and it has three child objects with warnings or alerts that have been triggered.

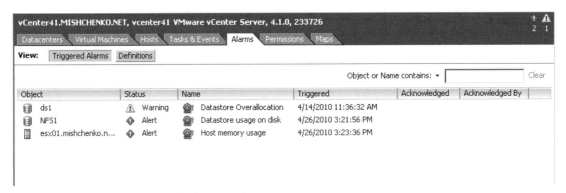

Figure 6.13   Viewing triggered alarms with vCenter Server.

When you select any vCenter object that has a triggered alarm for itself or a child object, the vSphere client displays either a warning or alert icon in the top-right corner of the content pane along with the number of warnings or alerts. This is also shown in Figure 6.13. If you click on the icons, the vSphere client switches to the Triggered Alarms view for that object.

Once you have reviewed the triggered alarms for an object, there are a number of actions that you can take. These include acknowledging the alarm, resetting the alarm, changing the alert, and disabling alarms.

Alarms that have a type of Monitor for Specific Conditions or State have typically been set up to monitor resource usage such as host CPU usage or space consumed on a datastore. With these alarms, as long as the condition that triggered the alarm persists, the alarm remains displayed in the Triggered Alarms view. Only after the alarm condition is resolved is the alarm removed from the list of triggered alarms. For these alarms, you can select the Acknowledge Alarm option. If you right-click on the triggered alarm, you have the option Acknowledge Alarm. Once you have selected the option, the Acknowledged column shown in Figure 6.13 is populated with the time stamp showing when the alarm was acknowledged, and the Acknowledged By column shows the user who acknowledged the alarm. The alarm still appears in the Triggered Alarms view, but it is grayed out. Once the alarm condition no longer exists, the alarm is removed from the view.

The other alarm type is set up to Monitor for Specific Events Occurring on This Object. Examples of this type of alarm include a virtual machine being powered off or a host being noncompliant with its host profile. With this type of alarm, you can also select the Acknowledge Alarm option or you can select the option Reset Alarm to Green as shown in Figure 6.14. This option is useful if vCenter Server does not retrieve an event that indicates that the alarm condition has returned to normal conditions. To reset an alarm right-click on the triggered alarm and select Reset Alarm to Green. The alarm is no longer displayed in the Triggered Alarms view until the alert condition reoccurs.

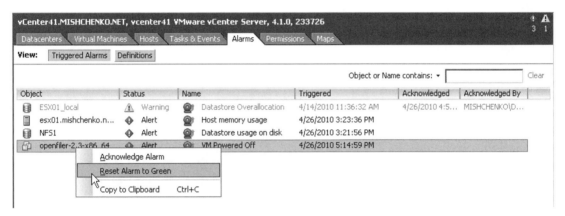

Figure 6.14   Resetting a triggered alarm to green.

In some cases, you might find it appropriate to disable alarm actions. This is a different option than editing an alarm and clearing the Enable This Alarm option. When you disable alarm actions, this is done on a vCenter object. Alarms are still triggered for an object, but the actions associated with the alarms no longer run. When you choose to disable alarm actions for an object, all alarm actions are disabled. However, alarm actions for child objects continue to execute. To disable alarm actions, right-click on the object when connected to vCenter Server and select Alarm > Disable Alarm Actions. You can enable alarm actions by right-clicking on the object again and selecting Alarm > Enable Alarm Actions.

While it is a useful option to disable alarm actions for an object, you may want to do so only temporarily. You can find objects that have had alarm actions disabled by looking in the following places in the vSphere client:

- In the General pane of the object's Summary tab.

- On the object's Alarm tab. If alarm actions are disabled, a warning message is displayed.

- In the Alarm Actions column of an object's child objects tab. This includes the Datacenters, Hosts, Virtual Machines, and Datastores tabs. Each item listed in the view has a status of either Enabled or Disabled for the Alarm Actions column.

Lastly, when managing your alarms, you may want to change an alert. After you create an alarm, you may find that you need to edit the trigger conditions to better match those that are true alarm conditions in your environment. To change an alarm, you select the Definitions view and then right-click on the alarm to select Edit Settings. If you see the View Settings option instead, the alarm has been defined on a parent object and should be edited at that level.

Finding Objects with Alarm Actions Disabled with PowerCLI If you need to find objects that have alarm actions disabled, it can be a tedious task if you have to rely on the vSphere client for that information. With a simple script, PowerCLI can provide a list of vCenter Server objects that have had alarm actions disabled. One of the properties of the get-view cmdlet is AlarmActionsEnabled, which carries a value of False if alarm actions have been disabled. The following sample script queries vCenter Server for a list of clusters, ESXi hosts, virtual machines, folder, datacenters, and datastores. Each list of objects is piped to the get-view cmdlet and the output is queried for objects where the AlarmActionsEnabled property is equal to false.

```
get-cluster | get-view | where {$_.AlarmActionsEnabled -eq $False} | Select
    Name, AlarmActionsEnabled
get-vmhost | get-view | where {$_.AlarmActionsEnabled -eq $False} | Select
    Name, AlarmActionsEnabled
get-vm | get-view | where {$_.AlarmActionsEnabled -eq $False} | Select Name,
    AlarmActionsEnabled
get-folder | get-view | where {$_.AlarmActionsEnabled -eq $False} | Select
    Name, AlarmActionsEnabled
get-datacenter | get-view | where {$_.AlarmActionsEnabled -eq $False} |
    Select Name, AlarmActionsEnabled
get-datastore | get-view | where {$_.AlarmActionsEnabled -eq $False} | Select
    Name, AlarmActionsEnabled

Name                              AlarmActionsEnabled
-----                             -------------------
esx01.mishchenko.net                    False
openfiler-2.3-x86_64                    False
BC                                      False
Toronto                                 False
```

The get-view cmdlet also includes the TriggerAlarmState property. If you query this property, you can find out whether any alarms have been triggered for your vCenter object. The follow example checks a host for any triggered alarms. Note that for each triggered alarm, the get-view cmdlet is called again to translate the alarm object ID, which appears something like alarm105-host18, to its more friendly display name.

```
$esx = Get-VMHost esx01.mishchenko.net | Get-View
    foreach($triggered in $esx.TriggeredAlarmState){
    $alarmDef = Get-View -Id $triggered.Alarm
    Write-Host $alarmDef.Info.Name
    }
```

Working with Performance Charts

Although vCenter Server alarms are great for alerting you to problem conditions or that certain conditions have occurred, the information that they provide is insufficient to deal with problems such as performance response. vCenter Server performance charts allow you to view CPU, disk, memory, and storage metrics for a number of vCenter objects. Chart types include bar charts for displaying datastore storage metrics in a selected datacenter; line charts for displaying metrics for a single inventory object such as network packets received by a host; pie charts for displaying storage metrics for a single datastore or virtual machine; and, lastly, stacked charts for displaying performance metrics for the child objects of a selected parent object.

Performance charts are available on the following vCenter objects: datacenters, clusters, hosts, resource pool, virtual machines, and datastores. When you select one of these options, the performance chart defaults to the Overview layout. The Overview layout summarizes a number of relevant performance metrics for that object. You can also select the Advanced layout. With this layout, you can see data point information for specific performance metrics, customize chart views, and export data for use with other applications. With vCenter Server 4.1, the Advanced layout is available for all of the previously mentioned objects except datastores.

Note: The Overview layout views on the Performance tabs are dependent on the VMware VirtualCenter Management Webservices service running on your vCenter Server host. If you receive any errors when accessing the Overview layout, make sure that the service is running. This is not the case for the Advanced chart layout, but is also the case for the Storage Views and Hardware Status tabs, which will be discussed later in this chapter.

Using the Overview Layout

The Overview layout is the default view when selecting a Performance tab for a vCenter object. It provides a high-level overview of the relevant performance metrics for the object you are viewing. A number of charts are shown at the same time, allowing you to do a side-by-side comparison of resource usage for your chosen vCenter object. Figure 6.15 displays the Space

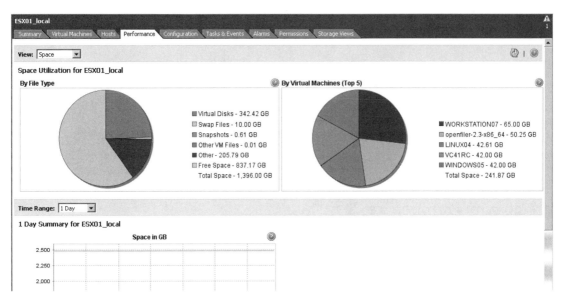

Figure 6.15   The Space view for a datastore on an ESXi host.

view for a datastore on an ESXi host. The two pie charts at the top of the Space view display the space utilization by file type and by the top-five space-consuming virtual machines. The Space view also includes a line chart that summarizes the space being used in the datastore. Most views contain a number of charts that extend beyond what the vSphere client can display, so in most views you need to use the scroll bars to view all the charts provided. Table 6.4 provides a summary of the available views for the vCenter objects for which an Overview performance layout is available. Each Overview layout provides at least one view and you can select the View dropdown menu to choose another view.

For some time-based line charts, you can select the range of data displayed. This is the case with the Space in GB chart shown in Figure 6.15. Depending on the object you are looking at, you can select a range of Realtime, 1 Day, 1 Week, 1 Month, 1 Year, or a custom period. The Realtime range displays the last hour of performance data that the host has generated.

Note: The Overview layout is available only when the vSphere client is connected to vCenter Server. If you are connected directly to an ESXi host, you will only have access to the Advanced layout and only for the host, resource pool, and virtual machine objects. When connected directly to an ESXi host, you are limited to viewing only real-time statistics, which includes the last one hour of performance data.

Table 6.4 Available Views for Various vCenter Objects When Using the Overview Performance Layout

Performance Tab	View Option	Description
Datacenter	Storage	The view summarizes datastore usage, including utilization by datastore, space used by datastore, and line charts showing changes in datastore space usage.
Cluster	Home	The Home view is the default view for clusters. Two charts summarize the CPU and memory usage for the cluster.
	Hosts	This view shows a number of CPU, memory, and disk charts for each host in the cluster. The view also summarizes CPU and memory usage for the top-10 consuming hosts in the cluster.
	Resource Pools & Virtual Machines	This view summarizes CPU and memory usage for resource pools and CPU, memory, and disk statistics for virtual machines. The view also summarizes CPU and memory usage for the top-10 consuming virtual machines in the cluster.
Host	Home	The Host Home view displays a number of summary charts for CPU, memory, disk, and network usage.
	Virtual Machines	This view summarizes CPU, memory, and disk statistics for virtual machines. The view also summarizes CPU and memory usage for the top-10 consuming virtual machines on the host.
Resource Pool	Home	On the Resource Pool Home view, two charts summarize the CPU and memory usage.
	Resource Pools & Virtual Machines	This view summarizes CPU and memory usage for resource pools and CPU, memory, and disk statistics for virtual machines. The view also summarizes CPU and memory usage for the top-10 consuming virtual machines in the resource pool.
Virtual Machine	Home	The Virtual Machine Home view displays CPU, disk, memory, and network performance metric charts for the virtual machine.
	Storage	The Virtual Machine Storage view shows the space utilization by file type, space utilization by datastore and a line chart showing the space used by the virtual machine over a period of time.

(Continued)

Table 6.4   (Continued)

Performance Tab	View Option	Description
Datastore	Space	The Space view is the default view for the datastore Performance tab. It displays the space utilization by both file type and top-five virtual machines. The view also shows a summary of space usage for a selected period of time.
	Performance	The Datastore Performance view includes a number of charts displaying storage-related performance metrics such as I/O operations per second (IOPS) and disk latency.

Using the Advanced Performance Layout

With advanced performance charts, you can customize your charts with the metrics you want to examine more closely. There are a number of customization options you can choose and you can export the performance data to a Microsoft Office Excel Workbook or a number of image file formats.

Figure 6.16 displays the Advanced layout for a VMware ESXi host. In the top-left corner of the image, you can see that the Power performance metrics are being displayed and that the data is being shown in real time. The Chart Options link allows you to configure the data shown in the

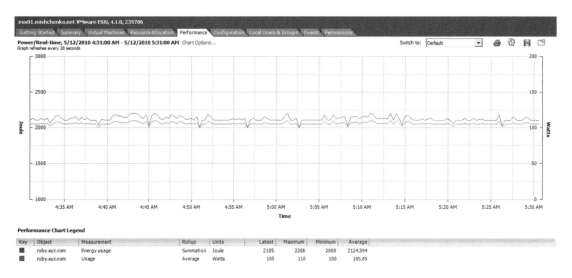

Figure 6.16   The Advanced performance layout for an ESXi host.

chart; you can select the performance metric group to display, the chart type to use, and the time period to display. To the right of the Chart Options link you can use the Switch To drop-down menu to select a performance metric group to display. The available performance metric groups displayed depend on the type of vCenter object that you have selected. A summary of those groups is available in Table 6.5. To the right of the Switch To menu are icons for printing the current chart, refreshing the chart data, saving the chart, and detaching the chart from the vSphere client. The option to detach the performance chart is helpful if you want to keep the performance chart open while you perform other tasks with the vSphere client. You can detach multiple performance charts for side-by-side comparisons. When you select to save a chart, you can save it as an image file or an Excel Workbook. When you save the chart as an Excel Workbook, the spreadsheet is populated with the data points that comprise the chart along with chart that is based on that data.

Enabling Virtual Machine Power Performance Counters VMware ESXi 4.1 introduces a number of new performance metric groups, including the Power group. This group includes the following counters:

- **Energy Usage.** This is the total energy used in watts since the counter was last reset.

- **Usage.** This is the current energy usage in watts.

- **Cap.** This is the maximum allowed power usage in watts.

By default, ESXi gathers Power performance data for the host, but not for any virtual machines. If you edit your performance chart and select to display Power counters for any virtual machines, the chart displays a value of zero for the virtual machine counters. With VMware ESXi 4.1, Power performance counters for virtual machines are supported experimentally. To track energy usage consumed by virtual machines, use the following process:

1. Select the Configuration tab for the host on which the virtual machines are running.

2. Select Software > Advanced Settings.

3. Find the setting Power.ChargeVMs.

4. Change the setting from 0 to 1.

5. Click OK to save your change.

Power charts for virtual machines will now begin to populate with data.

Table 6.5 Summary of vSphere Performance Metric Groups

Performance Tab	Description
Cluster Services	Displays aggregate CPU and memory statistics for DRS and HA failover statistics. This view is available for clusters and hosts that are part of a cluster. Cluster Services does not provide real-time statistics.
CPU	Shows various CPU statistics. Available for clusters, resource pools, hosts, and virtual machines.
Datastore	Displays counters related to datastore performance, such as IOPS and latency. This view is available for hosts and virtual machines. Only real-time statistics are available.
Disk	Storage performance statistics are displayed. This view is available for hosts and virtual machines.
Memory	Displays the amount of memory granted. Available for clusters, resource pools, hosts, and virtual machines.
Network	Shows various network performance statistics. This view is available for hosts and virtual machines.
Power	Displays real-time energy statistics for hosts and virtual machines.
Storage Adapter	Presents real-time write and latency statistics for a host's storage adapters.
Storage Paths	Shows real-time write and latency statistics for each storage path that a host has for each storage logical unit number (LUN).
System	Displays statistics for system availability, CPU usage, disk usage, and memory overhead. This view is available for hosts and virtual machines.
Virtual Disk	Provides real-time write and latency storage statistics for virtual machines.
Virtual Machine Operations	Displays counts for various virtual machine counters, such as power on count, cloning, and vMotion events.

When you select a group of performance counters to view with the Switch To menu, a set of default counters is displayed for the chosen performance metric group. You click on the Chart Options link to change the counters that are displayed as well as the chart type and time period shown. To customize your performance chart, you can follow this process:

1. Select the object you want to obtain performance data for and click the Performance tab.

2. Click Advanced and then select Chart Options.

3. Select the metric group to display.

4. Select a time range for the metric group. Some metric groups such as the Datastore group have only a real-time option, as shown in Figure 6.17. You can select Custom to specify your own time range if desired.

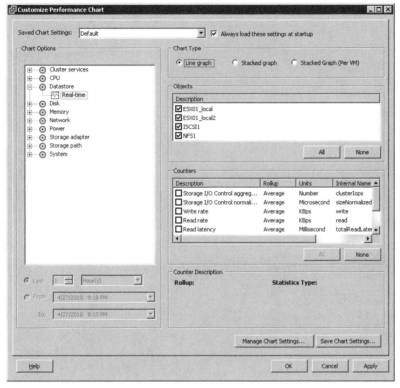

Figure 6.17   Using the Customize Performance Chart dialog box.

5. Select an appropriate chart type for your custom chart. When you select a stacked graph option, you may select only a single performance counter. If you are changing the chart options for a host, you also have the option Stacked Graph (per VM).

6. In the Objects pane, select the inventory objects to display in your chart.

7. In the Counters pane, select the performance counters to display. If you select a counter, information will be displayed about it in the Counter Description panel.

8. Click Apply to update your performance chart.

9. Click OK to close the dialog box and return to your performance chart.

If you plan to use the same chart settings on a continual basis, you can save your settings. Once you have configured your chart settings, click Save Chart Settings. Enter a new chart name in the dialog box that appears and then click OK to save the chart. You can select your new custom chart in the Saved Chart Settings drop-down menu and optionally check Always Load These Settings at Startup to make your new chart the default for when you select the Advanced layout for that specific vCenter object again. Chart settings are saved on a per-vCenter-object basis, so if you save a custom chart for one ESXi host, it will not be available for your other hosts. To delete a custom chart view, click Chart Options for the vCenter object and then select Manage Chart Settings. Select the chart to remove and click Delete. The chart will no longer be available on the Switch To menu.

On a performance chart, you can save the chart data to an Excel file that contains the data for that specific chart. You can also export all performance counters to an Excel file with the following steps:

1. Select the object in the inventory pane.

2. Select File > Report > Performance. The Performance menu option is available only if performance data is available for that specific vCenter object.

3. Select an export filename on the Export Performance dialog box, as shown in Figure 6.18.

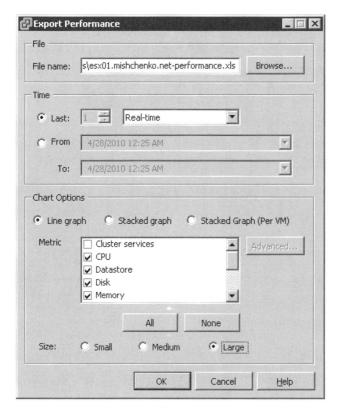

Figure 6.18 Exporting performance data with the vSphere client.

4. Choose a time range for the chart. If you are connected directly to your ESXi host, this option will not be available and you will only be able to download real-time data.

5. Select the chart type.

6. Select the performance metric groups to export. You can optionally click Advanced and then use the Customize Performance Chart dialog box as shown in Figure 6.17 to choose specific performance counters.

7. Select the size of the chart to be created in the exported files.

8. Click OK to export your data.

The export process creates an individual Excel file for each metric group and another Excel file that pulls each of those files into a single Excel workbook.

Note: If you have performed performance monitoring or troubleshooting with VMware ESX, one of the tools you may have used is `esxtop`. This tool is based on the Unix tool `top`. You can use `esxtop` to monitor real-time performance statistics for your host and the virtual machines running on it. As it is a Service Console tool, it is not available with ESXi (it is available in Tech Support Mode, but should not be used for regular production use). Instead, the vCLI provides the tool `rexstop` to use. You'll see how to use that tool in Chapter 8, "Scripting and Automation with the vCLI."

Using VMware Performance Counters with Microsoft Windows

One of the challenges of monitoring virtual machine performance in a virtualized environment is that the virtual machines are sharing various resources without knowing it. On a physical server, the operating system (OS) is aware of the total amount of physical memory that the host has. That's not the case for an OS running in a virtual machine. It is aware of how much memory has been allocated to it, but that memory could be physical memory allocated solely to that virtual machine, or physical memory shared with other virtual machines; or, if the host is running low on memory, the virtual machine's inactive memory may have been swapped by ESXi to disk. Thus when you're troubleshooting performance issues in a virtual machine, you cannot depend solely on the performance counters that the guest OS is reporting.

For Windows guests, VMware Tools includes virtual machine–specific performance counter libraries for the Windows Performance Monitor utility. With these performance counter libraries, you can accurately see virtual machine CPU and memory usage. To access these performance counters with Windows 2008 Server, use the following process:

1. On the Start menu, go to Administrative Tools > Reliability and Performance Monitor.

2. Select the Performance Monitor view.

3. In the Performance Monitor view, click Add.

4. In the Add Counters dialog box, select Local Computer as the source for counters.

5. Scroll down the list of performance metric groups to find VM Memory and VM Processor.

6. Select the performance counters you want to monitor and click Add.

7. Click OK to close the dialog box.

If you consider the issue described previously with memory, when you use native memory performance counters, you can ascertain what the OS believes is happening with memory. If it is low on memory, you can determine that the OS is starting to page memory to disk. But you will not be able to see what the host is doing with memory. With the VMware performance counters, you can see whether the host is swapping the virtual machine's memory to disk. You can also determine the share allocation for memory, if a limit exists and if the memory balloon driver is being used. Likewise, with the VMware CPU performance counters, you can determine things such as actual CPU usage, determine the time that the virtual machine was runnable but not scheduled to run, and whether a CPU limit exists.

---

vSphere 4.1 Memory Compression Memory compression is a new feature in vSphere 4.1 used to further enhance vSphere's ability to perform memory overcommitment and thus to increase the number of virtual machines running on a single host. With memory over-commitment, you can allocate more memory to virtual machines than exists on a host as there will typically be virtual machines that are not using the full allocation of memory granted to them.

With vSphere 4.0 and prior versions of ESXi and ESX, the following three methods were used to reclaim memory from virtual machines: sharing memory across virtual machines, using the memory balloon driver, and using swap files.

A typical workload running on VMware ESXi includes the same guest operating systems, the same applications, and common data. ESXi uses the transparent page sharing (TPS) technique to share memory between those virtual machines. ESXi runs a background TPS process to find and eliminate redundant copies of memory pages. With a fairly constant workload, ESXi can slowly increase the amount of free memory on the host, allowing you to run more virtual machines on that host.

Part of the installation of VMware Tools includes the driver vmmemctl, which enables the memory balloon driver. When a host is running low on physical memory, the memory balloon driver uses a proprietary ballooning technique that causes the guest operating system to determine that it is running low on memory. The guest OS then uses its own native memory management tools to determine which memory pages to reclaim and if necessary which memory pages to swap to its own memory swap file on its virtual disk.

If the `vmmemctl` driver is not responding or able to force the guest OS to free any additional memory, ESXi uses swap files to reclaim memory forcibly from virtual machines. For optimal performance, ESXi relies on the memory balloon driver to reclaim memory before it begins to use swap files.

With ESXi 4.1, compressed memory is a new level in the memory hierarchy existing between RAM and disk swap files. Memory compression is enabled by default, and if a host's memory becomes overcommitted, ESXi uses compression before it uses swap files, as accessing compressed memory is much faster than accessing the same memory page that has been swapped to disk. When a memory page in a virtual machine must be swapped, ESXi first attempts to compress the page. If the page can be compressed to 2KB or smaller, it is stored in the virtual machine's compression cache rather than being swapped to disk. Figure 6.19 shows the quantity of compressed memory per virtual machine for a host that is memory overcommitted.

Memory compression is controlled by using the Advanced Settings dialog box in the vSphere client. There are a number of settings that will control the behavior of memory compression on the host. The setting `Mem.MemZipEnable` is used to enable or disable memory compression and by default is enabled with a value of 1. The setting

Figure 6.19   Performance chart showing memory compression per virtual machine.

`Mem.MemZipMaxPct` is used to configure the size of the compression cache for the virtual machines on the host. The default value is 10 percent. With that value, for a virtual machine with 1000MB of memory, ESXi uses up to 100MB of memory for a compression cache.

Working with Storage Views

The last vCenter Server tool that this section examines is the Storage Views tab. With prior versions of vCenter Server, it was difficult to find information about disk utilization or snapshot usage. With the Storage Views tab, it is now possible to determine information such as the free space for all datastores, the snapshot space being used by individual virtual machines, and the status of all storage paths.

> **Note:** Several requirements must be met before you can use the Storage Views tab in the vSphere client. First, it is available only when connecting to vCenter Server. Second, it is dependent on the VMware VirtualCenter Management Webservices service that runs on your vCenter Server host. Last, the Storage Views tab is delivered as a vSphere client plug-in. The plug-in is installed by default when you install the vSphere client. If the tab is missing, go to Plug-ins > Manage Plug-in in the vSphere client and ensure that the vCenter Storage Monitoring plug-in is installed and enabled.

The Storage Views tab is available on the following vCenter objects: datacenters, datastores, clusters, hosts, resource pools, and virtual machines. The tab provides both a Reports view and a Maps view. The Reports view provides a number of relationship tables that display how the object is related to storage resources and summary storage usage for the object. The Maps view provides storage topology maps that represent the relationships between the vCenter object and its storage resources.

Using Storage Reports

The Reports view on the Storage Views tab provides a number of helpful reports on storage information. If you select the Datastore inventory view and then look at a specific datastore, you can quickly ascertain which virtual machines are using the datastore, which hosts have access to the datastore, and the status of all paths to the storage LUN. Figure 6.20 shows a report for a specific datastore. By default, the report shows which virtual machines are using the datastore, which host the virtual machine is on, what the multipathing status is, how many virtual disks for the virtual machine are on that datastore, the total datastore space used, and how much snapshot space is used for the virtual machine.

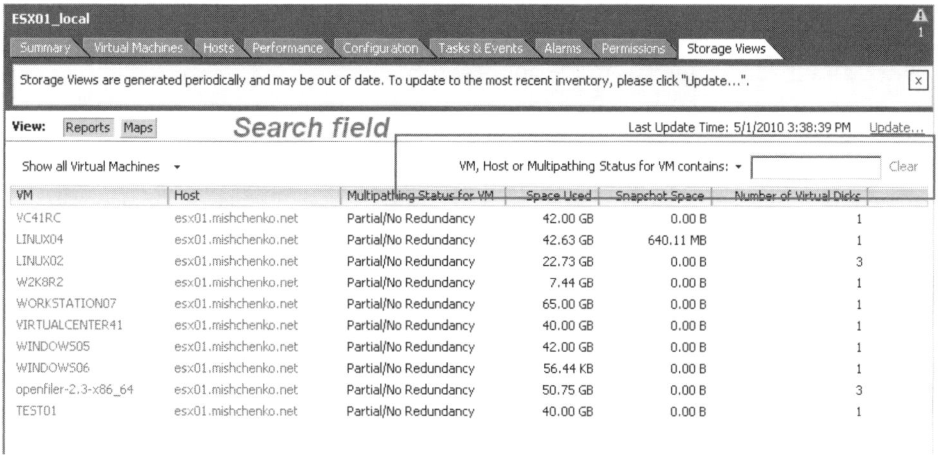

Figure 6.20   A Storage Views report showing space usage by virtual machines.

Note: You'll note in Figure 6.20 that the Last Update Time is displayed for the report. Report data is refreshed every 30 minutes, but you can click the Update link to refresh the data displayed manually.

For each vCenter object, there are a number of specific category report views that you can use. To change the report category, use the Show All < Category Name drop-down menu. Figure 6.20 has the Show All Virtual Machines category displayed, and depending on the vCenter object you have selected, you'll have the choice of the following categories:

- Show All Virtual Machines
- Show All Hosts
- Show All Resource Pools
- Show All Clusters
- Show All Virtual Machine Files
- Show All SCSI Volumes (LUNs)
- Show All SCSI Paths
- Show All SCSI Adapters

- Show All Targets (Array Ports)
- Show All network attached storage (NAS) Mounts

In certain report categories, you'll note that some items are highlighted in blue. In the case of Figure 6.20, the virtual machines and host are highlighted in such a manner. If you click on one of those items, the vSphere client will take you to the Storage Views tab for that specific object. You can also change the columns that are displayed for a specific category. Right-click on the column headings in the Report view and you will be presented with a list of columns to show or hide. With the Show All Virtual Machines category, you can select to view Virtual Disk Space, Uncommitted Space, and other columns relevant to virtual machine storage usage.

If you find that too much data is shown in a certain category report, you can filter the results using the search field shown in Figure 6.20. Click the search field arrow and select the attributes to include in the search. Type in a keyword and press Enter to search the Report view. You can click the Clear link to remove your search filter.

If you want to work with the data in the Report view in another application, you can easily export the data. Right-click below the table data and select Export List menu option. On the Save As dialog bog, enter a filename for your export file, select an appropriate file format, and click OK to save the file.

Using Storage Maps

Storage maps provide a visual representation of the relationships between the vCenter object that you select and the storage resources that it uses. The storage maps display only items relevant to the specific object and are object-centric. As with the Report view map, data is updated every 30 minutes but you can click the Update link shown in Figure 6.21 to refresh the data used to generate the map.

Figure 6.21 displays the storage map for a specific host. Using the Show options, the user has updated the display to show only the datastores available to the host and the virtual machines stored on those datastores. You can select any number of items in the Show area and then click Update Now to update the generated map.

In some cases, you may find the map so cluttered that you cannot properly view all the items. You can right-click on an item and select Hide Node to remove it from the map. To select multiple objects, press the Ctrl key while selecting the objects and then right-click to select Hide Node. To display any hidden objects, right-click on the map and select Show Hidden Nodes. For an alternative to hiding items, you can click one or more objects in the map to select them and then drag them to an empty space on the map.

You can export the map for use in other applications. Right-click on an empty space in the map and select Export Map. You can select among a number of image formats when saving the file.

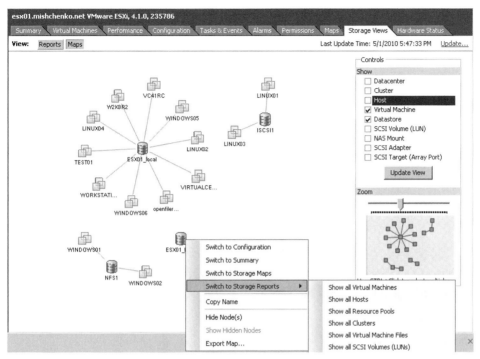

Figure 6.21   A storage map for a host showing connected datastores and virtual machines.

If you want to examine an object in the map more closely, you can right-click on an object to view a number of Switch To options on the context menu. In Figure 6.21, a datastore is selected and you can switch to the Configuration tab, Summary page, Storage Maps view, or one of the Storage Report views for the datastore.

Hardware Management

In earlier versions of ESX, if you wanted to monitor your hardware, you were required to install a Service Console–based agent. For example, if you wanted to monitor and manage an Emulex Host Bus Adapter (HBA), you would need to download and install Emulex's HBAnywhere agent and command-line interface (CLI) within the ESX Service Console. As VMware ESXi is designed to make the server a computing appliance, it runs more like the firmware you would find on a router or storage area network (SAN) rather than a traditional software package. Without the Service Console, it is no longer possible to install hardware agents on ESXi; thus VMware has provisioned Common Information Model (CIM) providers through which monitoring and management tasks can be accomplished. VMware partners are also able to add their own proprietary CIM providers. In the case of monitoring Emulex HBAs, an Emulex CIM provider is included on the ESXi installation media and you can manage your HBAs with HBAnywhere running on a remote management workstation.

What Is the Common Information Model?

To reduce the system footprint and eliminate the need for additional third-party agents, which can introduce instabilities and other problems, VMware has incorporated the standard CIM into ESXi and ESX. The CIM is an open standard that defines how managed elements in your information technology (IT) environment are represented as a set of common objects and the relationships among them. The CIM standard is defined and published by the Distributed Management Task Force (DMTF). Another DMTF standard used is the Web-Based Enterprise Management (WBEM), which defines a particular implementation of CIM, including protocols for discovering and accessing CIM implementations.

The CIM framework consists of CIM providers, which in this case are developed by VMware and its partners to enable management and monitoring of the hardware devices in your vSphere environment. As your hardware environment is represented using an open standard, any management tool that implements the CIM standard can manage your host. Management applications use protocols such as CIM Extensible Markup Language (CIM XML) and Web Services for Management (WSMAN) to monitor and manage the device information provided by the CIM providers. The ESXi CIM implementation consists of the components shown in Figure 6.22.

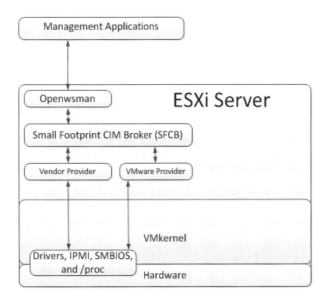

Figure 6.22   The ESXi CIM software architecture.

Providing data to the CIM providers are various components such as the drivers used to interact with your host's hardware, the host's Intelligent Platform Management Interface (IPMI), and the system management Basic Input/Output System (SMBIOS). The CIM providers are used to access the device drivers and the host's hardware. VMware writes providers that implement monitoring of hardware components, the storage infrastructure, and virtualization specific resources. Hardware vendors can also provide CIM providers for their specific devices. In some cases, these provide an interface that can be used to configure hardware devices, such as changing an array on a storage controller. In other cases, these providers extend the information that is available to management applications. While the VMware provider supplies basic information about a host's CPUs, the vendor provider includes CPU temperature and more detailed CPU model and version information. Vendor-supplied CIM providers will either be included on the installation media or added as described in the next section.

Managing the CIM providers is the CIM object manager (CIMOM). The CIMOM can also be referred to as a CIM broker. The CIMOM in ESXi implements the Common Manageability Programming Interface (CMPI) standard. The CMPI standard defines a common standard of interfacing between CIM providers and clients and the CIM broker. VMware ESXi uses the Small Footprint CIM Broker (SFCB), which is designed for environments with constrained resources.

The CIM client running in ESXi is Openwsman, which is an open source implementation of the Web Services Management specification. Openwsman communicates with the CIMOM via the CMPI standard. The Openwsman service in turn exposes CIM data to external CIM clients such as the vSphere client. Openwsman supports CIM connections over CIM XML, WSMAN, and the Service Location Protocol (SLP).

CIM Authentication and Lockdown Mode Before a CIM client can access data or perform operations on an ESXi host, it must first authenticate with the host. The client can authenticate directly with the host by using a login that has been defined locally. The client can also authenticate with a sessionID that is obtained from vCenter Server.

When you grant access to your hosts for a CIM client, it is not advisable to provide root credentials to the application. Instead, you should create a service account that is specific to the application. Whether you create the role directly on the host or in vCenter Server, it should have read-only access to CIM information. If the account requires write access to the CIM interface, the role should be granted the following rights: Host > Configuration > SystemManagement and Host > Config > CIMInteraction.

If you plan to use Lockdown Mode on your ESXi hosts, the CIM client will not be able to authenticate with your hosts directly using an account that is locally defined on the host. In such a case, the CIM client should be configured to authenticate with vCenter Server and it will have to support the ability to acquire a sessionID to be used to authenticate with the ESXi host when it is in Lockdown Mode.

Adding CIM Providers to Your ESXi Host

In Chapter 2, "Getting Started with a Quick Install," the section "Adding CIM Support to the Generic ESXi Installable Image" discussed how hardware vendors have begun to release offline update packages that add CIM support to the VMware release ESXi installation image. These packages use the vSphere Installation Bundle (VIB) format and can be installed on your host to augment the CIM data that will be provided to the CIM clients in your management infrastructure. Without the vendor-supplied CIM providers, you may not be able to obtain detailed health data for your servers and other hardware components.

The following process demonstrates the installation of the Dell OpenManage offline bundle for ESXi:

1. Download the most recent OpenManage offline bundle from Dell's Web site.

2. Place the host in maintenance mode.

3. Execute the following command:

    ```
    vihostupdate --server <IP address or hostname for your ESXi host> --install
      --bundle <path to OpenManage bundle>
    ```

4. Connect to the host with the vSphere client.

5. Select Software > Advanced Settings.

6. In the Advanced Setting dialog box, select UserVars on the left pane.

7. Find the value CIMOEMProvidersEnabled and change the value to 1.

8. Click OK to save your change.

9. Reboot your host.

Monitoring Health Status When Directly Connected to a Host

When you have connected the vSphere client directly to an ESXi host, you can view the health status for the host on the Configuration tab. After you have selected Health Status, the vSphere client displays the status for all hardware components detected by CIM providers, as shown in Figure 6.23.

Components that are functioning normally display a status indicator of green. If a component is not functioning properly or is exceeding a performance threshold, the status indicator changes to yellow or red. A yellow indicator indicates degraded performance, whereas a red indicator means that a component has failed or has exceeded its highest threshold. If the status column for a component is blank, the CIM providers have not been able to determine the status.

The Reading column displays the current value for the sensors. In Figure 6.23, the Reading column displays the temperature of the motherboard in the ESXi host.

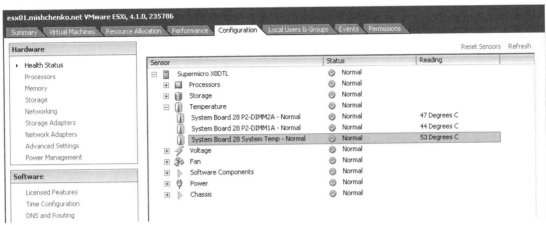

Figure 6.23 Viewing the Health Status page when directly connected to an ESXi host.

The data shown in the Health Status pages is refreshed automatically every few minutes. You can update the display manually by clicking the Refresh link. Some sensors display data that is cumulative over time. You can click the Reset link to clear the data for those sensors so that they begin to collect new data.

Querying Health Data with PowerCLI The sensor data that is displayed on the Health Status page can also be obtained with PowerCLI. The following sample script will retrieve a list of all sensors for the host; the current status of the sensors; and, if applicable, the reading value for the sensors. The script can be run directly against the ESXi host or with the PowerCLI session connected to vCenter Server.

```
$VMHostName = "esx01.mishchenko.net"
$HostView = Get-VMHost -Name $VMHostName | Get-View
$HealthStatusSystem = Get-View $HostView.ConfigManager.HealthStatusSystem
$SystemHealthInfo = $HealthStatusSystem.Runtime.SystemHealthInfo
ForEach ($Sensor in $SystemHealthInfo.NumericSensorInfo) {
 $Report = "" | Select-Object VMHost,Sensor,Status,Reading
 $Report.VMHost = $VMHostName
 $Report.Sensor = $Sensor.Name
 $Report.Status = $Sensor.HealthState.Key
 $Report.Reading = $Sensor.CurrentReading/100
 $Report
 }
```

A portion of the output from the script follows. Note that the output of the Reading column is divided by 100 to make the value returned match what you would see in the vSphere client.

VMHost	Sensor	Status	Reading
esx01.mishchenko...	System Board 28 ...	green	49
esx01.mishchenko...	System Board 40 ...	green	-11.9
esx01.mishchenko...	System Board 37 ...	green	12.29
esx01.mishchenko...	System Board 39 ...	green	5.08
esx01.mishchenko...	System Board 31 ...	green	4624
esx01.mishchenko...	VMware Rollup He...	green	0
esx01.mishchenko...	Management Contr...	green	0
esx01.mishchenko...	American Megatre...	green	0

Monitoring Health Status When Connected to vCenter Server

When you are connected to vCenter Server, the vSphere client no longer displays host health data on the Configuration tab. Rather, this data is now shown on the Health Status tab and the depth of information and functionality of the tab has expanded over what is available when directly connected to the host.

Figure 6.24 shows the hardware status for the same host as was shown in Figure 6.23. The Hardware Status tab includes a System Summary section showing the host's BIOS version, model, serial number, asset tag, and quantity of warnings or alerts. The sensor data is more detailed as well. Figure 6.24 shows the actual temperature for the host's motherboard along

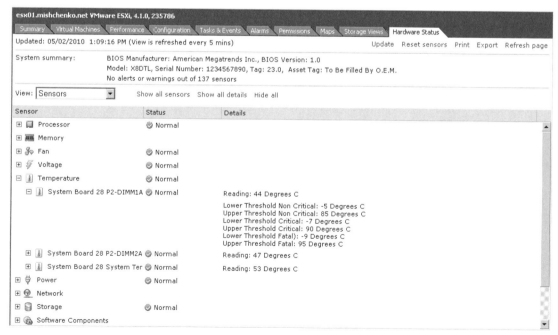

Figure 6.24   Viewing the Hardware Status page for a host when connected to vCenter Server.

with defined threshold values. The Sensors view also provides access to the server's IPMI event log and for this host information about the Baseboard Management Controller's IP configuration and Media Access Control (MAC) address. You can expand or minimize the data shown in the Sensors view by clicking on the following links: Show All Sensors, Show All Details, and Hide All.

The Hardware Status tab also includes two views that are not available when directly connected to your ESXi host. These are the Alerts and Warnings view and the System Event Log view. The Alerts and Warnings view filters all sensor data to display only those sensors that are registering a warning or alert condition. The System Event Log view displays the data in the host's IPMI system log. You can click the Reset Event Log link on that view to clear the IPMI log.

The data supplied in these views is updated every five minutes. You can click Update to update the data manually. Some host hardware sensors display data that is cumulative over time. Click the Reset Sensors link to clear the data for those sensors and begin collecting new data. Hardware Status tab views also include the option to print the data shown or to export the data to an XML file.

Integration with Server Management Systems

If you have a number of servers deployed, it is likely that you have also deployed a server management system. With Dell servers, you may be using Dell OpenManage Server Administrator and Dell Management Console, and with Hewlett-Packard (HP) servers, you may be using HP Systems Insight Manager (SIM) or Insight Control. These applications provide a central location to collect management data about your servers, including information about the base system, its processor, fan, power supply, memory, network, and storage subsystems. Information provided can include properties and health status for the individual devices in your infrastructure, as well as real-time event notifications.

If you've deployed VMware ESX in such a scenario, you have gone through the process of installing agent software in the Service Console, ensuring that dependent components were installed, and then configuring the Service Console firewall to allow agent network traffic to pass. This process can be complicated and lead to problems if you have a number of different agents to install.

With VMware ESXi, monitoring of the host is provided through the CIM interface as described in the previous section. CIM providers come embedded on the installation media. Hardware vendors can provide their own CIM providers to extend the hardware data that can be gathered. Those providers are distributed in easy-to-install VIB packages.

If you have used Dell OpenManage Server Administrator, you will be familiar with the Web-based interface that you access to obtain hardware information for your host and which can be used to manage your host. With ESXi, it is not possible to run the Web server at the console, so that component is moved to a management workstation. The process of providing an Open-Manage Server Adiminstrator interface to your ESXi hosts begins with installing the latest

CIM provider from Dell as was described in the "Adding CIM Providers to Your ESXi Host" section earlier in this chapter.

Once you have completed those steps, you next install the Dell OpenManage Server Administrator Managed Node package onto a Linux or Windows management workstation. The Web server that is installed as part of this package communicates with ESXi through CIM to obtain hardware information, which is then passed onto the Web client as shown in Figure 6.25. When you log in to the Managed Node Web interface, you will be prompted for a host to connect to and login information. You specify the IP address or hostname for your ESXi server and a login that exists locally on your ESXi host.

Figure 6.25 Viewing the Health Status page for a host when connected to vCenter Server.

You may find that not all options are available when accessing your ESXi host with your systems management software. With Dell OpenManage Server Administrator and ESXi 4.0, the following features are not available:

- Alert Management—Alert Actions

- Network Interface—Administrative Status

- Network Interface—DMA

- Network Interface—Internet Protocol (IP) Address

- Network Interface—Maximum Transmission Unit

- Network Interface—Operational Status

- Preferences—SNMP Configuration

- Remote Shutdown—Power Cycle System with Shutdown OS First

- About Details—server administrator component details are not listed under the Details tab

With some of these items, you may find alternative methods to obtain the data or functionality that is missing. SNMP alerts can be configured for ESXi and vCenter Server. Alerts can be configured within vCenter Server or with the host's remote management card.

Regardless of the systems management software that you use, to monitor ESXi the application will have to obtain its data via CIM. Thus it is important to ensure that your host is maintained with the latest CIM providers from your hardware vendor to ensure the most complete set of information is available within the management application. Figure 6.26 shows a typical management view with HP Insight Control/Virtual Machine Manager. Within a single management console, you are provided with a unified view of your physical hosts and the virtual machines running on them. You can manage virtual machines with operations such as start, stop, copy, and clone. If a predictive hardware failure is detected on a host, virtual machines can be automatically moved to other hosts in your infrastructure.

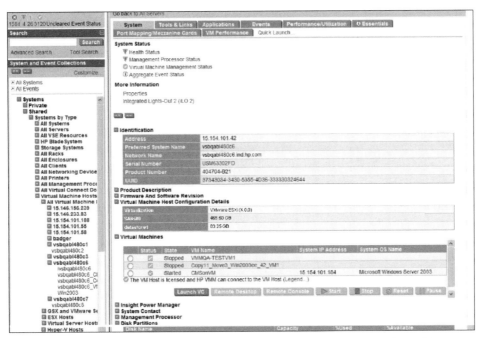

Figure 6.26   Managing your ESXi hosts with HP Insight Control/Virtual Machine Manager.

Host Backup and Recovery

One of the critical elements of managing your ESXi hosts is backup and recovery. Although elements of vCenter Server such as vMotion, High Availability, and Alarms can help mitigate the downtime on your virtual machines due to a host failure, recovery of a failed host is an inevitable task that you will have to perform at some point. This section of the chapter deals with backup and recovery for both your ESXi host and the virtual machines hosted on them.

ESXi Backup and Recovery

As discussed in Chapter 1, "Introduction to VMware ESXi 4.1," ESXi was designed to be more like an appliance firmware than a general-purpose operating system. The thin design to ESXi also applies to the configuration state of the host. Changes made to the configuration of an ESXi host through the application programming interfaces (APIs) are bundled into a single archive file that allows the configuration of a host to persist through a reboot. The data contained in the configuration file state.tgz will be discussed further in Chapter 11, "Under the Hood with the ESXi Tech Support Mode." For now, you only need to know that the single archive file contains the necessary configuration files for your host.

Although the improvements in scripted installs, host profiles, and vNetwork Distributed Switch may seem to negate the requirement to back up the configuration of your ESXi hosts, it is still a worthwhile endeavor to ensure that regular host backups are taken. Backup of an ESXi host is performed with the vCLI command vicfg-cfgbackup.

To back up the configuration of your ESXi host, run the vicfg-cfgbackup as shown in the following example:

```
vicfg-cfgbackup.pl --server esx05.mishchenko.net --save esx05.tgz
```

```
Saving firmware configuration to esx05.tgz ...
```

You will be able to open the backup file with any archive utility that can handle a GZIP-compressed TAR file.

If at some point your ESXi host will not boot into ESXi, you may need to restore your backup configuration, but first you may need to run the recovery process to restore the system files for ESXi. The recovery process is run by booting the ESXi installation media in repair mode. When the installer is run in repair mode, all host configuration data is overwritten by system defaults. If your original install location contained a Virtual Machine File System (VMFS) datastore, it will be preserved.

To run the recovery process on your ESXi host, follow these steps:

1. Boot your host with the ESXi installation CD.

2. At the installer welcome screen, press R to begin the repair process.

3.   Accept the VMware end-user license agreement by pressing F11.

4.   From the Select a Disk screen, choose the disk that contained the original ESXi installation.

5.   Press Enter on the Confirm Disk Selection screen to confirm your choice of the disk to be repaired.

6.   On the Confirm Repair screen, press F11 to process with the repair.

7.   Once the repair process has completed, a status of complete or incomplete will be displayed. In the case of an incomplete status, this may indicate that the repair process could not repair the partition table to recover any existing VMFS datastores. In such a case, you should contact VMware Support before proceeding if you need to recover virtual machine data on the installation target disk.

8.   Reboot the host.

When the host has rebooted, it will have no prior configuration information so it will attempt to acquire an IP address from a Dynamic Host Configuration Protocol (DHCP) server. If you have no DHCP server available, you should use the Direct Console User Interface (DCUI) to set a static IP address for the host. The root password will be blank when you log in to the DCUI. If you had installed custom VIB packages, reinstall those before proceeding. You should also patch the host to the same version of ESXi you used for the last backup. If the same version of ESXi is not installed, you need to use the `--force` option when you run the restore command.

You can then use `vicfg-cfgbackup` to restore a prior configuration backup, as shown in the following example:

```
vicfg-cfgbackup.pl --server 192.168.1.55 --load esx05.tgz

The restore operation will reboot the host.
Type 'yes' to continue:
yes
Uploading config bundle to configBundle.tgz ...
Performing restore ...
```

When the restore process has completed, the host will automatically reboot. After the ESXi host has rebooted, start the vSphere client and connect to vCenter Server. The host will appear grayed out and have a status of Not Responding. Right-click on the host and select Connect. In the Recent Tasks pane, you should see a Reconnect Host task running. If the host is part of a cluster, additional tasks may be initiated to correct the HA or DRS configuration on the host.

If you experience problems starting your host after you have applied a patch or VIB to your ESXi host, it may not be necessary to complete the entire recovery process. As you'll see in Chapter 11, it is possible to roll back to the previously installed version of ESXi.

Backup and Recovery for Virtual Machines

Numerous options are available for backing up your virtual machines. You can use traditional backup agent, custom scripts, or third-party products that utilize the VMware vStorage API for Data Protection. The following section will examine VMware Data Recovery, which is included with various editions of vSphere. Data Recovery is built on the VMware vStorage API for Data Protection and integrates into vCenter Server as a plug-in.

Data Recovery uses a virtual machine appliance to run backup operations and stores backup data within a store that utilizes data deduplication. The store can be on a storage area network (SAN), network attached storage (NAS), or Common Internet File System (CIFS)–based storage. Data Recovery supports Volume Shadow Copy Service (VSS) for Windows servers, including Windows 2008 and 2008 R2, to ensure that applications are properly quiesced to ensure consistent backups.

Installing VMware Data Recovery

Before you begin to install Data Recovery, you should estimate the amount of storage your deduplication stores will require. Each Data Recovery appliance can have two stores each up to 1TB. The total storage you allocate depends on the number of virtual machines you plan to back up, the frequency of backups, and the length of time backups are stored. You should allocate additional free space, which Data Recovery requires for overhead items such as indexing and restore point processing. For initial setup, you should provide a store that is equal to the amount of used disk space within your virtual machines. If you plan to backup 50 virtual machines that all have 40GB virtual disks that are approximately 50 percent full, you should allocate approximately 1TB of storage for your deduplication store.

You'll begin the installation process with the VMware Data Recovery plug-in. On a workstation where you have the vSphere client installed, insert the Data Recovery installation CD and start the installer for the Data Recovery plug-in. Once the installation is complete, you can start the vSphere client and log in to vCenter Server. You should see the VMware Data Recovery icon under Solutions and Applications on the Home page if you have successfully installed the plug-in.

The next step for the installation process is to add the Data Recovery appliance. This is supplied on the installation CD within the VMwareDataRecovery-ovf folder. The image is supplied in the Open Virtualization Format (OVF) format so you can select File > Deploy OVF Template to import the appliance into your vCenter infrastructure. The Data Recovery appliance needs access to port 902 on your ESXi hosts, so plan the network configuration for the appliances to allow that connectivity.

IP Address Allocation When you deploy the Data Recovery appliance, you will be prompted to configure the IP allocation policy to use. The following three choices exist: fixed IP address, IP address allocated by a DHCP server, and Transient. With the Transient policy, IP addresses are automatically allocated to the virtual machine from a vCenter Server–managed IP network range.

vCenter Server uses IP Pools to allocate IP addresses to virtual machines and essentially it acts as a DHCP server. IP Pools are configured at the datacenter level. They define IP and IPv6 address ranges, DNS settings, and proxy server settings. When you create a new pool, you can associate it with one or more virtual machine port groups.

When you import an appliance or vApp created by VMware Studio, you can configure it to use the Transient IP allocation policy. When configured with this policy, the appliance or vApp obtains IP addresses from vCenter Server.

The storage you use for your backup data can be on network storage or virtual disks attached to the Data Recovery appliance. If you plan to use virtual disks, edit the setting for the appliance and add the disk. You can add up to two virtual disks no larger than 1TB each.

Configuring VMware Data Recovery

Once you have completed the installation steps, you are ready to configure the Data Recovery appliance and connect it to vCenter Server. To configure the Data Recovery appliance, use the following process:

1. Power on the virtual appliance and open a console session to it.

2. Log in to the appliance at the console screen as shown in Figure 6.27. The default credentials are root for the username and vmw@re for the password.

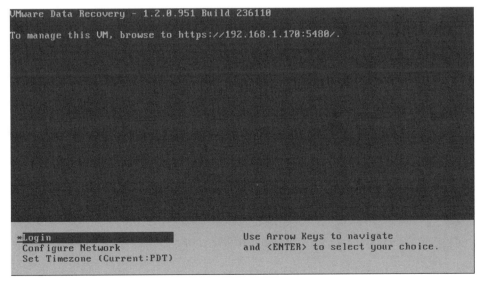

Figure 6.27 The VMware Data Recovery appliance console screen.

3.   Once you have logged in, change the password for the root account with `passwd`.

4.   Optionally you can configure the network settings for the appliance and set the time zone. The console also displays a URL that you can use to manage your appliance. You can log in at the URL to manage the network settings, change the time zone for the appliance, and reboot and shut down the appliance.

5.   Start the vSphere client and connect to vCenter Server.

6.   Select Home > Solutions and Applications > VMware Data Recovery.

7.   Select the Data Recovery appliance, or enter the IP address or hostname for it, and click Connect.

8.   Enter a set of credentials that are to be used to connect to vCenter Server for backup and restore operations.

The Data Recovery appliance is now connected to vCenter Server and ready to perform backups.

Note: When you look in the vSphere client at the status of the Data Recovery appliance, it will indicate that it is not managed by vSphere. This does not indicate that you should install VMware Tools within the appliance. Rather, it indicates that the virtual machine is being managed by Data Recovery.

To set up a backup job, you can use the Getting Started Wizard link found on the Configuration tab, as shown in Figure 6.28. The wizard will guide you through the following steps:

1.   Enter the credentials that the appliance will use to connect to your vCenter Server host for backup operations.

Figure 6.28 The VMware Data Recovery plug-in configuration tab.

2.   Select a backup destination. If you configured a deduplication store virtual disk earlier, this storage is displayed. Click the Format link to prepare it for use with Data Recovery. You'll also see links to Add Network Share and Mount. The Mount option is to attach a virtual disk that was previously used with Data Recovery but whose operation did not format the contents of the virtual disk. In place of virtual disk, you may also use Raw Device Mappings (RDMs).

3.   The Configuration Complete screen shows a summary of your setup and gives you the option to create a new backup job. Check the Create a New Backup Job after Completion option and click Close.

4.   The Backup Wizard starts. On the first screen, you can enter a job name and then click Next to continue.

5.   On the Virtual Machines screen, you can select the virtual machines to include in the backup job. You can use the Virtual Machine Name Contains filter to search for specific virtual machines. Click Next to continue once you have selected the virtual machines that you want to back up as part of this job.

6.   On the Destination screen, you can select a store to use for a backup file. You will have the same options on this screen as you did on the Backup Destination screen in step 2. Click Next to Continue.

7.   On the Backup Window screen, edit the displayed schedule to set backup periods for your backup job. If a backup window is not sufficient to back up all virtual machines, those virtual machines will be given a higher priority in the next backup window. Once you have set your backup windows, click Next.

8.   On the Retention Policy screen, specify the retention policy you want to employ. The retention policy determines how many backups to keep and how long to keep them. Older backups not protected by the retention policy are deleted to make room for new backups. You can select among the predefined policies of Few, More, or Many or create your own custom policy. For the predefined policies, the retention policy details are shown in the More Policy Details section of the screen. Click Next to proceed.

9.   On the Ready to Complete screen, a summary of the backup job is shown. Click Finish to save the backup job.

Once you have created your backup job, you select the Backup tab to view the status of the job. On that tab, you can edit the job, create new backup jobs, and delete existing jobs. You can manually start a backup job by right-clicking on the job and selecting Backup Now. On the Configuration tab shown in Figure 6.28, you can review details for the Data Recovery appliance, manage backup stores, view the time configuration for the appliance, and review the backup log.

Restoring Virtual Machines and Files with VMware Data Recovery

VMware Data Recovery supports restoring virtual machines and virtual disk files as well as individual files from Linux and Windows virtual machines. If you are restoring at the virtual machine level, you have the option to perform an actual restore of the virtual machine or you can run a rehearsal restore, which restores the backup data to another virtual machine to ensure that your backup data is consistent.

To perform a complete restore of a virtual machine, you begin by selecting the virtual machines to restore on the Restore tab of the Data Recovery screen. Then click the Restore link to begin the Virtual Machine Restore Wizard. The first screen of the wizard allows you to select the restore point to use. On the Destination Selection screen, you can change the virtual machine name; select the datastore to be used; and select a host, cluster, or resource pool in which the virtual machine will reside. You can also choose to power on the virtual machine after the restore is completed and whether the virtual network adapter for the virtual machine should be connected or disconnected. The Ready to Complete screen summarizes your restore options and displays how many virtual machines will either be created or overwritten. You can click Restore to begin the restore process. To monitor the progress of the restore job, select the Reports tab and view the Running Tasks report.

A rehearsal restore follows a process similar to the preceding one for restoring a virtual machine. To begin this process, you have to right-click on the virtual machine and select Restore to Most Recent Backup Rehearsal. The same Virtual Machine Restore Wizard runs, but in this case the virtual machine is automatically renamed, you have to select a datastore for the restore files, and the network adapter is set to be disconnected after the restore.

Restoring an entire virtual machine or disk file can be time consuming and cumbersome, and in some cases you may only need to recover a specific set of files. File Level Restore (FLR) provides a way to access individual files within a restore point for Linux and Windows virtual machines. With the FLR client, you can easily extract files from a backup and restore the files to the original or an alternative location.

The FLR client can be found on the Data Recovery installation CD. For the Linux client, you simply extract the TGZ file and execute the client. On Windows, you simply run the executable to start the client. Once the client has started, it can be run in one of two modes. In its regular mode, the FLR client connects to Data Recovery appliance and you can mount a restore point taken for the virtual machine on which you are running the client. If you check the Advanced option on the login screen, you can connect to vCenter Server to enumerate a list of virtual machines that have been backed up by the specific Data Recovery appliance.

After you have selected the mode to run the FLR client in, click Login to connect. You will then see a list of available restore points and virtual disks to use. If you have connected in Advanced mode, you can browse the navigation tree to find the virtual machine from which you want to restore files. Once you have selected the virtual disk to restore files from, click Mount. In Figure 6.29, the

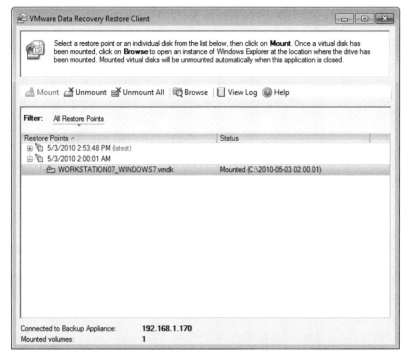

Figure 6.29   Mounting a restore point with the FLR client.

FLR client is running in regular mode on a Windows 7 virtual machine. A restore point has been selected and it is now mounted to the operating system at `C:\2010-05-03 02.00.01`.

Once a restore point is mounted, you can use any operating system tool to access the files in the restore point. The tools that you use have only read-only access to the files in the mounted restore point. If you're accessing restore points for another OS, your OS must be able to mount natively the file system that was used by that virtual machine.

Once you have completed restoring your files, you can click Unmount and then exit the FLR client. If necessary, you can mount multiple restore points and then click Unmount All to detach all the restore points that you have used.

Conclusion

VMware ESXi and vCenter Server provide a feature-rich and robust environment with which you can deploy your virtual infrastructure. ESXi and vCenter also provide a number of tools to help integrate your vSphere infrastructure into your management systems. ESXi can be easily configured to forward log data to a centralized syslog server, providing data for problem resolution and security analysis. Both products support SNMP traps and new to ESXi 4.1 is Active Directory Integration, which eliminates the need to use local accounts to manage your ESXi hosts directly.

vCenter Server provides powerful tools to manage your environment with alarms, performance charts, and storage views. Alarms can be configured to perform actions should certain events occur or be set to send alerts to other management systems. VMware Data Recovery is integrated into vCenter Server to provide a complete disk-based backup and recovery solution. The vCLI provides the ability to back up and restore the configuration of your ESXi hosts quickly. Leveraging the thin design of ESXi, hosts can be reinstalled and restored in a very short time.

VMware ESXi provides agentless monitoring via the implementation of CIM. Hardware vendors can augment the built-in hardware monitoring that ESXi includes by providing custom CIM providers for their specific hardware components. The health of your hardware can be monitored with vCenter Server and the vSphere client or any third-party management tool that supports CIM protocols.

7 Securing ESXi

One of the most critical aspects of managing your VMware ESXi environment is security. ESXi was designed with a focus on providing a secure and safe platform to host your virtual machines. Security is a very complex topic and not something that can be easily summarized with a single chapter. You have already seen a number of topics related to security discussed in earlier chapters, and that will continue to be the case for the remainder of this book. When considering the security of your vSphere environment, you should examine several components, including your ESXi hosts, vCenter Server, network setup, storage access, and virtual machine setup. This chapter will review some of the tools and techniques that are available to secure your environment.

The topics discussed in this chapter include the following:

- ESXi architecture and security features
- Network protocols and ports for ESXi
- Protecting your vSphere environment with firewalls
- Enabling ESXi Lockdown Mode
- Configuring authentication and users
- Replacing ESXi's self-signed SSL certificates
- Configuring IPv6 and IPSec
- Securing network storage
- Securing virtual networking
- Security and clustering
- Isolating virtual machine environments

ESXi Architecture and Security Features

There are two classifications of hypervisors. With a Type 2 or hosted hypervisor, a traditional operating system is installed directly onto the server hardware, and the hypervisor represents a distinct second layer of software. The guest operating systems running in the virtual machines then represent a third layer of software. Examples of Type 2 hypervisors include VMware Server and VMware Workstation. With a Type 1 or bare metal hypervisor, the first software layer is the hypervisor. Examples of Type 1 hypervisors include VMware ESXi, VMware ESX, and Microsoft Hyper-V. The hypervisor directly controls all hardware in the server without the performance impedance of running through a host operating system.

Bare metal hypervisors also enjoy a significant security advantage over Type 2 hypervisors in that they do not come with the security risks of a general operating system. Rather than also needing to provide network services such as file and print services, the hypervisor is designed exclusively for the purpose of running virtual machines. However, even within the available choices of Type 1 hypervisors, there are some significant differences in hypervisor architecture. Some hypervisors such as Hyper-V use a virtualized parent partition to manage the hypervisor layer. This adds another layer of security concern and opens the host to additional security risks that may be embedded within the operating system running in the parent partition. ESXi was designed to approach an embedded firmware model that does not include a management partition and the security risks inherent with that model.

The security focus in the design of ESXi is on the following three separate components: the VMkernel, virtual machines, and the virtual networking layer.

Security and the VMkernel

The VMkernel represents the heart of ESXi, and it is the component of ESXi that provides a virtual interface to the virtual machines that run on your hosts. The VMkernel manages interaction with the host's hardware devices, allocates memory to different processes, and schedules central processing unit (CPU) access. The VMkernel was designed for no other purpose than to run virtual machines, and the API that it exposes is limited to that purpose.

The VMkernel includes the following features to provide a secure environment for virtual machines: kernel module integrity, memory hardening, and the Trusted Platform Module (TPM).

Kernel module integrity consists of digital and module signing. Digital signing is used to ensure the authenticity of integrity of applications, drivers, and modules as they are loaded by the VMkernel. Module signing enables ESXi to identify the developers of applications, drivers, and modules and to verify whether VMware has approved those components.

The purpose of memory hardening is to use memory techniques and modern processor capabilities to protect the system from common buffer overflow attacks that can be used to exploit weaknesses in running code. ESXi uses Address Space Layout Randomization (ASLR) to load the VMkernel, user-mode applications, and executable components such as drivers and libraries at random and unpredictable memory locations. ESXi also takes advantage of Intel XD (eXecute Disable) and AMD NX (No eXecute) support to mark writable areas of memory as non-executable.

TPM provides platform verification during the boot process as well as cryptographic key storage and protection. TPM requires that the server have a special hardware chip installed that contains a unique Remote Supervisor Adapter (RSA) key. Ensure that TPM is properly enabled in the Basic Input/Output System (BIOS) of the host. During booting, ESXi measures the VMkernel using the TPM and stores the value in one of its platform configuration registers. TPM measurements are propagated to vCenter Server when the ESXi host has been added to vCenter, and the measurements can be obtained by third-party agents using the vCenter Server application programming interface (API). In addition to enabling TPM in the BIOS, enable the Misc.enableTboot option shown in Figure 7.1.

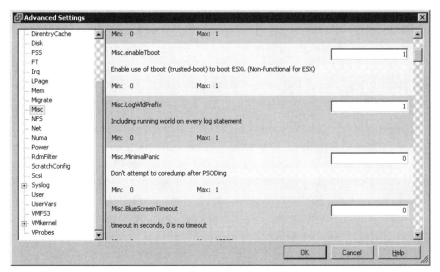

Figure 7.1   Enabling TPM on your ESXi host with the Misc.enableTboot setting.

Security and Virtual Machines

Virtual machines are software containers that encapsulate the necessary components for a guest operating system (OS) to execute. When a guest OS is being installed, it sees a CPU, memory, the network card, and the disk in the same way that it would on a physical host. But these resources are virtualized and thus the guest operating system does not have direct control of the hardware resources in the ESXi host. This design effectively isolates virtual machines from one another. In the case of an OS running on a physical server, an OS failure is isolated to a server's hardware and does not impact other hosts on the network directly. With a virtual machine, it is critical that a failure in the OS be limited to just the virtual machine and that the failure have no impact on the ESXi host or other virtual machines running on that host. The security design of ESXi virtual machines provides this protection.

This protection also ensures that one virtual machine cannot arbitrarily breach the security of another virtual machine or the host. A user operating in one virtual machine will not be able to take advantage of the fact that other operating systems are running virtual on the same host to circumvent their security unless the user has been granted specific privileges on the ESXi host. All access to hardware on the host is made through the VMkernel, which ensures that the environments are kept isolated and that one virtual machine will not be able to control or circumvent processes within another virtual machine.

Virtual machines require the ability to communicate with other virtual machines and physical hosts, and this is done through a virtual network interface card (NIC). A virtual network card (vmnic) is connected to a virtual switch (vSwitch), which can then provide access to your network when the vSwitch is linked to physical adapters in your ESXi host. A virtual machine with a vmnic is not able to bypass the security of your vSwitch design. If the vSwitch to which a virtual machine is connected has not been linked to your network, the virtual machine will effectively be isolated and only able to communicate with other virtual machines on the same vSwitch. Likewise, two virtual machines on different vSwitches on the same host will not be able to communicate with each other unless both vSwitches have been configured to be linked to your physical network through the network adapters in your ESXi host.

To protect virtual machines further, you should consider the use of limits, shares, and resource reservations. This topic was discussed briefly in Chapter 3, "Management Tools." By default, ESXi imposes a form of resource reservation to ensure that the resources of the host are divided equally among the virtual machines running on the host. If a virtual machine on the host were to be compromised by a denial-of-service (DoS) attack, the other virtual machines would be partially isolated from the resource drain caused by the DoS. You could further limit the impact of a problem virtual machine by setting specific reservation and limits. With a reservation, you ensure that a virtual machine has a guaranteed quantity of a specific resource and you could also use a limit to ensure that a virtual machine would not consume excessive hardware resources. For low-resource virtual machines that are accessible to the Internet, you may consider lowering the CPU shares or setting a CPU limit for the virtual machines. In the case of a compromise, the virtual machine would have limited CPU resources to attack other hosts and consume fewer CPU resources on the host.

Security and the Virtual Networking Layer

The virtual networking layer includes both the vmnics used in virtual machines and vSwitches. The networking layer provides network connectivity between virtual machines and other hosts on your network. The networking layer is not just limited to providing network service to virtual machines; ESXi uses it for management, communication with other ESXi hosts and vCenter Server, Internet Small Computer System Interface (iSCSI), and network attached storage (NAS).

With your implementation of ESXi, you need to spend some time carefully planning your network design to ensure that virtual machines are properly placed in the correct vSwitches and to ensure that virtual machines and other ESXi network components are properly isolated and protected from each other. ESXi supports 802.1q virtual local area networks (VLANs), which you can use to protect your virtual machines further and to isolate virtual machines and other ESXi network services even within the same vSwitch.

With the isolation that the virtual networking layer can provide, you can securely deploy ESXi to provide access to virtual machines that need to be placed into a demilitarized zone (DMZ) without compromising the security for your other virtual machines and, as important, without exposing management access to ESXi within the DMZ. DMZ virtual machines are typically exposed to the Internet and represent the virtual machines in your environment that are most open to attack by intruders. If you consider the default installation of ESXi, a single vSwitch is created with a virtual machine port group and a management port. If you want to place virtual machines within your DMZ, you don't want to unplug the network port linked to the management vSwitch and connect that to the DMZ. Rather, create a new vSwitch with a second network port on the host, which would be connected to the physical switch of your DMZ. On this second vSwitch, add a new virtual machine port group for the DMZ. The result would be two isolated vSwitches, and virtual machines on both would not be able to communicate to virtual machines on the other without routing their traffic through an established firewall on your network. Further, no management interface for ESXi would be exposed in the DMZ, and given what you've seen with virtual machine isolation, the ESXi host would be safe from attack from a compromised DMZ virtual machine.

As you add physical NIC ports to your host, you could also create additional vSwitches to isolate network traffic for other virtual machines on different network segments or to isolate ESXi storage network traffic. For additional reading on vSwitch design, an excellent online resource is http://kensvirtualreality.wordpress.com/2009/03/29/the-great-vswitch-debate-part-1/, and the ESXi Configuration Guide contains a best practice guide for various network scenarios.

In some scenarios, you may have a limited number of NIC ports on your ESXi host and with the emergence of 10GB networking, you may be consolidating the virtual networking layer onto fewer NICs. In such a case, you can configure your vSwitches with multiple port groups for various network services and then isolate each within the vSwitch with VLANs. The sample shown in Figure 7.2 has a single vSwitch connected to two physical NIC ports in the host. A number of different network services are provided in this scenario, including the management interface for ESX, the network storage interface for ESXi, and virtual machines hosted in a DMZ. Those are obviously not types of traffic that you would want to mix on the same network segment, as compromising a DMZ virtual machine would open the rest of your network infrastructure to attack. In this case, the traffic types are isolated through the use of VLANs.

You may be wondering about network communication between virtual machines on the same vSwitch. If the virtual machines are separated with VLANs, network traffic between the two virtual machines must leave the vSwitch and will be routed between the two subnets through an existing router or firewall. But for two virtual machines on the same VLAN and vSwitch, the network traffic that passes between the virtual machines receives no protection. You can consider deploying firewalls within your virtual machines or may consider employing virtual

Figure 7.2 Isolating network traffic on a vSwitch with VLANs.

firewalls. VMware vShield App is an example of a hypervisor-level firewall and provides connection control based on network, application port, protocol type, and application type. This product is discussed later in this chapter.

Network Protocols and Ports for ESXi

Network access to VMware ESXi, vCenter Server, and other components in your vSphere deployment is made over predetermined Transmission Control Protocol (TCP) and User Datagram Protocol (UDP) ports. As you explore employing firewalls to protect your infrastructure, identify which ports will have to be opened and how the components of your infrastructure will interact. Figure 7.3 displays the network ports used in a typical vSphere implementation.

vSphere client access is made over TCP port 443 and that can be directed at the vCenter Server or directly to a host if you are managing the host directly. But you should note that the vSphere client also connects to the ESXi hosts on port 902. This network traffic is for virtual machine console access. In the case of using vSphere Web Access, the Web interface is provided by vCenter Server, as this component is not included with ESXi. However, when a vSphere Web Access session opens a virtual machine console session, this connection is made directly to the ESXi, as is the case with vSphere client.

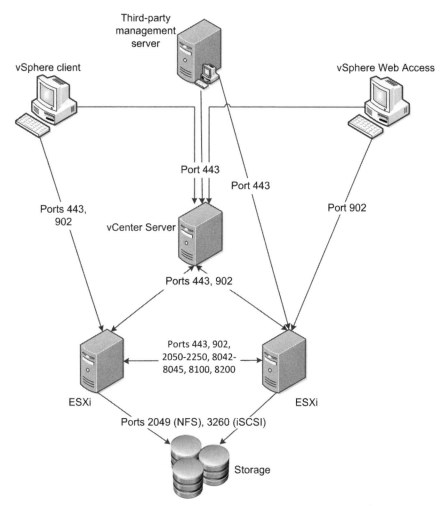

Figure 7.3 Network communication in a typical vSphere environment.

Communication between vCenter Server and the ESXi hosts is also made over ports 443 and 902. You will note that High Availability (HA) traffic is limited to the ESXi hosts only. Once you have configured HA on your hosts, which you'll learn how to do later in this chapter, it is communication among the ESXi hosts that determines HA actions, and the vCenter host is not involved. Your ESXi hosts will also communicate with network storage and, potentially, third-party management tools.

The common ports are summarized in Table 7.1. When configuring your firewalls, you will need to distinguish between TCP and UDP traffic and you should note that in most cases, traffic is unidirectional. The table is not meant to provide an exhaustive list of ports, nor does Figure 7.3 include all the ports that your vSphere environment will use. You can find an exhaustive list in this VMware Knowledge Base article: http://kb.vmware.com/kb/1012382.

Table 7.1 Network Ports for a Typical vSphere Implementation

Port	Description	TCP		UDP	
		Incoming	Outgoing	Incoming	Outgoing
80	HTTP access	X			
	Port 80 is redirected to the HTTPS landing page				
	Web Services for Management (WS-Management)				
123	NTP client				X
389, 636. 1024+	Communication between vCenter Server hosts for linked mode	X	X		
427	Service Location Protocol used by the CIM client to find CIM servers			X	X
443	HTTPS access	X			
	vCenter Server access to ESXi				
	SSL Web port				
	vSphere client access to vCenter Server				
	vSphere client access to ESXi				
	vSphere client access to vSphere Update Manager				
	vSphere Converter access to vCenter Server				
	WS-Management				

Port	Description				
902	ESXi to ESXi for migration and provisioning	X			X
	Authentication traffic for ESXi and remote console traffic				
	vSphere client access to virtual machine consoles				
	Heartbeat connection from ESXi to vCenter Server (UDP)				
1433	vCenter Server and Update Manager access to SQL Server		X		
1521, 1526	vCenter Server and Update Manager access to Oracle Database Server		X		
2049	VMkernel port to NFS storage	X	X		
2050-2250	Traffic for High Availability between ESXi hosts		X	X	X
3260	VMkernel port to iSCSI storage		X		
5900-5943	RFB protocol used by management tools such as VNC	X	X		
5989	CIM XML transactions over HTTPS	X	X		
8000	Requests for vMotion	X	X		
8042-8045	Traffic for High Availability between ESXi hosts		X	X	X
8100, 8200	Traffic for Fault Tolerance between ESXi hosts		X	X	X

Chapter 3 discussed syslogging. If you implement that, the ESXi hosts will be communicating with the syslog receiver over UDP port 514. Likewise, if you're using a third-party tool to monitor the hardware in your ESXi host with Common Information Model (CIM), the management server requires access on TCP port 443. If you enable e-mail alerting in vCenter Server, the server communicates with your mail server on TCP port 25. Chapter 4, "Installation Options," discussed the process for using a Preboot Execution Environment (PXE) server. If you plan to deploy servers via PXE, you need to open ports to the PXE server, the Dynamic Host Configuration Protocol (DHCP) server, and, optionally, a Web or Network File System (NFS) server if you're using scripted installations and a media depot. If you add VMware Data Recovery and Update Manager, they require another set of network ports. That includes both ports between the vSphere client and the server components of those products, between the ESXi hosts and those same server components, and between the server components and vCenter Server.

Protecting ESXi and vCenter Server with Firewalls

Once you have established a good understanding of the network access that various components of your vSphere environment will require, you will be able to plan your firewall deployment to protect those components. Earlier in this chapter, the importance of isolating various types of traffic was discussed. A DMZ virtual machine should have no access, for example, to your storage system. But it is important to consider any host as a potential threat to your vSphere infrastructure. Numerous studies point to insiders as the greater risk to network security than external hackers, and even a virus or instance of malware inadvertently introduced into your environment will pose a risk to any systems it can access.

Firewalls are used to control access to hosts and other network devices by closing all network ports and paths except those specifically configured for the network to function properly. ESXi does not include a firewall because it runs a limited set of well-known services and does not allow the addition of further services. With this design, the need to run a built-in firewall, as is the case with VMware ESX, is significantly reduced in ESXi.

Your deployment of firewalls to protect your vSphere deployment will depend on your security needs. Figure 7.4 shows a number of potential locations for firewalls in a typical vSphere deployment. In this example, all client traffic to the vCenter Server is routed through a firewall. This includes any management applications that will interact with vCenter Server. If you plan to provide remote console access to the virtual machines, you will further have to open your firewall to allow direct access from the client computers to the ESXi hosts for TCP port 902.

You may also consider a firewall between your vCenter Server host and your ESXi hosts. There are a limited number of ports that you have to open for this, but you should keep in mind that modules such as Update Manager and Data Recovery will require additional ports to be open. The sample configuration also has firewall protection between the ESXi hosts and storage devices. Between hosts, the traffic can be considered trusted, but if you have stringent security requirements and are concerned about a breach of your ESXi hosts, you can secure the network

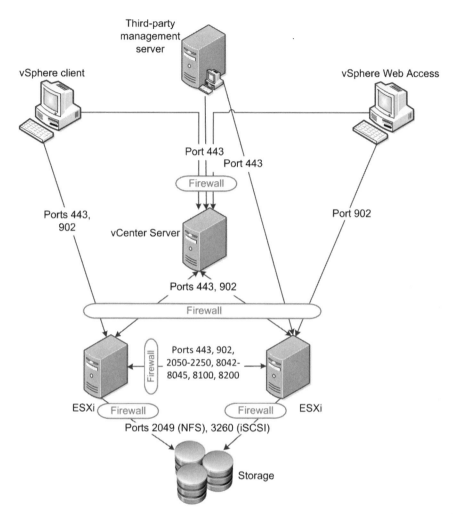

Figure 7.4   Potential firewall location for a typical vSphere deployment.

for HA, vMotion, Fault Tolerance, and other interhost communication. Given that the vCenter Server and vSphere client do not require access to the network used for interhost communication, you may consider physically isolating the network that is used for that traffic. The same consideration can be given to the network used to connect your ESXi hosts to your storage devices.

Caution: For some implementations, administrators are choosing to use a software initiator within a virtual machine to access iSCSI storage rather than relying on vSphere hosts to access the iSCSI logical unit numbers (LUNs) directly. In some cases, this is due to a performance improvement, whereas in others it is to overcome the 2TB LUN limitation of vSphere. If you choose to provide iSCSI storage access to your virtual machines, you should carefully consider the security implications and design your security to protect both your iSCSI servers and your ESXi host from an attack launched from a compromised virtual machine that has access to the storage network.

Modifying the hostd Service The hostd system process provides an interface to the VMkernel and is used by the vSphere client and other applications that access the vSphere API. This process authenticates users and keeps track of local privileges. The process also serves as a reverse proxy for a number of services. In this way, communication to the services can be encrypted as the traffic will be sent over a Secure Sockets Layer (SSL) connection and the services are not directly exposed on the network.

It is possible to edit the hostd configuration file to change the form of communication to a service or to disable external access to the service completely. The file can be copied from the ESXi to your management server with the following vCLI command:

```
vifs --server esx08.mishchenko.net --get /host/proxy.xml proxy.xml
```

To edit this file, you should review the guidelines documented in this Knowledge Base article: http://kb.vmware.com/kb/1017022. Each service is contained in an XML element as shown in this sample proxy.xml file:

```
- <ConfigRoot>
- <EndpointList>
  <_length>10</_length>
  <_type>vim.ProxyService.EndpointSpec[]</_type>
- <e id="0">
  <_type>vim.ProxyService.LocalServiceSpec</_type>
  <accessMode>httpsWithRedirect</accessMode>
  <port>8309</port>
  <serverNamespace>/</serverNamespace>
  </e>
- <e id="1">
  <_type>vim.ProxyService.LocalServiceSpec</_type>
  <accessMode>httpAndHttps</accessMode>
  <port>8309</port>
  <serverNamespace>/client/clients.xml</serverNamespace>
  </e>
- <e id="2">
  <_type>vim.ProxyService.LocalServiceSpec</_type>
  <accessMode>httpAndHttps</accessMode>
  <port>12001</port>
```

```
 <serverNamespace>/ha-nfc</serverNamespace>
 </e>
- <e id="3">
 <_type>vim.ProxyService.NamedPipeServiceSpec</_type>
 <accessMode>httpsWithRedirect</accessMode>
 <pipeName>/var/run/vmware/proxy-mob</pipeName>
 <serverNamespace>/mob</serverNamespace>
 </e>
- <e id="4">
 <_type>vim.ProxyService.LocalServiceSpec</_type>
 <accessMode>httpAndHttps</accessMode>
 <port>12000</port>
 <serverNamespace>/nfc</serverNamespace>
 </e>
- <e id="5">
 <_type>vim.ProxyService.LocalServiceSpec</_type>
 <accessMode>httpsWithRedirect</accessMode>
 <port>8307</port>
 <serverNamespace>/sdk</serverNamespace>
 </e>
- <e id="6">
 <_type>vim.ProxyService.NamedPipeTunnelSpec</_type>
 <accessMode>httpOnly</accessMode>
 <pipeName>/var/run/vmware/proxy-sdk-tunnel</pipeName>
 <serverNamespace>/sdkTunnel</serverNamespace>
 </e>
- <e id="7">
 <_type>vim.ProxyService.LocalServiceSpec</_type>
 <accessMode>httpsWithRedirect</accessMode>
 <port>8308</port>
 <serverNamespace>/ui</serverNamespace>
 </e>
- <e id="8">
 <_type>vim.ProxyService.NamedPipeServiceSpec</_type>
 <accessMode>httpsOnly</accessMode>
 <pipeName>/var/run/vmware/proxy-vpxa</pipeName>
 <serverNamespace>/vpxa</serverNamespace>
 </e>
- <e id="9">
 <_type>vim.ProxyService.LocalServiceSpec</_type>
 <accessMode>httpsWithRedirect</accessMode>
 <port>8889</port>
 <serverNamespace>/wsman</serverNamespace>
```

```
</e>
</EndpointList>
</ConfigRoot>
```

The file contains the following elements:

e id	This is the service ID. Each ID should be unique and if you remove a service, the remaining e id values should be renumbered so there are no skipped numbers.
_type	This is the name of the service.
accessmode	This dictates the form of communication allowed to the service. httpOnly provides only plain-text HTTP access to the service, httpsOnly configures the service to be HTTPS-accessible only, httpsWithRedirect dictates that the service is HTTPS only but will redirect requests to HTTP, and httpAndHttps configures the service to be accessible by both HTTP and HTTPS.
port	This configures the port used by the service.
serverNamespace	This is the namespace for the server that provides the service.

In a highly secured environment, consider allowing services to be accessible over HTTP. In other environments, you may choose to disable the Managed Object Browser service. This service provides an interface primarily for debugging the vSphere software development kit (SDK). This interface could potentially be used to perform malicious configuration changes or actions. To disable the service, remove the following section from proxy.xml:

```
-<e id="3">
  <_type>vim.ProxyService.NamedPipeServiceSpec</_type>
  <accessMode>httpsWithRedirect</accessMode>
  <pipeName>/var/run/vmware/proxy-mob</pipeName>
  <serverNamespace>/mob</serverNamespace>
</e>
```

Then you would have to renumber the subsequent e id values to ensure that the values are consecutive. After you have changed the file, you need to copy the file back to your ESXi host with the vifs command as shown in this example:

```
vifs --server esx08.mishchenko.net --put proxy.xml /host/proxy.xml
```

Once the file is in place, you can access the DCUI to restart the management services or restart the host to apply the configuration change.

Using ESXi Lockdown Mode

To enhance the security of your VMware ESXi hosts, you can enable Lockdown Mode when adding a host to your vCenter Server or after the vSphere client or the Direct Console User Interface (DCUI). Lockdown Mode restricts which accounts are able to manage the host via the following host services: the vSphere API, which is used by the vSphere Client, the vCLI, and other API clients; CIM; Tech Support Mode; and the DCUI. After you enable Lockdown Mode, no account other than vpxuser will have authentication permission or be able to perform operations directly on the host. This requires that you manage your ESXi host using vCenter Server rather than connecting directly with your management tools.

Caution: With ESXi 4.1, all accounts, regardless of privileges, are prevented from making direct host connections with the vSphere client, the vCLI, PowerCLI, or other management tools. This includes both local accounts on the ESXi host and Active Directory (AD) accounts that have been granted permissions directly on the host. Only connections made via vCenter Server, which uses the vpxuser account to connect, are allowed. This may impact other software or management tools that you want to use with ESXi. The root login and other accounts with root privileges may still log in at the DCUI to perform management tasks including disabling Lockdown Mode. This may be necessary in an emergency situation where your vCenter Server is not available.

When you enable Lockdown Mode, this does not affect the services running on the host. Local Tech Support Mode, Remote Tech Support Mode (SSH), and the DCUI services can still be started or stopped independent of Lockdown Mode. Login with either Local or Remote Tech Support Mode will not be possible when Lockdown Mode is enabled. In Local Tech Support Mode, you will receive the error `Login Incorrect`, and with Remote Tech Support Mode, you will receive the error `Access Denied`.

Lockdown Mode can be enabled when you add a host to vCenter Server, as shown in Figure 7.5. You can also enable and disable Lockdown Mode after a host has been added to vCenter Server using the vSphere client or the DCUI.

To enable Lockdown Mode on a host that has already been added to vCenter Server, you can use the following process:

1. Log in to your vCenter Server with the vSphere client.

2. Select the host in the inventory panel for which you wish to enable Lockdown Mode.

3. Select the Configuration tab and click Security Profile.

4. Click the Edit link next to Lockdown Mode.

5. Select Enable Lockdown Mode on the Lockdown Mode dialog box.

6. Click OK to complete the change.

The host enters Lockdown Mode immediately. Any connection made directly to the host via the vSphere API terminates after a short period. Existing Local and Remote Tech Support sessions are

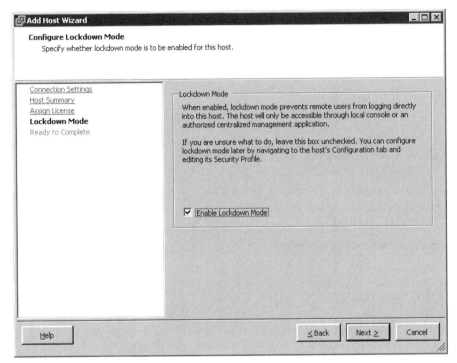

Figure 7.5   Enabling Lockdown Mode when adding a host to vCenter Server.

not closed automatically. If you attempt to log in directly with the vSphere client after Lockdown Mode is enabled, you will receive the error shown in Figure 7.6.

Tip: To audit the disabling of Lockdown Mode and access Tech Support Mode, see the section "Auditing Tech Support Mode" in Chapter 11, "Under the Hood with the ESXi Tech Support Mode."

You can also enable and disable Lockdown Mode with the DCUI. This may be necessary if your host is unable to communicate with vCenter Server and you need to connect with the vSphere client or other tools to correct the problem. The following process can be used to disable Lockdown Mode with the DCUI.

1.   Access the DCUI for your ESXi locally at the console or via a remote management card.

2.   Log in with an account such as root that has access to log in to the DCUI.

3.   Select Configure Lockdown Mode on the System Customization menu and press Enter.

4.   On the Configure Lockdown Mode dialog box, press the spacebar to uncheck the option Enable Lockdown Mode, as shown in Figure 7.7.

5.   Press Enter to complete the change.

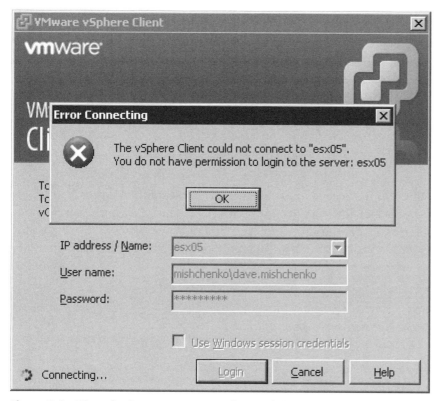

Figure 7.6   Direct login error message after Lockdown Mode is enabled.

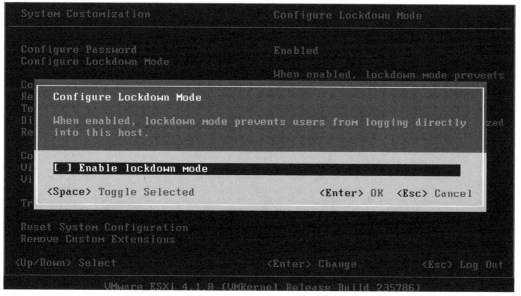

Figure 7.7   Disabling Lockdown Mode in the DCUI.

Caution: It is possible to deny access to the DCUI by stopping the associated service for it. This is possible on the Security Profile screen or with Host Profiles. If the DCUI service is stopped, you cannot log in to the DCUI. This may present a problem should you need to disable Lockdown Mode on a host to allow for a direct connection for troubleshooting purposes. Disabling the DCUI may be appropriate for your ESXi implementation. For example, if you have a host in a remote office, you may not be able to control physical access to that host. However, troubleshooting options may be limited if the host is not accessible via vCenter Server and you will not be able to use the DCUI.

At this point, you will not be able to manage Lockdown Mode as part of the vCLI or PowerCLI, but you will be able to query the lockdown setting with PowerCLI. The following script provides a list of all ESXi hosts that are part of your vCenter Server and displays the lockdown status for the hosts. The `Where { $_.Version -match "ESXi"}` clause ensures that vSphere ESX hosts are not included in the output from the script.

```
Get-View -ViewType HostSystem | Select Name,
@{N="Version";E={$_.Summary.Config.Product.Name}},
@{N="State";E={$_.Runtime.ConnectionState}},
@{N="LockedMode";E={$_.Config.AdminDisabled}} | Where { $_.Version -match "ESXi"}
```

Name	Version	State	LockedMode
esx01.mishchenko…	VMware ESXi	connected	False
esx05.mishchenko…	VMware ESXi	notResponding	False
esx02.mishchenko…	VMware ESXi	connected	False

The ability to enable or disable Lockdown Mode is available for PowerCLI as part of the virtual interface (VI) Toolkit for Windows Community Extensions project, which is available at http://vitoolkitextensions.codeplex.com/. The `Set-TkeVMHostLockdown` cmdlet is included, which allows you to enable Lockdown Mode with the following command:

```
Get-VMHost | Set-TkeVMHostLockdown $True
```

You can disable Lockdown Mode with this command:

```
Get-VMHost | Set-TkeVMHostLockdown $False
```

Comparing Lockdown Mode in ESXi 4.1 versus 4.0 and Earlier When Lockdown Mode was first introduced, the purpose was to prevent root-level access by the vSphere client and other vSphere API tools. With ESXi 4.0 and earlier releases, accessing the host directly would result in the error shown in Figure 7.6. With no locally defined users, the only option for management is through vCenter Server. However, you could still use any locally defined users to log in directly to the ESXi host. This design would prevent anonymous root-level interaction with the host. Effectively, users would have to interact with the host via vCenter or directly with a named account.

With ESXi 4.1, this design has changed, as has been discussed earlier in this section. When Lockdown Mode is enabled on an ESXi 4.1 host, no account other than the vpxuser account will be able to interact directly with the host. As the vpxuser account is encrypted and known only to the vCenter Server, all management tasks must be directed through vCenter Server and you cannot connect directly to the ESXi host with the vSphere client or other vSphere API tools.

The abilities in Normal and Lockdown Mode for user accounts are summarized in the following table:

Service	Normal Mode	Lockdown Mode
VIM	All based on hostd permissions	vCenter only (vpxuser)
CIM	Admin users	vCenter only
DCUI	Root and admin users	Root
Local Tech Support Mode	Admin users	None
Remote Tech Support Mode (SSH)	Admin users	None

Configuring Users and Permissions

With the default installations of VMware ESXi and vCenter Server, a fairly basic access structure is put in place. When connecting directly to your ESXi host with the vSphere client, you log in with the root account. If your host has been configured for AD Integration, as shown in Chapter 6, "System Monitoring and Management," accounts that are part of the AD group ESX Admins will be also able to log in to the host directly. In both cases, you will have full administrative rights on the host. With vCenter Server members of the local administrator, groups on the host will have full control of your vCenter structure. When adding a host to vCenter, the account vpxuser will be created on the host and granted the Administrator role at the host level. All interaction between your vCenter Server and ESXi hosts will be made with that user account.

It is unlikely that this default security implementation will be sufficient for your needs, so you will need to assign additional access to your hosts. VMware ESXi and vCenter Server will use a combination of user account, password, and permissions to determine the access for a user and the authorization that the user has to perform certain actions. Both ESXi and vCenter Server maintain separate user and access lists, but the process of managing users and permissions is the same with both. The next section will discuss the concepts and steps to maintain permissions on a standalone ESXi host. The following section in this chapter will review the processes for vCenter Server and highlight the differences and improvements over managing permissions on a standalone host.

Managing Permissions on a Standalone VMware ESXi Host

Each VMware ESXi host that you deploy will maintain its own list of users, groups, roles, and permissions. To view the default accounts on your host, select the Home > Inventory > Inventory view. Select the Local Users & Groups tab and click Users. You will see the list shown in Table 7.2, and as you will note, it is a much shorter list than with ESX due to the removal of the Linux-based Service Console in ESXi. ESXi likewise has far fewer locally defined groups than ESX. These groups include root, daemon, nfsnobody, nobody, tty, users, and vimuser.

Caution: The vpxuser and dcui users should not be altered in any way. Doing so can create problems when you try to manage the host with vCenter Server or with the DCUI.

Table 7.2 The Default ESXi User Accounts

User	Name	Description
root	Administrator	The root user has full administrative rights on the host. By default, this account will have a blank password and should be set after the installation. This account will be used during the process of adding your ESXi host to vCenter Server.
dcui	DCUI User	The DCUI user is granted the Administrator role at the host level on your ESXi host. The user's primary role is to configure hosts for Lockdown Mode from the direct console. The user is used as the agent for the DCUI and should not be modified or used to log in to your ESXi hosts.
nfsnobody	Anonymous NFS User	This is the system account used to access NFS datastores.
vimuser	vimuser	Vimuser was provided with ESX Server 3.i to allow you to configure a delegate user. This could be necessary when connecting to an NFS server with root squashing enabled. This was experimentally supported and is not available with VMware ESXi 4.1.
vpxuser	VMware vCenter administration account	This account is used by vCenter Server to issue commands to your ESXi host regardless of the end user that is connected to vCenter Server. This account is granted the Administrator role at the host level. This account will be discussed further in the following section.

To create a new user, you can use the following process:

1. Start the vSphere client and log in directly to the ESXi host.

2. From the Home screen, select the Inventory icon to view your ESXi host. You can also use the shortcut Crtl+Shift+H to switch to the Inventory view.

3. Select the ESXi host in the inventory tree and click the Local Users & Groups tab.

4. Ensure that the Users view is selected, and then right-click on a blank space in the Users view and select Add.

5. On the Add New User dialog box, you need to enter a login name and password. It is optional to enter a Username or UID (unique identifier). When the account is created, the next UID will be assigned to the account. You will also notice that there is no option to grant shell access as you would find when creating a local user on an ESX host.

6. You can optionally add to the user any groups that exist by default or that you have created.

7. Click OK to complete the creation of the new user account.

Changing Password Requirements for ESXi The password complexity requirements were discussed in Chapter 2, "Getting Started with a Quick Install." ESXi uses the pam_passwdqc.so module to check for the password strength and is configured with the following parameters:

pam_passwdqc.so retry=3 min=8,8,8,7,6

If your security policy dictates that these settings should be changed, you can edit the file /etc/pam.d/system-auth by accessing Tech Support Mode.

You can find more information on the syntax for the pam_passwdqc.so module at http://linux.die.net/man/8/pam_passwdqc. Modifying the password complexity settings may reduce the security of your ESXi environment. Any changes to the system-auth file should be carefully considered.

Merely adding an account will be insufficient to enable a user to log in to your ESXi host. The account must be granted a role on your ESXi host. Roles are a collection of privileges; when you assign user or group permissions to an object on your ESXi host, you'll grant the user or group a specific role to an object, and that role will define which privileges are granted to the object.

On an ESXi host, there are three predefined roles that cannot be modified or deleted. These roles can be used to assign privileges to your user or as models for more refined roles. Table 7.3 lists the default roles that you will find on your ESXi host.

Table 7.3 Default Roles on an ESXi Host

Role	Description
Administrator	This role has all privileges for all object types. This role allows a user or group to manage any object on the host and can be used to manage roles and permissions for other users. By default, the root login will have the role assigned at the host level. The same will be the case with the dcui user and vpxuser if the host has been added to vCenter Server. If you have enabled AD Integration, the AD group ESX Admins will also be assigned this role at the host level.
Read Only	This role allows a user to see all details and the state of the object to which the permission has been assigned. The user will not be able to perform any actions on the menus or toolbars nor access the console of a virtual machine.
No Access	The No Access role includes no privileges and can be used to deny access to an object. When you are granting permissions, the privileges in the role used are propagated to child objects by default. You can use the No Access role to deny a user access to an object when that user has been granted permissions to a parent object.

Use the following steps to create a new role:

1. Start the vSphere client and log in directly to the ESXi host.

2. From the Home screen, select the Role icon to view the roles defined on your host. You can also use the shortcut Crtl+Shift+R to switch to the Roles view.

3. Click the Add Role button.

4. On the Add New Role dialog box, enter a name for the new role. Then select the privileges that you wish to assign to the role. Figure 7.8 shows some of the privileges appropriate for a virtual machine administrator role.

5. Click OK to complete creating the new role.

When you create a new role, you will observe that there are a significant number of individual privileges that can be assigned to a role. When you select an individual privilege, a short description is shown for it. You can also refer to *The vSphere Datacenter Administration Guide* for a list of required privileges for common tasks.

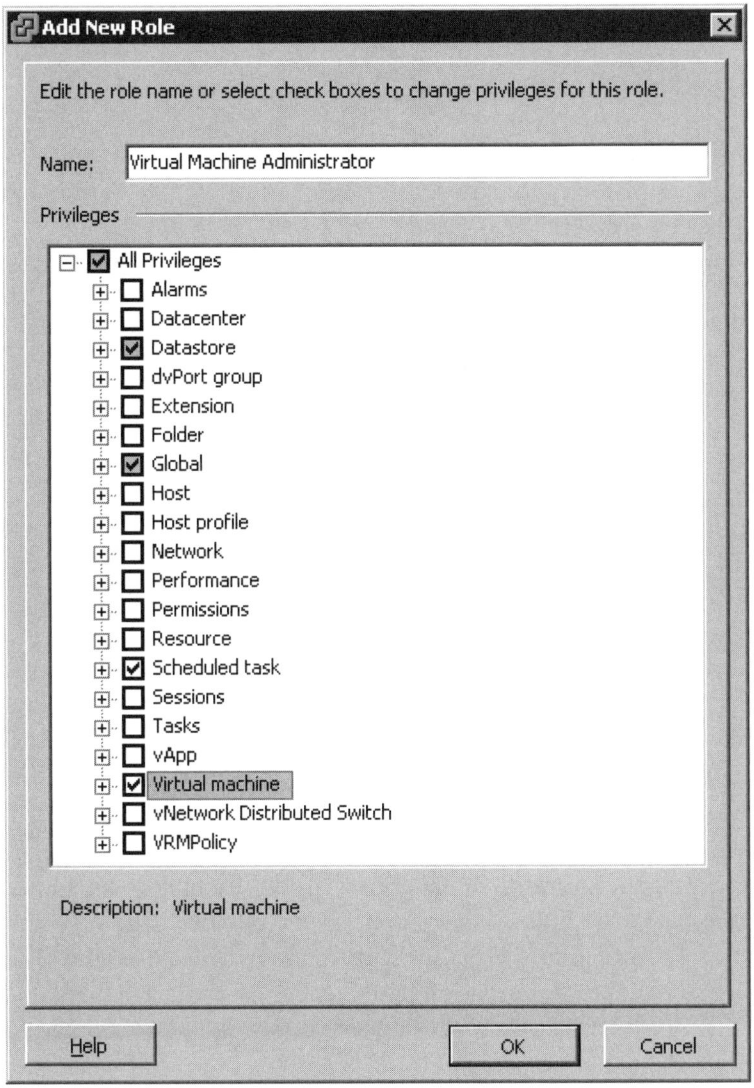

Figure 7.8   Creating a custom role on an ESXi host.

The final step in granting permissions to a user or group consists of granting that user or group a role for an inventory object. For a standalone ESXi host, you can assign permissions to the host, resource pools, or virtual machines. By default, the root and dcui accounts will have the administrator role on all objects on the host. The permission for these accounts is granted at the host level with the Propagate to Child Objects option enabled so that the accounts will have full control of all objects created on the host. When the host is added to vCenter Server, the vpxuser is granted the Administrator role at the host level as well. This is also the case for the AD group ESX Admins when you configure AD Integration.

To assign permissions to an object on your ESXi host, follow these steps:

1. Start the vSphere client and log in directly to the ESXi host.

2. From the Home screen, select the Inventory icon to view your host.

3. Select the object to which you want to grant a new permission and select the Permission tab to view the existing permissions for the object.

4. Right-click on the object and select Add Permission.

5. Click Add on the Assign Permissions dialog box to select the user or group.

6. The Select Users and Group dialog box will open. If you have AD Integration enabled, you can select your AD domain in the Domain drop-down box to select an AD user or group. Once you have selected your user or group, click OK to return to the Assign Permissions dialog box.

7. Select the role for the user or group as shown in Figure 7.9.

8. Click OK to complete assigning the permission.

For a user who has limited permissions on your host, the vSphere client will display only the objects for which the user has permissions assigned. In Figure 7.10, the vSphere client displays only the ESXi host and the specific virtual machine for which the user has been assigned a virtual machine administrator type role. If the user selects the host object, no information will be displayed, and he or she will see the error message You do not have the permissions to access this object. If the user right-clicks on the host, all options will be grayed out. The user will be able to control the virtual machine, but not perform any actions that require host permissions. For example, Figure 7.10 shows no datastore listed, as the required permissions have not been granted. Likewise, the user is not able to modify the permissions for the virtual machine. The Events tab and the Recent Tasks pane will filter information based on the user's permissions. If a user just has permission to a virtual machine, he or she will not see tasks and events related to the host or other virtual machines.

If you need to assign permissions to a number of virtual machines on your standalone host, you may find it cumbersome to manage permissions on each virtual machine. You can use a resource pool to create a folder for your virtual machines and then just assign permissions on the resource pool, which will propagate to each virtual machine. Use the following steps to create a resource pool and to move your virtual machines to it:

1. Start the vSphere client and log in directly to the ESXi host.

2. From the Home screen, select the Inventory icon to view your ESXi host. You can also use the shortcut Crtl+Shift+H to switch to the Inventory view.

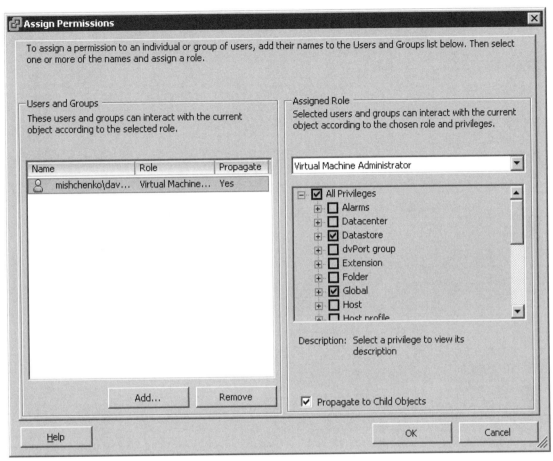

Figure 7.9   Assigning permissions on an ESXi host.

3.   Right-click on your host and select New Resource Pool.

4.   Enter a name for the resource pool. You can set resource limits and reservations, but in this case, doing so is not required, as you're only looking to organize your virtual machines into groups.

5.   Click OK to create the resource pool.

Note: If you are connected directly to an ESXi host that is a member of a cluster in your vCenter farm, you will not be able to create a resource pool directly on the host. For a clustered host, the resource pool should be created when connected to vCenter Server.

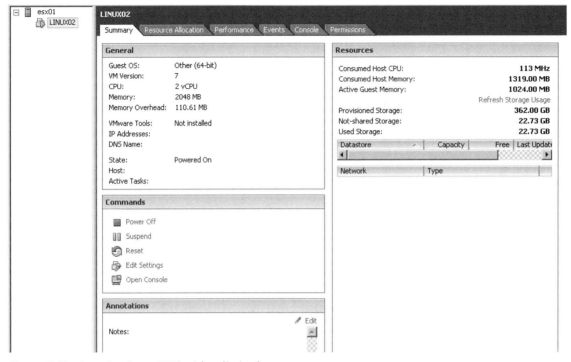

Figure 7.10 Logging in to ESXi with a limited account.

6. To move virtual machines to the resource pool, simply select the virtual machines in the navigation tree and drag and drop them into the resource pool.

7. Right-click on the resource pool and select Add Permissions.

8. Use the preceding process to add permissions to the resource pool. When assigning permissions, ensure that the Propagate to Child Objects option is enabled.

Once the resource pool has been set up with the appropriate virtual machines and permissions have been set for a user to manage the virtual machines in that resource pool, the user will log in with the vSphere client and be able to view only the resource pool and virtual machines in that resource pool. The user's capabilities will be the same as described previously when a user was set up with permissions for a single virtual machine and not the host, as shown in Figure 7.10.

When you move virtual machines, any permissions assigned to them will remain in place after the object is moved into a resource pool. If a virtual machine is assigned the No Access role to a specific user, the user will not have access to or be able to see the virtual machine, regardless of the permissions that were set on the resource pool.

Tip: With both VMware ESXi and vCenter Server, it is possible to assign permissions to both user and groups. As a best practice, it is recommended to use groups over users to assign permissions. This will not only make managing permissions easier but reduce the risk of an individual user maintaining permissions on the host when that is no longer part of the user's role.

After you have established your permissions, you may find the need to review, update, or remove permissions. In the vSphere client, select the Roles view to view the currently configured roles. If you select a role, you will see whether the role is unused and the objects to which the role is assigned. In Figure 7.11, you can see that the Virtual Machine Administrator role is assigned to the XP01 virtual machine and the Production Servers resource pool. A green arrow on the user or group indicates that the permission has been set with the Propagate to Child Objects option enabled. To change the privileges for the role, simply right-click, and then select Edit Role. You can also remove the role by right-clicking and selecting Remove. If the role is currently in use, you will be given the choice to remove role assignments or to reassign the affected users to another role.

Figure 7.11 Viewing permission assignments for a role.

To view permissions for an object in the vSphere client, you select the object, which in the case of a standalone host will be the host, a resource pool, or virtual machine, and then select the Permissions tab. You will be able to view the permissions set on that object and any permissions set on parent objects that have been propagated to the object you are viewing. To remove a permission, right-click on the entry and select Delete. To change the role for a user or group, right-click, and then select Properties. You can then select the new role to use and also change the Propagate to Child Objects option.

Granting DCUI Permissions The root account will be the login you use by default for accessing the DCUI. But your security requirements may prohibit use of the root account, so you will want to grant other logins the ability to use the DCUI.

Any user that is granted the Administrator role at the host level on your ESXi server will be able to log in at the DCUI and manage the host. You can also create a local user with no specific roles on the host, but adding it to the root group will provide the user with the rights to log in at the DCUI.

If you have enabled AD Integration and your account has been granted the Administrator role on the host, you will be able to use that account to log in to the DCUI. You will enter your account as domain\user or in the User Principal Name format of `user@domain`.

The DCUI will use the locally defined permissions on the host to authenticate. If your AD account has been granted the Administrator role in vCenter Server on the host but not on the host itself, you will not be able to log in to the DCUI.

Managing Permissions with vCenter Server

Managing permissions with vCenter Server follows the same process as with a standalone ESXi host. Users or groups are assigned a specific role to an object in vCenter Server. vCenter Server does not rely on the local account on your ESXi host, but rather the domain or workgroup accounts of which the vCenter Server is a member. The number of objects with a standalone host on which you can assign permissions is limited to the host, resource pools, and virtual machines. With vCenter Server, that list is significantly expanded to the following items:

- Clusters
- Datacenters
- Datastores
- Folders
- Hosts
- Networks (except vNetwork Distributed Switches)
- dvPort Groups
- Resource pools
- Templates
- Virtual machines
- Custom fields
- Licenses
- Roles
- Statistics intervals
- Sessions

Given the increase in the number of objects, it is more important to understand the hierarchical inheritance of permissions that is used with vCenter Server. With a standalone host, choosing the Propagate to Child Objects option on permissions causes permissions on the host to be propagated to resource pools and virtual machines. Those objects would have the same permissions as the parent object unless permissions were specifically set on an object. In that case, with both a standalone host and vCenter Server, the permissions on a child object always override the permissions that are propagated from parent objects. With vCenter Server, the permissions hierarchy is more complex and is shown in Figure 7.12. Permissions can be propagated from a number of parent objects, so it is important to review existing permissions carefully when making changes and to plan your hierarchy design carefully to minimize permissions complexity.

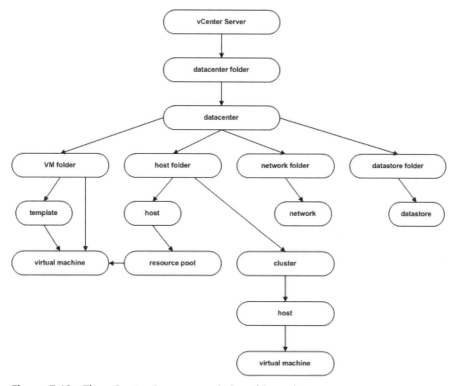

Figure 7.12   The vCenter Server permissions hierarchy.

When you first install vCenter Server and begin to configure it, one of the first things you have to do is to add a datacenter object. This is required before you can add your ESXi hosts. Your datacenter objects can be used to organize hosts by geographical location, department, or other methods of grouping. If your management needs vary by datacenter, you can then organize your permissions at the datacenter level to provide each with a unique set of permissions.

Folders are another addition in vCenter Server that allow you to organize your hierarchy. Folders can be created under the vCenter Server object as well as under any datacenter objects that you create. You can create multiple levels of folders. This expands your options for organizing your vCenter objects as you can create a folder structure to segment your datacenters and then use additional folders under the datacenters to organize clusters and hosts.

It is also worthwhile to be aware that folders can be created within a number of views. Generally, you may deal with the Hosts and Clusters view and create your folder structure there. But you can do the same in the following views: VMs and Templates, Datastores, and Networking. In each view, the folder structure below a datacenter object is unique to the view. In the VMs and Templates view, you can create a folder structure to organize your virtual machines as shown in Figure 7.13. You can also set permissions as appropriate on any of the folders in the hierarchy. The folder structure for the Hosts and Clusters view can reflect different organizational needs and you can set permissions on those folders as needed, as shown in Figure 7.14.

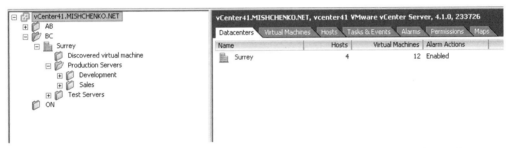

Figure 7.13 Organizing virtual machines with folders in the VMs and Templates view.

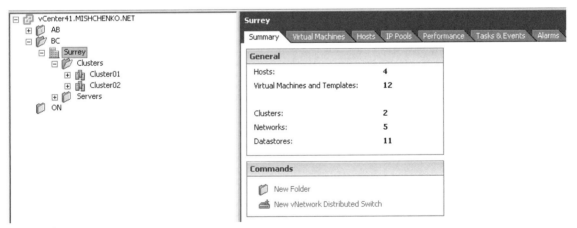

Figure 7.14 Organizing vCenter objects with folders in the Hosts and Clusters view.

With the flexibility that vCenter Server offers in setting permissions on various objects and in different views, it is important to understand how multiple permissions granted will interact. Permissions applied to a child object will always override permissions applied on any parent object. If no permissions are defined for the user or group, permissions propagated from parent objects will be applied. You should note that virtual machine folders and resource pools are equivalent levels in the hierarchy, as shown in Figure 7.12. Permissions for virtual machines will combine the propagating permissions from both objects. In the case of a user belonging to two or more groups that have permissions to an object, the following situations will apply:

- If a permission is defined for the user on that object, the user's permission will have precedence over any group permissions.

- If the user does not have a specific permission on the object, the user is assigned a set of privileges that combines all group roles on that object.

The following examples will demonstrate some various scenarios for permissions and how they interact in different situations. For each of these examples, the following will apply:

- User A belongs to both Group A and Group B.

- Role 1 has the Power On virtual machine privilege, which will allow a user or group to power on or resume on a virtual machine.

- Role 2 has the Create Snapshot privilege.

In the first example shown in Figure 7.15, Group A has been granted Role 1 at the virtual machine folder level, and Group B has been granted Role 2 at the same level. Both have the Propagate to Child Objects option enabled. User A does not have any specific roles granted on any of the objects shown. Since User A does not have any specific permission granted, the user inherits the combined permissions granted to Group A and Group B and is able to power on and create snapshots for both virtual machines.

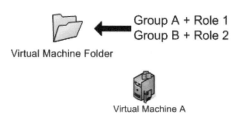

Virtual Machine Folder

Virtual Machine A

Virtual Machine B

Figure 7.15 Inheritance of multiple permissions.

In the second example shown in Figure 7.16, Group A has been granted Role 1 at the virtual machine folder level. Group B has been granted Role 2 on Virtual Machine B. User 1 does not have any specific roles granted on any of the objects shown. In this case, the user will have the ability to power on Virtual Machine A through permission inheritance. However, Role 2 is assigned at a lower point in the vCenter object hierarchy, as shown in Figure 7.12. Thus, for Virtual Machine B, the privileges of Role 2 override the privileges granted in Role 1 at the virtual machine folder level. User 1 is only able to create snapshots on Virtual Machine B.

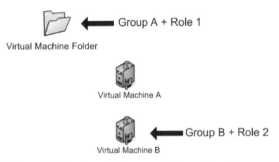

Figure 7.16 Overriding permission inheritance.

The last example, shown in Figure 7.17, demonstrates how user permissions will override group permissions. Group A has been granted Role 1 at the virtual machine folder level. User 1 has been granted the No Access system role at the same level. In this case, the permissions granted to the user override any group permissions and User 1 does not have any access to the folder or the virtual machines. In the vSphere client, the folder and virtual machines would not be visible. If User 1 had been granted the No Access role on Virtual Machine A, User 1 would have been able to power on Virtual Machine B, but would have no access to Virtual Machine A. In the vSphere client, Virtual Machine A would not be visible to User 1.

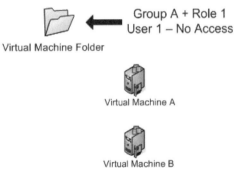

Figure 7.17 User permissions overriding group permissions.

When using vCenter Server and assigning permissions to AD users and groups, it is important to understand how vCenter Server interacts with AD to validate users and groups. vCenter Server validates with AD when the VMware VirtualCenter Server Windows service is started. This occurs when the vCenter host is restarted or if you manually start the service. vCenter Server also periodically validates with AD. The default setting for this is every 24 hours, as shown in Figure 7.18. If a user were to be deleted in the domain, the corresponding permissions in vCenter Server granted to the individual's user account would be removed at the next validation period. If a new account with the same name were to be added before the validation period had occurred, that new account would receive all permissions granted to the old account. Thus it is important to ensure that the Enable Validation setting is enabled and that the Validation Period is appropriate for your domain.

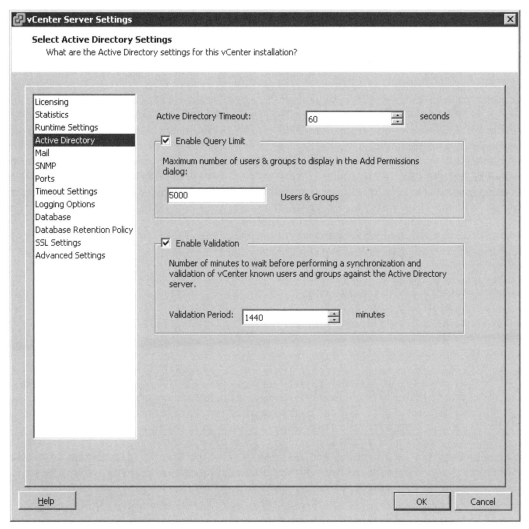

Figure 7.18   vCenter Server Active Directory settings.

To change the validation period for your vCenter Server, use the following steps:

1. Start the vSphere client and connect to vCenter Server.

2. From the Administration menu, select vCenter Server Settings.

3. Select the Active Directory list item.

4. Uncheck Enable Validation to disable periodic validation updates. AD users and groups will still be validated whenever the vCenter Server service is started.

5. If you have validation enabled, you can change the Validation Period by setting a time in minutes.

6. Click OK to save your changes.

The validation period will also have an impact on the removal of permissions granted to users or groups. If you change a group or user name in Active Directory, when vCenter Server validates with AD, it will assume the group or user has been deleted and remove any permissions granted to the AD object. Also when you remove an AD user or group, the permissions will remain listed in vCenter Server until the next validation period.

When assigning permissions with a domain that contains thousands of users or groups, you may find that searches of AD take a long time. You can adjust other settings on the Active Directory vCenter Server Settings screen, shown in Figure 7.18. The settings are listed in Table 7.4.

Managing Permissions with PowerCLI VMware PowerCLI includes a number of cmdlets that can be used to manage permissions with a standalone host or with vCenter Server. The list of cmdlets includes the following:

- New-VIPermission
- Remove-VIPermission

Table 7.4 Active Directory Search List Settings

Setting	Description
Active Directory Timeout	Searching a large domain can take a significant amount of time. This setting will set the maximum amount of time that vCenter Server will allow a search to run.
Enable Query Limit	If this setting is disabled, vCenter Server returns all users and groups from Active Directory.
Users & Groups	This setting specifies the maximum groups and users that vCenter Server displays if the Enable Query Limit option is enabled.

- Set-VIPermission

- Get-VIPrivilege

- Get-VIRole

- New-VIRole

- Remove-VIRole

- Set-VIRole

The following first account run queries the ESXi host for a list of local user accounts. The second command creates a new user account on the host.

```
Get-VMHostAccount
Id              Description              Groups
--              -----------              -------------
root            Administrator            {root}
nobody          Nobody                   {}
nfsnobody       Anonymous NFS User       {}
dcui            DCUI User                {}
daemon          daemon                   {}
vimuser         vimuser                  {}
vpxuser         VMware VirtualCen…       {users}


New-VMHostAccount -Id dave -Password SecUre34 -Description "Admin account"
Id        Description        Groups
--        -----------        --------
dave      Admin account      {users}
```

The Get-VIRole and Get-VIPermission are used to list the roles and permissions that exist on the host or vCenter Server. The output for Get-VIRole distinguishes between system and custom roles. As shown in the output for Get-VIPermission, the option Propagate to Child Objects is listed in the Propagate column:

```
Get-VIRole
Name              IsSystem
----              ----------
NoAccess          True
Anonymous         True
View              True
ReadOnly          True
Admin             True
VM Administrator  False
```

```
Get-VIPermission
EntityId              Role               Principal       IsGroup   Propagate
--------              ----               ---------       -------   ---------
VirtualMachine-48     Virtual Machine    MISHCHENKO      False     True
                      Admini…             \d…
Folder-ha-folder-…    Admin              vpxuser         False     True
Folder-ha-folder-…    Admin              dcui            False     True
Folder-ha-folder-…    Admin              root            False     True
Folder-ha-folder-…    Admin              MISHCHENKO\e…   True      True
```

The New-VIPermission cmdlet can be used to assign a role to an object. The -Entity option specifies the ESXi or vCenter Server object to which to assign the role. You can use get cmdlets such as Get-VMHost or Get-Datastores to list the entities for your host or vCenter Server. In the following listing, the first permission change grants the Read Only role to the user account at the host level. The second permission change grants the custom role VM Administrator to the account for a specific virtual machine:

```
New-VIPermission -Role ReadOnly -Principal dave -Entity esx01
EntityId              Role        Principal     IsGroup      Propagate
--------              ----        ---------     -------      ---------
HostSystem-ha-host    ReadOnly    dave          False        True


New-VIPermission -Role "VM Administrator" -Principal dave -Entity  LINUX02
EntityId              Role                      Principal IsGroup Propagate
--------              ----                      --------- ------- ---------
VirtualMachine-48     Virtual Machine Admini…   dave      False   True
```

You can then use the Get-VIPermission to query your host for permissions that have been granted. The following example uses the -Principal option to filter the output to a specific account:

```
Get-VIPermission -Principal dave
EntityId              Role                Principal       IsGroup    Propagate
--------              ---                 ---------       -------    ---------
VirtualMachine-48     VM Administator     dave            False      True
ComputeResource-h…    ReadOnly            dave            False      True
HostSystem-ha-host    ReadOnly            dave            False      True
ResourcePool-ha-r…    ReadOnly            dave            False      True
```

If you try to add permissions to vCenter Server, you will experience an error similar to the following example:

```
new-vipermission -role admin -principal "Mishchenko\Dave.Mishchenko" -Entity
   ESX05.mishchenko.net
New-VIPermission : 4/17/2010 5:26:19 PM   New-VIPermission       Could not
   find VIAccount with name 'Mishchenko\Dave.Mishchenko'.
```

At the time of writing, PowerCLI included a bug that would not correctly convert an AD principal into a VIAccount object. The following PowerShell function was provided on the VMware Communities forums and can be downloaded from http://poshcode.org/1517. A PowerShell function is code that you intend to use over and over. You can include this function in a script file or simply paste the code and execute it in your current PowerCLI session to have the function active within that session:

```
function New-VIAccount($principal) {
    $flags = '
        [System.Reflection.BindingFlags]::NonPublic    -bor
        [System.Reflection.BindingFlags]::Public       -bor
        [System.Reflection.BindingFlags]::DeclaredOnly -bor
        [System.Reflection.BindingFlags]::Instance
    $method = $defaultviserver.GetType().GetMethods($flags) |
        where { $_.Name -eq "VMware.VimAutomation.Types.VIObjectCore.get_
        Client" }
    $client = $method.Invoke($global:DefaultVIServer, $null)
    Write-Output '
        (New-Object VMware.VimAutomation.Client20.PermissionManagement.
        VCUserAccountImpl '
          -ArgumentList $principal, "", $client)
}
```

To add a permission in vCenter Server, you then process the account name with the New-VIAccount function and use the generated vCenter object within your New-VIPermission statement as shown in the following example:

```
$account = New-VIAccount "Mishchenko\Dave.Mishchenko"
Get-VMHost esx01.mishchenko.net | New-VIPermission -Role Admin -Principal
    $account
```

EntityId	Role	Principal	IsGroup	Propagate
HostSystem-host-18	Admin	MISHCHENKO\D...	False	True

Securing VMware ESXi and vCenter Server with SSL Certificates

Secure Sockets Layer (SSL) is a protocol originally designed by Netscape to enable servers and clients to securely pass information. SSL has been universally accepted on the Internet for authenticated and encrypted communication. The protocol makes use of a system of public and private keys to encrypt communication between hosts. The public key or certificate can be freely passed to any host, but the private key remains secured by the host that it was generated for and it is not shared with other hosts. To encrypt communication, the client and host use the SSL certificate in the following manner:

1. The client sends the server its SSL version number, cipher settings, some randomly generated data, and other information needed to communicate with SSL.

2. The server returns the same information along with its public certificate. If the server requires client authentication, it requests an SSL certificate for the client.

3. Using the data generated by the session, the client creates a premaster secret for the session, encrypts that with the server's public certificate, and sends the encrypted result back to the server.

4. If the server has requested client authentication, the server will attempt to authenticate the client. If the client is successfully authenticated, the server uses its private key to decrypt the premaster key. The server then generates a master secret.

5. Both the server and client use the master key to create session keys. These are symmetric keys used to encrypt and decrypt communication between the two hosts.

6. The client and server both send a message to the other indicating that future messages will be sent encrypted with the session key. A separate message is sent indicating that the handshake is complete.

7. With the handshake complete, the SSL session has begun. Both the client and server use the session keys to encrypt and decrypt data sent. Any data that fails to be decrypted by the session keys is discarded because it may indicate packet tampering by a third host.

Types of SSL Certificates

There are two kinds of SSL certificates that you may deal with in your vCenter Server infrastructure. Self-signed certificates have been generated by the server to which you are trying to connect. Use of self-signed certificates does not indicate that the session data will be less securely encrypted. The client host must implicitly trust the server host to be the server that it claims to be. Some applications will detect a self-signed certificate and warn the user of the situation. The following certificate error is generated when connecting with PowerCLI to a vCenter Server host with a self-signed certificate:

```
Connect-VIServer vcenter41.mishchenko.net
WARNING: There were one or more problems with the server certificate:
* The X509 chain could not be built up to the root certificate.
Name                         Port          User
----                         ----          ----

vcenter41.mishchenko.net     443           Administrator
```

The other kind of SSL certificate that you will encounter is one signed by a certificate authority (CA). A CA can be used by the client and server to confirm the validity of the SSL certificate being sent by the destination host. The CA used can be a well-known and publically trusted CA such as RSA or VeriSign, or it may be an internal CA set up as part of your company's information technology (IT) infrastructure. In either case, the client or server trust the CA to verify the certificate and thus confirm the identity of the other host involved in the SSL session.

SSL Certificates Used by ESXi and vCenter Server

As noted earlier in this chapter, SSL encrypted traffic is used between the vSphere client and hosts, between vCenter Server and ESXi hosts, and, in certain functions, between ESXi hosts. Both ESXi and vCenter Server support SSL v3 and Transport Layer Security (TLS) v1, which will both be referred to as SSL. SSL v3 was released in 1996 and replaced SSL v2, which contained a number of security flaws. TLS was defined in 1999 as an upgrade to SSL v3. The differences between the protocols are not significant, but they are sufficient to make it necessary to prevent interoperation between the two.

Both products also install with a self-signed certificate. In the case of a vCenter Server host, the certificate is issued to VMware Default Certificate and signed by the VMware Installer, as shown in Figure 7.19. With VMware ESXi, the certificate for a default installation is issued to localhost.localdomain, as that is the default hostname after an installation. With a scripted installation, if you set the hostname, the certificate will be issued to the hostname that you have set in the installation script.

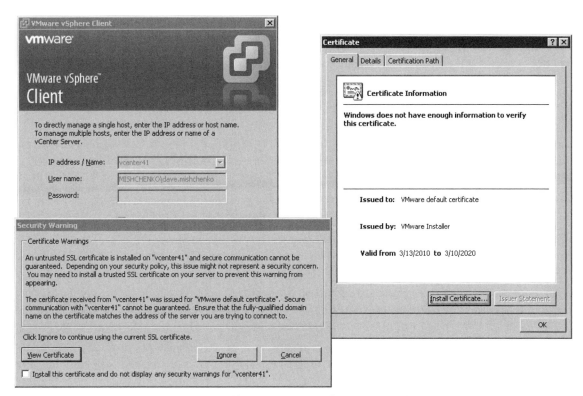

Figure 7.19   vCenter Server creates a self-signed SSL certificate during the installation process.

The Security Warning dialog box as shown in Figure 7.19 provides the following options when connecting to a host that has generated an SSL certificate warning:

- **Cancel.** If you are not expecting a security warning and cannot guarantee that you are connecting to the correct host, select Cancel to close the vSphere connection request.

- **View Certificate.** You can select the View Certificate to view details for the SSL certificate as shown in Figure 7.19. You can optionally choose Install Certificate on the Certificate dialog box to add this certificate to your Windows PC local certificate store.

- **Ignore.** You can select the Ignore option to bypass the warning message and continue connecting to the host. You should choose this option if you are able to verify that you are connecting to the correct host. You will receive the Security Warning dialog box on your subsequent login to the host.

- **Install the Certificate and Do Not Display Any Security Warnings.** If you select this option, an ignore entry will be stored in the registry of the Windows PC that you are using at the following location: HKEY_CURRENT_USER\Software\VMware\Virtual Infrastructure Client\Preferences\UI\SSLIgnore. The certificate will also be stored in the certificate store for the Windows PC running the vSphere client.

When you receive a security warning, the details should be carefully reviewed. In some cases, the warning is generated due to detection of a self-signed certificate. In other cases, it may be that the hostname to which you are connecting does not match the hostname on the SSL certificate. Or it could be that the SSL certificate has expired and thus is no longer valid.

Regardless of the case of using self-signed certificates or a security warning being generated due to an SSL certificate problem, choosing to ignore the warning opens the possibility of a Man in the Middle Attack (MiTM). As noted earlier, even with self-signed certificates, network communication is encrypted and thus protected from casual network sniffing. But if it is not possible to verify the identity of the client or server involved in the SSL handshake, there is the possibility that a third host may launch a MiTM attack.

Replacing the SSL Certificates Used by vCenter Server and ESXi

The following sections describe the process to replace the SSL certificates used by vCenter Server and ESXi with those generated by a trusted certificate authority. The processes use certificates created by a Windows 2003 Server certificate authority that has been set up as the enterprise CA for a Active Directory domain. The certificate requests are generated by the OpenSSL Toolkit, which you can download from this link: http://www.openssl.org/related/binaries.html. OpenSSL is run on a Windows server to generate the requests for both vCenter Server and the ESXi hosts, but you could follow the same process on a Linux server, and many distributions already include OpenSSL. You could likewise use certificates generated by a trusted, well-known CA. For additional information on the certificates used by vCenter Server and ESXi and the options to replace the certificates, you can refer to the *ESXi Configuration Guide* and http://www.vmware.com/pdf/vsp_4_vcserver_certificates.pdf.

To install OpenSSL on a Windows server, use the following process:

1. Open a Web browser and access the site http://www.openssl.org/related/binaries.html to find a download link for Windows binaries of OpenSSL.

2. Download a copy of the Microsoft Visual C++ 2008 Redistributable package. This can be found on http://www.microsoft.com.

3. After you have installed the C++ package, you can install OpenSSL. The default installation options are sufficient.

4. Optionally, you can edit the file openssl.cfg, which can be found in the `bin` folder of your OpenSSL installation. The configuration file contains a number of settings that you can update to match your environment more closely.

Replacing the SSL Certificate for vCenter Server

The certificate files for vCenter Server are stored in `C:\Users\All Users\VMware\VMware VirtualCenter\SSL\`. The files stored in that folder include the private key (`rui.key`), the certificate file (`rui.cer`), and the Personal Information Exchange (PFX) file (`rui.pfx`). Use the following process to create a new SSL certificate for your vCenter Server:

1. Open a command prompt and access the OpenSSL `bin` folder.

2. Run the following OpenSSL command to generate the private key file:

```
openssl genrsa 1024 > rui.key
Loading 'screen' into random state - done
Generating RSA private key, 1024 bit long modulus
..................++++++
............++++++
e is 65537 (0x10001)
```

3. Run the OpenSSL command again using the private key file to generate a certificate request. The critical parameter is the common name, which should match the fully qualified domain name (FQDN) for your vCenter Server host.

```
openssl req -new -key rui.key > rui.csr -config openssl.cfg

Loading 'screen' into random state - done
You are about to be asked to enter information that will be incorporated
into your certificate request.
```

```
What you are about to enter is what is called a Distinguished Name or a DN.
There are quite a few fields but you can leave some blank
For some fields there will be a default value,
If you enter '.', the field will be left blank.
- - - - -
Country Name (2 letter code) [AU]:CA
State or Province Name (full name) [Some-State]:BC
Locality Name (eg, city) []:Surrey
Organization Name (eg, company) [Internet Widgits Pty Ltd]:Mishchenko
Organizational Unit Name (eg, section) []:IT
Common Name (eg, YOUR name) []:vcenter41.mishchenko.net
Email Address []:

Please enter the following 'extra' attributes
to be sent with your certificate request
A challenge password []:
An optional company name []:
```

4. Open a Web browser and access the URL for the Enterprise CA. This is typically http://<CA server>/certsrv.

5. Select the option Request a Certificate and then choose the link to submit an Advanced Certificate Request.

6. Choose the link Submit a Certificate Request by Using a Base-64-Encoded CMC or PKCS #10 File, or Submit a Renewal Request by Using a Base-64-Encoded PKCS #7 File.

7. Copy the contents of the rui.cer file into the Saved Request field, choose a template of Web Server, and then click Submit Request.

8. On the Certificate Issued screen, select Base 64 Encoded and then download the certificate. Save the download to the OpenSSL bin folder and name it rui.crt.

9. Run the following OpenSSL command to create the PFX file:

    ```
    openssl pkcs12 -export -in rui.crt -inkey rui.key -name rui -passout
        pass:testpassword -out rui.pfx
    Loading 'screen' into random state - done
    ```

10. Copy the rui.key, rui.crt, and rui.pfx files to C:\Users\All Users\VMware\VMware VirtualCenter\SSL\.

11. Switch back to the command prompt and change to the vCenter Server folder. This will likely be C:\Program Files\VMware\Infrastructure\VirtualCenter Server. Run

the vpxd command as shown in the following listing to reinitialize the vCenter Server database with the new certificate. You will be prompted for a new vCenter database password.

```
C:\Program Files\VMware\Infrastructure\VirtualCenter Server>vpxd.exe -p
FILE: FileDeletionRetry unmapped error code 32

[2010-06-09 21:51:32.930 04180 info 'Libs'] FILE: FileDeletionRetry unmapped
    error code 32
[2010-06-09 21:51:32.930 04180 info 'App'] Current working directory:
    C:\Program Files\VMware\Infrastructure\VirtualCenter Server
[2010-06-09 21:51:32.930 04180 info 'App'] Log path:
    C:\ProgramData\VMware\VMware VirtualCenter\Logs
[2010-06-09 21:51:32.945 04180 info 'App'] Initializing SSL
[2010-06-09 21:51:32.945 04180 info 'Libs'] Using system libcrypto, version 9080BF
[2010-06-09 21:51:34.273 04180 info 'App'] Vmacore::InitSSL: doVersionCheck = true,
    handshakeTimeoutUs = 120000000
Enter new DB password:
again:
[2010-06-09 21:52:14.929 04180 info 'App'] Reset DB password succeeded.
```

12. Restart the VMware VirtualCenter Server service. This also restarts the VMware VirtualCenter Management Webservices service.

Once you have completed this process, you can start the vSphere client and connect to your vCenter Server. You should no longer experience a certificate error when you start the vSphere client. After you have logged in to vCenter Server, you will observe that all hosts are disconnected. vCenter Server uses the SSL certificate to encrypt and decrypt the password for the vpxuser account, which is used to connect to your ESXi hosts. With a change in SSL certificate, vCenter Server is no longer able to connect to the hosts and they appear disconnected. After you replace the SSL certificate on your hosts, you should reconnect the hosts. Ideally, the virtual machines on the hosts should be powered down for that operation. When you reconnect the hosts, you will be prompted for an administrator login to the host, and after you have authenticated with the host the vpxuser password is reset and saved to the vCenter Server database again after being encrypted with the new SSL certificate. Given the scope of this change, it is worthwhile to ensure that you have a backup of the vCenter Server host and the database before you attempt this procedure.

Replacing the SSL Certificate for Update Manager If you have installed Update Manager, you may have still noticed a certificate warning when connecting to your vCenter Server. This is due to Update Manager using its own self-signed certificate. There is not a supported method that is published at this time to replace your Update Manager SSL Certificate, but you can use the following process to accomplish that. This process assumes that the Update Manager database is hosted on a dedicated database server and that you are not using Microsoft SQL Express. Update Manager stores the SSL files for its services in `C:\Program Files (x86)\VMware\Infrastructure\Update Manager\SSL`. The installation process for Update Manager is documented in Chapter 10, "Patching and Updating ESXI."

1. If you're running Update Manager on the same host as vCenter Server, copy the SSL file that you generated using the process documented earlier to the folder `C:\Program Files (x86)\VMware\Infrastructure\Update Manager\SSL`. If you are running Update Manager on another host, use the same process to create a new set of files for the SSL certificate.

2. Uninstall Update Manager. To prevent a reboot of the host, stop the two Update Manager services before starting the uninstall process.

3. Reinstall Update Manager with the exact same settings that you used initially to install the product.

4. After you supply your Update Manager database credentials, you will see the Database Re-initialization Warning screen, as shown in Figure 7.20. Choose the default option of Do Not Overwrite, Leave My Existing Database in Place.

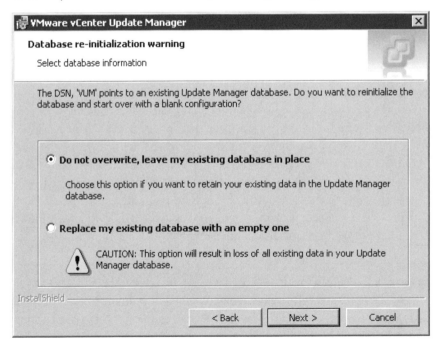

Figure 7.20 Keeping the existing database during the reinstallation of vCenter Update Manager.

5.   Complete the installation process.

6.   Start the vSphere client and connect to the vCenter Server with which Update Manager is registered. Verify that your previous configuration settings are still in place.

Replacing the SSL Certificate for ESXi

The process for replacing a certificate on an ESXi host is very similar to the process for vCenter Server. For ESXi, only the private key (rui.key) and the certificate file (rui.cer) file are copied to the ESXi host with vifs from the vCLI. ESXi does not require the PFX file (rui.pfx). These files are stored in /etc/vmware/ssl as well as in the configuration backup file that ESXi uses to maintain configuration settings between reboots. Use the following process to create a new SSL certificate for your ESXi host. You should generate a unique rui.key and rui.crs file for each of your ESXi hosts.

1.   Open a command prompt and access the OpenSSL bin folder.

2.   Run the following OpenSSL command to generate the private key file:

```
openssl genrsa 1024 > rui.key
Loading 'screen' into random state - done
Generating RSA private key, 1024 bit long modulus
..................++++++
.............++++++
e is 65537 (0x10001)
```

3.   Run the OpenSSL command again using the private key file to generate a certificate request. The critical parameter is the common name, which should match the fully qualified domain name for your vCenter Server host.

```
openssl req -new -key rui.key > rui.csr -config openssl.cfg

Loading 'screen' into random state - done
You are about to be asked to enter information that will be incorporated
into your certificate request.
What you are about to enter is what is called a Distinguished Name or a DN.
There are quite a few fields but you can leave some blank
For some fields there will be a default value,
If you enter '.', the field will be left blank.
- - - - -
Country Name (2 letter code) [AU]:CA
```

```
State or Province Name (full name) [Some-State]:BC
Locality Name (eg, city) []:Surrey
Organization Name (eg, company) [Internet Widgits Pty Ltd]:Mishchenko
Organizational Unit Name (eg, section) []:IT
Common Name (eg, YOUR name) []:esx08.mishchenko.net
Email Address []:

Please enter the following 'extra' attributes
to be sent with your certificate request
A challenge password []:
An optional company name []:
```

Note: ESXi does not support pass-phrase SSL certificates. Such a certificate will prompt a user for a password each time the server process using the certificate starts. With ESXi this will cause service failures, and the host will not operate properly. If you are using OpenSSL, you should enter nothing for the A Challenge Password field.

---

4. Open a Web browser and access the URL for the Enterprise CA. This is typically http://<CA server>/certsrv.

5. Select the option Request a Certificate and then choose the link to submit an Advanced Certificate Request.

6. Choose the link Submit a Certificate Request by Using a Base-64-Encoded CMC or PKCS #10 File, or Submit a Renewal Request by Using a Base-64-Encoded PKCS #7 File.

7. Copy the contents of the rui.cer file into the Saved Request field, choose a template of Web Server, and then click Submit Request.

8. On the Certificate Issued screen, select Base 64 Encoded and then download the certificate. Save the download and name it rui.cer.

9. Run the following command to convert the certificate to the x509 format:
    openssl x509 -in rui.cer -out rui.crt

10. Copy the rui.key and rui.crt to the host with vifs from the vCLI:
    vifs --server esx08.mishchenko.net --put rui.key /host/ssl_key
    Uploaded file rui.key to ssl_key successfully.
    vifs --server esx08.mishchenko.net --put rui.crt /host/ssl_cert
    Uploaded file rui.crt to ssl_cert successfully.

11. Access the DCUI and restart the management services for the host. The new certificate will be loaded when the services restart.

After you have replaced the SSL certificate on your host, you will need to reconnect your host to vCenter Server. Right-click on the ESXi host and select Connect. You will receive an error that the host cannot be reconnected due to a login failure. Click OK and the Add Host wizard will begin to allow you to reconnect your host.

Enabling Certificate Checking and Verifying Host Thumbprints

With vCenter Server, you can enable verification of host SSL certificates. This option is enabled by default and it is recommended to leave this setting enabled. The verification process affects operations such as adding a host, connecting to a virtual machine, and making virtual machine devices remotely available. This option is required for Fault Tolerance to operate.

To verify the SHA1 thumbprint of certificates on hosts, follow this procedure:

1. Start the vSphere client and connect to vCenter Server.

2. Select Administration > vCenter Server Settings.

3. Select SSL Settings in the left pane and check the vCenter Requires Verified Host SSL Certificates option.

4. For hosts that require verification, the SHA1 thumbprint will be displayed as shown in Figure 7.21. Compare that to the value shown in the DCUI as displayed in Figure 7.22. If you don't have DCUI access, you can download the certificate file from the ESXi host with `vifs` and then run the following OpenSSL command to generate the SHA1 thumbprint:

   ```
   openssl x509 - -in rui.crt - -fingerprint - -sha1 -noout
   ```

5. If the values match, check the Verified option.

6. Click OK to close the window.

Caution: If you enable the vCenter Requires Verified Host SSL Certificates option and then leave hosts unverified, those hosts will be disconnected from vCenter Server.

Configuring IPv6 and IPSec

Internet Protocol Security (IPSec) is a protocol suite designed to secure Internet Protocol (IP) communications by authenticating and encrypting each IP packet of a data stream between two hosts. IPSec includes protocols to establish mutual authentication between hosts at the start of a session and negotiation of cryptographic keys to be used to transmit data during a session. IPSec is integrated into the Internet layer (Layer 3 of the Open System Interconnection

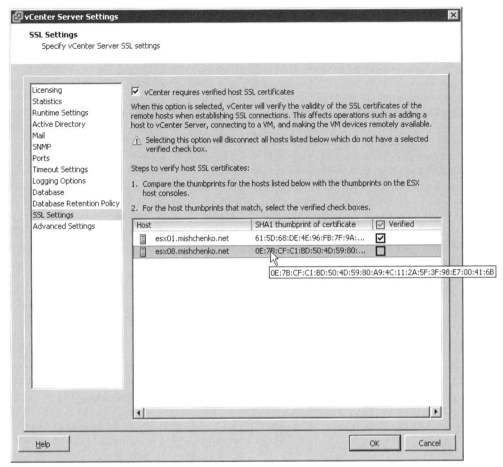

Figure 7.21   Enabling host certificate checking by vCenter Server.

model) and thus can function transparently to the applications that are running on the hosts. IPSec provides a defense in depth against the following security concerns:

- Data corruption
- Data theft
- User credential theft
- Network-based attacks from untrusted computers, such as denial-of-service attacks and replay attacks

To set up a secure path for communication using IPSec, two hosts perform the following tasks:

1.   The hosts agree upon a set of security protocols to use.
2.   The hosts decide on the specific security algorithm to use to encode data.

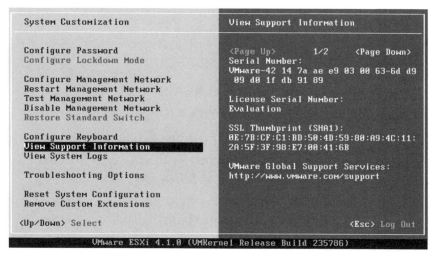

Figure 7.22 Checking an ESXi host's thumbprint in the DCUI.

3. The hosts exchange keys that are used to decrypt data that has been received from the other host.

4. After the IPsec session has been established, the hosts use the protocols, methods, and keys previously agreed upon to transfer data in a secure manner.

VMware ESXi 4.1 introduces support for IPSec using Internet Protocol version 6 (IPv6). IPSec is not supported for Internet Protocol version 4 (IPv4). The significant difference between IPv4 and IPv6 is the address length. IPv4 is limited to a 32-bit address whereas IPv6 uses a 128-bit address, which alleviates the current Internet problem of address exhaustion. The IPv6 implementation in ESXi supports addresses assigned by DHCP, configured by stateless configuration, sent by router advertisements, and entered statically. Before you can configure IPSec on your ESXi host, you must first enable IPv6, which is disabled by default. You can use the following process to enable IPv6 on your host. It is also possible to enable and configure IPv6 for the management network using the DCUI as shown in Chapter 3.

1. Start the vSphere client and connect to your ESXi host. You can connect directly to the host or to the vCenter Server managing the host.

2. Select the Configuration tab.

3. Select Networking under Hardware.

4. In the Virtual Switch view, click the Properties link.

5. Enable the option Enable IPv6 Support on This Host System and click OK as shown in Figure 7.23.

6. Right-click on the host and select Reboot.

7. After the host has rebooted, return to the Configuration tab for the host and select the Networking link again.

8. Click the Properties link for the virtual switch that contains the management network.

9. Select the Management Network port and click Edit.

10. Select the IP Settings tab and you will see the IPv6 configuration settings as shown in Figure 7.24. You can enable the host to obtain an IPv6 address from a DHCP server, through Router Advertisement, or set a static IPv6 address.

11. Optionally, you can click Edit to set an IPv6 VMkernel Default Gateway. You can click Advanced to view addresses assigned via DHCP or Route Advertisement.

12. Click OK and then Close to save your changes.

Figure 7.23   Enabling IPv6 support with the vSphere client.

Once you have enabled your ESXi host for IPv6, you are ready to configure IPSec. Configuration of IPSec is performed with the vCLI command `vicfg-ipsec`. In the following examples, a host is configured to secure vSphere client traffic with IPSec and also to block certain types of traffic and other hosts from communicating with your ESXi host.

When you enable IPsec on your host, you configure both authentication and encryption of incoming and outgoing network packets. There are two elements to enabling this setup. First, you create a security association that determines how the system will encrypt traffic. A security association includes the source and destination IPv6 addresses, encryption parameters, and a name for the security association. The second element is a security policy. The policy determines when the host should encrypt, discard, or allow traffic to pass unencrypted. A policy includes the source and destination IPv6 addresses, the protocol, and the direction of traffic that should be encrypted, and the mode and security association to use.

To begin the process of configuring IPSec, you run the following command to create a security association between the host, which has an IPv6 address of `2001:0F68::1986:69AF`, and the management server which has an IPv6 address of `2001:0F68::1986:69AD`:

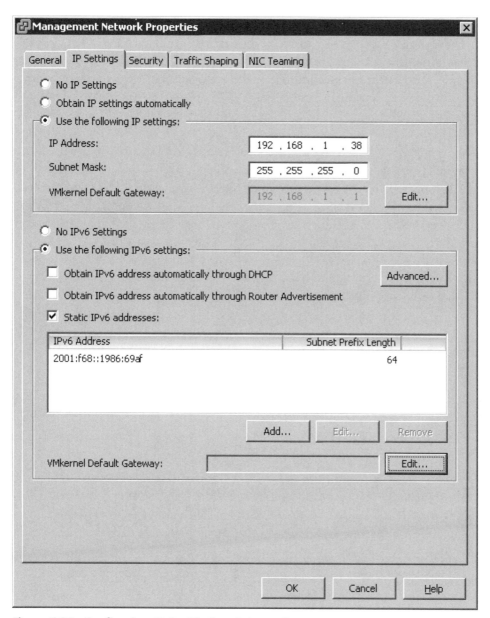

Figure 7.24   Configuring IPv6 with the vSphere client.

```
vicfg-ipsec --server esx08.mishchenko.net --add-sa --sa-src 2001:0F68::1986:69AD
    --sa-dst 2001:0F68::1986:69AF --sa-mode transport --spi 0x1000
    --ealgo 3des-cbc
    --ekey 0x6970763672656164796c6f676f336465736362636f757432
    --ialgo hmac-sha1 --ikey 0x6970763672656164796c6f67736861316f757432
    sa1
```

The parameter --add-sa indicates that the command is going to create a new security association on the host. The option --spi is used to create a security parameter index. The security parameter index is used to identify the security association to the host. It must be a hexadecimal value and a prefix of 0x. Each security association that you create on the host will have a unique combination of protocol and security parameter index. The --ealgo option indicates the encryption algorithm that will be used; you have an option between 3des-cdc, aes128-cbc, and none. The --ialgo parameter indicates the authentication algorithm, and the options are hmac-sha1 and hmac-sha2-256. The -ekey option is the encryption key used by this security association. The value is specified as a hex value and preceded with 0x. Lastly, the parameter -ikey is the authentication key. This is also a hex value. For authentication, ESXi supports the use of pre-shared keys. Both hosts involved in the IPSec session must be configured with the same authentication key. When establishing a session, the hosts compute and exchange a keyed hash of data that includes the pre-shared key. If the receiving host is able to create the same hash using its pre-shared key, it is able to determine that both hosts share the same authentication key. If your vicfg-ipsec command has a syntax error, the following error is returned. If the security association is created, no output will be generated.

```
Could not add Security Policy: A specified parameter was not correct.
```

To view the security association that you created, you can run the following command:
```
vicfg-ipsec --server esx08.mishchenko.net --list-sa
```

```
SA Name    Src Addr        Dst Addr        State    SPI
    Mode     Encrypt Algo  Auth Algo    Soft Lifetime Hard Lifetime
sa1       2001:f68::1986:69ad 2001:f68::1986:69af mature   0x1000
    transport 3des-cbc      hmac-sha1      infinite    infinite
```

IPSec Encryption Algorithms An IPSec session utilizes one set of algorithms for connection negotiation using the Internet Key Exchange (IKE) protocol and another set to encrypt all data traffic using the Encapsulating Security Payload (ESP) protocol.

For authentication purposes, the IPSec implementation in ESXi 4.1 can make use of HMAC-SHA1 and HMAC-SHA2. HMAC stands for Hash-based Message Authentication Code. HMAC-SHA1 and HMAC-SHA2-256 are key hash algorithms that are constructed from a Secure Hash Algorithm (SHA) hash function. The HMAC process mixes a secret key with data, hashes the result with the SHA hash function, mixes that hash value with the secret key again, and then applies the hash function a second time. The output hash is either 160 or 256 bits in length. The SHA computes a hash that is a unique value of fixed size representing a large amount of data. The SHA1 algorithm has a size of 160 bits, and for SHA2-256, the size is 256 bits. Any changes to the data result in a different hash, so tampering or corruption is easier to detect.

Since both hosts involved in the exchange of data share the same secret key, both can calculate the same hash values for the same data. When data is sent from one host to another, the sender calculates the hash value and sends it with the data. The receiving host recalculates the hash value and accepts the data as valid only if the sent and computed hash values match.

ESXi supports two algorithms for encryption. Triple DES (3DES) is the common name for the Triple Data Encryption Algorithm (TDEA). This algorithm applies the DES cipher three times to each data block. 3DES was designed as an improvement over DES to protect against the increasing risk of brute-force attacks, which require a completely redesigned cipher. The second algorithm, the Advanced Encryption Standard (AES), is a symmetric key encryption standard that has been adopted by the United States government. The AES algorithm starts with a random number and the data is then encrypted through a process of multiple mathematical processes.

When you create a security association for ESXi, each of the authentication and encryption algorithms requires an encryption key. These keys are required to be in hexadecimal format and require a specific key length. Those requirements are specified in Table 7.5.

Table 7.5 Algorithm Key Length Requirements

Algorithm	Number of ASCII Characters	Number of Hexadecimal Characters
hmac-sha1	20	40
hmac-sha2-256	xx	hh
3des-cbc	24	48
aes128-cbc	16	32

To create a security policy, you can use the `vicfg-ipsec` command with the option `--add-sp`. This policy enables IPSec encryption on vSphere client traffic coming from the management server to the ESXi host. The policy also includes the source and destination addresses, but in the case of creating the policy, you must include the prefix length as shown in the following example. The policy also includes the source and destination ports. The source port is specified as 0, as the originating port is dynamically allocated by the management computer when the vSphere client initiates a network connection. The `-ulproto` parameter specifies the upper-layer protocol; in this case, it is tcp. The traffic direction is specified by the --dir option, and in this case, the --action parameter is ipsec. Other options for --action include discard, which will drop the traffic matching the policy, and none, which allows matching traffic to pass unencrypted. The policy is set to use transport mode and it is linked to the security association called sa1. Lastly, the security policy is named sp1.

```
vicfg-ipsec --server esx08.mishchenko.net --add-sp
    --sp-src 2001:0F68::1986:69AD/128 --sp-dst 2001:0F68::1986:69AF/128
    --src-port 0 --dst-port 443 --ulproto tcp --dir in --action ipsec
    --sp-mode transport --sa-name sa1 sp1
```

Once you have created a security policy, you can run the following command to review the security policies that exist on the host:

```
vicfg-ipsec --server esx08.mishchenko.net --list-sp
```

```
SP Name    Src Addr           Src Port  Dst Addr           Dst Port
   Protocol  Flow     Action    Mode     SA Name
sp1        2001:f68::1986:69ad/128 0        2001:f68::1986:69af/128 443
   tcp      in       ipsec     transport sa1
```

At this point, your management server cannot connect to your ESXi host, as ESXi requires communication via IPSec with the vSphere client. When you attempt to connect with the vSphere client, an error message similar to Figure 7.25 is displayed. Setup of IPSec varies between operating systems and network devices. The following example shows the setup for IPSec on Windows 2008 Server. This setup assumes that IPv6 has already been correctly configured on the host.

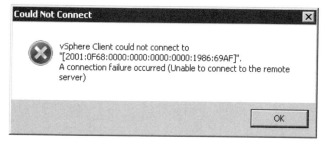

Figure 7.25 Connection error after IPSec is enabled only on the ESXi host.

1. Open a Microsoft Management Console (MMC) windows by selecting Start > Run and entering mmc.

2. Select File > Add/Remove Snap-in and then add the span-in IP Security Policy Management. The snap-in should be opened for the Local Computer.

3. Right-click on IP Security Policies on Local Computer and select Manage IP Filter Lists and Filter Actions.

4. On the Manage IP Filter Lists tab, click Add to create an IP filter.

5. Enter a Name and Description for the new filter. Then click Add to create the IP filter.

6. The IP Filter wizard starts. Optionally, enter a Description and click Next.

7. On the IP Traffic Source screen, change the Source Address to My IP Address and click Next.

8. On the IP Traffic Destination screen, select A Specific IP Address or Subnet and enter the IPv6 address for your ESXi host. Click Next to continue the wizard.

9. On the IP Protocol Type screen, you can change the Protocol Type to TCP and then click Next.

10. Select the option To This Port and enter a value of 443. The source port should be left as From Any Port. Click Next to complete the wizard and then Finish to close it.

11. You should now see the new IP Filter List as shown in Figure 7.26. Click OK to close the window.

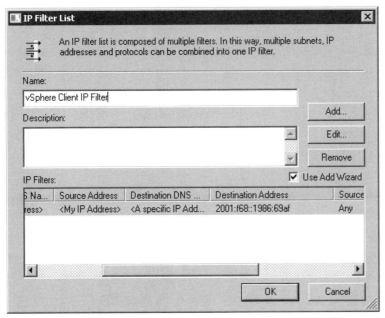

Figure 7.26   Creating an IP Filter List for IPSec on Windows Server 2008.

12. Select the Manage Filter Actions and click Add.

13. Enter a Name and Description for your filter action and click Next.

14. The default choice on the Filter Action General Options screen is Negotiate Security. Click Next to continue. Similar to the security policy you created on ESXi, the other action options are Block, to drop traffic that matches the filter, and Permit, to allow matching traffic to pass unencrypted.

15. The Do Not Allow Unsecured Communication is fine on the Communicating with Computers That Do Not Support IPSec screen. The other option to allow unsecured communication if a secure connection cannot be established will not work with the configuration that has been established on ESXi.

16. Choose the option Integrity and Encryption on the IP Traffic Security screen and click Next.

17. Click Finish to save your new IP Security Filter.

18. The Manage Filter Actions tab should now display the filter action that you created. Click Close to dismiss the Manage IP Filter Lists and Filter Actions window.

19. Right-click on IP Security Policies on Local Computer and select Create IP Security Policy.

20. The IP Security Policy wizard begins. Click Next to continue.

21. Enter a Name and Description for the policy and click Next.

22. Click Next on the Requests for Secure Communication screen as the default setting is sufficient.

23. Click Finish to close the wizard. The Edit Properties check box is enabled, which brings up the properties for the policy for further editing.

24. Click Add on the Rules tab to start the Security Rule wizard.

25. Click Next on the Security Rule welcome screen to proceed.

26. Click Next on the Tunnel Endpoint, as the default option of This Rule Does Not Specify a Tunnel is correct.

27. The default choice of All Network Connections on the Network Type screen is fine. Click Next to continue.

28. On the IP Filter List screen, select the IP filter that you created earlier and click Next.

29. On the Filter Action screen, select the filter action that you created and click Next.

30. On the Authentication Method screen, select the option Use This String to Protect the Key Exchange (Preshared Key). When you created the security policy on ESXi, the value specified for the pre-shared key was in hexadecimal format. The value that is entered on

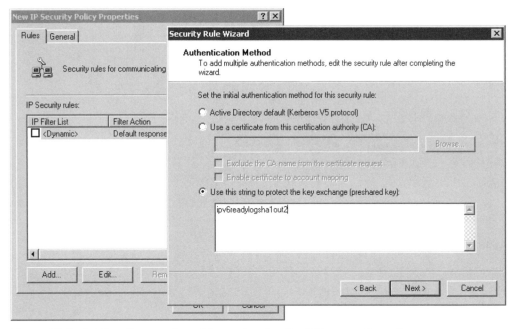

Figure 7.27   Setting the pre-shared key value for the IPSec security policy.

the Authentication Method screen is entered as ASCII text, as shown in Figure 7.27. Click Next to Continue.

31.   Click Finish to save the new security rule.

32.   The security policy dialog box should now display the new security rule, as shown in Figure 7.28. Click OK to close the window.

33.   To enable the security policy, right-click on the policy and select Assign.

After you have completed this setup, you can now attempt to connect with the vSphere client. If a connection is established, the traffic passed between your management computer and your ESXi host will be secured with IPSec. Should you experience any issues making the connection, you can use the Microsoft IPSec Diagnostic Tool, which is available from http://support. microsoft.com/kb/943862. This tool can display IPSec policy information for your computer, and it parses the IPSec logs to determine the potential cause of any IPSec failures.

You can also configure your host to block traffic from specific hosts or subnets. In the following example, the protocol setting has been changed to any and both the source and destination ports are set to 0. These settings impact all traffic coming from the host specified with the source parameter. The security policy has also been set to discard any traffic that meets the traffic filter.

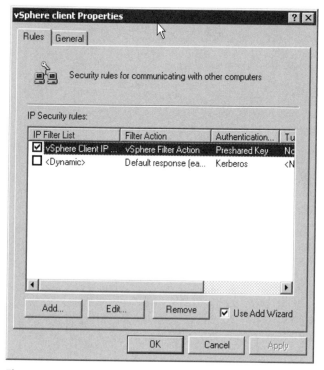

Figure 7.28   Creating a new IPSec policy on Windows Server 2008.

```
vicfg-ipsec --server esx08.mishchenko.net --add-sp
    --sp-src 2001:0F68::1986:69AE/128 --sp-dst 2001:0F68::1986:69AF/128
    --src-port 0 --dst-port 0 --ulproto any --dir in --action discard
    --sp-mode transport --sa-name sa1 sp2
```

Shortening IPv6 Addresses The IPv6 address size is 128 bits. This increase over the IPv4 value of 32 bits provides a practically unlimited pool of IP addresses to address the Internet shortage as an ever-increasing number of devices require Internet access. The preferred IPv6 address representation is eight blocks of four hexadecimal digits. An example of an address expressed in this format is 2001:0F60:0000:0000:0000:0000:0086:09AF.

IPv6 addresses can be shortened in the following ways. First, the address can be expressed without any leading zeros. The sample IPv6 address then becomes 2001:F60:0:0:0:0:86:9AF. Second, all consecutive zeros can be replaced with a double colon. In the case of the sample address, it is then expressed as 2001:F60::86:9AF.

Securing Network Storage

A single host deployment is likely to use local storage, and for the most part you need to be significantly concerned about the security of your storage. But as you add ESXi hosts, there are compelling reasons to move to some form of shared storage. ESXi supports Fibre Channel (FC) storage area network (SAN), iSCSI, and NFS storage. Practically, as you consolidate your storage, you can reduce your hardware costs, reduce your storage management overhead, and more effectively use your disk resources. Numerous vSphere features such as vMotion, High Availability, and Fault Tolerance require some form of shared disk resource.

This section of the chapter deals with some of the common security concerns with using shared storage. As has been mentioned earlier in this chapter, the key to securing your storage is isolation. Depending on your deployment, that will involve a mix of vSwitch design, employment of VLANs, and physical network separation. FC SAN, iSCSI, and NFS are all clear text protocols and thus vulnerable to MiTM attacks. With a packet sniffer, it is also possible to capture traffic, which allows for the discovery of classified data.

Note: One of the keys to security is physical security. If an intruder can gain physical access to a host, it becomes a very simple task to be able to remove the virtual machines running on that host. There are drivers that will allow a Linux or Windows machine to read a Virtual Machine File System (VMFS) datastore, in which case the virtual machines could be copied to another storage media or across the network to another device. It is even possible to create a Live CD that can be used to launch an independent copy of ESXi, which would then be able to run the virtual machines' hosts on the comprised host. If you cannot physically secure your ESXi hosts, consider using encryption within the guest operating system to add another layer of protection to your data.

Securing FC SAN Storage

With a traditional FC SAN deployment, each ESXi host contains an FC Host Bus Adapter (FC-HBA) that connects to an isolated storage network. Each FC-HBA has what is essentially a storage Media Access Control (MAC) address called a worldwide port name (WWPN). For security, the SAN presents a storage logical unit number (LUN) to the WWPN. The ESXi host with that FC-HBA is then able to access that storage LUN and use it as needed. The SAN can also be configured to provide access to a single LUN to a number of WWPNs. In this way, the LUN is configured to be shared among several ESXi hosts to allow for clustering. If a host fails, the FC-HBA can be moved to another host and the new host will have the same LUN access as the old host. While this is a benefit to recovery, it also poses a security concern, as the new host has no requirement to authenticate or validate its identity with the SAN. When configuring your SAN, you must carefully ensure that the LUNs are zoned to the appropriate WWPNs.

As Fibre Channel storage evolves as a technology, new security concerns come to light. With the emergence of Fibre Channel over Ethernet (FCOE), it is possible to send FC data over your Ethernet network. While this technology provides the opportunity to converge your network design, you must consider the risk of comingling your storage data with other network data types.

Another new Fibre Channel technology to be aware of is N_Port ID Virtualization (NPIV). With NPIV, a virtual machine can be granted an identity in the FC storage fabric. Instead of just granting access to a LUN to a host and all the virtual machines running on that host, the SAN administrator can grant access to a specific virtual machine. This provides an additional layer of LUN masking and allows the SAN administrator to identity traffic for that specific virtual machine.

Securing NFS Storage

VMware ESXi supports NFS version 3 over TCP. NFS storage is easy to set up, but it represents the least secure level of storage that you can use with ESXi. Authentication is often based upon an IP address, which can be spoofed. NFS is a clear text protocol, and ESXi authenticates with the NFS storage with the root login. Additionally, accessing NFS from ESXi requires that the no_root_squash option be enabled. With root squashing, the root account is mapped to another unprivileged account such as nobody on the NFS server to prevent root accounts on client machines from gaining privileged access to the NFS mounts. ESXi, however, requires read and write access to the mounts, so it is necessary to disable root squashing.

If you employ NFS storage, the primary concern is traffic isolation. If your environment requires physical separation, your NFS storage should be on a physically isolated network, and the vSwitch that connects to that network should have only a VMkernel port configured on it. No virtual machine port groups should be in that vSwitch, to prevent a virtual machine from attempting to attack or capture network traffic from the NFS server. You can also configure the NFS server to restrict access to the specific IP addresses of your ESXi host or use a firewall to restrict traffic to a specific host. If your NFS server supports IPSec, you might also consider configured IPSec for the traffic between your ESXi host and NFS server. If you are employing blade servers with a minimal number of NICs or 10GB networking, you should ensure that NFS traffic is isolated with a VLAN.

Security iSCSI Storage

Provisioning iSCSI storage is similar to Fibre Channel storage in that storage LUNs are presented to hosts that then choose how to partition and format the LUN. Access to your iSCSI storage can be via iSCSI Host Bus Adapters, which offload the overhead associated with iSCSI, or with standard NICs configured within your ESXi host's vSwitches.

Given that iSCSI traffic is over an IP-based network, it is vulnerable to the attacks discussed throughout this chapter. As with the other storage options, isolation is the first step to securing iSCSI. The iSCSI protocol supports the use of Challenge-Handshake Authentication Protocol

(CHAP), but post authentication traffic is sent in clear text. As is the case with NFS traffic, consider the use of IPSec to secure traffic between your ESXi hosts and iSCSI target. You might also consider the use of firewalls to protect the hosts involved. When you use iSCSI, ESXi does not open any ports to listen for network connections. This reduces the attack surface of your ESXi host, but you should still isolate the VMkernel port that is used for iSCSI access from general network traffic.

When designing your networking for iSCSI, it is ideal to be able to separate your iSCSI traffic either physically or with the use of a VLAN. If you are using iSCSI-HBAs, these devices will connect directly to your isolated network ports. If you're using the software iSCSI initiator within ESXi, you will configure a new vSwitch for storage traffic, and then configure this vSwitch to connect to the isolated storage network.

When configuring iSCSI storage for your ESXi hosts, you should enable CHAP authentication. When the ESXi initiator contacts the iSCSI target, the target responds with a predefined ID value and a random key. The initiator then creates a one-way hash value that it sends to the target. The hash contains the ID value, random key, and the CHAP secret that has been configured on both the ESXi host and iSCSI server. When the target receives the hash value, it computes its own hash value for the same elements. If both hashes match, the iSCSI target has verified the identity of the initiator.

ESXi supports both unidirectional and bidirectional CHAP. With unidirectional CHAP, only the iSCSI target authenticates the ESXi host. With bidirectional CHAP, the ESXi host also authenticates the iSCSI target providing an additional layer of security. It is possible to disable CHAP authentication, and the ESXi host will still authenticate in a very simple manner in that the iSCSI target will map a LUN to the unique iSCSI name for the host. This is not a recommended method to set up your iSCSI access.

To enable CHAP authentication, you can follow this process:

1. Start the vSphere client and connect either to your vCenter Server or directly to your ESXi host.

2. Select the Configuration tab for the host and then click the Storage Adapters link in the Hardware panel.

3. In the list of storage adapters, choose the iSCSI initiator and click Properties.

4. If the iSCSI initiator has been enabled, click CHAP.

5. Select an authentication option for CHAP (Target Authenticates Host), as shown in Figure 7.29. You have the following four options: Do Not Use CHAP, Do Not Use CHAP unless Required by Target, Use CHAP unless Prohibited by Target, and Use CHAP.

6. To use the iSCSI initiator name to identify the host to the iSCSI target, check the Use Initiator Name option. Otherwise, enter a name that the iSCSI target will be configured to recognize. Enter the Secret, which matches the password setup on the iSCSI target.

7. Optionally, you can configure the same settings for Mutual CHAP. The secret you configure for Mutual CHAP must be different from the one used for CHAP (Target Authenticates Host).

8. Click OK to close the CHAP Credentials window.

9. Click Close to close the Properties window for the iSCSI initiator. You will be prompted with a dialog box requesting a rescan of the host bus adapter due to the configuration change.

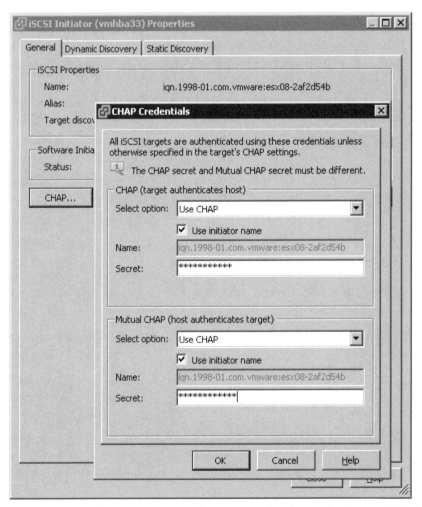

Figure 7.29 Configuring CHAP authentication for the ESXi software iSCSI initiator.

The preceding process configured CHAP authentication at the adapter level, and these settings and credentials would apply to all iSCSI targets that the host would attempt to access. You can also configure CHAP authentication on a per-target basis, which allows for greater security. When you add or modify a dynamic or static iSCSI target, you can click the CHAP button to access CHAP settings that will apply only to that specific target.

Securing Virtual Networking

A common theme throughout this chapter has been the need to isolate traffic types. You don't want DMZ virtual machines having access to your storage network, nor should the management interface for ESXi be exposed directly to your local area network (LAN). The same network principles that you'll use when designing your physical network security will apply when configuring vSphere networking. If your server design includes many network ports, it may be relatively easy to segment network traffic with the use of many vSwitches each connected to physically isolated networks. But as network speeds increase and hardware size decreases, it becomes more likely that you'll be running an ESXi host with only a few network ports. When configuring the security of your vSphere environment, networking represents the most significant avenue through which an attacker may impact not only your virtual machines but the network infrastructure surrounding them.

Security Virtual Networking with VLANs

In the cases where you have a limited number of network ports to configure, you have to rely on VLANs to segment your network traffic. There is a fair bit of debate of the security capabilities of VLANs, as they have been subject to attacks and circumventing in the past. However, the technology has matured and the vSwitch provides safeguards against certain threats to VLAN security, including the following:

- **MAC flooding.** This attack floods a switch with packets that contain MAC addresses from different sources. Switches track the source address for each packet, and if the MAC table fills, it is possible for the switch to enter a fully open state in which every packet is broadcast to all ports. In such a state, packet leakage across VLANs may occur. Although VMware vSwitches do track MAC addresses, the data does not come from observable traffic and thus a vSwitch is not vulnerable to this type of attack.

- **802.1q and Cisco Inter-Switch Link (ISL) tagging attacks.** These force a switch to redirect packets from one VLAN to another by tricking the switch into acting as a trunk. vSwitches do not perform the dynamic trunking required for this type of attack.

- **Double-encapsulation attacks.** These create a packet in which a VLAN tagged packet is encapsulated within another VLAN tagged packet. Some switches are configured to strip away the outer packet and pass on the inner VLAN tagged packet for backward compatibility. vSwitches drop any double-encapsulated packets that are sent.

- **Multicast brute-force attacks.** These involve sending a large number of multicast packets to a known VLAN almost simultaneously to overload the switch so that it inadvertently allows some of the packets to be broadcast to other VLANs. vSwitches do not allow packets to leave their correct broadcast domain (VLAN) and are not vulnerable to this attack.

The preceding list is not exhaustive and both technologies and security threats develop over time. However, use of VLANs in your vSwitches is a viable option for providing network isolation. Perhaps a more significant risk in using VLANs is the possibility of misconfiguration.

vSphere includes a number of improvements with permissions. An example includes the additional choices for network configuration for a virtual machine, as shown in Figure 7.30. In prior versions of ESXi and ESX, it was only possible to assign a Remove permission. With vSphere, you can also control the assignment of a virtual NIC to a vSwitch. You can also utilize Distributed Virtual Switches and Host Profiles to ensure consistent configurations across your ESXi host. There are also additional permissions you can control for Distributed Virtual Switches. Properly configured, these elements can help reduce the risk of a virtual machine or vSwitch being misconfigured either intentionally or accidentally, which could expose a virtual machine to an unauthorized VLAN.

You should also be aware that VMware vSwitches do not support the concept of a native VLAN. Native VLANs are used by switches for switch control and management. Native VLANs are not tagged with a VLAN ID in some switch implementations, and trunk ports treat all untagged packets as belonging to the native VLAN. If you have created a number of virtual machine port groups in your switch, assigned them VLANS, but left one port group as unset, traffic from that port group could end up on the native VLAN of your physical switches. If your physical switches use VLAN ID 1 for the native VLAN, you should configure your vSwitches with VLAN IDs in the range of 2 to 4094. If another VLAN ID is used for the native VLAN, you should avoid using that VLAN ID on your vSwitches.

Use of VLAN ID 4095 enables Virtual Machine Guest Tagging (VGT) mode. In this mode, the vSwitch port group passes packets to the virtual machines without modifying any VLAN tags. It is the responsibility of the guest operating system to assign a VLAN ID to packets that it sends. If enabled inappropriately, this could allow a virtual machine to interact with a VLAN for which it is not authorized.

Configuring vSwitch Security Properties

The properties for vSwitches and port groups include a number of security policies designed to safeguard your network. From the perspective of the guest operating system, the virtual NIC functions just as a physical NIC would, so a malicious program executing within the virtual machine is capable of forging MAC addresses or flooding the network to create a DoS attack. There are three security options that you can set to prevent malicious activity, and you can set limits on network traffic to prevent excessive network load.

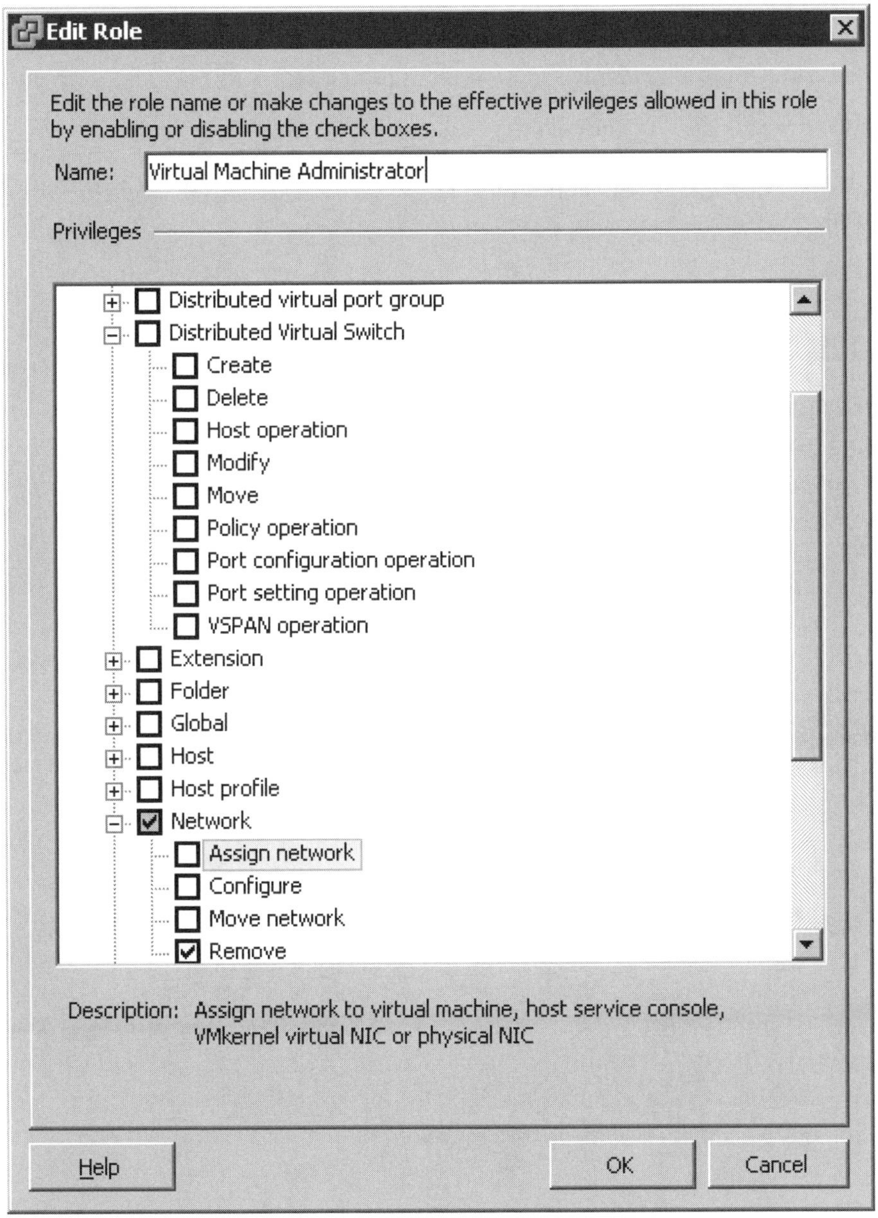

Figure 7.30 Configuring network permissions for a role.

To make changes to the security policy or traffic shaping policy of a vSwitch, you can follow these steps:

1. In the vSphere client, select the Configuration tab for a host and then select the Networking link in the Hardware pane.

2. For the vSwitch you wish to configure, select Properties.

3. Select the vSwitch port and click Edit.

4. Select the Security tab to display the security policy options shown in Figure 7.31.

5. Select the Traffic Shaping tab, shown in Figure 7.32. From this tab, you can configure the traffic settings for the vSwitch.

6. Make any desired changes and click OK, and then Close to complete the changes.

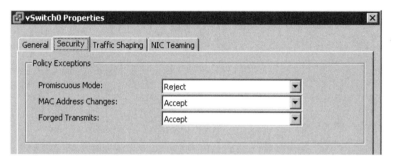

Figure 7.31   Configuring security policies on a vSwitch.

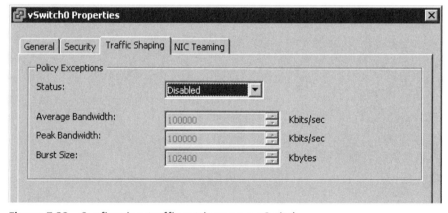

Figure 7.32   Configuring traffic settings on a vSwitch.

The first setting on the Security tab is Promiscuous Mode. The option is by default set to Reject. This eliminates the possibility that the virtual machine could be used to capture all traffic on the vSwitch, as the vSwitch will filter network traffic to ensure that the virtual machine receives only packets destined for that specific virtual machine. In some cases, if you are running a network sniffer or intrusion detection software, you may need to allow Promiscuous Mode on a vSwitch, but for most vSwitches, this setting can be left with the default setting.

The second option to configure is MAC Address Changes. This option is set to Accept. When a virtual NIC is added to a virtual machine, it is automatically assigned a MAC address. The guest operating system can change the MAC address and will begin to receive traffic destined for the new MAC address. This can be required in some situations such as using Microsoft Network Load Balancing in unicast mode. Additionally, the iSCSI initiator relies on being able to get MAC address changes from some types of storage. If the setting is change to Reject, ESXi will not honor a request by the virtual machine to change the MAC address from the initial value.

The last setting on the Security tab is Forged Transmits. When the option is set to Accept, ESXi does not compare source and effective MAC addresses. To protect against MAC impersonation, you can set this option to Reject. With that setting, ESXi compares the source MAC address as generated by the guest operating system with the effective MAC address for the adapters and drops the packet if there is not a match. This setting can impact applications that require a specific MAC address for licensing.

On the Traffic Shaping tab, you can set the traffic shaping policy for the vSwitch. This can be useful to ensure that a virtual machine is not used to saturate a vSwitch, which could create a DoS for other virtual machines or ESXi system services on that vSwitch. The traffic shaping policy is defined by the following three attributes: Average Bandwidth, Peak Bandwidth, and Burst Size. Average Bandwidth sets the bits per second to allow through the port averaged over time. Peak Bandwidth is the maximum number of bits per second allowed through the port when it is receiving or sending a burst of traffic. This setting, along with Burst Size, allows a vSwitch to transmit beyond the Average Bandwidth restriction. The Burst Size setting specifies the maximum number of bytes to allow in a burst of network traffic.

If you select the properties for a virtual machine port group or VMkernel port, the Security and Traffic Shaping tabs can also be found on these objects. You can check an option as shown in Figure 7.33 to override the setting enabled on the vSwitch. If you make no changes, the settings for the virtual machine port group or VMkernel port inherit the settings from the vSwitch.

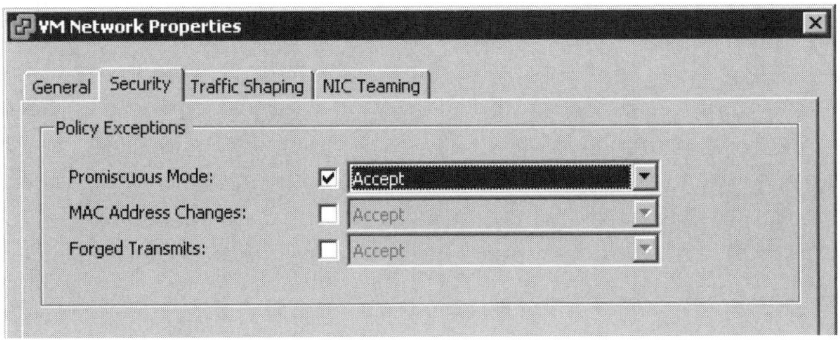

Figure 7.33 Overriding the security policy on a virtual machine port group.

The vSphere 4.0 Hardening Guide *The vSphere 4.0 Hardening Guide* was released by VMware in April 2010. This document is intended to provide guidance on securely deploying vSphere 4.0 in a production environment. The guide includes more than 100 recommendations for securing your environment and covers the following elements:

- Virtual machines

- Hosts (both ESXi and ESX)

- Virtual networking

- vCenter Server

- The ESX console operating system

Each guideline follows the same format and provides information on the nature of the risk, the potential severity in your environment, and steps to mitigate the problem. The guide is available at this link: http://www.vmware.com/resources/techresources/10109. It is a must-read as you implement your ESXi environment.

Security and Clustering

When used within a vSphere environment, the term *clustering* can refer to a number of different forms of clustering. At the host level, the most basic form of a cluster exists when two or more hosts share the same storage. ESXi supports shared storage using either VMFS-formatted LUNs or NFS mounts.

Many of the features in vSphere build upon the simple host clustering of storage. vMotion enables a running virtual machine to be migrated from one host to another while the virtual machine continues to execute uninterrupted. vMotion uses VMware's cluster file system to control access to the virtual machine's virtual disks. When a virtual machine is migrated from one host to another, the virtual machine's active memory and execution state are transmitted over the vMotion network to the new host. This transfer of data occurs in clear text. A number of technologies within vSphere are dependent on vMotion. Dynamic Resource Scheduling (DRS) is a feature that allows virtual machines to be migrated by vMotion to a less constrained host should the host running the virtual machine be low on CPU or memory resources. Distributed Power Management allows hosts within a cluster to migrate virtual machines and power down during off hours to conserve power resources. Storage vMotion allows not only the virtual machine to migrate to another host without interruption but also allows for the movement of the virtual machine's storage to another host datastore.

VMware High Availability (HA) is designed to detect the failure of a host or virtual machine. In the case of a virtual machine failure, it is restarted on the same host. With an unforeseen host failure, the virtual machines that were running on the failed host are restarted on other hosts within the HA cluster. VMware Fault Tolerance (FT) leverages HA clusters to create a shadow copy of a virtual machine on another host. The two virtual machines are kept in sync with VMware vLockStep technology. The secondary virtual machine executes the same sequence of virtual instructions as the primary guest. In the case of a failure or interruption in the primary virtual machine, the secondary guest completes outstanding input/output (I/O) requests, becomes the new primary virtual machine, and severs communication with the failed virtual machine.

Virtual machines can also be clustered in a number of different configurations. You may deploy some form of network load balanced (NLB) cluster or a shared disk cluster. A shared disk cluster could involve two virtual machines on the same host, virtual machines on two separate hosts, or a virtual machine paired in a cluster with a physical host.

A significant part of any cluster will be heartbeat traffic between the hosts or virtual machines involved in the cluster. These heartbeats will be used to determine the availability of services and control what actions are taken in the cluster. From a security perspective, it is critical to protect that heartbeat traffic, as it could provide an attack avenue for a DoS. With ESXi, VMware HA communication travels over VMkernel networks except those marked for use with vMotion. If there is only one VMkernel port, HA communicates over that network even if vMotion is enabled. If you have a number of VMkernel ports, you must enable the Management Network option as shown in Figure 7.34 to allow VMware HA to use this network. If you are not able to isolate the VMkernel port used for HA traffic, set up an additional VMkernel port on a secure network. Enable this new VMkernel port for management traffic to ensure that HA is not impacted by a DoS or similar attack.

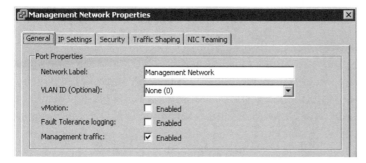

Figure 7.34   The Management Network setting enables VMware HA communication on a VMkernel port.

In some cases, a virtual machine cluster requires a private network for heartbeat communication. As is the case with VMware HA, you should isolate this traffic to ensure that the communication cannot be disrupted. As it will be a virtual machine or a physical node in a cluster sending this traffic, you should also isolate this traffic for other ESXi management traffic to ensure that a compromised virtual machine cannot then be used to attack your ESXi hosts. The virtual machine cluster may also require that you enable MAC address changes or forged transmits. If this is the case, you should set these options to Reject at the vSwitch level and then override them on virtual machine port groups specifically created for the virtual machines in the cluster.

The security concern with vMotion clusters is that information sent between hosts during a migration is sent in clear text. A person with access to the network would be able to capture this information flow and view the contents. The vMotion network should be isolated from your production network on an isolated segment. Only the ESXi hosts require a presence on the network. vCenter Server does not require an IP address on the vMotion. Ideally, this network should be nonroutable and configured within a separate vSwitch. If this is not possible, you should consider securing the vMotion network with a VLAN. You may also consider securing the vMotion network with IPSec, but this will require the use of IPv6 addresses, as IPSec is not supported for IPv4 addresses.

Isolating Virtual Machine Environments

A repeated topic throughout this chapter has been the need to isolate network traffic to protect data and sensitive systems. With proper vSwitch design and the use of firewalls, you can ensure that potentially hostile traffic is kept away from more sensitive networks, such as those used for management or storage. Even within a single vSwitch, you can employ VLANs to segment traffic. But within a single vSwitch without VLANs or within a single VLAN on a vSwitch, it becomes more difficult to see and control the network interaction between virtual machines. Although you may be able to design your networking to ensure that DMZ virtual machines are not able to communicate with other network segments, a vSwitch cannot control traffic within the vSwitch. A virtual machine compromised within the DMZ would be isolated from the rest of your network, but capable of attacking other virtual machines in the same VLAN on the vSwitch.

To protect virtual machines in such a situation, you can employ firewall software within each affected virtual machine. Most operating systems now include a rudimentary firewall enabled by default, or you can employ a third-party solution. The VMware vShield family includes vShield App, which provides visibility into the network communication for your virtual machines and provides an application-aware firewall with deep packet inspection and connection control based on destination and source IP addresses. The vShield family also includes vShield Edge, which provides network perimeter security, and vShield Endpoint, which enables antivirus and anti-malware scanning of virtual machines from a hardened security appliance. As these solutions are hypervisor based, they are protected from attacks that would comprise the same type of solution operating as an agent service within the virtual machine.

When deployed within your environment, vShield App consists of the vShield Manager appliance, which provides the centralized management component for vShield. The vShield Manager communicates with vShield App appliance, which runs on each ESXi host that you intend to protect with vShield App. These components communicate with hosts and virtual machines through the vSphere API and are compatible with other VMware features such as vMotion and HA. vShield App integrates with vCenter Server and can be managed via a plug-in for the vSphere client.

To begin using vShield App, you can select vShield application on the Home screen when you're connected to your vCenter Server Host. At the datacenter, cluster, and virtual machine levels, you can select the Flow Monitoring tab to display information about the network connections that are occurring at that level. Figure 7.35 displays the network traffic to a virtual machine by traffic type, application type, and source and destination IP address or MAC address. Traffic data can also be displayed in a chart format.

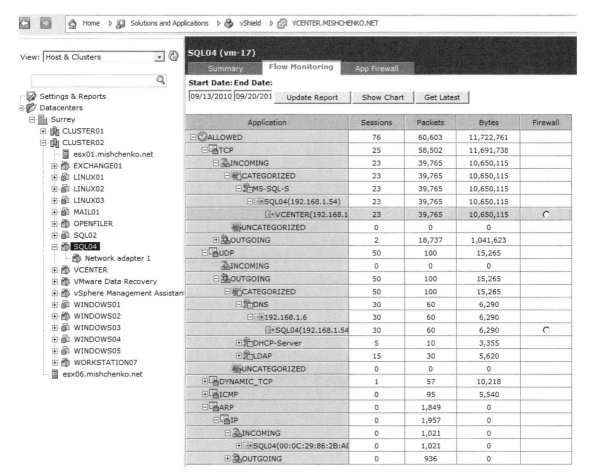

Figure 7.35   Analyzing traffic flow for a virtual machine with vShield App.

Once you have an understanding of your network traffic, you can begin to configure rules to manage traffic to and from your virtual machines. To ease management, you can group virtual NICs from many virtual machines into security groups and use those as the source or destination addresses in the rules that you create. Rules can be created at the datacenter, cluster, and network port group levels. To create a rule, you can select the App Firewall tab and then add a new entry specifying the source and destination addresses, ports, application, protocol, and action as shown in Figure 7.36. You can also create rules directly from the Flow Monitoring tab by clicking the radio button for a specific destination address.

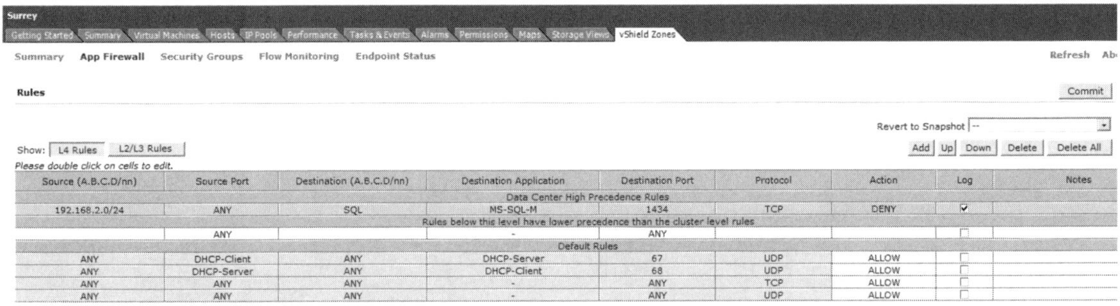

Figure 7.36   Creating a firewall rule with vShield App.

Conclusion

VMware ESXi was designed from the bottom up to provide a secure environment in which to host your virtual machines. The hypervisor, virtual machine, and virtual networking layers of ESXi enable virtual machines to operate in an isolated manner to ensure that malicious code within a virtual machine cannot be used to breach the hypervisor to attack the host or other virtual machines. You can employ resource limits and reservations further to ensure that virtual machines have adequate resources to perform.

This chapter has reviewed a number of tools that can be used to secure your environment. Traffic between your client PC and vCenter Server and between vCenter Server and ESXi hosts is secured with SSL certificates. With ESXi 4.1, you can further encrypt sensitive IPv6 traffic with IPSec. Careful planning and use of vSwitches and VLANs can ensure that your sensitive data and traffic are isolated from prying eyes. Update Manager and the vCLI provide the necessary tools to keep your hosts up to date on patches. You can employ permissions to secure vCenter Server and ensure that end users are limited in what tasks they can perform within your vSphere environment. vShield App provides the capability to protect individual virtual machines within a vSwitch and to gain a better view of the network traffic passing through your virtual networking infrastructure.

Security is a broad topic and certainly not one that can be conclusively discussed within a chapter, or even a single book for that matter. Nor is security a single step within your implementation plan, but rather an ongoing concern and something that requires periodic review. *The vSphere Hardening Guide* provides a great checklist to use, whether you're planning your implementation or already using VMware ESXi. VMware's Security Center can be found at http://www.vmware.com/security; it contains the latest security alerts, documentation, and tools.

8 Scripting and Automation with the vCLI

W hen VMware first released ESXi 3.5, the Remote Command Line Interface (RCLI) was also introduced to provide a replacement mechanism for administrators accustomed to using the Service Console on ESX. Significant improvements have been made in the last two releases of this interface, and with the release of vSphere the RCLI was renamed to the vSphere Command Line Interface (vCLI). The vCLI is available for both Linux and Windows.

VMware also created a virtual appliance called the vSphere Management Assistant (vMA). The vMA includes the vCLI and adds the vi-fastpass authentication component and the vi-logger component. The vi-fastpass component eliminates the need to supply credentials when executing vCLI commands, whereas the logging component captures log files from ESXi for further analysis.

Both the vCLI installation package and the vMA include the vSphere Software Development Kit (SDK) for Perl. The vSphere SDK for Perl provides an easy-to-use Perl scripting interface to the vSphere application programming interface (API). A number of sample scripts are included, and you can use the SDK to build utilities to configure and manage your ESXi hosts. The vSphere SDK for Perl includes the Web Services for Management (WSMAN) component, which can be used to create scripts that retrieve health data from ESXi hosts and vCenter Server.

This chapter examines the following items:

- Installing the vCLI on Linux and Windows

- Importing and configuring the vMA

- Using the commands of the vCLI

- Using the authentication and logging components of the vMA

Installing the vCLI on Linux and Windows

The installation of the vCLI includes both the vCLI commands and the vSphere SDK for Perl. For Windows installations, these components and a number of required components are all included in the installation package. For Linux, the following prerequisite packages are required before the installer can proceed:

- **OpenSSL.** This component is used to provide Secure Sockets Layer (SSL) communications with the vSphere API running on ESXi and vCenter Server.

- **LibXML2.** This package is required for Extensible Markup Language (XML) parsing.

- **e2fsprogs.** This package contains utilities for maintaining `ext2`, `ext3`, and `ext4` filesystems. It is required by the Universally Unique Identifier (UUID) Perl Module, which the vCLI package installs if it does not find it on the system.

If you start the Linux installer and any of these packages are missing, it reports an error and terminates the installation. On a Red Hat Linux machine, you can install OpenSSL and LibXML2 with the following command:

```
yum install openssl-devel libxml2-dev
```

For other Linux distributions, you can consult your documentation for the appropriate installation command.

The Linux installer for the vCLI also checks for the following components:

- Crypt_SSLeay_0.55 (0.55_0.9.7 or 0.55_0.9.8)

- IO_Compress_Base_2.005

- Compress_Zlib_2.005

- IO_Compress_Zlib_2.005

- Compress_Raw_Zlib_2.017

- Archive_Zip_1.26

- Data_Dumper_2.121

- XML_LibXML_1.63

- libwww_perl_5.805

- XML_LibXML_Common_0.13

- XML_NamespaceSupport_1.09

- XML_SAX_0.16

- Data_Dump_1.15

- URI_1.37

- UUID_0.03

- SOAP_Lite_0.710.08

- HTML_Parser_3.60

- version_0.78

If any of these components is not found, the vCLI installer adds the package to your system. If a different version is found on your system, the installer still proceeds. At the end of the installation process, the installer informs you that the correct version of the component is not installed and specifies the version that the vCLI was tested with.

You can download the latest release of the vCLI from the following Web uniform resource locator (URL): http://www.vmware.com/support/developer/vcli/. You can use the following steps to install the vCLI on your Linux computer:

1. Uninstall an existing version of the vCLI or RCLI with the command `/usr/bin/vmare-uninstall-vSphere-CLI.pl`.

2. Extract the vCLI download with this command: `tar /zxvf VMware-vSphere-CLI--4.1-0-254719.x86_64.tar.gz`. This creates the folder `vmware-vsphere-cli-distrib`.

3. Ensure that you are logged in as a superuser and start the installation with the command `sudo vmware-vsphere-cli-distrib/vmware-install.pl`.

4. Type `yes` and press Enter to accept the license terms.

5. Specify an installation folder or accept the default of `/usr/bin`.

If the installer detected an incorrect version for the components listed previously, a warning message is displayed. Otherwise, a success message is shown and you are returned to the command prompt. With the default installation, the components of the vCLI can be found in the following locations:

- vCLI scripts: `/usr/bin`

- vSphere SDK for Perl utility applications: `/usr/lib/vmware-vcli/apps`

- vSphere SDK for Perl sample scripts: `/usr/share/doc/vmware-vcli/samples`

Tip: If you uninstall a prior version of the vCLI and then install the vCLI to a different folder, you must reset the `PATH` environment variable. You can do this before or after upgrading the vCLI. If you do not update the path, the system may search the old location for vCLI commands.

The vCLI installation for Windows can be downloaded from the link provided earlier. It includes the ActivePerl runtime from ActiveState Software and the required Perl modules. The vCLI is supported on the 32-bit versions of Windows XP, Vista, and 2003 and the 64-bit version of Windows 2008.

Use the following steps to install the vCLI on a Windows computer:

1. Start the installation package for the vCLI. If a prior version is detected, it is automatically uninstalled.

2. Click Next on the Welcome screen to proceed.

3. Accept the license agreement and click Next.

4. Select the installation folder and click Next.

5. Click Install to begin the installation.

6. Click Finish to complete the installation.

The vCLI installation on Windows makes changes to the system path. You should log off and back in again to pick up those changes before testing your installation. The components of the vCLI are installed to the following locations with a default installation. The folder where the vCLI scripts are located is not added to the system path. When you attempt to run those commands, you should either make that your current directory in the command prompt or add the `bin` folder to the system path.

- vCLI scripts: `C:\Program Files\VMware\VMware vSphere CLI\bin`

- vSphere SDK for Perl utility applications: `C:\Program Files\VMware\VMware vSphere CLI \Perl\apps`

- vSphere SDK for Perl sample scripts: `C:\Program Files\VMware\VMware vSphere CLI\Perl \samples`

Tip: The commands included with the vCLI are Perl scripts and when executed on Windows require the addition of the `.pl` extension. The samples in this chapter do not include the extension, but you need to include it when running the vCLI on Windows. The exception is for `esxcli`, which is a precompiled executable.

After you install the vCLI, you can quickly test your installation to ensure that it has installed correctly. Open a command prompt and then navigate to the `bin` folder on your Linux or Windows system. vCLI command scripts follow this format:

```
<command> <connection_options> <parameters>
```

To view the virtual machines registered on an ESXi host, you can run the following command:

```
vmware-cmd --server esx01 -1
```

You will be prompted for a login and password. If the command is entered correctly, a list of virtual machines is displayed. If you have made an error with the command, the help file showing the command syntax is displayed.

Note: Although the vCLI allows configuration of Internet Protocol Version 6 (IPv6) on your ESXi hosts, communication with the hosts is supported only on Internet Protocol Version 4 (IPv4).

Installing and Configuring the vMA

The vMA is a CentOS-based virtual machine that includes the vCLI and vSphere SDK for Perl. It also extends the vCLI with an authentication component that allows you to run scripts against ESXi or vCenter Server without authenticating each command and a logging component for gathering ESXi and vCenter Server logs. The vMA can be joined to your Active Directory domain, which eliminates the need to maintain local accounts and enables you to pass your credentials through to the ESXi and vCenter Server hosts that you interact with.

The vMA comes preconfigured with the following two user accounts: vi-admin and vi-user. With the vi-admin account, you can perform administrative operations on the vMA such as adding target servers for the authentication component. The vCLI commands that you run with this account also execute with administrative privileges on the added target hosts. The vi-user account is disabled by default. When enabled, it can be used to run vCLI commands but those execute only with read-only privileges on the target hosts. The root account does exist in the vMA, but it is disabled. To run privileged commands, you can use sudo and by default this is limited to the vi-admin account. Sudo (super user do) allows users to run programs with the security rights of another user, which in this case is the root account. Throughout this chapter, a number of examples are shown where sudo is required.

As it is packaged as a virtual machine, the vMA can be run on an ESXi or any other VMware product. The guest operating system (OS) is 64-bit so the host must be capable of running 64-bit guests. The vMA does include VMware Tools, so you can control the power state of the vMA just as you would with any other virtual machine.

Included with the vMA is a Simple Network Management Procotol (SNMP) server that enables monitoring of the vMA. The vMA can't proxy SNMP data about the hosts it manages or export a configuration using SNMP. The SNMP Management Information Bases (MIBs) included with the vMA allow you to gather data about the vMA host, including its resources, resource usage, and networking setup.

You can find the download for the vMA at http://www.vmware.com/support/developer/vima/. It can be downloaded to your management system as either a ZIP file containing the Open Virtualization Format (OVF) package for the vMA or you can use a Web URL to import the OVF package directly to your ESXi host. Use the following process to import the vMA from a URL:

1.   Start the vSphere client and connect to vCenter Server or an ESXi host.

2.   Select File > Deploy Template.

3.   Once the Deploy OVF Template wizard appears, enter the URL for the OVF download and click Next.

4.   The details of the OVF package are displayed, as shown in Figure 8.1. Click Next to continue.

5.   Accept the license agreement.

6.   You can optionally specify a name for the virtual appliance or accept the default of vSphere Management Assistant (vMA).

7.   Select the location for the appliance. Depending on your configuration, this may include selecting an appropriate cluster, host, and resource pool.

8.   If the destination host has multiple datastores, select a location to store the vMA file and click Next.

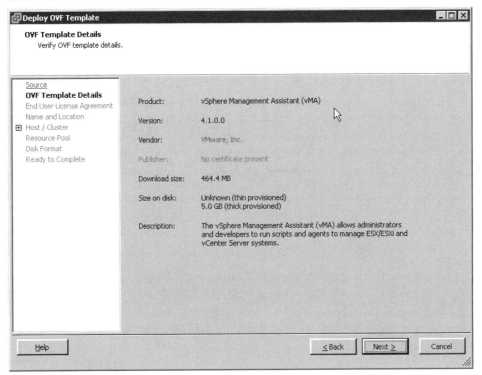

Figure 8.1 OVF template details for the vMA 4.1 download.

9. Select a disk format for the virtual disk of the vMA.

10. Choose the network mapping for the vMA. The vMA should have network access to the management port of your ESXi hosts if you plan to run commands directly against ESXi.

11. Review the information for the import and click Finish.

Once the vMA has been deployed to your ESXi host, you need to perform some initial configuration steps. If you need the vMA to connect to multiple networks, you should first edit the vMA virtual machine and add the additional virtual network adapter.

To configure the vMA, follow these steps:

1. In the vSphere client, right-click on the vMA virtual machine and select Power > Power On.

2. Open a console session for the virtual machine.

3. The initial configuration begins with a network configuration wizard. For each network adapter in the vMA, you can choose between using Dynamic Host Configuration Protocol (DHCP) and setting a static Internet Protocol (IP) address.

4. Enter a primary and secondary domain name service (DNS) server to use for the vMA. The default values are populated from information obtained from a DHCP server.

5. Select a hostname for the virtual machine.

6. A summary of your configuration settings is displayed, as shown in Figure 8.2. Type yes and press Enter to confirm the settings.

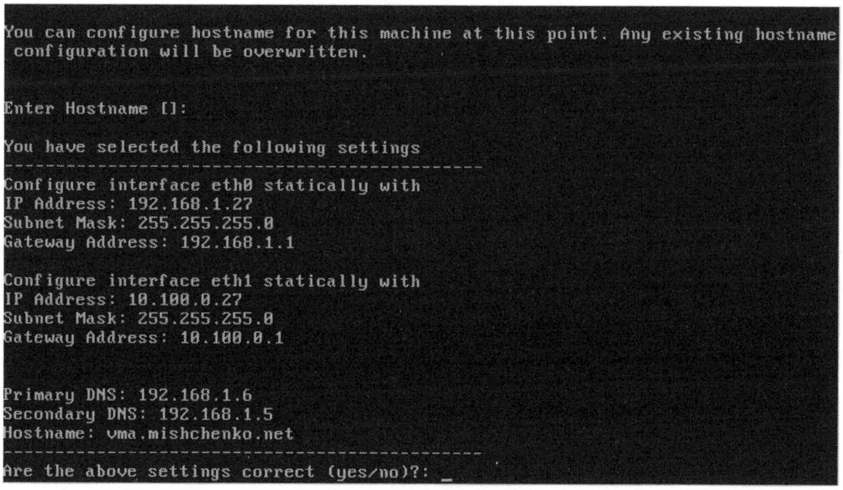

```
You can configure hostname for this machine at this point. Any existing hostname
 configuration will be overwritten.

Enter Hostname []:

You have selected the following settings
---------------------------------------------------
Configure interface eth0 statically with
IP Address: 192.168.1.27
Subnet Mask: 255.255.255.0
Gateway Address: 192.168.1.1

Configure interface eth1 statically with
IP Address: 10.100.0.27
Subnet Mask: 255.255.255.0
Gateway Address: 10.100.0.1


Primary DNS: 192.168.1.6
Secondary DNS: 192.168.1.5
Hostname: vma.mishchenko.net
---------------------------------------------------
Are the above settings correct (yes/no)?: _
```

Figure 8.2 Reviewing the network configuration for the vMA appliance.

7. Next you are prompted for a password for the vi-admin account. The prompt uses the Linux `passwd` utility and requires a sufficiently secure password. If you enter a password that is not complex, you may receive the `Bad Password` error.

8. After you have entered a password, the configuration wizard completes and a welcome screen is displayed.

Once the vMA is configured, you can log in locally at the virtual machine console by pressing Alt+F2 or remotely via Secure Shell (SSH). To change the password for the vi-admin user, enter the command `passwd`. To restart the network configuration wizard, run the following:

```
cd /opt/vmware/vma/bin
sudo ./vmware-vma-netconf.pl
```

Patching the vMA The vMA includes the `vma-update` utility to keep your appliance current with updates and security fixes for the VMware components in the vMA, the Java Runtime Environment, and CentOS. The `vma-update` utility can download patches and perform upgrades between releases of the vMA, such as upgrading from vMA 4.0 to vMA 4.1.

By default, `vma-update` is configured to download patches from an online VMware patch depot. The configuration setting for obtaining patches is stored in the file `/etc/vmware/esxupdate/vmaupdate.conf`. The vMA requires a direct connection to the Internet to download patches. If your network environment requires the use of a proxy server, you can edit this file to update the configuration with the URL and port of your proxy host. If your security policies do not permit the vMA to access the Internet, you can create an internal patch depot and update `vmaupdate.conf` to access the URL of your internal depot.

To query the patch depot for applicable updates, you can use the `scan` option as shown in the following example. In this case, the command is running on the vMA version 4.0 and the upgrade for 4.1 has been found. Note that although the command used in the following samples is `vima-update`, this command has been renamed `vma-update` in vMA 4.1.

```
sudo vima-update scan

Applicable bulletins with updates are listed.
Bulletin ID ---Date--- -----Summary--------------
VIMA410-GA 2010-07-13 VIMA 4.1 GA update
```

To get more information on bulletins that are available, you can issue the following command:

```
sudo vima-update info
```

```
    Id          - VIMA410-GA
    Releasedate - 2010-07-13T00:00:00-08:00
    Vendor      - VMware, Inc.
    Summary     - VIMA 4.1 GA update
    Severity    - critical
    Category    - critical
    Installdate -
    Description - This upgrade patch updates vMA 4.0 appliance to vMA 4.1 GA. See
                  more details at http://www.vmware.com/support/developer/vima/
    Kburl       - http://kb.vmware.com/kb/
    Contact     - http://www.vmware.com/support/contacts/
    List of constituent VIBs:
      rpm_python_2.4.3-24.el5_3.6@x86_64
      rpm_lsof_4.78-3@x86_64
      ...
      rpm_newt_0.52.2-12.el5_4.1@x86_64
      rpm_elfutils-libelf_0.137-3.el5@i386
```

To install available bulletins, you can issue the following command:

```
sudo vima-update update
```

The `vma-update` command downloads all components listed in the bulletin and then installs them on your vMA system. After the process has completed, restart your virtual machine with the following:

```
sudo reboot
```

If you wish to install a specific update, you can specify the bulletin ID with the `update` option. For the update shown earlier, you would issue the following command to install that specific update:

```
sudo vima-update -b 'VIMA410-GA' update
```

Running vCLI Commands

Before you begin to look at the commands included with the vCLI, it is worthwhile to understand the connection options that are used by the vCLI commands. With all the commands, you must authenticate with either ESXi or vCenter Server. The connection options allow you to specify the authentication method and other options such as the port used for the vSphere API. Table 8.1 summarizes the connection options for the vCLI.

Table 8.1 vCLI Connection Options

Option	Description
`--config <config file with path>` `VI_CONFIG=<config file with path>`	This option uses the specified file for connection options
`--credstore <credential store file with path>`	With this option, the credentials are stored in a file. The vSphere SDK for Perl documents how to manage the credential store file.
`--encoding <encoding>` `VI_ENCODING=<encoding>`	This option specifies the encoding to use when run on a foreign language system. Options include `ISO-8859-1` (German), `Shift_JIS` (Japanese), and `cp936` (Simplified Chinese).
`--passthroughauth` `VI_PASSTHROUGHAUTH`	The Microsoft Windows Security Support Provider Interface (SSPI) is used to pass authentication. This option is available only on Windows systems. If an untrusted account is used, the user is prompted for credentials.
`--passthroughpackage <package>` `VI_PASSTHROUGHPACKAGE=<package>`	Use this option with `-passthroughauth` to specify the domain-level authentication protocol that is configured for Windows. The default for SSPI is the Negotiate protocol, which means that the server and client attempt to negotiate a protocol that both can support.
`--password <password>` `VI_PASSWORD=<password>`	This option is used with the `--username` option to log in to vCenter Server or ESXi. You should use credentials that are appropriate to either vCenter Server or ESXi and that correspond to what you have entered with the `--server` option. If you don't specify this option, the system prompts you for your password.
`--portnumber <number>` `VI_PORTNUMBER=<number>`	This specifies the port to connect to on the vCenter Server or ESXi host if you have changed from the default of 443.
`--protocol <HTTP|HTTPS>` `VI_PROTOCOL=<HTTP|HTTPS>`	You can connect to the vSphere API over HTTP or HTTPS. HTTPS is the default and the recommended option.
`--savesessionFile <file>` `VI_SAVESESSIONFILE=<file>`	You can save your authentication with a host to a session file.
`--server <server>` `VI_SERVER=<server>`	This option specifies the host to run the command against. If you connect to vCenter Server, you must also use the `--vihost` option.
`--servicepath <path>` `VI_SERVICEPATH=<path>`	This option uses the specified service path to connect to on your ESXi host. The default is `/sdk/webService`.

Table 8.1   *(Continued)*

Option	Description
`--sessionfile <file>` `VI_SESSIONFILE=<file>`	This option uses a saved session file to load a previous authentication session.
`--url <url>` `VI_URL=<url>`	With this option, you can specify the vSphere Web Services SDK URL.
`--username <username>` `VI_USERNAME=<username>`	This option specifies the username to use to authenticate to the host. If you are connecting to vCenter Server, you should use an account that has been granted privileges on vCenter Server. If you are connecting to an ESXi host, use an account with local privileges.
`--vihost <host>`	If the `--server` option is pointing to vCenter Server you must use the `--vihost` option to specify the ESXi host to run the command against. Note that this option is not supported for all vCLI commands.
`--h <host>`	

To view the connection options at a command prompt, you can use the `--help` option, which displays the connection options and command-specific help. Two other helpful options include `-verbose`, which displays additional debugging information, and `-version`, which shows the version information for the command and the vSphere SDK for Perl as shown in the following example:

```
vicfg-nics --version
vSphere SDK for Perl version: 4.1
Script 'vicfg-nics' version: 4.1
```

Most of the connection options in Table 8.1 deal with the method of authentication and it is worthwhile to examine how the vCLI orders the authentication methods that are available. If you're migrating scripts from ESX to ESXi, you don't want to embed passwords into your scripts. Rather, you want to use one of the methods that the vCLI provides, such as employing interactive logins, using a session file, or authenticating with your Windows credentials.

When you execute a vCLI command, authentication happens in the order shown in Table 8.2. This order is hard-coded and cannot be altered.

When you're using the command-line option, you can either specify the username and password in the command or use a session file. Using the `--password` option in a script is not recommended as it exposes the password to anyone with access to the script. When you're using the command-line options, you should enclose any special characters with single quotes on

Table 8.2 vCLI Authentication Precedence

Authentication Method	Description
Command line	The vCLI uses either the `--password` or `--sessionfile` options.
Configuration file	The password is stored in a configuration file.
Environment variable	The password is specified as an environment variable.
Credential store	The command retrieves the password from a credential store file.
Windows account	Windows SSPI passes the user's Windows credentials to the host.
Prompt for password	The user interactively enters the password, which is not echoed to the screen.

Linux and double quotes on Windows. You can also use the backslash (\) as an escape character, as shown in these examples:

Linux:

```
vicfg-nics --server esx01 --username 'user-1' --password 's@f#t&'
vicfg-nics --server esx01 --username user\-1 --password s\@f\#t\&
```

Windows:

```
vicfg-nics --server esx01 --username "user-1" --password "s@f#t&"
```

A more secure option for the command line is to use the save session script. This is an application of the vSphere SDK for Perl and is located in /usr/lib/vmware-vcli/apps/session for Linux and C:\Program Files\VMware\VMware vSphere CLI\Perl\apps\session for Windows. When you create a session file, the credentials stored in the file are valid for 30 minutes.

To create a session file, open a command prompt and go to the folder where the save_session script is stored. Run the following command to create a session file:

```
save_session --savesessionfile /tmp/session --server esx01 --username root
```

You can optionally include the --password parameter with the command, but if you don't, the system prompts you to enter the password. The saved session file does not contain the password but rather has the following information:

```
#LWP-Cookies-1.0
Set-Cookie3: vmware_soap_session="\"52ce644b-288d-12c9-d91f-6d6a48f832aa\"";
    path="/"; domain=esx01.local; path_spec; discard; version=0
```

To run commands, you may now reference the session file and other connection options are ignored:

```
vicfg-nics --sessionfile /tmp/session -l
```

With configuration file authentication, a plain text file contains the connection options shown in Table 8.1. A sample file would include the following items:

```
VI_SERVER = esx01
VI_USERNAME = root
VI_PASSWORD = Secret
VI_ENCODING = cp936
```

To execute a command, you would only have to reference the configuration file for your connection options, as is shown in this example:

```
vicfg-nics --config '/home/vi-admin/config' -l
```

Environment variables present a similar way to fix connection options. On a Linux system, you can set an environment variable in your command-line session with the following command:

```
export VI_SERVER=esx01
```

You can do the same in a Windows command prompt session with this command:

```
set VI_SERVER=esx01
```

After you have set the environment variables, you can issue the vCLI commands and omit the options. In the following example, the `--server` option is omitted as it is already set as an environment variable:

```
vicfg-nics --username root -l
```

With credential store authentication, the vSphere SDK for Perl is used to store and retrieve credentials from local database files. The vMA authentication component is an example of an application that uses a credential store. This is discussed further in the following section.

Tip: The credentials stored on the vMA are encrypted using standard encryption algorithms. There is a risk that a malicious user could obtain the virtual disk files for the vMA and then decrypt the passwords. To add an additional layer of security, it is possible to encrypt the filesystem in which the credentials and vMA database files are stored. That procedure is documented in this Knowledge Base article: http://kb.vmware.com/kb/1017669.

The last authentication method is to use Window SSPI and the `--passthroughauth` option to authenticate with vCenter Server. This option is not supported if you are connecting directly to ESXi. After you authenticate with vCenter Server, you do not have to supply credentials again for that session. You may have to set the `--passthroughauthpackage` option when authenticating in this manner. The default setting for this option is `Negotiate`, but for some systems you may have to change this setting to `Kerberos`.

In the following example, the option is used with the first vCLI command run and it is not required with subsequent commands:

```
vicfg-nics --server vcenter --vihost esx01 --passthroughauth
   --passthroughauthpackage "Kerberos" -l
vicfg-nas --server vcenter --vihost -l
```

The vCLI and ESXi Lockdown Mode As you have seen with the connection options, it is possible to run the vCLI commands directly against your ESXi hosts. This requires access to the management port on your hosts, which may be discouraged. If your organization has enabled Lockdown Mode, you can run the vCLI command only directly against vCenter Server. This can create a problem in that several of the vCLI commands may be executed only directly against an ESXi host. Those commands include the following:

- `vicfg-snmp`
- `vifs`
- `vicfg-user`
- `vicfg-cfgbackup`
- `vihostupdate`
- `vmkfstools`
- `esxcli`
- `vicfg-ipsec`

When you execute a command against a host that is in Lockdown Mode, you receive the following error:

```
vicfg-nics --server esx01 -l
```

```
Error: Permission to perform this operation was denied.
```

If you need to run these commands, you must first disable Lockdown Mode. The process to disable Lockdown Mode with the vSphere client was discussed in Chapter 7, "Securing ESXi." The script `vicfg-legacylockdown`, available with the Knowledge Base article at http://kb.vmware.com/kb/1017628, provides a useful sample of a script that makes use of the vSphere SDK for Perl. The purpose of the script is to revert the behavior of Lockdown Mode for ESXi 4.1 to the settings for ESXi 4.0. The differences were discussed in Chapter 7. The script can also be used to enable and disable Lockdown Mode. To disable Lockdown Mode on a host, run the command with the following syntax:

```
vicfg-legacylockdown --server vcenter41 --vihost esx01.mishchenko.net --disable
    --username mishchenko\dave.mishchenko
    --viadminuser mishchenko\dave.mishchenko
```

To enable Lockdown Mode again after you have run your scripts, run the preceding command but change `--disable` to `--enable`.

Configuring vMA Components

The vMA contains two additional components over the vCLI: the vi-logger component, which captures ESXi and vCenter Server log data, and the vMA authentication component, which stores credentials to enable passthrough authentication.

Configuring vi-fastpass Authentication

The vMA authentication component allows you to authenticate with target hosts using vi-fastpass or Active Directory. When adding a server as a target, you can configure which authentication method to use. If you use vi-fastpass authentication, the credentials that you have for vCenter Server or ESXi are stored in a local credential store. If you use Active Directory authentication, no credentials are stored locally, but the user authenticates with an Active Directory server.

When using vi-fastpass with an ESXi host, two accounts with encrypted passwords are created on the ESXi host. The account vi-admin is created with administrator rights, whereas the vi-user account is created on ESXi with read-only privileges. That password information is stored locally in a credential store. To enable a number of vMA appliances to manage the same ESXi host, each vMA appliance creates the accounts in the format of `vi-admin<XX>` and with a unique login name, as shown in Figure 8.3.

esx01.mishchenko.net VMware ESXi, 4.1.0, 235786

| Summary | Virtual Machines | Resource Allocation | Performance | Configuration | Local Users & Groups | Events | Permissions |

View: Users Groups

UID	User	Name
99	nobody	Nobody
504	vi-admin01	ESXID=523a507d-7f03-e517-91f3-6a080feebe90;VIMAID=421D45B7-A5E2-FF00-5E11-CA266CDDE296;
501	vi-admin00	ESXID=525c660e-30bd-671c-9f28-f2ae25df27db;VIMAID=564D4CEB-9777-B949-9839-2FDCBD5EB8AC;
100	dcui	DCUI User
503	admin1	Linux User,,,
500	vpxuser	VMware VirtualCenter administration account
0	root	Administrator
2	daemon	daemon
65534	nfsnobody	Anonymous NFS User
502	vi-user00	ESXID=525c660e-30bd-671c-9f28-f2ae25df27db;VIMAID=564D4CEB-9777-B949-9839-2FDCBD5EB8AC;
505	vi-user01	ESXID=523a507d-7f03-e517-91f3-6a080feebe90;VIMAID=421D45B7-A5E2-FF00-5E11-CA266CDDE296;
12	vimuser	vimuser

Figure 8.3   Each vMA appliance creates a unique instance of vi-admin and vi-user on an ESXi host.

If Active Directory is used to connect to the target host, the accounts are not created and no credentials are stored. It is necessary to set up the vMA to join the Active Directory (AD) domain.

Once you have configured your target hosts, you can issue the `vifptarget` command to start an authenticated session with the host. Subsequent vCLI commands that you run do not require the `--server` option or any authentication options.

Configuring Prerequisites for Active Directory Authentication

If you wish to use AD authentication, join the vMA appliance to your domain. When you configured the vMA appliance initially, you should have specified the DNS hosts for your domain and matched the domain name for the vMA appliance to your AD domain. It is also worthwhile to ensure that the time in the vMA is set to sync with your domain's Network Time Protocol (NTP) server. You can use these steps to configure the NTP setting on your vMA appliance:

1.   Run the command `sudo nano /etc/ntp.conf`.

2.   Add your NTP hosts under the following section: `# Use public servers from the pool.ntp.org project`. Press Ctrl+X and then enter Y for Yes to save and exit.

3.   Configure the `ntpd` daemon to start automatically with the command `sudo /sbin/chkconfig ntpd on`.

4.   Restart the `ntpd` daemon with the command `sudo /sbin/service ntpd restart`.

Before you begin the process to join the vMA appliance to your AD domain, you should ensure that you can resolve vCenter Server and domain controllers by their fully qualified domain names. Then use the following steps to add the vMA appliance to your domain:

1.   Log in to the vMA appliance with vi-admin.

2.   Enter the command to join the domain as shown in the following example:

     `sudo domainjoin-cli join mishchenko.net mishchenko\dave.mishchenko`

3.   When the system prompts you to do so, enter the password for the administrator account that you used for the command.

4.   Restart the vMA appliance.

After you have joined the domain, you can use the `query` option with `domainjoin-cli` to display the domain information and the `leave` option to remove the vMA from the domain. If you are having trouble joining the domain, ensure that the DNS settings are correct. It may also help to ensure that the time zone of the vMA appliance matches the time zone of the domain controllers. As an example, you can change the time zone to Pacific Standard Time (PST) with the following commands:

```
sudo rm /etc/localtime
sudo ln -s /usr/share/zoneinfo/America/Vancouver /etc/localtime
```

You can also begin to log in to the vMA appliance with your AD login. Then you can execute commands with the --passthroughauth option and your Windows credentials are passed through to vCenter Server and your ESXi hosts.

The second configuration item of AD authentication is to configure unattended authentication to AD targets. This process uses the Ktpass tool from Microsoft, which enables an administrator to configure a non-Windows Kerberos service as a security principal within AD. Without this setup, the vMA is not able to generate authentication tickets with AD that it uses to authenticate with vCenter Server or ESXi when it is enabled for AD integration. In the following example, the domain account is dave.mishchenko and the domain is MISHCHENKO.NET:

1. Download the Ktpass tool from microsoft.com and install it on a Windows computer that is part of the domain.

2. Run the Ktpass command with the following syntax:

    ```
    ktpass /out mishchenko.keytab /princ dave.mishchenko@mishchenko.net /pass ca...
        /ptype KRB5_NT_PRINCIPAL -mapuser mishchenko\dave.mishchenko
    ```

3. Copy the file to the folder /home/local/MISHCHENKO/dave.mishchenko.

4. Ensure that the owner is set to match the domain account by running the following command:

    ```
    sudo chown 'MISHCHENKO\dave.mishchenko'
        /home/local/MISHCHENKO/dave.mishchenko/mishchenko.keytab
    ```

5. Create the file /etc/cron.hourly/kticket-new and add the following text. Note the use of the \ escape character.

    ```
    #!/bin/sh

    su - MISHCHENKO\\dave.mishchenko -c '/usr/kerberos/bin/kinit -k
      -t /home/local/MISHCHENKO/dave.mishchenko/mishchenko.keytab dave.mishchenko'
    ```

The cron job that is created renews the Kerberos ticket for the specified account each hour. You could also add the script to /etc/init.d to refresh tickets when the vMA appliance is started. If you plan to use multiple accounts to add target hosts to your vMA appliance, you need to create a keytab file for each account and update the script in step 5 to refresh the Kerberos ticket for each user account.

Adding and Managing Target Servers

In this section, you examine the steps to add the target host to your vMA appliance. The recommended method is to use AD authentication, as no passwords are stored on the vMA appliance. If the AD setup in the preceding section had not been performed, it would require adding targets with credentials that would be stored locally. In the following example, a vCenter Server and ESXi host are added as targets on the vMA appliance. The `vifp` command is used with the `addserver` option to add the hosts as targets. In both cases, the authentication policy for vi-fastpass is set to `adauth` (AD authentication).

```
vifp addserver vcenter.mishchenko.net --authpolicy adauth
   --username 'MISHCHENKO\dave.mishchenko'
vifp addserver esx01.mishchenko.net --authpolicy adauth
   --username 'MISHCHENKO\dave.mishchenko'
```

To query the hosts that have been added as targets, you use the `listservers` option:

```
vifp listservers --long
vcenter.mishchenko.net     vCenter  adauth
esx01.mishchenko.net       ESXi     adauth
```

To begin using vi-fastpass, you issue the `vifptarget` command and set a target. No authentication is required and once you set a host with `vifptarget`, all subsequent commands run against that host. To switch to another target, you must issue the `vifptarget` command again:

```
vifptarget --set esx01.mishchenko.net
vicfg-nics -l
vifptarget -s vcenter.mishchenko.net
vicfg-nics --vihost esx02.mishchenko.net -l
```

In the case of a vMA appliance without the preceding AD configuration, you must use the `fpauth` authentication option as shown in the following example. Note the security warning that is displayed and the requirement to provide a password for the AD account.

```
vifp addserver vcenter.mishchenko.net --authpolicy fpauth
   --username 'MISHCHENKO\dave.mishchenko'
MISHCHENKO\dave.mishchenko@vcenter.mishchenko.net's password:
This will store username and password in credential store which is a security risk.
Do you want to continue?(yes/no): yes
vifp addserver esx01.mishchenko.net --authpolicy fpauth
   --username 'MISHCHENKO\dave.mishchenko'
MISHCHENKO\dave.mishchenko@esx01.mishchenko.net's password:
```

Running a query of the targets set up on the vMA appliance, as in the following example, shows the authentication method used for these hosts, but no authentication is required as expected when setting the hosts as targets, as was the cause with the preceding AD configuration.

```
vifp listservers --long
vcenter.mishchenko.net      vCenter   fpauth
esx01.mishchenko.net        ESXi      fpauth

vifptarget --set esx01.mishchenko.net
vicfg-nics -l
vifptarget -s vcenter.mishchenko.net
vicfg-nics --vihost esx02.mishchenko.net -l
```

In addition to the difference in authentication, one other difference with using vi-fastpass authentication is the setup of the accounts vi-admin and vi-user on any ESXi targets that you define. The vi-admin account is granted the Administrator role on the ESXi host, whereas the vi-user account is granted the Read-Only role. By default, the vi-user account on the vMA appliance is disabled. You can enable it by setting a password for the account. To do this, log in with the vi-admin account and run the command `sudo passwd vi-user` and then follow the prompts. When users log in to the vMA appliance with the vi-user account, they can only execute read-only commands against ESXi hosts set up with vi-fastpass authentication. If the account is used to run a command against an ESXi host set up with AD authentication or a vCenter Server host with any authentication mode, the user is prompted for another username and password. The vi-user account is not able to execute any commands using `sudo`.

The `vifp` command also includes the `reconfigure` option. This option can be used for the following purposes:

- To change the authentication mode used with a target.

- To change the user configured for an AD target.

- To recover users for a vi-fastpass target. A user needs to be recovered if the vMA credential store is corrupted or if the user accounts on the ESXi host are updated without a corresponding change made on the vMA appliance.

To change the authentication policy from vi-fastpass to AD, you can issue the following command:

`vifp reconfigure esx01.mishchenko.net --authpolicy adauth`

To change the configured user or recover users, issue this command:

`vifp reconfigure esx01.mishchenko.net`

You may also have to use the `removeserver` option to manage hostname changes and before you delete a vMA appliance. If you change the hostname for one of your ESXi hosts, you should use the option to delete the target and then add the target again with its new hostname. You should also issue the command when you plan to delete the vMA appliance, as removing a target ESXi host deletes the vi-admin and vi-user accounts that were created when the host was first made a vi-fastpass target.

The last option for `vifp` to be aware of is `rotatepassword`. When you use the vi-fastpass authentication option, by default the passwords for the accounts created on your ESXi hosts are never changed. You can enable password changing by setting a password rotation policy. If you run the command `vifp rotatepassword -- now`, the passwords for vi-admin and vi-user on all your ESXi hosts are updated and the changed passwords are recorded in the local credential store. You can also append the `--server` option to `--now` to change the passwords for a specific ESXi target. The `--days` option is used to set the frequency of password changes, whereas `--never` disables password changes. If you use `rotatepassword` without any options, the current rotation policy is displayed.

Capturing ESXi Logs with vi-logger

With the vi-logger component, you can capture log files from vCenter Server and ESXi. Use of vi-logger is suitable for small and medium-sized environments, but for large environments, you should consider using an enterprise-scale log collection tool rather than vi-logger. From vCenter Server, you can gather the `vpxd.log` file, which contains logging data for the vCenter Server Windows service. For ESXi, you can capture the following log files:

- **/var/log/messages.** This log file contains the VMkernel logs and warnings, host daemon messages, and other user-level daemon messages. This log file contains the same data you would find in `vmkernel`, `vmkwarnings`, and `hostd` log files on an ESX system.

- **/var/log/vmware/hostd.log.** This is the host agent log file.

- **/var/log/vmware/vpx/vpxa.log.** This is the vCenter Agent log file.

The heart of the vi-logger component is the `vilogd` daemon, which is responsible for log collection. The daemon is set to start automatically each time the vMA virtual machine is started. When you are logged in with the vi-admin account, you can control and check the start of the `vilogd` daemon. To check the status of the service, run the following command:

```
/sbin/service vmware-vilogd status
vmware-vilogd is running
```

To restart the daemon, you can issue this command:

```
sudo /sbin/service vmware-vilogd restart
Stopping vmware-vilogd:                    [ OK ]
Starting vmware-vilogd:                    [ OK ]
```

To configure hosts for log collection, you use the command `vilogger`. Prior to adding a host, you must configure it as a vMA target, as shown in the previous section. When you want to start capturing data, you first need to enable logging for some or all of your vMA targets. To accomplish this, you run `vilogger enable`, and you can include the options in Table 8.3 to customize the logging configuration. If you run `vilogger enable` with no options, all your vMA targets are enabled for logging with the default values for the options in Table 8.3.

Table 8.3 vilogger enable Command Options

Option	Description
server	This specifies the hostname or IP address for the vMA target. If this option is omitted, all vMA targets are added.
logname	You can specify a log file to capture. The default value is to enable all log files.
collectionperiod	This option specifies how often a log file should be collected. The default value is 10 seconds and you can use a value between 10 and 3600.
maxfilesize	With this option, you set the maximum size for log files before rollover. The default value is 5MB and you can set the value between 1 and 1024.
numrotation	This option sets the number of log files to keep before the oldest is deleted. The default is 5 and you can configure this option with a value between 1 and 1024.

You can use any combination of options to customize the logging level for each host. In the following example, the first command gathers all log files on an ESXi host and collects data every 60 seconds. The second command collects the vpxd.log file from vCenter Server and retains 100MB worth of logged data, using 10 log files.

```
vilogger enable --server esx01.mishchenko.net --collectionperiod 60

Target Server: esx01.mishchenko.net
hostd       ... Enabled
messages    ... Enabled
vpxa        ... Enabled


vilogger enable --server vcenter.mishchenko.net --numrotation 10 --maxfilesize 10

Target Server: vcenter.mishchenko.net
vpxd        ... Enabled
```

To review the logs being collected by the vilogd daemon, you can issue the command vilogger list. You can optionally include --server or --logname to filter the output. The output of vilogger list is shown in Figure 8.4.

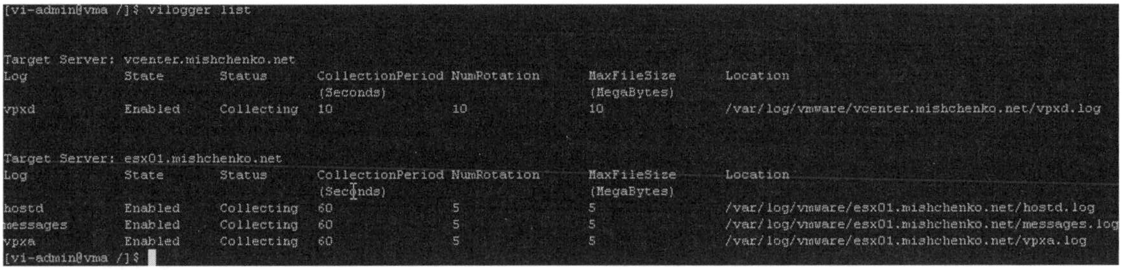

Figure 8.4 Displaying the `vilogger` configuration with `vilogger list`.

Tip: As mentioned in an earlier chapter, when ESXi logs data, the time stamps are in the Coordinated Universal Time (UTC) time zone. You can change the vMA to have the same time zone with the following commands:

```
sudo rm /etc/localtime
sudo ln -s /usr/share/zoneinfo/UTC /etc/localtime
sudo reboot
```

To update log collection for a vMA target, you can use `vilogger updatepolicy`. This command uses the options shown in Table 8.3. To update the logging configuration for the ESXi host used in the preceding example, you would issue the following command:

```
vilogger updatepolicy --server esx01.mischenko.net --collectionperiod 30
```

With this command, all logs being gathered for the ESXi host would now be collected every 30 seconds. If you need to disable logging, you can use `vilogger disable`. This command takes the options of `--server`, `--logname`, and `--force`. The `--force` option should be used when the vMA target is unreachable; otherwise, the `vilogger disable` command fails. In the first example, logging of the message's log file for an ESXi host is disabled; in the second example, all logging for an ESXi host is disabled; and in the last example, all logging on the vMA appliance is disabled.

```
vilogger disable --server esx01.mishchenko.net --logname messages
vilogger disable --server esx01.mishchenko.net
vilogger disable
```

Increasing Storage in the vMA If you're collecting log data for a number of hosts, you may find that the partition allocated for storage of log data is too small. You can use the following process to add additional space for the storage of log files captured by the `vilogd` daemon:

1. Start the vSphere client and connect to vCenter Server or your ESXi host running the vMA virtual machine.

2. Right-click on the vMA and select Power > Shut Down Guest.

3. Right-click on the vMA and select Edit Settings.

4. Add an additional virtual disk to the vMA.

5. Power on the virtual machine.

6. Log in to the vMA with vi-admin.

7. Format the new disk with the following command: `sudo fdisk /dev/sdb`.

8. In the `fdisk` session, press the following key sequence: n to create a new partition, p to create a primary partition, 1 to make it partition1, Enter to accept the default first cylinder, and Enter to accept the default for the last cylinder.

9. You can press p to verify that a partition has been created on the disk.

10. Press w to write the partition table to the disk and to exit.

11. Execute the following command to format the partition: `sudo mkfs -t ext3 /dev/sdb1`.

12. Enter the command `sudo nano /etc/fstab`. Add the following line and then press Ctrl+X, and then y to save the file.

    `/dev/sdb1    /var/log/syslog    ext3    defaults,auto    1 2`

13. Enter the command `cd /var/log` and then `sudo mkdir syslog`.

14. Run the command `sudo chown vi-admin:root /var/log/syslog`.

15. Mount the new disk with `sudo mount /var/log/syslog`.

16. Run the command `sudo nano /etc/vmware/vMA/vMA.conf` to edit the `vilogd` daemon configuration file.

17. Change each location entry to be the following:

    `<location>/var/log/syslog</location>`

    Then press Ctrl+X and y to save the change and exit.

18. Restart the `vilogd` daemon with the command `sudo service vmware-vilodg restart`.

Managing vSphere with the vCLI

The vCLI includes many commands to make the transition from managing your ESX hosts at the console to managing ESXi with the vCLI an easy road. Version 4.1 of the vCLI includes new commands to configure AD integration, configure Internet Protocol Security (IPSec), and to manage the state of your hosts. Use of some of the vCLI commands has already been discussed in other chapters, so we won't repeat their discussion here. Rather, this section highlights some of the commands that are available and discusses the new vCLI features for ESXi 4.1. For a more complete reference to the vCLI, you can consult the vSphere Command-Line Interface Manual and the vSphere Command-Line Interface Reference. Both can be found at the following URL: http://www.vmware.com/support/developer/vcli/.

A list of the vCLI commands can be found in Table 8.4. For the most part, these commands may be run against ESX(i) 3.5, ESX(i) 4.x, and vCenter Server. The commands that must be executed directly against an ESXi host were noted earlier in this chapter. If you are starting to migrate from ESX 3.5 to ESXi 4.1, you can begin to use the vCLI on your existing ESX hosts and start to convert your scripts to execute with the vCLI instead of the Service Console. If you review the vCLI commands in the vCLI `bin` folder, you can see that many of the commands exist both with an `esxcfg` and a `vicfg` prefix. The `esxcfg` commands are included to provide backward compatibility for the scripts you may have. On Linux systems, the `esxcfg` commands exist as symbolic links to the corresponding `vicfg` commands. If you are developing new scripts for the vCLI, it is recommended to use the `vicfg` commands, as the `esxcfg` commands may not be included in the future. New commands added to the vCLI such as `vicfg-hostops` do not include an `esxcfg` equivalent.

Table 8.4 vCLI Command Summary

Option	Description
`esxcli`	Provides a command-line interface to access components called namespaces. Some of the namespaces allow management of elements such as storage multipathing, software iSCSI, and virtual machines.
`resxtop`	Monitors ESXi hosts in real-time or Batch Mode.
`svmotion`	Migrates a virtual machine's configuration file and disks between datastores that the virtual machine is running.
`vicfg-advcfg`	Configures advanced options, including enabling and disable Common Information Model (CIM) providers.
`vicfg-authconfig`	Enables the configuration of an ESXi host for AD integration.
`vicfg-cfgbackup`	Backs up and restores the system configuration files for an ESXi host.

Table 8.4   (*Continued*)

Option	Description
vicfg-dns	Configures the DNS settings for an ESXi host.
vicfg-dumppart	Manages the diagnostic partitions.
vicfg-hostops	Performs host operations, including rebooting hosts and placing a host in Maintenance Mode.
vicfg-ipsec	Secures IP communication by enabling IPsec for IPv6.
vicfg-iscsi	Configures iSCSI storage.
vicfg-module	Manages VMkernel modules.
vicfg-mpath	Configures storage arrays.
vicfg-mpath35	Configures storage arrays for ESX(i) 3.5 hosts.
vicfg-nas	Configures network attached storage (NAS) for use as datastores.
vicfg-nics	Manages your ESXi host's physical network interface cards (NICs).
vicfg-ntp	Configures NTP settings for your host.
vicfg-rescan	Rescans your storage configuration for changes and new storage.
vicfg-route	Changes the routes used for the VMkernel on ESXi.
vicfg-scsidevs	Lists available logical unit numbers (LUNs).
vicfg-snmp	Configures SNMP on your ESXi host.
vicfg-syslog	Configures the syslog server and port to which your ESXi host forwards log files.
vicfg-user	Manages users and groups defined locally on ESXi.
vicfg-vmknic	Configures the VMkernel network interfaces.
vicfg-volume	Manages duplicate Virtual Machine File System (VMFS) volumes, including resignaturing, mounting, and unmounting.
vicfg-vswitch	Manages virtual switches (vSwitches) on the ESXi host.
vifs	Performs filesystem operations such as uploading files to a datastore.
vihostupdate	Updates ESXi 4.x hosts.
vihostupdate35	Updates ESXi 3.5 hosts.
vmkfstools	Manages virtual disks, datastores, and storage devices.
vmware-cmd	Manages virtual machines, including starting and stopping them.

Managing ESXi Hosts

The host-related commands can perform a number of management and configuration tasks on your ESXi hosts. You have already seen examples of a number of these commands used in previous chapters, such as `vicfg-authconfig` for enabling AD integration, `vicfg-ipsec` for configuring IPsec, and `vicfg-ntp` for enabling NTP synchronization. In the following section, you learn about the other host-related vCLI commands.

One of the new vCLI commands in vSphere 4.1 is `vicfg-hostops`. To shut down a host, you can issue the following command:

```
vicfg-hostops --operation shutdown --force.
```

With the `--force` option, the command shuts down all running virtual machines and then the host. You can omit this option if you've put the host into Maintenance Mode. With this command, you can also use the `--cluster` or `--datacenter` options to shut down entire clusters or datacenters as required.

Note: Throughout this section and the following sections, connection options are not displayed with the commands. If you are not using vi-fastpass authentication or another method to specify the connection options discussed earlier, you need to add those options.

You can also use the `reboot` option, which works in the same manner as `shutdown` and accepts the same options. Prior to issuing a reboot or `shutdown` command, a host should be placed in Maintenance Mode. For a host that is a member of a Distributed Resource Scheduler (DRS) cluster, the virtual machines running on the host migrate to other hosts before the server can enter Maintenance Mode. If the host is not a member of a DRS cluster, `vicfg-hostops` suspends any running virtual machines. A host remains in Maintenance Mode until you take it out of Maintenance Mode, and no virtual machines can be started on a host in Maintenance Mode. Run the following command to place a host into Maintenance Mode:

```
vicfg-hostops --operation enter
```

You can also use the `--cluster` or `--datacenter` options with this operation. To take a host out of Maintenance Mode, you can substitute the option `exit`. When you put a host in Maintenance Mode, you can get the status of that operation with the `info` option. This option also displays information about the host's central processing unit (CPU), memory, whether vMotion is enabled, and the last boot time. An example of the output for the `info` option follows:

```
vicfg-hostops --operation info
```

```
Host Name        : esx01.mishchenko.net
Manufacturer     : Supermicro
Model            : X8DTL
```

```
Processor Type      : Intel(R) Xeon(R) CPU E5520 @ 2.27GHz
CPU Cores           : 4 CPUs x 2266 GHz
Memory Capacity     : 8182.8359375 MB
vMotion Enabled     : yes
In Maintenance Mode : yes
Last Boot Time      : 2010-07-27T06:10:48.791755Z
```

> **Note:** One of the sample scripts included with the vSphere SDK for Perl is a utility called hostops. In addition to providing the operations performed by vicfg-hostops, this utility includes the following operations: add_standalone, disconnect, addhost, reconnect, removehost, moveintofolder, and moveintocluster. You can find more information about this utility in this document: http://www.vmware.com/support/developer/viperltoolkit/viperl41/doc/hostops.html.

Each of your ESXi hosts should be configured with a dump partition. The command vicfg-dumppart is used to display the configuration of the dump partition and to make changes to it. The dump partition is used to store core dumps should your host fail and display a purple screen. You can modify the dump partition to be located on a Fibre Channel or iSCSI LUN, but the iSCSI LUN should be accessible via a hardware iSCSI adapter.

To display the current configuration, issue the following command:

```
vicfg-dumppart --get-active
```

To display the potential targets, you can use the --find option. The active dump partition is shown as well as all potential partitions. The output may display partitions accessible via the ESXi software iSCSI adapter, but these should not be used for the dump partition. To change the dump partition, you first run vicfg-dumppart with the --deactivate option. Then use the --set option and specify one of the available partitions to set and activate the new dump partition.

From time to time, you may find that you have to set advanced configuration options on your ESXi host. This can be accomplished with the vSphere client, as shown in Figure 8.5. You may be instructed by VMware support to make such a change or you may be following a Knowledge Base article.

These configuration changes can also be made with the command vicfg-advcfg. The following commands are used to increase the number of Network File System (NFS) mounts that an ESXi host can support:

```
vicfg-advcfg -s 32 NFS.MaxVolumes
Value of MaxVolumes is 32

vicfg-advcfg -s 120 Net.TcpipHeapMax
Value of TcpipHeapMax is 120
```

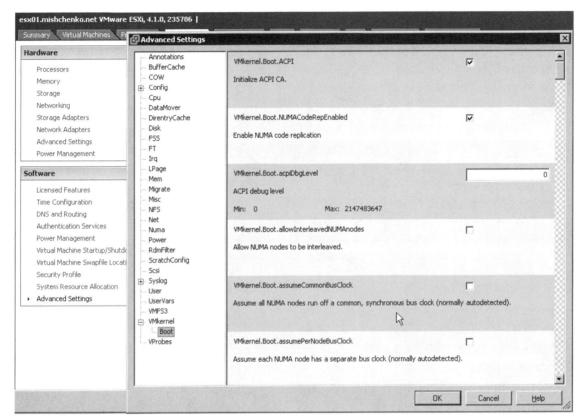

Figure 8.5 Adjusting advanced configuration settings with the vSphere client.

Tip: Another useful sample script in the vSphere SDK for Perl is `mcli`, which is found in `/opt/vmware/vima/samples/perl`. This script can be used to execute a command against a number of hosts. First generate a text file containing the hostnames of your ESXi scripts. Then run the script with the following syntax to run the `vicfg-advcfg` command against all the hosts listed in the text file.

```
mcli <file containing ESXi server list> vicfg-advcfg -s 32 NFS.MaxVolumes
```

The `vicfg-module` command is used to set and retrieve VMkernel module options. The `--list` and `--query` options display the modules that the VMkernel has loaded. You can change options for a module with the `--set-option` option. The following example changes the queue depth for all Emulex Fibre Channel adapters using the specified module:

```
esxcfg-module --set-option 'lpfc_lun_queue_depth=20' lpfc820.o
```

After you have set an option, you can use the following command to query the module to verify the change:

```
esxcfg-module --get-option lpfc820.o
```

The final command for managing your host that this section discusses is vicfg-user. This command is used to manage accounts and groups that are locally defined on your ESXi host. With this command, you can assign users and groups to a role, but you cannot create or manage roles with it. Table 8.5 lists the command's options. The command is always issued with the following format:

```
vifcg-user --entity <user | group> --operation <add | modify | delete | list>
```

To create a user, you can use the following command:

```
vicfg-user --entity user --operation add --login user1 --newpassword Secret45
```

Table 8.5 vicfg-user Command Options

Option	Description
--entity <group|user>	The object to perform the operation on. This is either user or group.
--operation	The operation to perform. This can include add, delete, list, or modify.
--addgroup <group_list>	Comma-separated list of groups to add a user to.
--adduser <user_list>	Comma-separated list of users to add to a group.
--group <name>	The name of the group.
--groupid <group_id>	The group ID for the group.
--login <login_id>	Login ID of the user.
--newpassword <p_wd>	Password for the target user.
--newuserid <UUID>	New UUID for the target user.
--newusername <name>	New username for the target user.
--removegroup <group_list>	Comma-separated list of groups to remove a user from.
--removeuser <user_list>	Comma-separated list of users to remove from a group.
--role <admin|read-only|no-access>	Role to assign user to. The valid options are admin, read-only, and no-access.

The command does not include the `--role` option, so this new login does not have access to the ESXi host. To verify that the user was created, you can change the operation to `list` to view all users defined on the host:

```
vicfg-user --entity user --operation list
```

To change the role for an existing user, change the `operation` to `modify`, as the following example shows:

```
vicfg-user --entity user --operation modify --login user1 --role admin
```

The `vicfg-user` command script is coded to accept only `admin`, `read-only`, and `no-access` as valid roles even if you have defined other roles on the host. If you are interested in learning more about scripting with the vSphere SDK for Perl, you can start by modifying an existing script such as `vicfg-user` to meet your needs.

To manage groups with `vicfg-user`, you change the `--entity` option to `group`. If you require a number of local users on your ESXi hosts with the same permissions, it is easier to create a group, assign permissions to the group, and then to add users to the group. To create a new group and assign a role to it, issue the following command. You can optionally add the `--groupid` parameter to assign a group ID to the new group.

```
vicfg-user --entity group --operation add --group ESXiAdmins --role admin
```

To add a user to that group, you can issue the following command:

```
vicfg-user --entity group --operation modify --group ESXiAdmins --adduser admin1
```

To add a number of users to the group in one command, you list the users separated by a comma:

```
vicfg-user --entity group --operation modify --group ESXiAdmins
    --adduser admin1, admin2, admin3
```

Although such use is not documented as being officially supported, you can use `vicfg-user` to manage AD users if the host has been enabled for AD integration. You cannot create an AD user or group on your ESXi, but you can assign a role to the account or group.

```
vicfg-user --entity user --operation modify -login 'MISHCHENKO\dave.mishchenko'
    --role admin
Updated user MISHCHENKO\dave.mishchenko successfully.
Assigned the role admin
vicfg-user --entity user --operation delete -login 'MISHCHENKO\dave.mishchenko'
Removed the user MISHCHENKO\dave.mishchenko successfully.

vicfg-user --entity group --operation modify --group 'MISHCHENKO\Domain Admins'
    --role admin
Assigned the role admin
```

```
Vicfg-user --entity group --operation delete --group 'MISHCHENKO\domain^admins'
Deleted MISHCHENKO\domain^admins successfully.
```

Note that although the commands to add an AD user or group are not case-sensitive for the username or group name, it is case-sensitive when the commands are deleting the user or group. When adding a user or group with a space in the name, ESXi replaces the space with the ^ character. When you delete the user or group, you must include this as shown in the removal of the domain admins group in the preceding example.

Managing Virtual Machines

The vCLI includes a version of vmware-cmd, svmotion, which allows you to migrate virtual machines, and the esxcli command has been improved to allow the forcible termination of virtual machines. The vmware-cmd enables the following virtual machine functions:

- Start, stop, and reset virtual machines

- List and register virtual machines

- Manage virtual machine snapshots

- Retrieve virtual machine attributes

- Connect and disconnect virtual devices

- Retrieve user input

When using vmware-cmd, you follow this syntax for entering commands:

```
vmware-cmd <virtual machine config file> <operation> <operation options>
```

To view a list of virtual machines registered on your ESXi host, you run the following command. The output lists the full path to the virtual machines configuration file, including the datastore UUID rather than the datastores logical name.

```
vmware-cmd -l
/vmfs/volumes/4a7cf921-017eb919-bb32-000423e540c6/SQL04/SQL04.vmx
```

When entering vmware-cmd commands that require the virtual machine's configuration file, you can enter the full path as shown in the preceding example. Alternatively, you can use the datastore logical name in either of the following formats. If you are using the first method shown, you need to enclose the path in quotes appropriate to the OS that you are running the vCLI on.

```
[datastore1] SQL04/SQL04.vmx
/vmfs/volumes/datastore1/SQL04/SQL04.vmx
```

To register a virtual machine, you can use the -s option, as shown in this example:

```
vmware-cmd -s register vmfs/volumes/datastore1/SQL04/SQL04.vmx
```

For `vmware-cmd` commands, a 1 is returned for a successful operation and a 0 for a failure.

You can use `vmware-cmd` to obtain information about the virtual machine and the host that it is running on. Table 8.6 summarizes the operations that are available.

Table 8.6 vmware-cmd Attribute Operations

Operation	Description
getuptime	This displays virtual machine uptime is seconds
getproductinfo product	This lists the VMware product that the virtual machine is running on.
getproductinfo platform	This lists the host platform such as Linux or Windows for VMware Workstation or vmnix-x86 for ESXi.
getproductinfo build, majorversion, minorversion	These options return build information about the platform hosting the virtual machine.
getstate	This returns information about the state of the machine, which can be on, off, suspended, or unknown.
gettoolslastactive	This returns the state of VMware Tools and the time interval since the last VMware Tool heartbeat. The values for the statistics of VMware Tools are 0 (VMware Tools is not installed or running), 1 (the guest OS is responding okay), 5 (there is an intermittent heartbeat, which could indicate an issue), and 100 (there is no heartbeat, which may indicate that the guest OS has stopped responding).

To start the virtual machine, you can use the following command. To stop the virtual machine, you change the operation to `stop`, but you also must specify an operation option of `soft` or `hard`. For the `soft` option, ESXi attempts to perform a clean shutdown of the guest OS via VMware Tools. With the `hard` option, ESXi simply powers down the virtual machine. The other power operations are `suspend` and `reset`.

```
vmware-cmd /vmfs/volumes/datastore1/SQL04/SQL04.vmx start
```

In some cases, you may find that you cannot power down a virtual machine or reset it. On ESX, you may have followed a process of accessing the Service Console, using the `ps` command to find the process ID for the virtual machine and then issuing a `kill` command on that process ID. With ESXi and the vCLI, you can use `esxcli` to accomplish the same process. `esxcli` is a new interface for vSphere that provides modular access to various components called namespaces. `esxcli` accesses an unpublished API to perform high-level configuration, such as iSCSI configuration and storage multipathing, and management of various components, such as core storage commands.

To use `esxcli` to kill an unresponsive virtual machine, you first need to determine the World ID. Run the following command to return a list of running virtual machines on the host:

```
esxcli vms vm list
SQL04
  World ID: 9577
  Process ID: 0
  VMX Cartel ID: 9576
  UUID: 56 4d 2e 83 2f 38 ff 7f-ff f8 62 58 03 86 2b a0
  Display Name: SQL04
  Config File: /vmfs/volumes/4a7cf921-017eb919-bb32-0423e540c6/SQL04/SQL04.vmx
```

After you have the World ID, you can issue the `kill` command:

```
esxcli --server esx01 vms vm kill --type hard --world-id 9577
true
```

The `kill` command requires the option `--type` to specify the nature of the `kill` operation to perform. The following three options are available and should be executed in sequential order:

- `soft`. This option attempts to shut the virtual machine down cleanly similar to using `kill` or `kill -SIGTERM` with ESX.

- `hard`. This stops the VMX process immediately like `kill -9` or `kill -SIGKILL`.

- `force`. This option should be used if the other two options are not able to shut down the virtual machine.

The `svmotion` command allows you to move a virtual machine's configuration file and optionally its virtual disks to another datastore while the virtual machine is running. You can choose a single location for the configuration file and virtual disks or choose separate locations for each. You can't change the host that the virtual machine is running on with `svmotion`.

The `svmotion` command can be run in one of two modes. In Noninteractive Mode, you specify the new location for the configuration file and optionally new locations for one or more of the virtual disks:

```
svmotion --datacenter=<datacenter name>
   --vm <virtual machine configuration datastore path>:<new datastore>
   [--disks <virtual disk datastore path>:<new datastore>,
   <virtual disk datastore path>:<new datastore>]
```

With Interactive Mode, you add the `--interactive` option, in which case all other options are ignored. In this mode, the script prompts you for each required parameter. The parameters that you enter are validated as you enter them; because of this, you cannot, for example, enter a datastore name that does not exist. This option can be useful for troubleshooting if you are having problems with Noninteractive Mode. For either mode, you should ensure that you enclose parameters in quotes if they contain special characters.

Managing Host Networking

With the vCLI networking commands, you can manage the configuration of your host's networking services. The vCLI includes the following four commands for networking: `vicfg-nics`, `vicfg-vswitch`, `vicfg-vmknic`, and `vicfg-route`.

To manage the physical NICs in your host, you use the command `vicfg-nics`. The `--list` option provides a list of the NIC ports that are visible to your host, as shown in Figure 8.6. You may need to obtain this information before you can begin to create vSwitches.

```
Name    PCI      Driver    Link Speed     Duplex MAC Address       MTU   Description
vmnic0  06:00.0  e1000e    Up   1000Mbps  Full   00:30:48:db:68:88 1500  Intel Corporation 82574L
vmnic1  07:00.0  e1000e    Up   1000Mbps  Full   00:30:48:db:68:89       Intel Corporation 82574L
```

Figure 8.6 A list of physical NIC ports generated by `vicfg-nics`.

Should you need to configure the speed or duplex settings for a NIC, you can use the `--speed` and `--duplex` options. To set the speed and duplex for the vmnic0 of the host, you would issue the following command:

`vicfg-nics --duplex full --speed 1000 vmnic0`

A NIC can be set to auto negotiation with this command:

`vicfg-nics --auto vmnic0`

The `vicfg-vswitch` command is used to manage both standard vSwitch and Distributed Virtual Switches (dvSwitch). With dvSwitches you must create a dvSwitch and then add hosts to it with the vSphere client when connected to vCenter Server. You can then manage ports and properties with `vicfg-vswitch`.

To create a new vSwitch, you can issue the following command. No output is displayed unless there is an error.

`vicfg-vswitch --add vSwitch1`

To create a port group on that vSwitch, you issue the following command:

`vicfg-vswitch --add-pg iSCSI1 vSwitch1`

Tip: If you're scripting creation of vSwitches and port groups, you can check for the existence of either before issuing the command to create them. The check returns a value of 1 if the object exists and 0 if it does not.

```
vicfg-vswitch --check vSwitch1
1
vicfg-vswitch --check-pg PortGroup1 vSwitch1
0
```

To link a vSwitch to a physical network port, you can use the command that follows. You can also link a NIC port to a specific port group.

```
vicfg-vswitch --link vmnic2 vSwitch1
Updated uplinks: vmnic2
```

Should you require the setup of virtual local area networks (VLANs) on your port groups, use the --vlan option. You can configure a specific VLAN, use 0 to disable the VLAN for a port group, or use 4095 to allow VLAN tags set by the guest OS to pass through the vSwitch unchanged. The following example sets the VLAN to 100 for the port group created earlier:

```
vicfg-vswitch --vlan 100 -pg PortGroup1 vSwitch1
```

Once you have configured your vSwitch, you can review the settings with the --list option. If you want to enable jumbo frames, you may also change the maximum transmission unit (MTU) for the vSwitch with the --mtu option. If you're using Cisco switches, you can enable the Cisco Discovery Procotol with --set-cdp.

To configure VMkernel networking, you use the vicfg-vmknic command. With ESXi, you have no Service Console ports, but rather you create a VMkernel port for management traffic, vMotion traffic, and IP storage. If you're configuring iSCSI storage, you can first create a VMkernel port and then bind it for iSCSI usage with esxcli, as you can see in the next section, "Managing Host Storage."

To add a new VMkernel port, you supply an IP address, subnet mask, and name, as in the following example. The name should be an existing port group that you've created with vicfg-vswitch.

```
vicfg-vmknic --add --ip 192.168.1.105 -n 255.255.255.0 iSCSI1
Added the VMkernel NIC successfully
```

To change the IP address for a VMkernel port, you can issue the following command. You can either specify an IP address or DHCP if you plan to use that.

```
vicfg-vmknic --ip 192.168.1.110 iSCSI1
```

Some of the other options for the command include --enable-vmotion, --mtu to set the MTU, and --tso to disable Transmission Control Protocol (TCP) Segmentation Offload (TSO) for the

VMkernel port. If you plan to use IPv6 with your VMkernel networking, you must first enable IPv6 on the VMkernel port. To enable IPv6, you can issue the following command sequence:

```
vicfg-vmknic --enable-ipv6 true iSCSI1
Please reboot the system now for the change to take effect.
vicfg-hostops --operation enter
Host esx10.mishchenko.net entered into maintenance mode successfully.
vicfg-hostops --operation reboot
Host esx10.mishchenko.net rebooted successfully.
```

After the host has rebooted, you can set an IPv6 address on a VMkernel port using the `--ip` option used earlier for an IPv4 address. The valid options for setting an IPv6 address are to use a static IPv6 address, `DHCPv6` for a DHCP IPv6 address, and `AUTOCONF` to obtain an IPv6 address via router advertisement. Don't forget to take the host out of Maintenance Mode.

To disable IPv6 on the host, you first remove the IPv6 address and then use the `--enable-ipv6` option to disable it:

```
vicfg-vmknic --unset-ip 2001:10:20:253::20/64
vicfg-vmknic --enable-ipv6 false iSCSI1
```

To manage the VMkernel gateway or routing, you can use `vicfg-route`. If the command is run without any options, the IPv4 default gateway is shown. Use the `--family v6` option to configure or display the IPv6 gateway. To set the default VMkernel gateways for IPv4 and IPv6, run the following commands:

```
vicfg-route --add default 192.168.1.1
vicfg-route --family v6 --add default 2001:10:20:253::1
```

To change the default gateway, you must first delete the existing gateway and then add the new one. Use the following command to delete the default IPv6 gateway:

```
vicfg-route --family v6 --delete default 2001:10:20:253::1
WARNING! Removing the default route for system!
Removing the default route may result in lost network connectivity
Are you sure you wish to proceed? (y/n) y
```

To add routes to your ESXi host, you can use the following commands:

```
vicfg-route --add 192.168.2.0/24 192.168.1.2
vicfg-route --family v6 --add 2000:10:20:254::/64 2001:10:20:253::2
```

One of the new namespaces added to `esxcli` for vSphere 4.1 is `network`. This namespace allows you to list information about the current IP connections and the active Address Resolution Protocol (ARP) table for the host. The first execution of `esxcli network` that follows uses the `connection` application with the `list` command. This displays the current connections for the host in numeric format and is the equivalent to running `netstat -tuwln` at the console of an ESX host. It is possible to filter the output by using the `-t | --type` option and specifying a type of `ip`, `tcp`, `udp`, or `all`. In the second instance of `esxcli network`, the `neighbor` application is run with the `show` command. This displays the active ARP table entries. You can use the option `-v | --version` with the switches of 4, 6, or `all` to filter IPv4 and IPv6 addresses.

```
esxcli network connection list
```

Proto	Recv-Q	Send-Q	Local Address	Foreign Address	State	World ID
tcp	0	492	127.0.0.1:51002	127.0.0.1:8307	ESTABLISHED	899921
tcp	0	0	192.168.1.30:443	192.168.1.27:35438	ESTABLISHED	902512
tcp	0	0	127.0.0.1:5988	127.0.0.1:63363	FIN_WAIT_2	0
tcp	0	0	127.0.0.1:63363	127.0.0.1:5988	CLOSE_WAIT	899919
tcp	0	0	127.0.0.1:5988	127.0.0.1:52581	TIME_WAIT	0
tcp	0	0	192.168.1.30:49154	192.168.1.5:389	TIME_WAIT	0
tcp	0	0	192.168.1.30:443	192.168.1.225:60225	ESTABLISHED	902510
tcp	0	0	192.168.1.30:902	192.168.1.225:60211	ESTABLISHED	0
tcp	0	0	192.168.1.30:894	192.168.1.100:2049	ESTABLISHED	0
tcp	0	0	192.168.1.30:61602	192.168.1.105:3260	ESTABLISHED	4967

```
esxcli network neighbor list
```

Neighbor	Mac Address	vmknic	Expiry(sec)	State
192.168.1.1	00:04:5a:fb:a9:2d	vmk0	1169	
192.168.1.5	00:10:a4:f2:30:a5	vmk0	1195	
192.168.1.100	00:0e:0c:c2:ce:fb	vmk0	1014	
192.168.1.105	00:0c:29:35:9e:49	vmk0	1118	
192.168.1.225	00:23:54:06:f3:a6	vmk0	1178	
fe80::230:48ff:fedb:6888	00:30:48:db:68:88	vmk0	0	Reachable

Managing Host Storage

The vCLI contains a number of commands to manage storage devices, datastores, and files. These can be used to manage local, Fibre Channel, iSCSI, and NFS storage for your hosts.

With the support of vMotion, DRS, and High Availability on NFS volumes, NFS is increasingly becoming the choice of storage for ESXi hosts. ESXi supports NFS version 3 over TCP/IP. After you have your networking set up for access to your NFS server, you can use `esxcfg-nas` to configure the NFS share as a datastore. The following command is used to list any existing NFS datastores:

```
vicfg-nas --list
NFS1 is /NFS1 from 192.168.1.100 mounted
```

To add another datastore, you use the --add option as shown in this example and add the NFS server hostname or IP address, the share name, and the datastore name to use. You can add the -y option to make the mount read-only, which would be appropriate for a datastore storing ISO images:

```
vicfg-nas --add -y --nasserver 192.168.1.100 --share /NFS2 NFS2
```

The following steps use vicfg-iscsi to enable and configure the ESXi software iSCSI initiator to create a new datastore on an iSCSI server. One of the significant iSCSI improvements in vSphere is iSCSI multipathing. With ESX 3.5, the iSCSI initiator can establish only a single TCP connection to each iSCSI target. Thus iSCSI traffic is limited to a single NIC port within a vSwitch, even though the vSwitch may be linked to multiple NICs. If your environment has required greater throughput, you may have configured your iSCSI storage with multiple iSCSI targets and your hosts with a number of VMkernel ports to be able to initiate multiple iSCSI sessions to your iSCSI storage. The default behavior with vSphere is the same as with ESX 3.5 to allow for a simple upgrade from ESX 3.5. But you can enable multipathing with esxcli to enable multiple connections to the same iSCSI target.

To begin, vicfg-iscsi is used to enable the software iSCSI initiator on ESXi. The subsequent commands verify that the initiator is enabled and determine the Host Bus Adapter (HBA) ID.

```
vicfg-iscsi --swiscsi --enable
Enabling software iSCSI...

vicfg-iscsi --swiscsi --list
Software iSCSI is enabled.

vicfg-iscsi --adapter --list
vmhba33            iSCSI Software Adapter
```

You can optionally set an alias for an iSCSI HBA. The iSCSI name generated for the iSCSI HBA is similar to iqn.1998-01.com.vmware:esx10-627fb181. An alias provides a more manageable name for the device and can be changed with the following command. You can also change the iSCSI name, but you must ensure that you assign a name that is unique within your organization.

```
vicfg-iscsi --swiscsi --iscsiname --alias ESX10_vmhba33 vmhba33
```

After you have enabled the iSCSI software initiator, you can add a discovery target. The target can be dynamic or static. With dynamic discovery, all storage targets associated with a hostname or IP address are discovered. With static discovery, you specify the hostname or IP address and the iSCSI name of the storage target. The following example adds an iSCSI target with dynamic discovery:

```
vicfg-iscsi --server esx10 --username root --password '' --swiscsi --discovery
    --add --ip 192.168.2.105 vmhba33
```

```
Adding discovery address 192.168.2.105:3260 ...
A rescan of the host is recommended for this configuration change.
```

To secure access to your iSCSI targets, you may employ the Challenge-Handshake Authentication Protocol (CHAP). With CHAP authentication, both the ESXi host and iSCSI target share a common username and password. During iSCSI login, the ESXi host authenticates with the iSCSI target. You can also enable mutual authentication in which the iSCSI target is also required to authenticate with the ESXi host. When configuring CHAP authentication, one of the levels shown in Table 8.7 is required.

Table 8.7 Supported Levels for iSCSI CHAP

Level	Description
chapProhibited	The host does not use CHAP authentication. You can use this option to disable authentication if it has been enabled.
chapDiscouraged	The host uses a non-CHAP connection but allows CHAP if required by the iSCSI target.
chapPreferred	The host attempts a CHAP connection but fails to achieve a non-CHAP connection if the iSCSI target does not support CHAP.
chapRequired	The host requires successful CHAP authentication.

To enable authentication with an iSCSI target, you can issue the following command. In this case, CHAP is required and the ESXi host authenticates with the iSCSI target at 192.168.2.105 with a username of user1 and a password of pass5. This example sets CHAP authentication for a specific iSCSI target. If the -i option were excluded, CHAP authentication would be enabled for all iSCSI targets. This mimics the behavior of the vSphere client, with which you can enable CHAP settings on both the HBA and target levels.

```
vicfg-iscsi --authentication -c chapRequired -m CHAP -u user1 -w pass5
    -i 192.168.2.105 vmhba33
```

If you need to enable mutual CHAP, you should first enable CHAP before running the command that follows. The username and password used for mutual authentication do not need to match the values that you used to set up CHAP authentication. However, the CHAP level must match. Note that the command syntax is nearly identical, but it adds the -b option for mutual authentication.

```
vicfg-iscsi --authentication -c chapRequired -m CHAP -b -u user3 -w pass4
    -i 192.168.2.105 vmhba33
```

To review the authentication settings for the HBA you have configured, you can issue this command:

```
vicfg-iscsi --authentication --list vmhba33
```

Tip: If you configure Advanced Settings for your iSCSI connections using the vSphere client as shown in Figure 8.7, you can also configure those with `vicfg-iscsi` using the `-W` option.

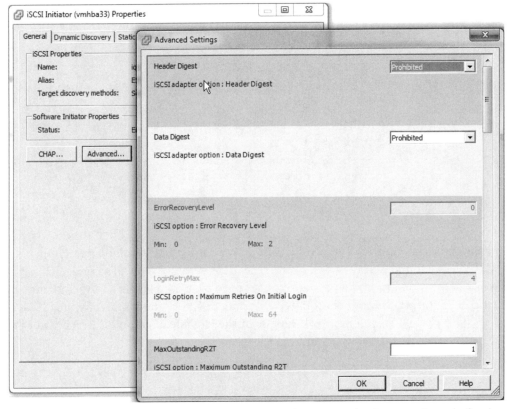

Figure 8.7   iSCSI Advanced Settings in the vSphere client may also be set using `vicfg-iscsi`.

After you have completed the setup for your iSCSI connected storage, you can issue the following command to rescan for new LUNs. `vicfg-rescan` should be run each time you make a storage configuration change.

```
vicfg-rescan vmhba33
Scan operation succeeded.
```

You can then use `vicfg-scsidevs` to view the storage LUNs that have been discovered. With this command, you can display data such as the UUID, device type, display name, and multipathing plug-in. With that information, you can utilize `vmkfstools` to format the LUN as a VMFS datastore or to create a raw device mapping. With `vmkfstools`, you can manage datastores, including extending datastores and virtual disks in the same manner in which you would use `vmkfstools` at the Service Console.

With the preceding setup, the iSCSI initiator makes a single connection to the iSCSI target. In the following example, `vSwitch1` has been created for iSCSI storage and it is linked to `vmnic2` and `vmnic3`. As the following output from `resxtop` shows the network traffic for the iSCSI target is passing through `vmnic2` while `vmnic3` is idle. `resxtop` is discussed later in the chapter.

```
    PORT-ID     USED-BY  TEAM-PNIC  DNAME       PKTTX/s   MbTX/s
   16777217  Management       n/a  vSwitch0       0.00     0.00
   16777218     vmnic0         -   vSwitch0    1089.87     0.74
   16777219       vmk0    vmnic0   vSwitch0    1089.87     0.74
   33554433  Management       n/a  vSwitch1       0.00     0.00
   33554434     vmnic2         -   vSwitch1     522.65   125.30
   33554435     vmnic3         -   vSwitch1       0.00     0.00
   33554441       vmk1    vmnic2   vSwitch1     522.65   125.30
   33554442       vmk2    vmnic3   vSwitch1       0.00     0.00
```

With `esxcli` from the vCLI, you can enable iSCSI multipathing. As you have seen previously, `esxcli` can be used to kill a virtual machine, but it can also be used to configure and manage a wide range of storage options, including iSCSI sessions and storage path policies. It is worthwhile to review the vCLI guides provided by VMware to gain a full understanding of the power of the vCLI utility.

Before enabling multipathing, you should configure your vSwitch so that each VMkernel port is set to be active on only one of the physical NIC links. Figure 8.8 shows that the iSCSI1 VMkernel port has been set to be active on `vmnic2` and not to use `vmnic3`. The iSCSI2 VMkernel port is set in a similar manner to be active on `vmnic3` and not to use `vmnic2`.

To configure multipathing, you must first determine the VMkernel interface names for the iSCSI port groups that have been created on the vSwitch. The command to display those interface names follows. Those interface names are then used with `esxcli` to add the VMkernel port to the software iSCSI HBA.

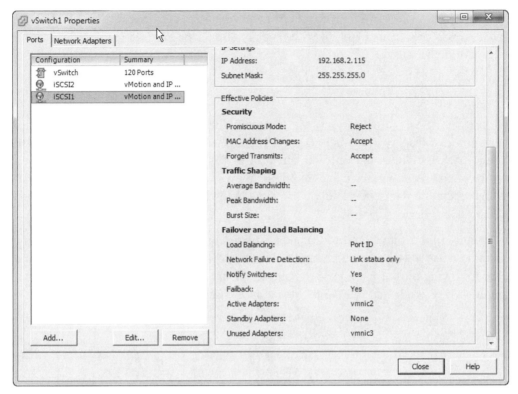

Figure 8.8   Preparing your vSwitch for iSCSI multipathing.

```
vicfg-vmknic --list
Interface  Port Group/DVPort   IP Family  IP Address               Netmask
vmk0       Management Network   IPv4       192.168.1.40             255.255.255.0
vmk0       Management Network   IPv6       fe80::20c:29ff:fe3f:dab0 64
vmk1       iSCSI1               IPv4       192.168.2.115            255.255.255.0
vmk1       iSCSI1               IPv6       fe80::250:56ff:fe72:d55e 64
vmk2       iSCSI2               IPv4       192.168.2.116            255.255.255.0
vmk2       iSCSI2               IPv6       fe80::250:56ff:fe73:834  64

esxcli swiscsi nic add -n vmk1 -d vmhba33
esxcli swiscsi nic add -n vmk2 -d vmhba33
```

To verify your setup, you can use the list option to display the VMkernel ports that have been bound to the HBA. If the settings are correct, you can issue the rescan command to discover the new paths to your iSCSI target:

```
esxcli swiscsi nic list -d vmhba33
vicfg-rescan vmhba33
Scan operation succeeded.
```

Managing Files

To manage files on your ESXi host, the vCLI includes the command `vifs`. If you're copying or cloning virtual disks on your datastores, `vmkfstools` is still the command to use. However, with `vifs` you can create folders, manage all file types, and copy files between your ESXi host and your management computer. This is one of the significant differences you'll find with using the vCLI to manage your host. With the service console on ESX, you access and edit files directly. With ESXi, you need to copy those files to your management computer, edit the files locally, and then copy those files back to the host with `vifs`.

`vifs` can be used to access host files such as `esx.conf`, which is discussed further in Chapter 11, "Under the Hood with the ESXi Tech Support Mode." When accessing files on a datastore, you should specify the path in either the datastore format of `[datastore] path/file` or with the full path, such as `/vmfs/volumes/datastore/path/file`. To avoid problems with special characters or spaces, ensure that you enclose the path in quotes.

To list the datastores for your ESXi host, issue the following command:

```
vifs --listds
```

To create a directory and then copy the file from your computer to your host, you would use the following commands:

```
vifs --mkdir '[datastore1] ISO_images'
vifs --put Linux.iso '[datastore1] ISO_images/Linux.iso'
```

Note that when you copy of a file to a datastore, you must specify the destination file name.

If you have an existing virtual machine and want to make a copy of it, you would follow this procedure:

1. Copy the vmx file to your management computer to update any configuration settings:

    ```
    vifs --get '[Datastore1] LINUX01/LINUX01.vmx' LINUX02.vmx
    ```

2. After you have edited the vmx file, you need to copy it back to the ESXi host. Execute the following commands to create a folder for the new virtual machine and to copy the vmx file to that folder:

    ```
    vifs --mkdir '[Datastore1] LINUX02'
    vifs --put LINUX02.vmx '[Datastore1] LINUX02/LINUX02.vmx'
    ```

3. Next, copy the virtual disk file with the following command. If the source virtual machine is running, you should first create a snapshot with `vmware-cmd`:

    ```
    vmkfstools -i '[Datastore1] LINUX01/LINUX01.vmdk'
        '[Datastore1] LINUX02/LINUX02.vmdk'
    ```

4. Once the virtual disk has been cloned, you can register the new virtual machine with the following command:

    ```
    vmware-cmd -s register '[datastore1] LINUX02/LINUX02.vmx'
    ```

5. The last step is to start the virtual machine using the following commands. It is necessary to use the `answer` option with `vmware-cmd` because the host may recognize the new virtual machine as a copy of the source virtual machine:

    ```
    vmware-cmd '[datastore1] LINUX02/LINUX02.vmx' start
    vmware-cmd '[datastore1] LINUX02/LINUX02.vmx' answer
    ```

Monitoring Performance with resxtop

`resxtop` is included with the vCLI to provide detailed information on how ESXi is using resources in real time. You can use the utility in one of three modes: Interactive, Batch, and Replay. Replay Mode is covered further in Chapter 11. `resxtop` is included with the vCLI to replace `esxtop`, which you execute in the Service Console for ESX. With `resxtop`, you can quickly determine whether a certain resource is the cause of performance problems. `resxtop` is not available on the Windows version of the vCLI. For more information about interpreting the statistics that `resxtop` records, you can consult this VMware Communities document: http:// communities. vmware.com/docs/DOC-11812. The Performance community on VMware's forums contains a number of documents on troubleshooting specific performance issues.

With vSphere 4.1 `resxtop` has been enhanced and includes a number of improvements, such as the addition of NFS performance statistics. It is now possible to monitor NFS storage at the datastore level for a host, and at the datastore and virtual disk levels for a virtual machine.

When you start `resxtop`, it begins in Interactive Mode and displays CPU statics for the ESXi host. The data is refreshed every five seconds, but you can change that setting by pressing s and then entering the new interval in seconds. Be aware that excessive sampling, especially in Batch Mode, imposes a CPU load on the host.

To change views, you can use the following keys:

- c: CPU
- m: Memory
- n: Network
- i: Interrupts
- d: Disk adapter
- u: Disk device
- v: Disk for virtual machines

- p: Power management

- V: Display only virtual machine worlds

You can press h to get a full list of command options. You may choose to re-sort the column order, sort the data in a specific order, or remove some columns. To save the customizations that you make, press W and you are prompted to save a configuration file, as follows:

```
Save config file to (Default to : /home/vi-admin/.esxtop41rc):
```

With Batch Mode, you can capture data for further performance analysis. The following command enables Batch Mode with the -b option. The -c option specifies the configuration file to use, -n instructs resxtop to collect 500 iterations of data, and -d sets the collection delay to five seconds. The command collects 2500 seconds of performance data and pipes the data to the file output.csv.

```
resxtop -b -c .esxtop41rc -n 500 -d 5 > output.csv
```

After you have collected the data, you can use tools such as Windows Performance Monitor, Microsoft Excel, and esxplot to analyze the data. esxplot is available at http://labs.vmware.com/flings/esxplot and runs on Linux, OSX, and Windows. Start the esxplot application, select File > Import > Dataset and select the data file generated by resxtop. Then double-click on the hostname and select a performance metric to display as shown in Figure 8.9.

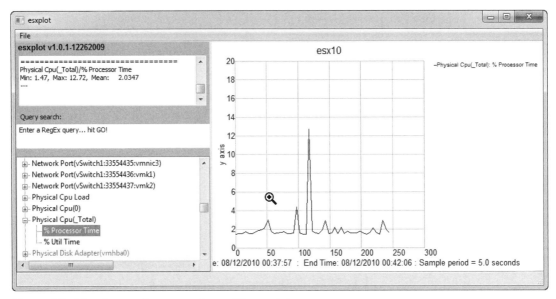

Figure 8.9 Viewing performance data with esxplot.

Scripting with the vCLI and the vSphere SDK for Perl

Many of the commands provided in the vCLI are useful for step-by-step troubleshooting or setup, but you will likely want to create more complex scripts to automate post-installation configuration or to update multiple hosts with the same change. The `mcli` utility from the vSphere SDK for Perl is useful for executing single commands against many hosts. Likewise, it is fairly straightforward to string together the vCLI commands into a single script. However, to exploit the power of the vSphere SDK for Perl, which is utilized by the vCLI, it is necessary to delve into Perl scripting and the SDK documentation.

With a simple loop in a script, you can execute your commands against a number of hosts, as shown in the following example:

```
#!/usr/bin/perl -w
for $i in "esx01" "esx02" "esx03"
    do
    echo "Adding NAS datastore for $i..."
    vicfg-nas --server $i --add --nameserver 192.168.1.100 --share /NFS2 NFS2
    vicfg-nas --server $i -l
done
```

You can also use the programing depth of the SDK to create scripts for functionality not provided for in the vCLI. For example, with the `vicfg-user` command, you can assign permissions only at the host level. With the script found in the VMware Communities discussion at http://communities.vmware.com/message/1560327, you can grant a user a role on any virtual machine running on your ESXi host. The script takes the options `--vmname`, `--rolename`, and `--setuser`.

```
setRoleToVM.pl --vmname SQL01 --rolename LocalAdmin
    --setuser "Mishchenko\dave.mishchenko"
```

```
Assign role LocalAdmin to user Mishchenko\dave.mishchenko
Authorization Role LocalAdmin Added To Mishchenko\dave.mishchenko Successfully.
```

In Chapter 3, "Management Tools," the new vSphere feature Storage input/output (I/O) Control was discussed. This is configured at the datastore level with the vSphere client, which can be tedious if you have a large number of datastores to configure. With the script provided at http://www.virtuallyghetto.com/2010/07/script-automate-storage-io-control-in.html, the configuration of Storage I/O Control is accomplished with a vSphere SDK for Perl script. You can enable, configure, or disable the feature, and because the change is made in a script, it can be run repeatedly with little chance of error.

As you look to develop your own scripts, you should also review the utilities that are included with the SDK. These tend to be less host-centric than the vCLI commands and expose the richness of functionality that is available with the SDK. Documentation on the SDK utilities can be found at http://www.vmware.com/support/developer/viperltoolkit/viperl41/doc/vsperl_util_index.html.

For more reference material on the vSphere SDK for Perl, you can refer to this link: http://www.vmware.com/support/developer/viperltoolkit/.

Conclusion

Since the initial release of the RCLI for ESX and ESXi 3.5, VMware has made significant strides to provide feature parity in the vCLI when compared with the Service Console on ESX. With this release of the vCLI and vSphere 4.1, veteran users of the Service Console can find a suitable replacement.

With the vMA VMware provides an easy to deploy appliance that includes the vCLI and the vSphere SDK for Perl. The additional components of vi-fastpass and vi-logger, which are based on the SDK, provide convenient tools to handle authentication and logging.

To extend your scripting capabilities beyond the vCLI, VMware provides the vSphere SDK for Perl. With the SDK, you can automate many of the tasks you perform manually with the vSphere client.

9

Scripting and Automation with PowerCLI

Throughout this book, you've seen numerous PowerCLI scripts that can perform complex tasks with a minimal amount of code. Microsoft PowerShell was designed to help system administrators manage their systems more efficiently and easily. VMware PowerCLI extends that ease of management to your VMware infrastructure.

Have you ever had to make a simple change such as updating the network connection for a number of virtual machines? If so, you know it is time consuming and tedious and opens the possibility of misconfiguration if you need to reconfigure a large number of virtual machines. With PowerCLI, such a change can be made on any number of targets with a simple, one-line script.

The following topics are discussed in this chapter:

- Learn to install PowerShell and PowerCLI

- Understand the basics of using PowerCLI

- Manage virtual machines with PowerCLI

- Manage ESXi hosts and vCenter Server with PowerCLI

- Extend PowerCLI with other tools

Installing vSphere PowerCLI

PowerCLI is supported on a wide range of Windows versions, from Windows XP to Windows Server 2008 R2. Both 32- and 64-bit versions of Windows are supported. Documentation and the download for PowerCLI can be found at this link: http://www.vmware.com/go/powercli. Prior to your installation, you should ensure that the computer has the following prerequisites:

- Microsoft .NET 2.0 SP1

- Windows PowerShell 1.0/2.0

For Windows XP, Vista, and Server 2003, you can download PowerShell from Microsoft's Web site. PowerShell is included with Windows 7 and Server 2008 R2 and is available as an Optional Feature in Server Manager on Windows Server 2008.

The computer running PowerShell also requires HTTPS or HTTP access to your vCenter Server or ESXi. You can test connectivity by accessing the vSphere Managed Object Browser (MOB) on the hosts that you plan to manage with PowerCLI. It is redundant to test connectivity if you're already using the vSphere client or other tools on your computer to manage your vSphere infrastructure. However, accessing the MOB provides valuable information about the objects in your vCenter datacenter and their properties.

Accessing the vSphere Managed Object Browser

The vSphere MOB is not a well-known tool, but it is available on both your ESXi hosts and vCenter Server. A Web-based tool, the MOB provides a graphical visualization of the vSphere entities that are available in the vSphere application programming interface (API). The MOB can be used to display the properties of a certain object and reveal the relationships to other vSphere API objects. The relationships between objects in the MOB are reflected in the way that the various cmdlets of the PowerCLI interact to create complex actions with relatively short scripts.

To access the MOB, you can use the following steps:

1. Open a Web browser on your management computer.

2. Access the MOB by using the hostname or Internet Protocol (IP) address, as shown here:

   ```
   https://vcenter.mishchenko.net/mob
   ```

3. Enter a username and password. This account should have access to your ESXi host or vCenter Server.

4. If you have not replaced the self-signed certificate on the host, you can disregard the warning message regarding the Secure Sockets Layer (SSL) certificate and proceed to the MOB.

On the start page, find the Content property and then click on the Content link in the Value column. A list of vCenter objects are displayed, as shown in Figure 9.1. If you click on the About property, you are shown a list of properties about the vCenter Server host, including the version and build for vCenter Server. If you navigate back to the Content page, you can find the rootFolder property. Then click on the value for rootFolder, which in Figure 9.1 is group-d1. The page shown for group-d1 contains the objects that are directly related to the vCenter Server. These include alarms that are defined at the vCenter object level, datacenters, and permissions. The objects that are linked to the vCenter object are the same ones that are available in the vSphere client. On the rootFolder page, you can also find a section called Methods. The methods are the functions that can be performed on this object. These include adding hosts, creating clusters,

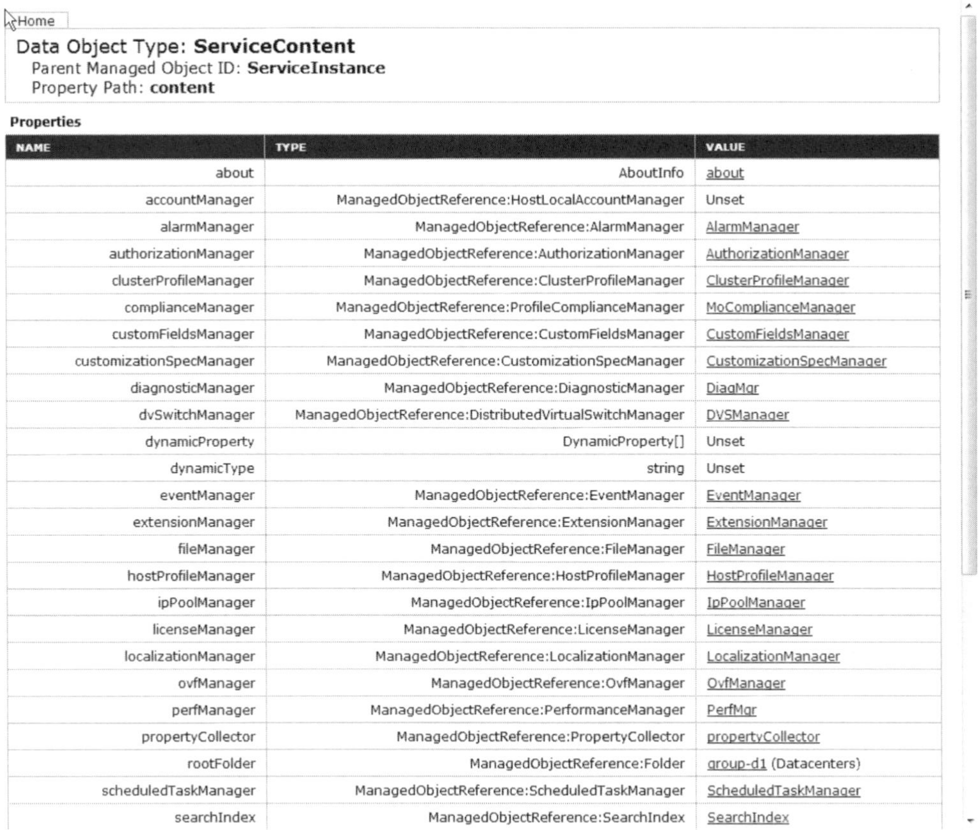
Home

Data Object Type: **ServiceContent**
Parent Managed Object ID: **ServiceInstance**
Property Path: **content**

Properties

NAME	TYPE	VALUE
about	AboutInfo	about
accountManager	ManagedObjectReference:HostLocalAccountManager	Unset
alarmManager	ManagedObjectReference:AlarmManager	AlarmManager
authorizationManager	ManagedObjectReference:AuthorizationManager	AuthorizationManager
clusterProfileManager	ManagedObjectReference:ClusterProfileManager	ClusterProfileManager
complianceManager	ManagedObjectReference:ProfileComplianceManager	MoComplianceManager
customFieldsManager	ManagedObjectReference:CustomFieldsManager	CustomFieldsManager
customizationSpecManager	ManagedObjectReference:CustomizationSpecManager	CustomizationSpecManager
diagnosticManager	ManagedObjectReference:DiagnosticManager	DiagMgr
dvSwitchManager	ManagedObjectReference:DistributedVirtualSwitchManager	DVSManager
dynamicProperty	DynamicProperty[]	Unset
dynamicType	string	Unset
eventManager	ManagedObjectReference:EventManager	EventManager
extensionManager	ManagedObjectReference:ExtensionManager	ExtensionManager
fileManager	ManagedObjectReference:FileManager	FileManager
hostProfileManager	ManagedObjectReference:HostProfileManager	HostProfileManager
ipPoolManager	ManagedObjectReference:IpPoolManager	IpPoolManager
licenseManager	ManagedObjectReference:LicenseManager	LicenseManager
localizationManager	ManagedObjectReference:LocalizationManager	LocalizationManager
ovfManager	ManagedObjectReference:OvfManager	OvfManager
perfManager	ManagedObjectReference:PerformanceManager	PerfMgr
propertyCollector	ManagedObjectReference:PropertyCollector	propertyCollector
rootFolder	ManagedObjectReference:Folder	group-d1 (Datacenters)
scheduledTaskManager	ManagedObjectReference:ScheduledTaskManager	ScheduledTaskManager
searchIndex	ManagedObjectReference:SearchIndex	SearchIndex

Figure 9.1 Using the vSphere MOB Web interface to browse vCenter objects.

and creating datacenters. If you click the CreateDatacenter link, you are taken to the Invoke Method page for CreateDatacenter method. Required parameters for creating the object are listed, which in the case of a datacenter is only a name. If you enter a Value for the Name parameter and click the Invoke Method link, a new datacenter is created on your vCenter Server host. The Invoke Method page will refresh to display a link to the new datacenter object. You can click that link to display the Object page for the new datacenter and to see the objects that are linked to it. On a datacenter Object page, you can access objects such as the network, datastores, and hosts that are a part of that datacenter.

The vSphere MOB certainly isn't intended as a day-to-day management tool, but it does provide a valuable source of information on the objects in vCenter and the properties for those objects. For more information on the vSphere API, you can consult the vSphere Web Services software development kit (SDK) documentation at the following link: http://www.vmware.com/support/developer/vc-sdk/.

Installing and Testing PowerCLI

To install PowerCLI, you can follow these steps after you have installed the prerequisites:

1. Start the installation by double-clicking on the executable that you have downloaded.

2. You may receive a warning that the installation requires the component VMware VIX. Click OK to continue.

3. Click Next on the Welcome screen to proceed with the installation.

4. Accept the license agreement, then click Next.

5. Select the installation path for the installation and continue. The default location is `C:\Program Files\VMware\Infrastructure\vSphere PowerCLI\`.

6. On the Ready to Install the Program screen, click Install.

7. Click Finish to complete the installation process.

During the installation, the warning dialog box shown in Figure 9.2 may appear. You can click Do This for Me to change the execution policy or click Continue to proceed with the installation without making changes to the execution policy. By default, PowerShell is configured to have a policy of Restricted. With this policy, no scripts can be run and you can use PowerShell only in interactive mode. The other policies are the following:

- AllSigned: Only scripts signed by a trusted publisher can be executed.

- RemoteSigned: Downloaded scripts must be signed by a trusted publisher before they can be run.

- Unrestricted: Any PowerShell script can be executed.

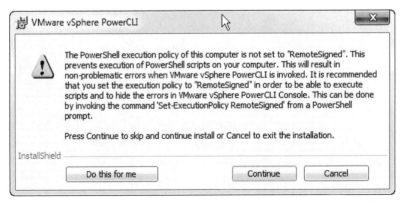

Figure 9.2 Changing the PowerShell execution policy during the PowerCLI installation.

If you select Continue on the execution policy screen during the installation, you need to set the policy in a PowerCLI console window before you can begin using the PowerCLI cmdlets. To start a PowerCLI console window, click Start and select All Programs > VMware > VMware vSphere PowerCLI > VMware vSphere PowerCLI. In the console window that opens, a warning message is displayed about the execution policy. Run the following command to set the policy to RemoteSigned, which is the recommended setting for using PowerCLI. With some version of Windows, you have to start the PowerCLI console window as an administrator to be able to execute the following command:

```
Set-ExecutionPolicy RemoteSigned

Execution Policy Change
The execution policy helps protect you from scripts that you do not trust.
Changing the execution policy might expose you to the security risks described
    in the about_Execution_Policies help topic. Do you want to change the execution
    policy?
[Y] Yes  [N] No  [S] Suspend  [?] Help (default is "Y"): Y
```

Tip: If you use the RemoteSigned policy and download a script to use from the Internet, you may receive the error message The File Is Not Signed. On Windows Vista, 7, and 2008, open Windows Explorer, right-click on the file, and click Unblock.

To test your installation, you can issue the Connect-VIServer cmdlet to open a session to vCenter Server or your ESXi host. If you have just set the execution policy, then you need to restart your PowerCLI console session. The Connect-VIServer cmdlet takes the following parameters:

```
Connect-VIServer -Server <hostname or IP address> -Protocol <HTTPS or HTTP>
    -User <username> -Password <password>
```

If you are connecting to your vCenter Server host, you can merely use the -Server parameter and your Windows credentials are used for authentication. For an ESXi host, you can use your Windows credentials if the host has been configured for Active Directory integration, but you need to enter that account and password in the login dialog box that comes up. If your workstation does not trust the SSL certificates installed on vCenter Server or your ESXi hosts, then you receive a warning message about this after you log in. When you successfully log in to your host, the hostname, the port, and your username are displayed as follows:

```
Name                    Port        User
-----                   ------      ------
vcenter.mishchenko.net  443         MISHCHENKO\Dave.Mishch...
```

To access PowerCLI cmdlets with other tools such as the PowerGUI or the PowerShell shortcut, you run the following cmdlet:

```
Add-PSSnapin VMware.VimAutomation.Core
```

You can optionally execute the `Initialize-VIToolkitEnvironment.ps1` script, which is found in the PowerCLI installation folder. This script initializes the PowerShell environment to run PowerCLI cmdlets; these cmdlets perform such actions as creating aliases and functions. The `Get-VICommand` cmdlet is a function defined in this script, which executes the following to return only PowerCLI cmdlets:

```
Get-Command -PSSnapin VMware.VimAutomation.Core
```

The aliases `Get-ESX`, `Get-VC`, and `Get-VIServer` are defined in the script to point to the cmdlet `Connect-VIServer`. You can edit this script to include functions and aliases that you intend to use frequently to manage your ESXi hosts.

In addition to `Get-Command`, another cmdlet that you will use frequently is `Get-Help`. This is used to display help for a cmdlet that you specify. To display help for `Get-VMHost`, you execute the following command:

```
Get-Help Get-VMHost
```

You can optionally add the parameters `-examples` to view samples for the cmdlet; `-detailed` to see more help information, including parameter descriptions and examples; and `-full` to see the entire help file for the cmdlet, including technical information about the parameters.

Understanding the Basics of PowerShell and PowerCLI

When you first open the PowerCLI window, you may find that it appears to be similar to the standard Windows command prompt. Common commands such as `dir` and `cd` can be executed and you can launch other applications from the PowerCLI window. But if you compare the output of the `dir` command run in a regular command prompt session with the output produced by PowerCLI, the differences become evident. With the output of the command from the regular command prompt, you have plain text output showing a list of files and folders. This list is difficult to manipulate should you want to perform additional tasks on the files and folders that were displayed.

PowerShell Objects and Pipelines

When you execute the PowerShell cmdlet `dir`, the output is a number of objects that represent folders and directories. These objects have properties that describe the object and methods that define the actions that can be taken on the objects. The cmdlet `Get-Member` can be used to display the properties and methods for an object. The following command displays the members for the `dir` command. The output has been truncated and shows some of the actions and properties for file and folder objects. You can use the `Get-Member` with any of the PowerCLI cmdlets such as `Get-VM`.

```
Dir | Get-Member
   TypeName: System.IO.DirectoryInfo
Name              MemberType       Definition
------            --------------   ---------------
Mode              CodeProperty     System.String Mode{get=Mode;}
Create            Method           System.Void Create(System.Security....
Delete            Method           System.Void Delete(), System.Void D...
CreationTime      Property         System.DateTime CreationTime {get;s...
Exists            Property         System.Boolean Exists {get;}
Name              Property         System.String Name {get;}
   TypeName: System.IO.FileInfo
Name              MemberType       Definition
------            --------------   --------------
CopyTo            Method           System.IO.FileInfo CopyTo(string de...
Create            Method           System.IO.FileStream Create()
DirectoryName     Property         System.String DirectoryName {get;}
Exists            Property         System.Boolean Exists {get;}
Name              Property         System.String Name {get;}
```

If you execute Get-VM | Get-Member, you'll find that many of the properties for Get-VM are similar to the properties that you see in the vSphere client. The properties include such items as the virtual machine name, the host, the configured memory, and the power state. With the PowerShell pipeline, you can pass the output of one cmdlet and direct it to be the input for another cmdlet. If you just run Get-VM, you are shown a list of virtual machines, their power state, the number of virtual CPUs, and the configured memory. If you want to start all your virtual machines, you can use Start-VM and use the output of Get-VM as the input list of virtual machines to start. Your command will look like the following:

```
Get-VM | Start-VM
```

The preceding command may be of limited use as you may not always want to start all your virtual machines; also, any virtual machines that are already running will cause an error message to be generated by Start-VM. You can use Where to filter the output generated by Get-VM before it is sent to Start-VM. To start all virtual machines that are currently powered down, you can use the following command. The output from Get-VM remains the same and a complete list of virtual machines is sent to the next cmdlet in the pipeline. But in this case, Where filters that list and its output is only a list of virtual machines that are powered off. That is the output that is then sent to Start-VM.

```
Get-VM | Where { $_.PowerState -eq "PoweredOff" } | Start-VM
```

PowerShell Variables

With PowerShell, all variables start with a dollar sign ($). As you begin to script with PowerCLI, you'll find it worthwhile to begin using variables and PowerShell supports a number of data types, including Boolean, char, date, decimal, integer, and object. When you create a variable, you don't have to assign a data type to it. So your script could set the variable $number = "ABC", which may result in errors later in the script. To ensure that a variable is assigned only a specific type, you can define the data type when you create the variable; for example, the following variable restricts the values that can be assigned to the variable to integers:

```
[int]$number = 10
```

You can also create an array by assigning a variable to be equal to a number of objects. If you run $hosts = Get-VMHost, the variable contains a list of your hosts and all the object properties for the host object. To see the complete list of hosts, you can run $hosts. Each item in the array has a unique index number and you could display the fifth item by running $hosts[5].

The preceding example with Get-VM includes the special variable $_. The $_ symbol is an automatic variable that refers to the current object. In that example, the current object is a virtual machine and $_.name signifies the name property for that object. The sample also uses -eq as the comparison operator. When you compare expressions in PowerShell, you can use the operators found in Table 9.1.

Table 9.1 PowerShell Comparison Operators

Operator	Description
-eq	Equals
-ne	Not equals
-gt	Greater than
-ge	Greater than or equal to
-lt	Less than
-le	Less than or equal to
-is	Returns true if the value is a certain data type
-isnot	Returns true if the value is not a certain data type
-like	Use with a wildcard for pattern matching
-notlike	Use with a wildcard to find nonmatching expressions
-match	Finds a match using regular expressions
-notmatch	Returns true when a match is not made
-contains	Returns true when a collection contains a given item
-notcontains	Returns true when a collection does not contain a given item

> Note: The operators in Table 9.1 are not case sensitive. That also applies to object data and all cmdlets. If you need to compare case-sensitive data, you can prefix the comparison operator with c. For example -cmatch and -cgt perform case-sensitive comparisons.

Formatting Output

If you're writing reports with PowerShell, you will find that it is sometimes necessary to format the output from your scripts to produce a report that is more easily read. The default output for Get-VM may truncate the virtual machine name and the default columns displayed may not contain the data you're looking for. The two common cmdlets that you can use to format output are Format-Table and Format-List. If you run Get-VM | Format-Table -AutoSize, PowerShell calculates the best column width to use based on the data that will be displayed. You can also use the -Property parameter to select which properties of an object to display. The following example displays a list of virtual machines and the hosts they are running on. You can alternatively use -GroupBy to group the output by a parameter, as shown in the second example.

```
Get-VM | FT -Property Name, Host
Name                                    Host
------                                  ------
WINDOWS02                               esx01.mishchenko.net
WINDOWS03                               esx01.mishchenko.net
WINDOWS01                               esx01.mishchenko.net
C:\> Get-VM | FT Name -GroupBy Host


   Host: esx01.mishchenko.net
Name
------
WINDOWS02
WINDOWS03
WINDOWS01
```

If the number of columns you wish to display will not fit into a table format, then you can use Format-List. The output generated will be similar to the following example. To display all properties for an object, you can use Format-List *.

```
Get-VM | FL
Name          : WINDOWS05
PowerState    : PoweredOff
NumCpu        : 1
MemoryMB      : 1024
HardDisks     : {Hard disk 1}
CDDrives      : {CD/DVD Drive 1}
FloppyDrives  : {Floppy drive 1}
```

```
NetworkAdapters : {Network adapter 1, Network adapter 2}
UsbDevices      : {}
Host            : esx01.mishchenko.net
Id              : VirtualMachine-vm-27
Notes           :
```

Creating and Managing Aliases So far in this chapter, you've seen a number of examples of aliases, such as FL and FT for Format-List and Format-Table. Likewise, Where is an alias of Where-Object and dir is an alias of Get-ChildItem. To view a list of aliases that are available in your session, run Get-Alias.

The following examples create two aliases. The first is an alias for Get-VMHost and the second an alias to run Notepad:

```
New-Item Alias:gvh -Value Get-VMHost
New-Item Alias:np -Value c:\windows\system32\notepad.exe
```

When you create an alias in your PowerShell session, it exists until the session is closed. You can import and export aliases between sessions with Export-Alias and Import-Alias. You can also edit your profile file to add alias definitions. Your profile is a PowerShell script that is loaded each time you start a session. To determine the location of your profile file, run the following command:

```
$profile
C:\Users\dave\Documents\WindowsPowerShell\Microsoft.PowerShell_profile.ps1
```

The WindowsPowerShell folder may not exist, so you may have to create the folder before you create the profile file. You can also use this file to define PowerShell functions or to control the appearance of your PowerShell window.

Managing Connections

When you first open a PowerCLI session, your first task is likely to connect to either your vCenter Server host or one of your ESXi hosts. You can check which host you're connected to by running $DefaultVIServers. You may need to work with multiple vCenter Server hosts or ESXi hosts that are not managed by vCenter Server, in which case you can enable multisession management. The default setting for PowerCLI is to allow only a single connection at one time. If you run Connect-VIServer again in your session, your current session is closed to allow the new session to be opened. To change that behavior, you can run the following command:

```
Set-PowerCLIConfiguration -DefaultVIServerMode Multiple
Proxy Policy      Default Server
                  Mode
---------------   -------------------
UseSystemProxy    Multiple
```

Now when you connect to another host both are displayed with $DefaultVIServers. Any commands that you issue are executed on both hosts. The data is returned as one set of objects so the output of Get-VM, for example, displays a single list of virtual machines.

Developing Scripts with WhatIf

One of the most useful options that you can use when developing scripts is -WhatIf. In the following sample, the script is designed to stop and remove all virtual machines in a test cluster. First, an array is created containing a list of virtual machines in a cluster. Each virtual machine is then powered off if it is running and then deleted from a cluster. The great thing about Power-CLI is that a simple script can perform complex operations on a large number of objects. The danger with PowerCLI is also that you can easily perform powerful commands on the wrong objects. If the wrong cluster name is entered, then the cmdlet that deletes virtual machines could instead be run on production virtual machines. That's where the -WhatIf option comes in handy. Rather than actually performing the action of the cmdlet, the option generates a message specifying which operation is to be performed, as shown in the following example. After you have confirmed that the script performs as expected, you can remove the -WhatIf option and rerun the script.

```
$VMs_to_delete = Get-Cluster -Name "Cluster02" | Get-VM
$VMs_to_delete | ForEach {
   If ($_.PowerState -eq "PoweredOn")
      {
      Stop-VM -VM $_.Name -Confirm:$False -WhatIf
      }
   Remove-VM -VM $_.Name -Confirm:$False -WhatIf
   }
What if: Performing operation 'Removing VM from inventory.' on VM 'TEST01'
What if: Performing operation 'Removing VM from inventory.' on VM 'TEST02'
What if: Performing operation "Stop-VM" on Target "VM ' TEST02'".
What if: Performing operation 'Removing VM from inventory.' on VM 'TEST03'
```

Finding PowerCLI Cmdlets

As you start with PowerCLI, you'll find that you come back again and again to Get-Command to find the cmdlets that you'll use in your scripts. On its own, Get-Command produces a very long list of cmdlets. To view only the VMware cmdlets that include network in its name, you can run the following command. You can further limit the output by piping the output to Select -First 10 to limit the list to 10 cmdlets.

```
Get-Command *network* -PSSnapin vmware*
```

As PowerShell cmdlets are comprised of a verb-noun pair, you can group the cmdlets by either the verb or noun. The following sample groups all VMware cmdlets by verb. Some of the output is truncated so you can also pipe the output to Format-List.

```
Get-Command -PSSnapin vmware* | Group-Object Verb | FT -AutoSize'
   | Select -First 15
Count Name       Group
------- ------    -------
   3   Add        {Add-PassthroughDevice, Add-VMHost, Add-VmHostNtpServer}
   2   Apply      {Apply-DrsRecommendation, Apply-VMHostProfile}
   1   Attach     {Attach-Baseline}
   1   Connect    {Connect-VIServer}
   3   Copy       {Copy-DatastoreItem, Copy-HardDisk, Copy-VMGuestFile}
   1   Detach     {Detach-Baseline}
   1   Disconnect {Disconnect-VIServer}
   1   Dismount   {Dismount-Tools}
   1   Download   {Download-Patch}
   2   Export     {Export-VApp, Export-VMHostProfile}
  75   Get        {Get-Annotation, Get-Baseline, Get-CDDrive, Get-Cluster...}
   2   Import     {Import-VApp, Import-VMHostProfile}
   1   Install    {Install-VMHostPatch}
```

Tip: VMware provides a poster of Power CLI 4.1 cmdlets, and it is available for download from the following URL: http://communities.vmware.com/servlet/JiveServlet/download/ 1597600-42488/PowerCLI-Poster-4.1.pdf.

Using PowerShell Drives

PowerShell Drives, or PSDrives, extend the concept of drive letters into your PowerShell session. At a command prompt, you are used to navigating drives and folders and to mapping a drive to a network resource. With PSDrives, that concept is extended to other elements such as the registry, Active Directory, and the certificate store. To view the list of PSDrives, run the following command:

```
Get-PSDrive | FT -AutoSize
Name     Used (GB)    Free (GB)    Provider     Root     CurrentLocation
-----    -----------  -----------  -----------  -----    --------------------
A                                  FileSystem   A:\
Alias                              Alias
C        206.91       258.75       FileSystem   C:\      tmp\delete
cert                               Certificate  \
D                                  FileSystem   D:\
Env                                Environment
Function                           Function
HKCU                               Registry     HKEY_CURRENT_USER
```

```
HKLM                          Registry      HKEY_LOCAL_MACHINE
Variable                      Variable
vi                            VimInventory  \LastConnectedVCenterServer
vis                           VimInventory  \
vmstore                       VimDatastore  \LastConnectedVCenterServer
vmstores                      VimDatastore  \
WSMan                         WSMan
```

To access the HKEY_CURRENT_USER registry hive, you enter the command cd HKCU:. You can then browse HKCU as if it were a file system and use cmdlets such as cd, dir, mkdir, and copy.

With PowerCLI, two PSDrive providers are included. The Inventory Provider (VimInventory) is designed to provide a raw inventory view of your vCenter environment. You can create a PSDrive on a managed object such as a datacenter and then manipulate objects with commands to move, rename, and delete child objects. Two inventory drives are shown in the preceding output: vi and vis. The vis drive contains the inventory of all vSphere servers to which you are connected in the current PowerCLI session. The vi drive displays the objects for the server to which you most recently connected.

If you want to create a new PSDrive, you can issue the following command. In this example, Surrey is a datacenter and CLUSTER01 is a cluster. If you execute dir within a datacenter, you will see that the child objects are vm, host, and datastore.

```
New-PSDrive -Name Cluster01 -PSProvider VimInventory`
  -Root "vi:\Surrey\host\CLUSTER01"
```

After you have created the PSDrive, you can access it with the command cd Cluster01:. You can view resource pools, hosts, and virtual machines in the cluster. To start a group of virtual machines that start with Windows, you can issue the following command:

```
dir Windows* | Start-VM
```

Note: It was noted earlier that the names of PowerShell cmdlets and objects are not case sensitive. One exception to this is object names accessed with the VMware PSDrive providers. When referring to objects such as a host, virtual machine, or folder, you must match the case of the name as it is displayed in the PSDrive.

The second PSDrive provider included with PowerCLI is Datastore (VimDatastore). This provides access to the datastores within your virtual environment. Two datastore PSDrives are created by default when you connect to vCenter Server or your ESXi host. The vmstore drive displays the datastores for the last host that you connected to. The vmstores drive displays all datastores for all the servers that you have connected to within that PowerCLI session. After you have accessed a datastore PSDrive, you can manipulate folders and files in the same way as you would with a regular filesystem. You can copy files and folder between datastores and even to your local drive, as shown in the following example:

```
vmstore:\Surrey\NFS1\LINUX01> Copy-DatastoreItem LINUX01.vmx c:\tmp\LINUX01.vmx
```

You'll note that the `Copy-DatastoreItem` cmdlet is used instead of `copy`, which is the alias for `Copy-Item`. When moving objects between different providers—in this case, the VimDatastore and FileSystem providers—objects may not be compatible between different providers and `Copy-Item` thus generates an error.

Tip: Access to the VMware PSDrives is available only from within the PowerCLI session. When a session is started, the current provider is the Microsoft FileSystem provider. If you issue a command such as `notepad script.ps1`, the file is opened in Notepad, as the application is able to access the absolute path to the script file. If you execute the same command when accessing a folder within `vmstore:`, Notepad is able to access the file that you have referenced.

Managing Virtual Machines with PowerCLI

This section of the chapter deals with some of the aspects of managing virtual machines, including virtual machine creation and reporting. You have already seen a number of examples using `Get-VM`. The following list displays a number of cmdlets that are used to manage virtual machines:

Get-NetworkAdapter	New-OSCustomizationSpec	Set-Template
Get-VM	New-Snapshot	Set-VM
Get-VMGuest	New-Template	Set-VMStartPolicy
Mount-Tools	New-VM	Start-VM
Move-VM	Remove-Snapshot	Stop-VM
New-HardDisk	Set-CDDrive	Suspend-VM
New-NetworkAdapter	Set-Network Adapter	Update-Tools

For an updated list of all cmdlets, you can check the Online Cmdlet Reference, which is found at the following URL: http://www.vmware.com/support/developer/PowerCLI/PowerCLI41/html/index.html.

Creating Virtual Machines

Creating new virtual machines is done with the cmdlet New-VM. When you look at the options for this command, the list is somewhat overwhelming as the cmdlet may be used to create a new virtual machine, to clone an existing virtual machine, to create a virtual machine from a template, or to register a virtual machine. You can organize the parameters with the cmdlet Get-Parameter, which is available for download from http://halr9000.com/article/507. Running the following command groups the parameters for each of the previously mentioned functions for New-VM. You can use Get-Parameter to produce an easy-to-read list of options for any Power-CLI cmdlet.

```
.\Get-Parameter.ps1 New-VM default | FT -GroupBy ParameterSet
```

Creating a single virtual machine with New-VM may not be a significant time saver, but by using New-VM with Import-CSV, it's possible to create a countless number of virtual machines with minimal effort. Import-CSV is used to read a comma-delimited file into a variable. In the following sample file, the first row defines the parameters that are used within the script:

```
Name    NumCPU  DiskMB  MemoryMB  GuestID
App10   1       20      512       winNetEnterprise64Guest
App11   1       20      512       winNetEnterprise64Guest
App12   2       30      1024      winNetEnterprise64Guest
App13   2       20      1024      rhel6_64Guest
App14   1       15      512       rhel6_64Guest
App15   4       60      4096      rhel6_64Guest
```

The following script requires the $ImportFile parameter, which specifies the file to import. When you run this script, the command takes the following format:

```
.\import.ps1 VM_list.csv
```

In this format, VM_list.csv is a file containing the list of virtual machines that are created by the script. Some parameters, such as those for adding a CD-ROM to the virtual machine or specifying which datastore to use, are fixed within the script. When you create scripts and decide to word-wrap a command, it is important to include the back tick operator ('), as shown in this script:

```
Param ( $ImportFile)
$ImportList = Import-CSV $ImportFile
$ImportList | ForEach-Object {
            New-VM -Name $_.Name '
            -NumCPU $_.NumCPU '
            -DiskMB $_.DiskMB '
            -MemoryMB $_.MemoryMB '
            -GuestID $_.GuestID '
```

```
-Floppy:$False '
-CD:$False '
-ResourcePool "Production App" '
-Datastore "Production" '
-VMHost "esx01.mishchenko.net" '
-RunAsync
}
```

Tip: The name for the `RunAsync` parameter is an abbreviation of "run asynchronously." Without this parameter, the script waits while each virtual machine in the preceding script is created. When you use `-RunAsync`, a task is created with vCenter Server and the task ID is returned by the cmdlet. You can use `Get-Task` to query the status of the task and use `Wait-Task` to determine whether your script requires the completion of that step before proceeding further.

Creating Virtual Machines from Templates

If you're using virtual machine templates and the guest customization wizard in vCenter Server to deploy new virtual machines, you can also employ that strategy from PowerCLI. To clone an existing virtual machine to a template, you can use `New-Template` as shown in the following example:

```
New-Template -VM W2K3R2_x64 -Name TEMPLATE_W2K3R2_x64 -Location Surrey
```

At this time, PowerCLI does not include a cmdlet to convert a virtual machine to a template, but you can easily accomplish that with the following script:

```
$ConvertToTemplate = Get-VM W2K3R2_x64 | Get-View
$ConvertToTemplate.MarkAsTemplate()
```

To deploy a new virtual machine from this template, you can issue the following command. You can use `Get-Parameter` (which was discussed earlier) to obtain a list of parameters that can be used when creating a new virtual machine from a template.

```
New-VM -Name CLUSTER03 -Template (Get-Template TEMPLATE_W2K3R2_x64) '
  -VMHost esx01.mishchenko.net -RunAsync
```

Tip: If you plan to customize Windows XP, 2000, or 2003, you must download the appropriate Sysprep files to your vCenter Server host. You can find the appropriate locations for these files and download links at the following URL: http://kb.vmware.com/kb/1005593.

To manage and create guest operating system (OS) customization specifications, you can use the following cmdlets:

`Get-OSCustomizationNicMapping`	`Remove-OSCustomizationNicMapping`
`Get-OSCustomizationSpec`	`Remove-OSCustomizationSpec`
`New-OSCustomizationNicMapping`	`Set-OSCustomizationNicMapping`
`New-OSCustomizationSpec`	`Set-OSCustomizationSpec`

To apply a customization specification to a virtual machine, you can use either `New-VM` when creating new virtual machines or `Set-VM` for existing virtual machines, as shown in the following example:

```
Set-VM -VM App10 -OSCustomizationSpec Windows2003_x64
```

PowerCLI includes a number of cmdlets to manage your virtual machines after they are deployed. Those include cmdlets for managing virtual hardware, installing VMware Tools, migrating virtual machines, and managing snapshots.

Managing Virtual Machine Snapshots

Snapshots are a useful tool, especially in test or development environments and in production, to provide an easy method to reverse changes to virtual machines. PowerCLI includes the following cmdlets to manage snapshots: `Get-Snapshot`, `New-Snapshot`, `Set-Snapshot`, and `Remove-Snapshot`. To create a snapshot on a virtual machine, issue the following command. The `-Memory` parameter causes the memory state to be saved with the snapshot if the virtual machine is powered on, and the `-Quiesce` parameter instructs VMware Tools to pause disk activity momentarily while the snapshot is created.

```
Get-VM -Name Windows01 | New-Snapshot -Name (Get-Date) -Memory -Quiesce
```

To manage the name and description for a snapshot, you use `Set-Snapshot`. To revert a virtual machine back to a prior snapshot, you use `Set-VM`. In the first example that follows, the snapshots for a virtual machine are obtained and then passed to `Set-VM`. You are prompted to select a snapshot to revert to. The snapshots are listed from oldest to newest.

```
Get-VM Windows01 | Get-Snapshot | Set-VM -VM Windows01

Confirmation
Reverting VM 'WINDOWS01' to snapshot 'Pre-Upgrade'.
[Y] Yes [A] Yes to All [N] No [L] No to All [S] Suspend [?] Help
(default is "Y"):N
```

```
Confirmation
Reverting VM 'WINDOWS01' to snapshot '09%2f14%2f2010 12:20:54'.
[Y] Yes [A] Yes to All [N] No [L] No to All [S] Suspend [?] Help
(default is "Y"):Y
```

Removing snapshots is accomplished with Remove-Snapshot. The following example uses Sort-Object to find the oldest snapshot on a virtual machine and passes that snapshot alone to Remove-Snapshot. Removing a snapshot can be time consuming, so -RunAsync is used to obtain a task ID for the removal instead of waiting for the task to complete.

```
$Oldest_Snapshot = Get-VM -Name Windows01 | Get-Snapshot | Sort-Object
  -Property "Created" | Select -First 1
Remove-Snapshot $Oldest_Snapshot -Confirm:$false -RunAsync
```

Get-Snapshot is used to obtain snapshot information, as the preceding examples have shown. It can also be used to generate a report of all virtual machines with a snapshot. The Addday() method is used to subtract seven days from the current date so the script displays snapshots that are older than seven days. In a more complex example (which you can download from http://www.virtu-al.net/2009/06/22/powercli-snapreminder/), PowerCLI is used to query the vCenter task history and Active Directory to send an e-mail to users who have created snapshots that have not been deleted:

```
Get-VM | Get-Snapshot | Where-Object { $_.Created -le '
  ((Get-Date).AddDays(-7)) } | FT Name, Created, Description -GroupBy VM


   VM: WINDOWS03
Name                  Created               Description
------                ----------            ---------------
Patches installed     8/10/2010 9:01:47 AM
WINDOWS03_vm-22_1     9/9/2010 7:40:15 AM   VMware vCenter Update Manager...


   VM: LINUX01
Name                  Created               Description
------                ----------            ---------------
LINUX01_vm-30_1       9/9/2010 7:41:39 AM   VMware vCenter Update Manager...
```

Interacting with VMware Tools

A number of PowerCLI cmdlets, such as the following, interact with VMware Tools to provide access to the guest operating system. With these cmdlets, you can control the power state of the guest OS, change network settings, and even copy from and to the virtual machine without having a network connection to it.

Copy-VMGuestFile

Get-VMGuest

Get-VMGuestNetworkInterface

Get-VMGuestRoute

New-VMGuestRoute

Remove-VMGuestRoute

Restart-VMGuest

Set-VMGuestNetworkInterface

Set-VMGuestRoute

Shutdown-VMGuest

Suspend-VMGuest

Get-VMGuest can be used to retrieve information from the guest OS, including IP addresses and disk usage:

```
Get-VMGuest CLUSTER04 | FL *
```

```
OSFullName       : Microsoft Windows Server 2003, Enterprise Edition (64-bit)
IPAddress        : {172.16.1.134, 192.168.1.134, 192.168.1.144}
State            : Running
Disks            : {VMware.VimAutomation.ViCore.Impl.V1.VM.Guest.DiskInfoImpl,
  VMware.VimAutomation.ViCore.Impl.V1.VM.Guest.DiskInfoImpl,
  VMware.VimAutomation.ViCore.Impl.V1.VM.Guest.DiskInfoImpl,
  VMware.VimAutomation.ViCore.Impl.V1.VM.Guest.DiskInfoImpl...}
HostName         : cluster04.MISHCHENKO.NET
Nics             : {Public, Private}
ScreenDimensions : {Width=640, Height=480}
VmId             : VirtualMachine-vm-103
VM               : CLUSTER04
VmUid            : /VIServer=@vcenter:443/VirtualMachine=VirtualMachine-vm-103/
VmName           : CLUSTER04
Uid              : /VIServer=@vcenter:443/VirtualMachine=VirtualMachine-vm-103
  /VMGuest=/
GuestId          : winNetEnterprise64Guest
ExtensionData    : VMware.Vim.GuestInfo
```

If you want to create a report about the disks in your virtual machines and their utilization, the information you need is available with Get-VMGuest, but as shown in the preceding example, that information is not usable in its default format. If you use the vSphere MOB discussed earlier, you will find that this property should display the disk path, total capacity, and free space. You can also obtain that information by looking up the DiskInfo type at http://www.vmware.com/support/developer/PowerCLI/PowerCLI41/html/index.html. To extract that information, you can use the ExpandProperty parameter from Select-Object, as shown in the following example:

```
$diskinfo = Get-VMGuest Cluster04 | Select -ExpandProperty Disks
$diskinfo | FT -AutoSize
```

```
Path   Capacity      FreeSpace
------ -----------   -------------
C:\    42935926784   37148037120
F:\    21467947008   21399695360
M:\    26839052288   26770636800
N:\    26839052288   26770636800
Q:\     1071627264    1063469056
```

The ExpandProperty parameter is also useful for string items such as IPAddress in the preceding Get-VMGuest example. The three IP addresses are contained in a single string, which makes it difficult to pass the IP addresses on to subsequent cmdlets in a pipeline or script. In the following example, three IP addresses are returned instead of a single string value:

```
$IPAddresses = Get-VMGuest Cluster04 | Select -ExpandProperty IPADdress
$IPAddresses
172.16.1.134
192.168.1.134
192.168.1.144
```

The following script uses the disk data obtained with ExpandProperty to produce a report of disk size and space utilization for virtual machines:

```
$VMList = Get-VM  | Where { $_.PowerState -eq "PoweredOn"} | Get-View | `
                                Where { $_.GuestHeartbeatStatus -ne "gray"}

$VMList | ForEach {
            Write-Host "Virtual Machine:  " $_.Name
            $Drives = @(Get-VMGuest $_.Name | Select -ExpandProperty Disks)
            $Drives | Select-Object Path, `
                @{Name="Capacity(GB)"; Expression={"{0:n1}" `
                                            -f ($_.Capacity/1GB)}},`
                @{Name="% Utilized"; Expression={"{0:p0}" `
                            -f (($_.Capacity-$_.FreeSpace)/$_.Capacity)}} `
                | FT -AutoSize
                }

Virtual Machine:  VCENTER
Path      Capacity(GB)    % Utilized
------    ----------------  -------------
C:\       40.0            45 %

Virtual Machine:  VMware Data Recovery
Path      Capacity(GB)    % Utilized
------    ----------------  -------------
/         3.7             32 %
/boot     0.1             9 %
/SCSI-0:1 499.7           11 %
```

```
Virtual Machine:  vSphere Management Assistant (vMA)
Path              Capacity(GB)  % Utilized
------            ----------------  -------------
/                 3.3           42 %
/var/log          0.5           20 %
/boot             0.1           12 %
/var/log/syslog   9.8           1 %
```

The first statement in the script uses Get-VM to obtain a list of virtual machines and then filters the list for virtual machines that are running. Get-View is used to filter the list further for virtual machines that do not show a gray status for VMware Tools. This would indicate that VMware Tools is not running or installed within the virtual machine. The other status values for VMware Tools are red (no heartbeat), yellow (intermittent heartbeat), and green (the guest OS is responding normally). As Get-VMGuest relies on VMware Tools to interact with the virtual machines, this filtering is required to prevent errors in the output of the script. Get-View is an excellent tool in addition to the MOB and PowerCLI Online Cmdlet Reference to determine the properties that are available on a vCenter object.

For each virtual machine, disk information is then obtained and stored in an array. Select-Object is used to display data from the array. The Name and Expression operators are used to calculate and format the data that is displayed. The disk size information is returned as integers that would be difficult to read if displayed without changes. The Name operator specifies a new column name. Expression formats the data using "{0:n1}" -f and "{0:p0}" -f. The initial number, 0 in both cases, is used as an index marker to identify multiple formatting strings in a single statement. N and P indicate that the value is a number or percentage, and the last number specifies the number of decimal places to use.

Measuring PowerCLI Query Time As you work with PowerShell and PowerCLI, you will find that there are often a number of methods to use to accomplish a task you may need to solve. In the preceding example, the following statement was used to generate a list of virtual machines that were powered on and running VMware Tools:

```
Get-VM | Where { $_.PowerState -eq "PoweredOn"} | Get-View | '
                              Where { $_.GuestHeartbeatStatus -ne "gray"}
```

The query can be rewritten to exclude Get-VM and rely entirely on Get-View instead. The output is the same, but the time to execute the statements is vastly different.

```
Get-View -ViewType "VirtualMachine" -filter @{"Guest.GuestState"="running"} '
     | Where {$_.GuestHeartbeatStatus -ne "gray"}
```

To measure the difference in performance, you can use Measure-Command. Measure-Command takes a statement or script as its parameter and outputs the time that a script has taken to run. As you can see in the following example, the statement without Get-VM runs significantly faster. Performance improvements such as this one can make a significant difference when a script is run against an environment with hundreds or thousands of virtual machines.

```
Measure-Command {Get-View -ViewType "VirtualMachine" -filter '
    @{"Guest.GuestState"="running"} | Where {$_.GuestHeartbeatStatus '
    -ne "gray"}} | Select TotalSeconds
Measure-Command {Get-VM | Where { $_.PowerState -eq "PoweredOn"} | Get-View '
    | Where { $_.GuestHeartbeatStatus -ne "gray"} } | Select TotalSeconds
TotalSeconds
-------------
0.4492601
3.2450127
```

Managing ESXi Hosts and vCenter Server with PowerCLI

As in the case with virtual machines, PowerCLI includes a wide range of cmdlets that enable configuration, management, troubleshooting, and reporting of your ESXi hosts and vCenter Server. PowerCLI includes cmdlets to configure and manage networking, storage, clusters, and many other aspects of ESXi and vCenter Server. In this section, you'll look at configuring a new ESXi host, applying host profiles with PowerCLI, configuring vCenter Server alarms to use PowerCLI, and using some troubleshooting cmdlets for ESXi. For a complete guide to managing hosts with PowerCLI, check out the book *Managing VMware Infrastructure with Windows PowerShell: TFM* by Hal Rottenberg.

Configuring Your ESXi Hosts with a PowerCLI Script

When deploying a new host, you can use host profiles, a scripting install, and the vCLI to automate aspects of the configuration for a new host. PowerCLI presents another tool to use to configure your host. The following is a sample of a script that can be used to configure a new ESXi host:

```
# Set variables
$user = "root"
$password = ""
$newhost = Read-Host Enter the IP address of the new ESXi host
$newpassword = Read-Host -AsSecureString Enter a new password for the root '
  account

# Connect to the target ESXi Host
Write-Host  Connecting to ESXi server
Connect-VIServer $newhost -User $user -Password $password

# Change the password for root
Write-Host  Changing the password for root
Set-VMHostAccount $user -Password $newpasswd
```

```
# Set the hostname and domain name
$newhostname = Read-Host Enter a new hostname
$newdomainname = Read-Host Enter the host's domain name
Write-Host   Configuring the host and domain name
Get-VMHostNetwork | Set-VMHostNetwork -DomainName $newdomainname -HostName
$newhostname

# Configure DNS settings
$dns = Read-Host Enter the DNS server for the host
Get-VMHostNetwork | Set-VMHostNetwork -DnsAddress $dns
Sleep 15

# Set NTP Server
Write-Host   Configuring NTP and restarting service
$NTPServers = "0.pool.ntp.org", "1.pool.ntp.org"
Add-VMHostNTPServer -NTPServer $NTPServers -Confirm:$false
$ntpd = Get-VMHostService -VMHost $newhost  | where {$_.Key -eq 'ntpd'}
Restart-VMHostService $ntpd -Confirm:$false
Set-VMHostService -HostService $ntpd -Policy "Automatic"

# Enable Active Directory Integration
$domain = Read-Host Enter the domain for the host to join
$account = Read-Host Enter an account with permissions to join the host to `
   the domain
$ADpassword = Read-Host -AsSecureString Enter the password for that account
$_AD =Get-View -Id 'HostActiveDirectoryAuthentication-ha-ad-auth'
$_AD.JoinDomain_Task($domain, $account, $ADpassword)
Sleep 60

# Assign Active Directory group administrative rights to the host
Get-VMHost $newhost  | New-VIPermission -Role Admin `
   -Principal "Mishchenko\ESX Administrators"

# Delete the default VM port group
Write-Host   Removing the default virtual machine port group
Get-VirtualPortGroup -Name "VM Network" | Remove-VirtualPortGroup -Confirm:$false

# Create a new VMkernel port for vMotion on vSwitch0, set the vLAN for it
$vMotionIP = Read-Host Enter the vMotion IP address
$vMotionSubnet = Read-Host Enter the vMotion network subnet mask
$vSwitch = Get-VirtualSwitch -name vSwitch0
New-VMHostNetworkAdapter -PortGroup 'vMotion' -VirtualSwitch $vSwitch -IP $vMotionIP `
    -SubnetMask $vMotionSubnet -vMotionEnabled:$true
$vMotionPG = Get-VirtualPortgroup -Name 'vMotion'
Set-VirtualPortGroup -VirtualPortGroup $vMotionPG -VlanId 125
```

```
# Set vSwitch0 to use vmnic0 and vmnic1
Set-VirtualSwitch -VirtualSwitch $vSwitch -Nic vmnic0,vmnic1
# Set vMotion vmnic1 active vmnic0 standby
get-virtualportgroup -name vMotion | Get-NicTeamingPolicy | `
   Set-NicTeamingPolicy -MakeNicActive vmnic1
get-virtualportgroup -name vMotion | Get-NicTeamingPolicy | `
      Set-NicTeamingPolicy -MakeNicStandby vmnic0
# Set Management Network vmnic0 active, vmnic1 standby
get-virtualportgroup -name 'Management Network' | Get-NicTeamingPolicy | `
      Set-NicTeamingPolicy -MakeNicActive vmnic0
get-virtualportgroup -name 'Management Network' | Get-NicTeamingPolicy | `
      Set-NicTeamingPolicy -MakeNicStandby vmnic1

# Configure vSwitch1 with vmnic2, vmnic3
New-VirtualSwitch -Name vSwitch1 -Nic vmnic2,vmnic3
Get-VirtualSwitch -Name vSwitch1 | New-VirtualPortGroup -Name"DMZ" -VLANID 500
Get-VirtualSwitch -Name vSwitch1 | New-VirtualPortGroup -Name"LAN" -VLANID 400
Get-VirtualSwitch -Name vSwitch1 | New-VirtualPortGroup -Name"DEV" -VLANID 600
Sleep 15

# Reboot Host
Write-Host   Rebooting Host
Set-VMHost -state "Maintenance"
Restart-VMHost -Force:$true -Confirm:$false
Sleep 60

# Check to see if host is up
Connect-VIServer -Server $newhost -User root -Password $newpasswd
While ($? -ne $true ) {
            Sleep 30; write-host  Waiting for host to respond ...; `
            Connect-VIServer -Server $newhost -User root -Password $newpasswd
            }

# Connect to vCenter and join new ESXi to it
Disconnect-VIserver $newhost
$vCenter = Read-Host Enter the network name of your vCenter Server
$datacenter = Read-Host Enter the datacenter for the ESXi host
Add-VMHost $newhost -Location $datacenter -User root -Password $newpassword
```

At the beginning of the script, some variables are set. To make the script dynamic, Read-Host is used to prompt the user to enter items such as the IP address for the new host. The parameter -AsSecureString is used to mask sensitive input such as passwords. The script then opens a connection to the host that was specified.

As a default installation of ESXi leaves the host with a blank password for root, the first configuration change that the script makes is to change the root password. Subsequent connections to the host in the script make use of the new password.

The script then sets the hostname, domain name, and domain name service (DNS) server for the new host. Get-VMHostNetwork and Set-VMHostNetwork can be used to query and configure a number of networking settings for ESXi, including IPv4 and IPv6 management IP addresses, the host and domain name, and the VMkernel gateway. This section of the script also uses Sleep. This pauses the script for the number of seconds specified and is used throughout the script to allow configuration changes to have effect.

The following section configures Network Time Protocol (NTP) settings on the host. After the script has set the NTP servers with Add-VMHostNTPServer, Restart-VMHostService is used to restart the NTP service to ensure that the host's time is properly set. This is critical for the next portion of the script. The service is set to start automatically with Set-VMHostService.

The next commands in the script enable Active Directory integration on the host. As there is no PowerCLI cmdlet to enable this, Project Onyx was used to obtain the PowerShell code required to perform this action. Project Onyx is explored in detail later in this chapter. Sleep is issued again and then Set-VIPermission is used to grant an Active Directory group the Administrator role on the ESXi host.

A good portion of the script is then devoted to configuring the networking on the host. The following steps are taken:

1. The default virtual machine port group VM Network is deleted from vSwitch0 as this virtual switch (vSwitch) is only to be used for management purposes.

2. The user is queried for vMotion IP address information. That input is used to create a vMotion port. The vMotion port is configured with the VLAN ID of 125.

3. vSwitch0 is reconfigured to include vmnic1. By default, only vmnic0 is connected to vSwitch0.

4. Get-NicTeamingPolicy and Set-NicTeamingPolicy are used to configure the active and standby network interface card (NIC) ports for the vMotion and management traffic ports on vSwitch0.

5. A new virtual switch is created for virtual machines and it is linked to vmnic2 and vmnic3.

6. Three virtual machine port groups are created for various traffic types.

After the networking on the host has been configured, the script pauses before restarting the host. Before the host is restarted, it is placed into maintenance mode with Set-VMHost. Restart-VMHost is used to reboot the host.

The script then pauses on the Sleep command and afterward attempts to reconnect to the ESXi host after its reboot. If Connect-VIServer fails to connect, the While statement repeats again. This block of script could be rewritten as the following:

```
$i = 0
Do {
    Sleep 30; write-host  Waiting for host to respond ...; '
    Connect-VIServer -Server $newhost  -User root -Password $newpasswd ;$i++}
While ($i -le 10)
```

The advantage of using a Do ... While loop is that it executes only a finite number of times. If a host were to fail to come back online, the script would loop endlessly until terminated. With Do ... While, additional error-handling code could be added to generate a meaningful error message and the script would be able to continue processing.

The final step of the script uses Add-VMHost to join the ESXi host to vCenter Server. You can specify any folder or datacenter for Location. The script first uses Disconnect-VIServer to close the PowerShell connection to the ESXi host. The script then opens a session with the vCenter host. As you'll recall from earlier in the chapter, PowerCLI can be configured to connect to several vCenter and ESXi hosts simultaneously. Running the disconnect statement ensures that Add-VMHost is not executed on the ESXi host in addition to the vCenter Server host.

Managing Host Profiles with PowerCLI

If you're using Host Profiles to ensure configuration compliance of your ESXi hosts, PowerCLI includes the following cmdlets to help you automate that task:

Apply-VMHostProfile	New-VMHostProfile
Export-VMHostProfile	Remove-VMHostProfile
Get-VMHostProfile	Set-VMHostProfile
Import-VMHostProfile	Test-VMHostProfileCompliance

Configuring and managing Host Profiles using the vSphere client was discussed in Chapter 3, "Management Tools." After you have configured one of your ESXi hosts to serve as the baseline for your profile, you can create a profile with the following statement:

```
Get-VMHost esx01.mishchenko.net | New-VMHostProfile -Name "DMZ Host Profile" '
    -Description "This profile is for hosts running DMZ virtual machines"
```

To view the profiles that have been created, you can use Get-VMHostProfile. To filter your list of profiles, you can use the -ReferenceHost parameter to display only the profiles created from certain hosts. If you have to move profiles between vCenter Server hosts, you can use `Export-VMHostProfile` and `Import-VMHostProfile`.

To check whether a host is compliant with a profile, you must first attach the profile to the host. You can do that with the following command. You could substitute `Get-Cluster` for `Get-VMHost` to associate the profile with all the hosts in a cluster.

```
Get-VMHost esx02.mishchenko.net | Apply-VMHostProfile -AssociateOnly `
  -Profile "DMZ Host Profile"
```

You can then use `Test-VMHostProfileCompliance` to test the ESXi host. If no output is returned, then the host has passed the check. In the following example, the cmdlet reports that the host is not compliant due to a vSwitch configuration issue:

```
Test-VMHostProfileCompliance -VMHost esx02.mishchenko.net
VMHostId              VMHostProfileId          IncomplianceElementList
----------            ---------------------    ---------------------------------

HostSystem-host-9  HostProfile-hostprofile-1  {network.vswitch["key-vim-profil...
```

To apply a profile to a host that has failed the compliance test, you must first place it in maintenance mode with `Set-VMHost`. You can then run `Apply-VMHostProfile` again without the `-AssociateOnly` parameter to apply the profile. After this step has been completed, you can run `Test-VMHostProfileCompliance` to verify the status of the host.

```
Get-VMHost esx02.mishchenko.net | Apply-VMHostProfile `
  -Profile "DMZ Host Profile"
```

Integrating PowerCLI with vCenter Server Alarms

If you're employing vCenter Server alarms, you may want to employ PowerCLI scripts to enable more complex actions to be taken in the event of an alarm. vCenter Server can currently be configured to send an e-mail alert, generate a Simple Network Management Procotol (SNMP) notification, or to run a command. The command options are limited to EXE or BAT files. To run a PowerCLI script, you must create a small batch file that when executed spawns a PowerShell process that can run your script. The batch file should contain the following commands. Note that the location of the PowerShell executable may differ from the path shown in the following example.

```
set POWERSHELL=C:\WINDOWS\system32\windowspowershell\v1.0\powershell.exe -nologo
    -noprofile -noninteractive
start %POWERSHELL% -command "&"%1""
```

When you create the action for the alarm, you enter the path to the batch file and the name of the script as shown in Figure 9.3. If the alarm is triggered, the batch file is passed the path and

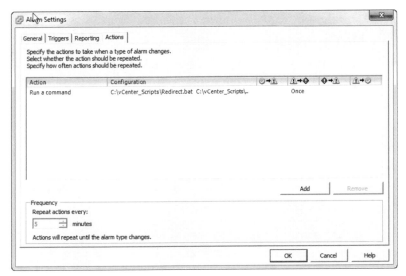

Figure 9.3   Configuring a vCenter alarm to execute a PowerCLI script.

filename for the script file as a parameter. The batch file then launches PowerShell and passes the script file name and path to it.

If you do use this method to run PowerCLI scripts, you need to consider how your scripts authenticate with the hosts to which they connect. The vCenter Server service typically runs with the LocalSystem account. Ideally, the scripts should not include any credentials. If you set your vCenter Server service to use an Active Directory account, you'll be able to log in without credentials to vCenter and ESXi hosts configured for Active Directory Integration. If you need to stick with LocalSystem, then you can employ a PowerShell script called Export-Credentials, which you can access at this URL: http://halr9000.com/article/531.

Troubleshooting Your ESXi Hosts

If you need to perform troubleshooting on your ESXi environment, PowerCLI includes some cmdlets that can assist you with that task. Get-VIEvent is used to query vCenter Server or ESXi to retrieve events. Each action you take in your environment is recorded as an event, and searching through your event data may provide some clues to the problem you are experiencing. Events that occur are categorized with the following three types: info, warning, and error.

Run on its own, Get-VIEvent retrieves the last 100 events for your vCenter Server or ESXi host. That may not always be helpful and instead you may wish to be able to search for specific events. You can filter the output with the parameters in Table 9.2.

Table 9.2 Parameters for Get-VIEvent

Parameter	Description
Entity	Specify objects such as virtual machine, host, or resource pool.
Start	Specify the start date of events you want.
Finish	Specify the end date of events you want.
Username	Specify the user who initiated the event.
MaxSamples	Limit the events to retrieve. The default value is 100 and you can retrieve up to 1000 events.
Types	Specify the types of event you want to collect. The types include info, warning, and error.

It is also possible to search by the event description. The following script creates a file in which you will find the event name, the category of the event (info, warning, or error), and a description of the event:

```
$report = @()
$eventMgr = Get-View EventManager
$eventMgr.Description.EventInfo | %{
$row = "" | Select Name, Category, Description
$row.Name = $_.Key
$row.Category = $_.Category
$row.Description = $_.Description
$report += $row
}
$report | Export-Csv "C:\events.csv" -NoTypeInformation
```

If you want to filter events to find who created a virtual machine, you want to use the event VmCreatedEvent. As you examine the events generated by the preceding script, note that there are similar events for virtual machine creation such as VMClonedEvent, VMDeployedEvent, and VMRegisteredEvent. Your script should take into consideration that a task may have different event types depending on how the task is performed. After you have identified the correct event type, you can run the following script to find the user who created a virtual machine:

```
Get-VIEvent | Where { $_.Gettype().Name -eq "VMCreatedEvent"} `
| Select CreatedTime, UserName, FullFormattedMessage
```

To obtain log files from vCenter Server and ESXi, you use Get-LogType and Get-Log. Get-LogType is used to obtain a list of log types that are available on the host to which you are connecting. The first list shown is for a vCenter Server host and the second is for an ESXi host.

```
Key                     Summary
----                    ---------
vpxd:vpxd-28.log        vCenter server log in 'plain' format
vpxd:vpxd-29.log        vCenter server log in 'plain' format
vpxd:vpxd-alert-7...    vCenter server log in 'plain' format
vpxd:vpxd-profile...    vCenter server log in 'plain' format
vpxd-profiler:vpx...    vpxd-profiler

Key                     Summary
----                    ---------
hostd                   Server log in 'plain' format
messages                Server log in 'plain' format
vpxa                    vCenter agent log in 'plain' format
```

Get-Log is used to retrieve the contents of the log file. The only required parameter is -Key, which you determine from the output of Get-LogType. To retrieve the VMkernel log from an ESXi host, issue the following command:

```
$Log = Get-Log -Key messages
```

This generates the array $Log, which is an array of strings that represents the contents of the log file. Each entry within the array contains one entry from the log file. The first command can be used to display the last 20 entries in the log file. The second command searches the log for entries with word "warning."

```
$Log.Entries[-1..-20]
$Log | ? { $_.Entries | Select-String warning }
```

Get-Log can also be used to obtain a VM-support log bundle. The following example generates a log bundle in the temp folder and uses -RunAsync, as the process can take some time:

```
Get-Log -Bundle -DestinationPath c:\temp -RunAsync
```

Extending PowerCLI with Other Tools

The following section discusses three graphical tools that you can use with PowerCLI. It may seem strange to discuss graphical tools with a shell-based product, but these applications can accelerate your learning of PowerCLI and help you develop complex scripts.

The Integrated Shell Environment

Included with PowerShell 2.0 is the Integrated Shell Environment (ISE). It provides a simple editor for developing your scripts, as shown in Figure 9.4. The ISE consists of a script pane for creating and editing scripts, an output pane where the output from your scripts or commands are displayed, and a command pane where you can enter commands as you would in a regular PowerShell session.

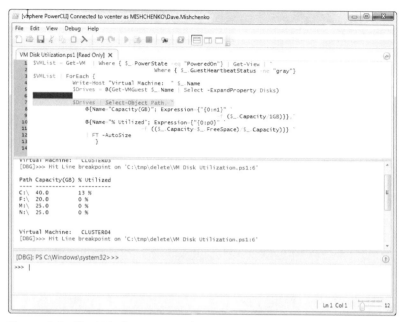

Figure 9.4   The Windows PowerShell Integrated Shell Environment.

Tip: When you're using tools like the ISE, the VMware PowerCLI cmdlets may not be available until you run `Add-PSSnapin VMware.VimAutomation.Core`.

One of the benefits to using a PowerShell-aware editor is that the scripts are colored-coded to make reading much easier. You can also set breakpoints within a script. With a breakpoint, PowerShell pauses execution of the script. You can use the command pane to check the values of variables. To set a breakpoint with ISE, right-click on the command where you want the script to pause and select Toggle Breakpoint. Start the script by pressing F5. The script will pause at the breakpoint and you can query the current values of any variables that the script has defined. You can then press F5 to continue executing the script until the next breakpoint is encountered, or press one of F10, F11, or Shift+F11 to step through the individual lines of the script. To remove a breakpoint, right-click on it and select Disable Breakpoint.

VMware Project Onyx

VMware Project Onyx is a tool that captures Simple Object Access Protocol (SOAP) traffic between the vSphere client or a PowerCLI session and your vCenter Server host or ESXi server. The traffic can be translated to PowerShell, SOAP, C#, and JavaScript code. With this tool, you can capture your actions within the vSphere client and have them translated to PowerShell code, which you can then copy to your own scripts.

The Connect icon

Figure 9.5 Starting a new session with VMware Project Onyx.

Project Onyx can be downloaded from http://www.vmware.com/go/onyx. After you have extracted the ZIP package, start Onyx.exe and accept the license agreement. On the main screen, shown in Figure 9.5, change the Output mode to PowerCLI.NET. Click the Connect icon to open a session to vCenter Server or ESXi and enter the host to establish a connection with. Optionally check the Launch a Client after Connection checkbox, select either VMware VI Client or VMware PowerCLI, and enter appropriate credentials.

When you click Start, Onyx opens a connection to your host over an SSL connection and begins to listen on port 1545 on your management computer. If you manually connect to Onyx, you should specify your hostname or IP address and port 1545 in the IP Address/Name field of the vSphere client. When you log in, you will receive an error about the traffic not being secure. This refers only to the connection between the client you use and Onyx. Communication between Onyx and vCenter or ESXi is secure. If you connect with PowerCLI, you should issue the following command:

```
Connect-VIServer 192.168.1.225 -Protocol http -Port 1545
```

Note: Some modules within vCenter, such as Update Manager or VMware vShield, may make an independent connection that bypasses Onyx. Some plug-ins such as License Reporting Manager and vCenter Hardware Status do not connect over the SSL default port and fail to connect through Onyx. Check the Plug-In Manager for the status of any plug-ins that you are using.

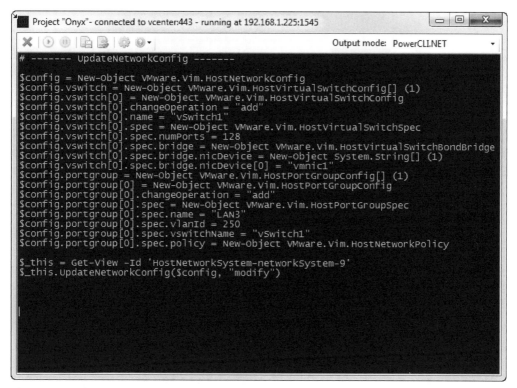

```
# ------- UpdateNetworkConfig -------
$config = New-Object VMware.Vim.HostNetworkConfig
$config.vswitch = New-Object VMware.Vim.HostVirtualSwitchConfig[] (1)
$config.vswitch[0] = New-Object VMware.Vim.HostVirtualSwitchConfig
$config.vswitch[0].changeOperation = "add"
$config.vswitch[0].name = "vSwitch1"
$config.vswitch[0].spec = New-Object VMware.Vim.HostVirtualSwitchSpec
$config.vswitch[0].spec.numPorts = 128
$config.vswitch[0].spec.bridge = New-Object VMware.Vim.HostVirtualSwitchBondBridge
$config.vswitch[0].spec.bridge.nicDevice = New-Object System.String[] (1)
$config.vswitch[0].spec.bridge.nicDevice[0] = "vmnic1"
$config.portgroup = New-Object VMware.Vim.HostPortGroupConfig[] (1)
$config.portgroup[0] = New-Object VMware.Vim.HostPortGroupConfig
$config.portgroup[0].changeOperation = "add"
$config.portgroup[0].spec = New-Object VMware.Vim.HostPortGroupSpec
$config.portgroup[0].spec.name = "LAN3"
$config.portgroup[0].spec.vlanId = 250
$config.portgroup[0].spec.vswitchName = "vSwitch1"
$config.portgroup[0].spec.policy = New-Object VMware.Vim.HostNetworkPolicy

$_this = Get-View -Id 'HostNetworkSystem-networkSystem-9'
$_this.UpdateNetworkConfig($config, "modify")
```

Figure 9.6 Reviewing PowerShell code generated by Onyx for creating a new vSwitch.

When you're ready to capture your actions in Onyx, click the Start button. In the example shown in Figure 9.6, a new vSwitch has been created. Note that New-Object has been used to create the object $config, which stores the configuration settings for the new vSwitch. The task UpdateNetworkConfig has been used to create the vSwitch. You may have expected to see New-VirtualSwitch and New-VirtualPortGroup. But those cmdlets send the same underlying code to the host to create a new vSwitch. If you capture a PowerCLI session, you will see the same code captured when using those cmdlets. The PowerCLI cmdlets merely wrap that code into easy-to-use commands. For more information on the objects and methods used for the actions that you capture, you can refer to the vSphere API SDK at http://www.vmware .com/support/developer/vc-sdk/visdk41pubs/ApiReference/index.html.

While PowerCLI does include a wide range of cmdlets, they do not encompass all the actions that are available within the vSphere client. As noted earlier, there is no cmdlet to convert a virtual machine into a template. The two lines of code to accomplish that are easily captured with Onyx and you can use that code directly in your PowerShell scripts.

As you use Onyx, you may notice that it is not capturing all your actions. By default, Onyx ignores certain methods, such as those used by Get-VM. To control the methods that are displayed, click the Settings icon and edit the Ignored Methods list on the Output tab. In the Settings screen, you can also change the port that Onyx listens on and configure Onyx to mask security-sensitive commands such as the creation of users and the transmission of passwords.

PowerWF

PowerWF is an application that leverages Windows Workflow Foundation to provide a drag-and-drop environment for developing and debugging your PowerCLI scripts. Figure 9.7 shows a graphical representation of the virtual machine disk utilization report discussed earlier in this chapter. You can add PowerCLI and PowerShell cmdlets merely by dragging them into the script from the Toolbox pane.

One of the best features of the product is that you can import existing PowerShell scripts. This can be a significant benefit if you're trying to understand a complex script. As you develop your workflow, you can use PowerWF's built-in debugger or open a PowerShell session within the application. After you have completed your workflow, you can deploy it to a number of options, including a cmdlet, a PowerShell snap-in, a standalone application, or you can deploy it for integration with Microsoft System Center.

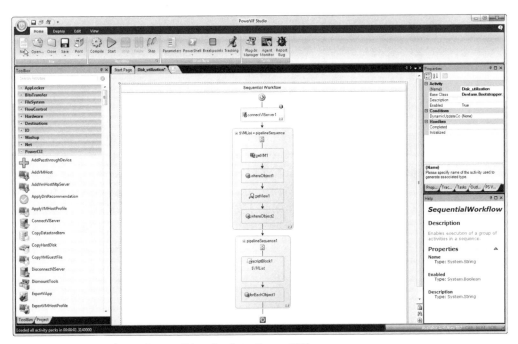

Figure 9.7   Importing a PowerCLI script into PowerWF.

Conclusion

Together, PowerShell and PowerCLI represent a powerful tool that you can use to manage your vSphere environment. You can use it to automate configuration of vCenter Server, your ESXi hosts, and virtual machines. Management tasks that may have taken hours in the vSphere client can be accomplished quickly with PowerCLI, using scripts that eliminate the risk of misconfiguration.

10 Patching and Updating ESXi

An essential task in maintaining any software installation is the application of patches. Firmware updates are provided periodically for ESXi to correct software bugs, implement new functionality, and remove new security risks. With ESXi 4.1, it is possible to patch your hosts with vCenter Update Manager (VUM), PowerCLI, or with the vCLI command `vihostupdate`. This chapter will step through the processes required to patch your ESXi hosts with these methods.

Installing Patches for ESXi

The process of installing patches for ESXi differs from that for ESX in several significant ways. Patches for ESX are released with only the necessary code changes to fix or secure a specific issue. They can vary significantly in size and more importantly have dependencies on previously released patches. Thus, it is necessary to track which patches are installed on an ESX host and ensure that all necessary patch dependencies are tested within your test environment to make certain that patches are properly installed and that dependencies do not harm your environment.

ESXi patches are released as complete firmware updates. Any patch or update release contains at least one of the following two bundles to update the following components of ESXi:

- The ESXi firmware
- VMware Tools ISO images

As a single ESXi patch includes all the necessary software components to run ESXi, an ESXi patch does not have any dependencies on prior patch releases. Rather, a single patch in a cumulative package contains all previously released bug and security fixes. Installing the latest patch ensures that you have all the latest updates installed on your host.

The second significant difference between patches for ESX and ESXi is the reboot requirements. With ESX, a patch may make only a minor change and not require a reboot of the host. With an ESXi patch, the firmware component will always be replaced, which necessitates a host reboot. The virtual machines running on the host will need to be stopped and the host must be placed into maintenance mode before the patch can be applied. After the patch has been applied, a reboot is required so that the new firmware version can be loaded. If your host is part of a fully automated Dynamic Resource Scheduling (DRS) cluster, the virtual machines running on the host will be migrated when the host is placed in maintenance mode. Otherwise, you can manually migrate your virtual machines with vMotion to ensure that the patch process does not interrupt their availability. For a standalone ESXi host, you must shut down any running virtual machines before placing the host in maintenance mode, so you should plan on shutting them down appropriately before applying the latest patch to the host.

Information about the patches available for ESXi can be found at this link: http://www.vmware.com/patch/download/. On that page, you can select to view all patches for a specific product and version. If you select a product of ESXi (Embedded and Installable), a version of 4.0.0, and then click Search, a list similar to that shown in Figure 10.1 is displayed. Patch bulletins follow a specific naming convention; an example of a bulletin name is ESXi400-201005401-SG. The ending of the name signifies the type of bundle that you may download. The ending of SG means that the bundle contains security fixes, and an ending of BG indicates that the bundle provides bug fixes. With ESXi, an update release will also be listed on the patch download page

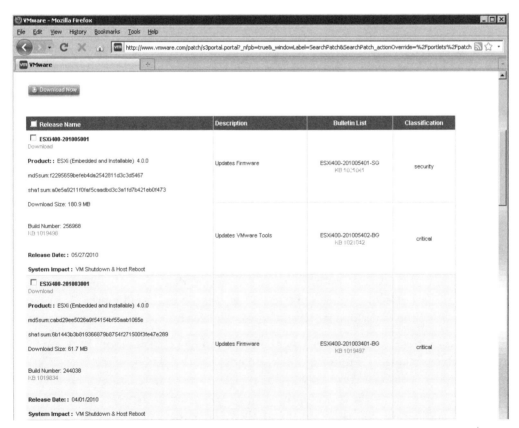

Figure 10.1 Patch downloads for VMware ESXi.

and be bundled in the same format. The download for an update will have a UG suffix and be installed with the same processes described later in this chapter.

Patching ESXi with the vCLI Command vihostupdate

The vCLI includes the command `vihostupdate`, which can be used to install patches and updates on your ESXi host. You can download patches to the computer on which you have the vCLI installed or use a media depot to store the bundle files. In the case of downloading the patch file to your computer, the `vihostupdate` command uses the actual ZIP file as an argument for the `--bundle` option. If you plan to use a media depot, which can be accessed by `vihostupdate` with HTTP, HTTPS, or File Transfer Protocol (FTP), you have to extract the ZIP file and use the `--metadata` option.

If you are not using a media depot, you just run `vihostupdate` with the `--bundle` option to patch an ESXi host, as shown in this example:

```
vihostupdate.pl --server esx08 --install --bundle c:\tmp\ESXi400-201005001.zip
```

The following steps demonstrate how to patch an ESXi host using a media depot.

1. Open a Web browser and access the uniform resource locator (URL) http://www.
   vmware.com/patch/download/.

2. Change the product type to ESXi (Embedded and Installable) and then select the appropriate version for the host you will be patching. You can optionally select a patch classification to filter only general, security, or critical patches. Click Search to produce a list of applicable downloads.

3. Select the patch release you wish to download and click Download Now. As mentioned previously, the most recent patch will include all prior bug fixes, security patches, and feature enhancements.

4. Extract the ZIP file to your media depot. The files extracted include `metadata.zip` and a folder structure containing one to three vSphere Installation Bundle (VIB) files. The VIB files will correspond to the two software components of ESXi discussed earlier in this section of the chapter.

5. Put the ESXi host in maintenance mode, as shown in the following example:

   ```
   hostops.pl --server vcenter41.mishchenko.net --operation enter_maintenance
        --host esx08.mishchenko.net
   Putting host esx08.mishchenko.net in maintenance mode
   Host entered maintenance mode successfully
   ```

   If the host is part of a fully automated DRS cluster, any virtual machines running on the host will be migrated to other hosts in the cluster. Otherwise, you can manually migrate the virtual machines with the vSphere client or by using the `hostevacuate` script that is included with the vCLI before you issue the command. If the host cannot be put in maintenance mode, an error message is displayed informing you that certain VIBs in the patch package require the host to be in maintenance mode before the patch can be installed.

6. Run the `vihostupdate` command to start the patching process. As the patch is being installed from a media depot, the `--metadata` option is used.

```
vihostupdate --server esx08.mishchenko.net --install
      --metadata
      http://server02.mishchenko.net/patch/ESXi400-201005001/metadata.zip
Please wait patch installation is in progress …
The update completed successfully, but the system needs to be rebooted for the
changes to be effective.
```

7. Use the `hostops` command again to restart the host:

```
hostops.pl --server vcenter41.mishchenko.net --operation reboot
      --host esx08.mishchenko.net
Rebooting host esx08.mishchenko.net…done
Host 'esx08.mishchenko.net' exited maintenance mode successfully
```

8. After the host has been restarted, you can verify that the patch bundle has updated correctly on your host by using the `--query` option:

```
vihostupdate --server esx08.mishchenko.net --query
--------Bulletin ID-------- ------Installed------------- ---------Summary------
ESXi400-201005401-SG       2010-06-03T03:35:54 Updates   Firmware
ESXi400-201005402-BG       2010-06-03T03:35:54 Updates   VMware Tools
```

Patching ESXi with the vCenter Update Manager

vCenter Update Manager (VUM) is designed to provide a centralized and automated patching tool for vSphere administrators. With VUM, it is possible to scan and patch hosts, virtual machines, templates, and virtual appliances. Supported virtual machines for patching include Windows machines and a number of Linux distributions. It is possible to patch both running and offline guests, and VUM uses snapshots to revert virtual machines back to their prior condition should an upgrade or patch fail to install properly. VUM can also be used to update VMware Tools and the virtual hardware of virtual machines.

VUM integrates tightly with vCenter Server. The VUM server component can be installed on the same host that is running vCenter Server or on another host if you plan to patch a large number of hosts and virtual machines. If it is installed on another host, network connectivity is required with the vCenter Server. If you are using vCenter Server in vCenter Linked Mode, you need to install and register VUM for each vCenter Server, as each installation of VUM is associated with a single vCenter Server instance. The VUM client consists of a vSphere client plug-in, which must be installed on any computer that will be used to configure and manage VUM.

A typical installation of VUM requires Internet access to obtain information about patches for your hosts and virtual machines as well as to download the actual patch files. If you are deploying VUM in a secure network without Internet access, you can use the VUM Download Service on another host with access to download patch metadata and path files.

The following sections provide the necessary steps to set up and configure VUM, create a baseline, scan your ESXi hosts, and apply patches to your hosts.

Installing vCenter Update Manager

Prior to running the installation program for VUM, it is necessary to set up a database that will be used by VUM and an Open Database Connectivity (ODBC) data source name (DSN) that VUM will use to connect to the database. If you have a smaller deployment of up to 5 hosts and 50 virtual machines, you can use Microsoft SQL Server Express, which can be installed and configured when you run the installation for VUM. Otherwise, you must create a database with Microsoft SQL Server or Oracle. You can use the following process to create the DSN and database for Microsoft SQL Server:

1. Start SQL Server Management Studio and connect to the SQL instance that will host your database for VUM.

2. Create a database that will be used for VUM.

3. Create a new SQL login that VUM will use to connect to the database. Set the default database for the login to be the database that you created in step 2.

4. The login should be updated to have the db_owner fixed database role in both the VUM database and the MSDB database.

Note: Both the installation and upgrades for VUM create and modify SQL Server scheduled jobs, which are stored in the Microsoft System Database (MSDB) database. Thus it is necessary to grant the SQL login the db_owner role for the MSDB database during those processes. Alternatively, you can grant the login the sysadmin server role. After completing the installation or upgrade, you can remove the role for the MSDB database.

---

5. Run the 32-bit ODBC Administrator application. The server component is a 32-bit application that requires a 32-bit ODBC connection. If you are installing the server component on a 32-bit server, the installation program will not be able to find a 64-bit ODBC connection, which will be created if you use the ODBC Data Source

Administrator application found in Administrative Tools. The 32-bit ODBC Administrator application can be found at <Windows>\ SysWOW64\odbcad32.exe.

6. Select the System DSN tab.

7. Click Add to start the wizard to create a new ODBC connection. Select SQL Native Client as the driver type and click Finish. Enter a name for the ODBC connection and specify the SQL Server to which to connect. Click Next to continue configuring the connection. Change the authentication setting to With SQL Server Authentication Using a Login ID and Password Entered by the User. Enter the SQL login and password you created earlier in this process, and then click Next. If you set up the login correctly, the default database should be listed as the database you created to store VUM data. Click Next to continue. Click Finish to complete creating the ODBC connection.

After you have created the ODBC connection and the database, you should review the database settings for the connection and also ensure that the database is properly maintained. This maintenance should include regular backups and ensure that indexes are regularly rebuilt to optimize database performance. You can then follow this process to install the VUM server component:

1. Start the VMware vCenter Installer application on the vCenter Server installation media.

2. Click the link to start the vCenter Update Manager product installer.

3. Select the appropriate language to use and click OK.

4. Click Next on the Welcome page to start the installation.

5. Review the license agreement and click Next.

6. Enter the connection information for your vCenter Server host and an account with vCenter Server administrative privileges. Click Next to continue.

7. Select the database storage option for VUM. You can choose between installing an instance of SQL Server Express and connecting to a database with the ODBC connection that you created earlier. If you select the SQL Server Express option, the installer launches a process to install SQL Server Express. Otherwise, choose the ODBC connection that you created earlier and then click Next. If you do not see the connection that you created, ensure that you used the 32-bit version of the ODBC Administrator application and then restart the VUM installer.

8. Enter the SQL login and password for the VUM database and click Next.

9. On the VMware vCenter Update Manager Port Settings screen, shown in Figure 10.2, select the network identity that vCenter Server and your hosts will use to connect to the VUM service. This can be the fully qualified domain name for the host as shown in

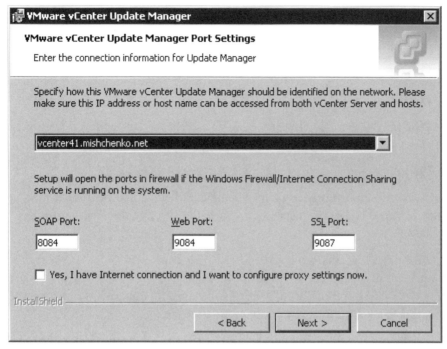

Figure 10.2   The VMware vCenter Update Manager Port Settings installation screen.

the figure or the IP address for one of the host's network interfaces. If you have Windows Firewall or other firewall software running on the host, you should open the ports shown to allow connectivity to the service. You may also wish to modify the ports used should your security requirements necessitate a change. You can check the box Yes, I Have Internet Connection and I Want to Configure Proxy Settings Now if the VUM service will have to use a proxy server to obtain patches for your host and virtual machines.

10.   On the following screen, you can select the location for the VUM installation and for the patches download directory. The default location for downloading patches is `C:\ProgramData\VMware\VMware Update Manager\Data\`. You should ensure that the volume has sufficient space for storing patches for ESXi, ESX, and any guest operating systems that you will patch with VUM. A sizing estimator can be found at http://www. vmware.com/support/vsphere4/doc/vsp_vum_40_sizing_estimator.xls, which provides some information on database and disk sizing as well as database and service placement. After you have confirmed the locations, click Next.

11.   Click Install to begin the installation.

12.   Click Finish to complete the install process.

To access VUM functionality within the vSphere client, you must enable the VUM client plug-in. This is required on any workstation that will be used to manage VUM. After VUM has been installed, you can use the following procedure to enable the plug-in:

1. Start the vSphere client and connect to the vCenter Server with which the VUM service is registered.

2. Select Plug-Ins > Manage Plug-Ins. The VMware vCenter Update Manager should be listed under Available Plug-ins, as shown in Figure 10.3.

3. Click Download and Install to begin installation of the plug-in.

4. The vCenter Update Manager Client installation begins. You can select the default options to step through the wizard and click Finish once the installation has completed.

5. On the Manage Plug-Ins screen, the VUM plug-in should now have a status of Enabled. You may also receive a security warning about an untrusted Secure Sockets Layer (SSL) certificate if you're still using the default vCenter Server SSL certificates. Click Ignore to close the security warning.

6. Close the Manage Plug-Ins screen. Select the Home screen in the vSphere client. You should now see an Update Manager icon under Solution and Applications.

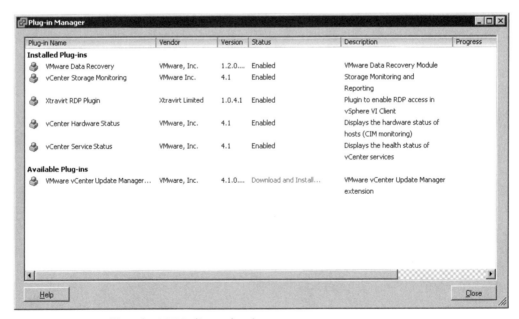

Figure 10.3 Installing the VUM client plug-in.

Note: If you plan to use VUM to patch Linux and Windows virtual machines, the VMware vCenter Update Manager Guest Agent will be installed within the guest operating systems. The installation of the agent occurs the first time a patch remediation is scheduled or when you start a patch scan on a powered-on virtual machine. The Guest Agent is required for scanning and remediation of a virtual machine.

Configuring vCenter Update Manager

Several configuration options require review before you can begin to use VUM. From the Home page of the vSphere client, select the Update Manager icon to access the VUM screens. Select the Configuration tab to see areas of configuration, as shown in Figure 10.4. The screen displays the ports and hostname used for VUM communication. If any changes are made on this screen, it is necessary to restart the Windows service VMware vCenter Update Manager Service.

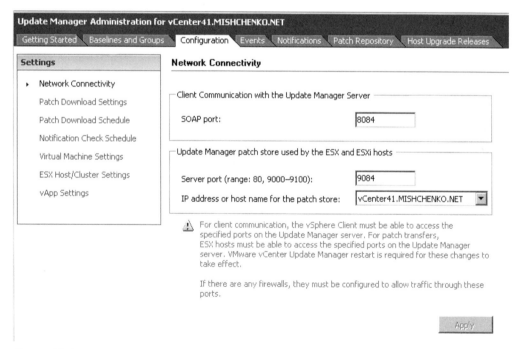

Figure 10.4   VMware vCenter Update Manager Configuration options.

If you plan to use VUM just to update your ESXi host, it is worthwhile to edit the Patch Download Sources on the Patch Download Settings screen. By default, VUM downloads patches for ESX(i) 4.x, ESX(i) 3.x, Linux, and Windows, as shown in Figure 10.5. You will also notice a

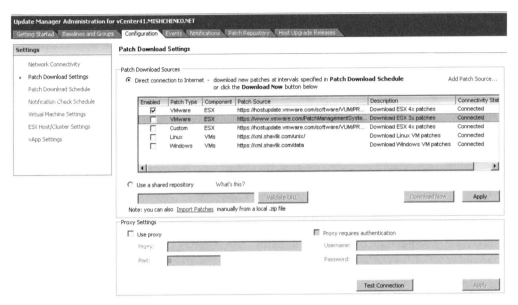

Figure 10.5 Changing patch download settings for VMware vCenter Update Manager.

Custom patch type with a download URL of https://hostupdate.vmware.com/software/VUM/ PRODUCTION/csco-main-index.xml. This patch download source allows for the downloading of patches for the Cisco Nexus 1000V virtual switch. To conserve space and bandwidth only, the VMware patch type for ESX 4x patches should be left enabled. Click Apply to save your configuration change.

On the Patch Download Settings screen, you can also add your own third-party patch source and configure or update proxy settings that the VUM service will use to connect to the Internet. On this screen, you can also manually import patches. If you have downloaded an ESXi patch, as was done in the section "Patching ESXi with the vCLI Command vihostupdate," you can click the Import Patches link and a wizard will guide you through the process of importing the patch into the VUM patch repository. You can also set the VUM service to use a shared repository to obtain patch files should the VUM host not have Internet connectivity. The shared repository is populated by the Update Manager Download Service, which can be installed on a host with Internet access if your security requirements prohibit the VUM host from having direct Internet connectivity. The repository can be a local directory or HTTP URL.

On the Patch Download Schedule screen, you can set a schedule for downloading software patch definitions. When setting the schedule, you can also include a notification e-mail address that is notified when VUM downloads new updates. The notification process is dependent on the e-mail notification setup in vCenter Server that was discussed in Chapter 6, "System Monitoring and Management." On the Notification Check Schedule screen, you can schedule a job that checks for new patches as well as enables e-mail notification for when new patches are available.

The vApp Settings and Virtual Machines Settings screen relates solely to options for virtual machines and vApps. On the vApp Settings screen, you can check the option Enable Smart Reboot after Remediation. This option will ensure that the virtual machines that are part of a vApp are rebooted in such an order as to maintain startup dependencies. On the Virtual Machines Settings screen, you can control how snapshots are maintained for virtual machines that are going to be patched. The default settings are to take a snapshot of the virtual machine before patches are applied and not to delete the snapshots taken. You can choose not to take snapshots before patches are applied and also set the length of time that snapshots are kept after patches are installed.

The final configuration screen is ESX Host/Cluster Settings. Before a host can be patched, it must be placed in maintenance mode. If the host cannot be placed into maintenance mode, the default settings shown in Figure 10.6 specify that the operation will be retried another three times with a 30-minute delay between attempts. You can change the Failure Response setting to the following:

■ **Fail Task.** The attempt to patch the host will be logged as a failure and no further attempts will be made.

■ **Retry.** This is the default setting. You can set a delay period and total number of retry attempts.

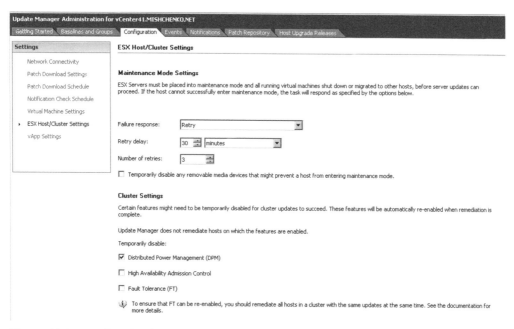

Figure 10.6   Configuring host and cluster settings for VMware vCenter Update Manager.

- **Power Off Virtual Machines and Retry.** All virtual machines on the host will be powered off and the host will be put into maintenance mode. The Retry Delay and Number of Retries settings will be used with this option.

- **Suspend Virtual Machines and Retry.** The virtual machines running on the host will be suspended and VUM will retry to place the host in maintenance mode according to the retry settings.

You may also want to check the option Temporarily Disable Any Removable Media Devices That Might Prevent a Host from Entering Maintenance Mode. If your host is part of a vMotion-capable cluster, a virtual machine may not be able to migrate if it is configured with a virtual floppy or CD-ROM device that is not available on the destination host. If you check this option, those devices will be disabled, which will allow the virtual machine to be migrated to another host.

To allow a host to enter maintenance mode, it may also be necessary to disable certain features of the cluster. For example, in a High Availability (HA) cluster, the Admission Control policy may not allow a host to be placed in maintenance mode, as there would then be insufficient failover capacity in the cluster. Thus it is necessary to disable Admission Control temporarily while the host is being remediated. After the patch process is complete, Admission Control can then again be enabled. The following cluster options can be disabled to allow hosts to enter maintenance mode successfully:

- Distributed Power Management (DPM)

- High Availability Admission Control

- Fault Tolerance (FT)

Creating a vCenter Update Manager Baseline

VUM uses baselines to keep hosts and virtual machines up-to-date with patches, updates, and extensions. A baseline is a collection of one or more patches, service packs, extensions, or upgrades. You can create either a host baseline or one for virtual machines and appliances. Host baselines can be one of three types: patch, upgrade, or extension. When you create baselines, you can also specify whether the baseline will be fixed or dynamic. A fixed baseline for patching an ESXi host would include a specific patch or patches and would not change over time. A dynamic baseline would include patches based on a defined criteria and change over time. As you typically want to run the latest patches on your ESXi hosts, creating a dynamic baseline is the best option for your hosts.

VUM comes with a number of predefined fixed and dynamic baselines for both host and virtual machines. For hosts, this includes the baselines Critical Host Patches and Non-Critical Host Patches. As you begin to use VUM, you may find that it is necessary to create some additional baselines, as the defaults may not meet your needs. To create a new baseline that includes only ESXi patches, use the following process:

1. Start the vSphere client and connect to the vCenter Server where VUM has been registered. On the Home page, select the Update Manager icon.

2. On the Baselines and Groups tab, click the Create link.

3. Enter a Name and Description for your new baseline. The Baseline Type should be set to Host Patch. Click Next to continue.

4. On the Patch Options screen, you can select between a Fixed and Dynamic baseline type. As this baseline should ensure that your ESXi hosts are patched to the most recent version, you should choose the Dynamic option.

5. On the Criteria screen, you have a number of options to filter the patches that will be included in the baseline. The sample in Figure 10.7 has been set to a Patch Vendor of VMware, Inc., as the Cisco Nexus module is not in use, to include patches for only the

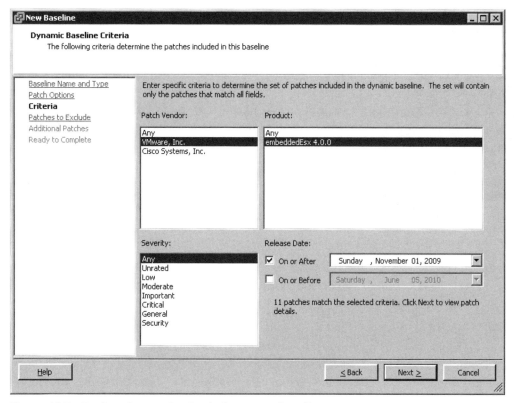

Figure 10.7   Setting the patch criteria for a new baseline.

embeddedEsx 4.0.0 product and to include patches with any severity rating released after November 1, 2009.

6.   On the Patches to Exclude screen, you can remove any patches that should be permanently excluded from the baseline. As the remediation process will exclude any outdated patches from the ESXi patching process, you can click Next to continue without excluding any patches.

7.   Click Next on the Additional Patches screen, as it is not necessary to add additional patches to the baseline.

8.   Click Finish on the Ready to Complete screen. You may also expand the Patches to view the list of patches that are part of this dynamic baseline at the present time.

After you have created a baseline, you will be able to attach the baseline to various vCenter objects to determine which hosts are noncompliant and require patching. You will also have noticed the Baseline Groups section on the Baselines and Groups tab. Groups can be used to create a set of nonconflicting baselines. The group can then be assigned to vCenter objects to allow you to scan and remediate multiple baselines at the same time. If you create a group with both the default baselines of Critical Host Patches and Non-Critical Host Patches when that baseline group is applied on an ESXi host, it will ensure that all patches are installed to that host.

To attach a baseline to a vCenter object, you use the Update Manager tab for that object. You can attach a baseline to a specific host, but it is more efficient to attach the baseline at the cluster, datacenter, or vCenter Server levels. If you are using vCenter Server in vCenter Server Linked Mode, you will attach baselines and baseline groups to the vCenter Server with which VUM is registered. Baselines and groups are specific to the VUM instance that is registered with a specific vCenter Server. Use the following process to attach the baseline that you created at the vCenter Server level:

1.   Start the vSphere client and connect to the vCenter Server where VUM has been registered. Select the Host and Clusters icon.

2.   Select your vCenter Server object and then the Update Manager tab.

3.   Click the Attach link to see the list of available baselines and baseline groups that you can attach to the vCenter Server object. Check the baseline that you created earlier and click Attach.

4.   After you have attached the baseline, Update Manager summarizes the compliance to the baseline for the applicable hosts, as shown in Figure 10.8. The figure shows that three hosts have not been scanned and thus the Patches status is set to Unknown. The hosts are considered to be 0 percent compliant.

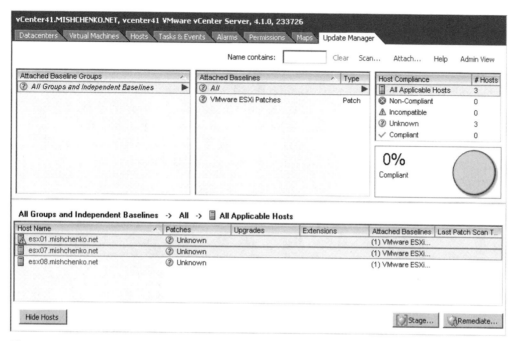

Figure 10.8   Attaching a baseline to the vCenter Server object.

Scanning and Remediating ESXi with vCenter Update Manager

After a baseline has been attached to your hosts, the next step is to scan the hosts for compliance. You can initiate this scan manually or schedule it to run at a more convenient time. After the scan has been completed, you can determine which hosts will need to be patched. As an optional step, you can stage patches to your ESXi host. This essentially copies the patches to the host and does not require the host to be in maintenance mode to copy the patches locally. Once the host is being patched, the process will complete more quickly, as the patches are already stored locally on the ESXi host. Remediation is the final step in patching your ESXi hosts. Again, this step can be manually started or scheduled to occur at an appropriate time.

To scan your hosts manually, you can follow these steps:

1. Start the vSphere client and connect to the vCenter Server where VUM has been registered. Select the Host and Clusters icon.

2. Select your vCenter Server object and then click the Update Manager tab.

3. Click the Scan link.

4. On the Confirm Scan screen, the Patches and Extensions option will be enabled. Click Scan to begin the process.

You can also right-click on the vCenter object and select Scan for Updates. If you have attached a baseline on the Update Manager tab of a parent object, any child objects to which the baseline will apply also show the baseline on the Update Manager tab as well as the status for any child objects. After the scan is complete, the Update Manager tab displays the compliance status for the hosts that you have scanned, as shown in Figure 10.9. Two of the three hosts listed are shown as being compliant. In the case of one of the hosts, it was already up-to-date with patches. The second compliant host was running ESX 4.0 and thus none of the patches in the baseline was applicable. If you are running a mixed environment of ESXi and ESX hosts, you should carefully set up your baselines so that you do not create such a false positive.

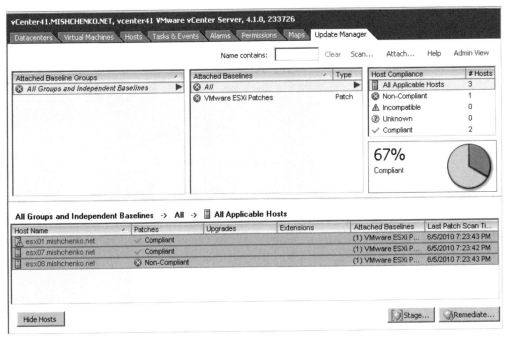

Figure 10.9 Reviewing patch compliance on the Update Manager tab.

You can also easily schedule a periodic scan to ensure that all hosts are up-to-date. Use the following process:

1. Start the vSphere client and connect to the vCenter Server where VUM has been registered. Select the Home > Management Scheduled Tasks.

2. Click New in the toolbar to open the Select a Task to Schedule dialog box.

3. Select the option Scan for Updates and click OK.

4. The Schedule a Scan wizard opens. Select a Scan Type of ESX/ESXi Hosts and click Next.

5. Select the vCenter object to scan. This can be vCenter Server, a folder, a datacenter, a cluster, or a host.

6. Select the Patches option on the Update Types screen and click Next.

7. Enter a Task Name, Description, and Schedule for the task and click Next.

8. Optionally, you can check the Send Email option and then enter a notification e-mail that should be used when the task is complete. Click Next to continue.

9. Click Finish after reviewing the details of the new task on the Ready to Complete screen.

After your scans have been completed and you have identified the hosts that require patching, you can choose to stage the patches to the host before remediation happens. The process of staging the patches to the host essentially copies the patches to the host in advance so you can minimize the patch time later on. The host does not have to be in maintenance mode to have patches staged to it. To stage patches to a host, you can follow these steps:

1. Select the Update Manager tab to which you've attached and scanned a baseline; then click Stage. The Stage button will be grayed out if all the hosts are compliant.

2. The Stage Wizard starts as shown in Figure 10.10. On the Baseline Selection screen, select the baseline to use for staging and the hosts that will be staged. Click Next to continue.

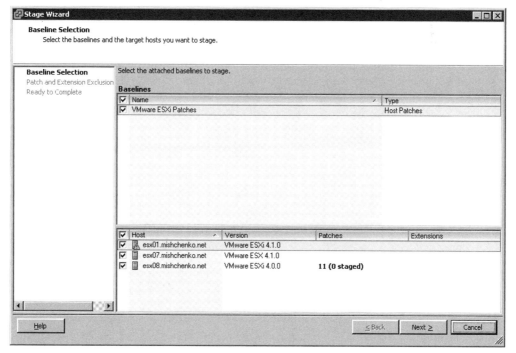

Figure 10.10 Staging patches to a VMware ESXi host.

3. On the Patch and Extension Exclusion screen, you can select which patches should not be staged. Your list may include a number of patches for ESXi that no longer apply because they have been replaced with newer versions. It is not necessary to uncheck those patches, as VUM will stage only the latest patch for the firmware, VMware Tools, and vSphere client components for ESXi. Click Next to continue.

4. The Ready to Complete screen displays a summary of the patches to be staged. Click Finish.

Several staging tasks are initiated for each host that the process will affect. After the patches have been copied to the ESXi hosts, the tasks should display a Completed status, as shown in Figure 10.11. The patches are uploaded to /tmp/updatecache on the hosts. If you examine the file location on your host after the staging is complete, you will find that only the most recent patches for the host have been staged. As mentioned previously, VUM does not apply any patches for ESXi that have been superseded by a newer version.

Recent Tasks							
Name	Target	Status	Details	Initiated by	Requested Start Ti...	Start Time	Completed Time
Stage	esx08.mishchenko.net	Completed		com.vmware....	6/5/2010 9:28:27 PM	6/5/2010 9:28:27 PM	6/5/2010 9:30:34 PM
Stage patches to entity	vCenter41.MISHCHENKO.NET	Completed		MISHCHENK...	6/5/2010 9:28:13 PM	6/5/2010 9:28:13 PM	6/5/2010 9:30:42 PM

Figure 10.11 Staging tasks with a Completed status.

The final step in patching your ESXi hosts is to run the remediation process. You can initiate this process manually on the Update Manager tab or by right-clicking on a vCenter object and selecting Remediate. You can also schedule remediation using a process similar to the one used to schedule scanning for your hosts. To remediate the ESXi hosts that the Update Manager tab displays as being noncompliant, use the following steps:

1. Select the Update Manager tab to which you've attached and scanned a baseline, and then click Remediate. The Remediate button will be grayed out if all the hosts are compliant.

2. The Remediate wizard is started. On the Remediation Selection screen, select the baselines to be used for patching as well as which hosts should be patched. As shown in Figure 10.12, noncompliant hosts list the number of patches that are missing along with the number of patches that are already staged on the host. Click Next to continue the process.

3. You can deselect any patches on the Patch and Extension Exclusion screen. VUM automatically skips any patches for ESXi that have been replaced with newer versions. You can simply click Next on this screen.

4. On the Host Remediation Options screen, you can set a Task Name and Description for the remediation process. You can choose between running the task immediately or

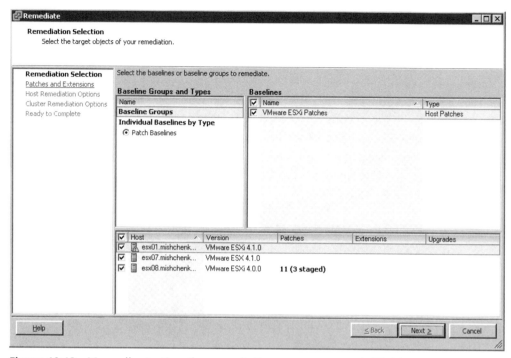

Figure 10.12 Manually starting the remediation process to patch ESXi hosts.

scheduling it to occur at a later date. You can also define the maintenance mode options. These are the same options as were discussed in the "Configuring vCenter Update Manager" section earlier in this chapter. Click Next to continue.

5. On the Cluster Remediation Options screen, you can select whether or not to disable DPM, Admission Control, or FT, as discussed in the "Configuring vCenter Update Manager" section. You also have the option to click Generate Report to see a list of configuration changes that will be made by the Host and Cluster Remediation Options.

6. On the Ready to Complete screen, you can review the settings to be used and then click Finish to start the remediation process.

A number of tasks are generated to begin the installation of patches. Any impacted hosts are placed in maintenance mode. After the patches have been installed and the host rebooted, the remediate task takes the hosts out of maintenance mode. If the patches have been completed successfully, the Update Manager tab should now show the impacted hosts as compliant with the patch baseline that you created.

As mentioned earlier, it is also possible to schedule a remediation task. Select Home > Management > Scheduled Tasks and then click New Task to start the wizard to create a new scheduled task. Select a type of remediation and the wizard that is used will be the same that you used to start the previously described remediation process manually. You should note that unlike the Scan task, which can be scheduled to occur regularly, when you create a remediation task, it can be scheduled to run only once.

The vSphere Host Update Utility The Host Update Utility was included with the vSphere client installation for versions 3.5 and 4.0. This utility could be used to connect directly to an ESXi 3.5 or 4.0 host and apply patches as shown in Figure 10.13. The tools could also be used to upgrade an ESXi host from version 3.5 to 4.0. This utility is no longer included with the vSphere client. You can use `vihostupdate` from the vCLI as an alternative for patching standalone ESXi hosts.

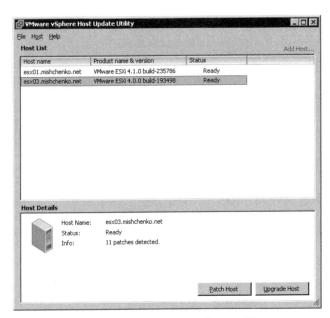

Figure 10.13 The vSphere Host Update Utility.

Patching ESXi with PowerCLI

PowerCLI provides two methods to patch VMware ESXi. The cmdlet `Install-VMHostPatch` can be used to patch hosts directly. You can use this cmdlet as part of a script to automate the patching of your hosts. VMware has also released the vCenter Update Manager PowerCLI. The VUM PowerCLI installs cmdlets that enable you to interact with your Update Manager installation.

Updating a Host with Install-VMHostPatch

The `Install-VMHostPatch` cmdlet can be used to install patches that are located on your management server, on a Web server, or on the filesystem accessible to your ESXi hosts. When you use the -LocalPath or -WebPath options, the patch contents are copied to your ESXi host. Your host may not have sufficient free space for the largest ESXi patches, so it is best to upload the patch to a datastore and then use the -HostPath parameter.

In the following example, an ESXi host is updated from version 4.0 Update 1 to Update 2 with the patch copied to a datastore accessible by the host:

1. Download the patch from VMware and extract the contents to a folder on your management server.

2. Start a PowerCLI session with vCenter Server or your ESXi host.

3. Use the following commands to access the datastore. The first command accesses the datastore provider, the second accesses the appropriate datacenter, and the last accesses the datastore.

    ```
    cd vmstore:
    cd Surrey
    cd NFS1
    ```

4. Run the following commands to create a folder on the datastore and then to copy the contents of the patch folder to the datastore. The -Recurse option instructs cmdlet to copy the entire contents of the ESXi4.0U2 folder.

    ```
    mkdir Patch
    cd Patch
    copy-datastoreitem C:\tmp\ESXi4.0U2 . -Recurse
    ```

5. Use the Set-VMHost cmdlet to put the host in maintenance mode. For a host that is part of a fully automated DRS cluster, you can add the -Evacuate option to migrate virtual machines from the host.

    ```
    Set-VMHost -VMHost esx10.mishchenko.net -State Maintenance -Evacuate
    ```

6. Run the Install-VMHostPatch cmdlet to update the host. When the host has completed installing the patch, the following warning message is displayed:

    ```
    Install-VMHostPatch -VMHost esx10.mishchenko.net
        -HostPath /vmfs/volumes/NFS1/ESXi4.0U2/metadata.zip
    WARNING: The update completed successfully, but the system needs to be rebooted
    for the changes to be effective.
    ```

7. Issue the following command to restart the host:

    ```
    Restart-VMHost -VMHost esx10.mischenko.net
    ```

8. After the host has rebooted, you can take it out of maintenance mode with the Set-VMHost cmdlet:

    ```
    Set-VMHost -VMHost esx10.mishchenko.net -State Connected
    ```

If you're patching a number of hosts, you can easily embed these commands into a single script to patch all your hosts. If you're not using a DRS cluster, you can use the `Move-VM` cmdlet to migrate virtual machines between hosts with vMotion.

Updating a Host with VUM PowerCLI

The vCenter Update Manager PowerCLI provides a number of cmdlets for managing your VUM installation. The VUM PowerCLI is available for download from http://www.vmware.com/go/powercliupdate. Both PowerShell and PowerCLI must be installed before you run the installation. The cmdlets included with vSphere 4.1 are listed in Table 10.1.

In the following example, a new baseline will be created to patch ESXi hosts in a cluster called Cluster01:

1. Begin the process by creating a new baseline. The following example creates a dynamic baseline for ESXi 4.0:

    ```
    New-PatchBaseline -Dynamic -Name "ESXi Patches" -TargetType Host
        -SearchPatchProduct "embeddedEsx 4.0.0"
    ```

Table 10.1 vCenter Update Manager PowerCLI Cmdlets

Cmdlet	Description
Attach-Baseline	Attaches baselines to Cluster, Datacenter, Folder, Template, VApp, VirtualMachine, and VMHost objects.
Detach-Baseline	Detaches baselines from the specified inventory objects.
Download-Patch	Downloads new patches into the Update Manager repository.
Get-Baseline	Displays the baselines specified by the provided cmdlet parameters.
Get-Compliance	Obtains compliance data for the specified object.
Get-Patch	Retrieves all available patches or those specified.
Get-PatchBaseline	Retrieves patch baselines.
New-PatchBaseline	Creates a new patch baseline.
Remediate-Inventory	Remediates an inventory object against the specified baselines.
Remove-Baseline	Deletes the specified baselines.
Scan-Inventory	Scans objects for baselines attached to them.
Set-PatchBaseline	Modifies the properties of a patch baseline.
Stage-Patch	Initializes staging of a patch that allows you to download patches from Update Manager to your ESXi hosts without applying the patch.

2. Attach the baseline to the cluster:

    ```
    Attach-Baseline -Entity (Get-Cluster 'CLUSTER01')
        -Baseline (Get-Baseline 'ESXi Patches')
    ```

3. Scan the cluster to determine compliance with the attached baseline:

    ```
    Get-Cluster -Name CLUSTER01 | Scan-Inventory
    ```

4. Query the compliance of hosts within the cluster with the following command. The output shows that the host is not compliant.

    ```
    Get-Compliance -Entity (Get-Cluster 'CLUSTER01')
    ```

    ```
    Entity                      Baseline                Status
    -------                     ---------               -------

    esx10.mishchenko.net        ESXi Patches            NotCompliant
    ```

5. Use the `Remediate-Inventory` cmdlet to install patches to the ESXi host. Before performing remediation on a cluster, you must temporarily disable the DPM, HA Admission Control, and FT features on the cluster. After the remediation task is complete, the features will be automatically reenabled.

    ```
    Remediate-Inventory -Entity (Get-Cluster 'CLUSTER01')
        -Baseline (Get-Baseline 'ESXi Patches')
        -ClusterDisableDistributedPowerManagement:$true
        -ClusterDisableHighAvailability:$true
        -ClusterDisableFaultTolerance:$true
    ```

Once you execute the remediation task, you will find a number of new tasks in vCenter Server, including reconfiguring the cluster, putting the host in maintenance mode, and patching the host. After the process is complete, the host and cluster are returned to their prior states.

In some cases you may have hosts at remote sites with low bandwidth connections. It may not be desirable to send patches to those hosts during business hours. vCenter Server does not currently include the capability to schedule a stage patch job, but you can schedule `Stage-Patch` with a third-party tool. The main parameter for `Stage-Patch` is `-Entity` and this can be a host, cluster, or datacenter. The cmdlet also accepts the parameters `-Baseline` which you can use to filter the patch baselines that should be used, and `-ExcludePatch` to specify which patches to exclude from staging.

Conclusion

Maintaining any software system requires patching to ensure that the system stays secure. The vCLI and PowerCLI include the necessary commands to patch your ESXi hosts. This chapter has shown the process for using each tool. The process can be easily automated to patch a large number of hosts. With Update Manager, you have an automated patch system for keeping your hosts up-to-date and you can further automate Update Manager with vCenter Update Manager PowerCLI.

11 Under the Hood with the ESXi Tech Support Mode

As you migrate your environment from VMware ESX to ESXi, what was your stable ESX environment will become your stable ESXi environment. Your management methods may change, but you'll slowly grow accustomed to the nuances of managing ESXi.

If you have to perform low-level troubleshooting of your ESXi hosts, the differences in architecture will become quite obvious and you'll be in a situation where some aspects are familiar, but others quite different. In this chapter, you explore the following aspects:

- Accessing Tech Support Mode

- Auditing access to Tech Support Mode

- Exploring the boot process and filesystem for ESXi

- Understanding standing system backups and repairs

- Using Tech Support Mode to troubleshoot your hosts

Accessing Tech Support Mode

The Direct Console User Interface (DCUI) provides a local user interface to the console of an ESXi host. As discussed in Chapter 3, "Management Tools," the DCUI is a simple, menu-driven interface that you can use to configure and manage components, including performing the following actions:

- Configuring the password for the root account

- Configuring the Internet Protocol (IP) settings and network interface cards (NICs) used for management access

- Viewing system logs

- Restarting management services

With the DCUI, you can control access to Tech Support Mode (TSM), whether that be for local access or remote access via Secure Shell (SSH). To enable TSM with the DCUI, follow these steps:

1. Access the DCUI for the host and press F2 to open the System Customization menu.

2. Select Troubleshooting Options and press Enter.

3. Select either the Enable Local Tech Support Mode or Enable Remote Tech Support Mode (SSH). If either option starts instead with the word "Disable," this indicates that the option has already been enabled.

4. Press Enter to enable the service.

5. Select the Modify Tech Support Timeout option and press Enter.

6. Enter a value between 0 and 1440 to set the timeout value for TSM in minutes. Setting the timeout value to 0 disables the timeout option.

Once you have enabled TSM, you can press Alt+F1 to access Local TSM or use an SSH client to access Remote TSM via SSH. You require a login that has been granted the Administrator role on the host or a local user that is a member of the root group. If Local TSM is not enabled when you press Alt+F1, you receive the error message Tech Support Mode Has Been Disabled by the Administrator. For Remote TSM, the connection is refused as ESXi does not have the port for SSH enabled unless the Remote TSM service is running. If you have Lockdown Mode enabled on the ESXi host, you are prevented from using TSM. In that case, the error message is Login Incorrect for Local Tech Support Mode and Access Denied for Remote TSM.

Note: The timeout value sets the number of minutes that can elapse before you must log in to TSM. If the timeout expires, you must enable TSM again before you can log in. If you have an existing session open to TSM when the timeout value expires, that session is not closed.

TSM may also be enabled with the vSphere client, both manually and using Host Profiles. To enable TSM manually, use the following process:

1. Log in to your ESXi host or vCenter Server with the vSphere client.

2. Select the Configuration tab for the host and click Security Profile.

3. Click the Properties link to access the Services Properties screen.

4. Select either Local Tech Support or Remote Tech Support (SSH) and click Options.

5. On the Options screen, click Start. You can optionally configure the startup policy for the service.

6. After the service has started and is showing a Status of Running, click OK to close the Options screen.

7. Click OK to close the Services Properties screen.

You can also enable the TSM timeout value in the vSphere client. On the Configuration tab, select Advanced Settings in the Software section. Find the `UserVars.TSMTimeOut` parameter and set it to a value between 0 and 86400 seconds. A value of 0 disables the TSM timeout.

Tip: Setting a short timeout value between one and two minutes ensures that you have ample time to connect to TSM, but safeguards that the service is not left running after you have connected.

If you're using host profiles, you can configure the settings for TSM mode as shown in Figure 11.1. In this example, the Remote TSM is set to have a startup policy of Off and the Advanced Setting `UserVars.TSMTimeOut` has been set to 120 seconds. Note that Host Profiles does not check for the status of the TSM services to verify if they are stopped or running.

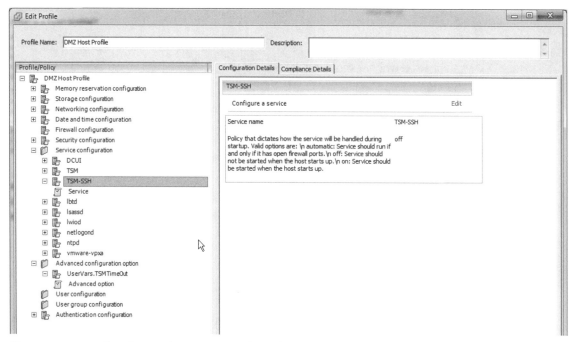

Figure 11.1 Configuring Tech Support Mode with vSphere Host Profiles.

You can also configure the TSM services with PowerCLI. The next example connects to each ESXi host and stops the Local or Remote TSM services if they are running. The startup policy for the services is set to Start and Stop Manually, and the timeout value is set to 2 minutes.

```
$VMhosts = Get-VMHost
ForEach ($VMhost in $VMhosts)
{
Set-VMHostService -HostService (Get-VMHostService -VMHost $VMhost | '
    Where {$_.key -eq "TSM-SSH"}) -Policy "Off"
Set-VMHostService -HostService (Get-VMHostService -VMHost $VMhost | '
    Where {$_.key -eq "TSM"}) -Policy "Off"

$status = Get-VMHostService -VMHost $VMhost | Where {$_.key -eq "TSM-SSH"}
    If ($status.Running -eq "True") {Stop-VMHostService -HostService '
    (Get-VMHostService -VMHost $VMhost | where {$_.key -eq "TSM-SSH"} ) }
$status = Get-VMHostService -VMHost $VMhost | Where {$_.key -eq "TSM"}
    If ($status.Running -eq "True") {Stop-VMHostService -HostService '
    (Get-VMHostService -VMHost $VMhost | where {$_.key -eq "TSM"} ) }

If((Get-VMHostAdvancedConfiguration -VMHost $VMhost -Name '
    UserVars.TSMTimeOut).Values -ne 120 ){Set-VMHostAdvancedConfiguration '
    -VMHost $VMHost -Name UserVars.TSMTimeOut -Value 120 '
    -Confirm:$False
  }
}
```

Note: TSM can be used when testing and debugging the pre-boot, post-boot, or first boot portions of the automated installation scripts for ESXi. This is not recommended for production environments. To enable Remote TSM during your installation script, you can add the following lines to the appropriate section for when you want to enable Remote TSM:

```
vim-cmd hostsvc/enable_remote_tsm
vim-cmd hostsvc/start_remote_tsm
```

To enable Local TSM with your installation script, you can add the following lines:

```
vim-cmd hostsvc/enable_local_tsm
vim-cmd hostsvc/start_local_tsm
```

You can also set the TSM timeout value within your installation script. The following command sets the timeout value to 300 seconds:

```
vim-cmd hostsvc/advopt/update UserVars.TSMTimeOut long 300
```

Auditing Tech Support Mode

If you're managing a large environment, you may wish to take steps to ensure that TSM is not improperly used. Although TSM provides an important tool for troubleshooting, problems can result if it is used for other management tasks that can be performed with the vSphere client or automated with the vCLI or PowerCLI.

One line of defense to ensure that TSM is not casually accessed is to enable Lockdown Mode. As discussed in Chapter 7, "Securing ESXi," Lockdown Mode prevents all user access to both Local and Remote TSM. However, if users have access to log in to the DCUI or can access the Configuration tab for the host, they can disable Lockdown Mode, then access TSM. To monitor for a change in Lockdown Mode, you can use the following process to enable a vCenter Server alert:

1. Start the vSphere client and connect to vCenter Server.

2. At the appropriate level, select the Alarms tab and click Definitions.

3. Select File > New > Alarm.

4. Enter an Alarm Name and Description for the new alarm.

5. Select an Alarm Type of Host and check the option Monitor for Specific Events Occurring on This Object.

6. Select the Triggers tab.

7. Click Add to create a new trigger.

8. Set the Event to Host Administrator Access Enabled.

9. On the Action tab, configure an appropriate Action for your alarm.

10. Click OK to create the new alarm.

Caution: When you disable Lockdown Mode in the DCUI, a corresponding event is not currently logged with vCenter Server. If you are sending syslog data to a management server, you can look for a rapid succession of log entries containing `vim.Authorization Manager.setEntityPermissions`. You can also monitor for a number of login events by the dcui account as shown in Figure 11.2. When you enable Lockdown Mode, you should be aware that it does not terminate existing TSM sessions to the host.

If you prefer using PowerCLI rather than vCenter Server alarms, you can use `Get-VIEvent` to monitor for the event that indicates that Lockdown Mode has been disabled. The following script checks all hosts connected to your vCenter Server for this event. When Lockdown Mode is enabled, the event `HostAdminDisableEvent` is generated.

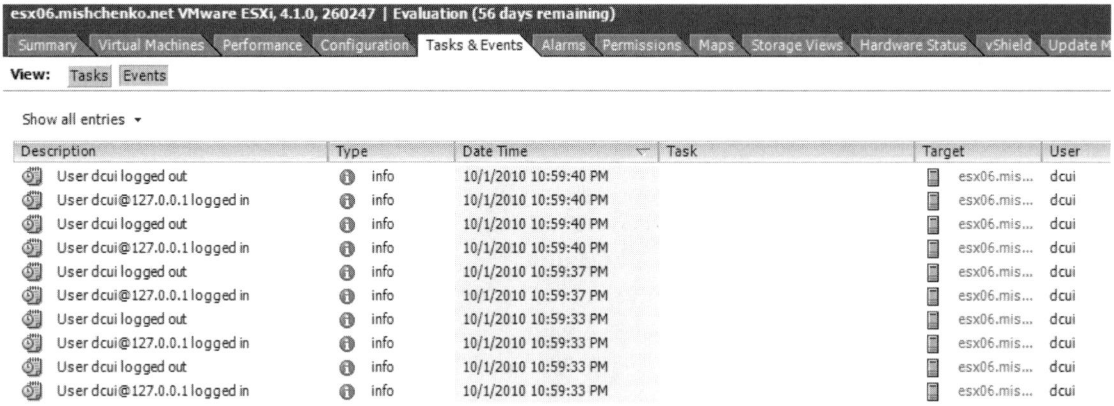

Figure 11.2 Disabling Lockdown Mode with the DCUI does not generate a specific event within vCenter Server.

```
Get-VIEvent -Entity $_.Name | Where { $_.Gettype().Name '
              -eq "HostAdminEnableEvent"} '
              | Select CreatedTime, UserName, FullFormattedMessage
```

PowerCLI may also be used to query for the events related to enabling Local and Remote TSM. The following script queries vCenter Server for events of the type LocalTSMEnabledEvent and RemoteTSMEnabledEvent:

```
Get-VIEvent -Entity $_.Name | Where { ($_.Gettype().Name '
              -eq "LocalTSMEnabledEvent") -Or ($_.Gettype().Name '
              -eq "RemoteTSMEnabledEvent") } '
              | Select CreatedTime, UserName, FullFormattedMessage
```

Caution: If you enable TSM in the DCUI or when connected directly to the host with the vSphere client, vCenter Server records the LocalTSMEnabledEvent and RemoteTSMEnabledEvent type of error. If you start the TSM services via vCenter Server, a Service Start task is recorded instead of the TSM events. You will also note some differences in how the user is recorded when TSM is enabled. When TSM is enabled in the DCUI, the event is recorded by ESXi and vCenter Server as having been initiated by the DCUI user. When the change is made by a user connected directly to the ESXi, both ESXi and vCenter Server record the actual user that initiated the change. Lastly, if the change is made when connected to vCenter Server, vCenter Server records the actual user, but ESXi records the task as initiated by the vpxuser account.

The last option for auditing TSM and the actions taken in TSM is to use syslog. Setup of syslog is discussed in Chapter 6, "System Monitoring and Management." The following events correspond with TSM being enabled. You could create an alert that would be triggered based on the event text VMware Tech Support Mode available:

```
Oct  1 23:13:17 Hostd: [2010-10-01 23:13:17.147 23506B90 verbose 'ServiceSystem'
     opID=E3CD7415-0000012C] Invoking command /bin/ash /etc/init.d/TSM start
Oct  1 23:13:17 root: TSM Displaying TSM login: runlevel =
Oct  1 23:13:17 init: init: process '/sbin/initterm.sh TTY1 /sbin/techsupport.sh
     ++min=0,swap' (pid 579733) exited. Scheduling it for restart.
Oct  1 23:13:17 init: init: starting pid 584732, tty '/dev/tty1': '/bin/sh'
Oct  1 23:13:17 root: techsupport VMware Tech Support Mode available
```

The following events record a user's session with TSM. The initial dropbear events record a remote SSH session initiated from a remote host. This corresponds with the warning message that the user receives when accessing TSM shown in Figure 11.3. Note that the commands executed by the user in TSM are logged from a source of shell. The last event records the end of the user's TSM session.

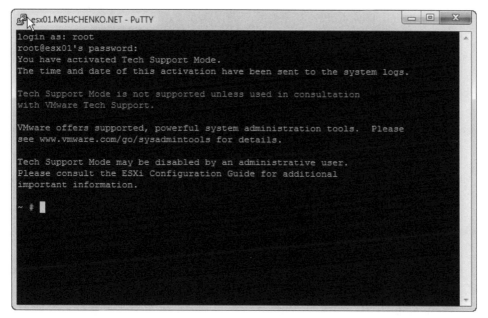

Figure 11.3 When TSM is accessed, a warning message is issued and the event is logged to the VMkernel log file.

```
Oct  1 22:46:44 dropbear[582158]: Child connection from 192.168.1.225:62951
Oct  1 22:46:51 dropbear[582158]: pam_per_user: create_subrequest_handle():
     doing map lookup for user "root"
Oct  1 22:46:51 dropbear[582158]: pam_per_user: create_subrequest_handle():
     creating new subrequest (user="root", service="system-auth-generic")
```

```
Oct 1 22:46:51 dropbear[582158]: PAM password auth succeeded for 'root' from
    192.168.1.225:62951
Oct 1 22:46:51 shell[582159]: Interactive shell session started
Oct 1 22:50:13 shell[582378]: esxcfg-nics -l
Oct 1 22:50:21 shell[582378]: vdf -h
Oct 1 23:47:35 dropbear[582158]: exit after auth (root): Exited normally
```

Exploring the File System

ESXi was designed to be easily deployed to thousands of nodes and at the same time to enable the deployment of very small turnkey installations. As you've seen in prior chapters, ESXi can be preinstalled on a flash device or installed to a small local or remote hard drive. In the future, you can expect to see ESXi booting on completely diskless systems. These design goals required a change in the way that the boot files are stored, and ESXi differs significantly from how a traditional operating system (OS) is installed or even how ESX is installed and boots.

Note: VMware Auto Deploy is an experimental product from VMware Labs that enables automatic Preboot Execution Environment (PXE) boot and customization for VMware ESXi. With Auto Deploy, you can use completely diskless and stateless ESXi hosts. Each time an ESXi host boots from the PXE server, it is automatically configured by Auto Deploy using Host Profiles and other information stored within vCenter Server. The host can then join a cluster and begin to handle your virtual machine workload. VMware Auto Deploy is not supported in production environments, but provides a preview of how you might deploy your ESXi hosts in the future. It is available for download from http://labs.vmware.com.

The system partitions for ESXi are summarized in the following list. The partition layout is the same whether you're using ESXi Embedded or Installable. The system partitions include the following:

- Bootloader partition. This 4MB partition contains SYSLinux, which is used as a bootloader to start ESXi.

- Boot bank partition. This 250MB partition stores the required files to boot VMware ESXi. The partition is also referred at as Hypervisor1.

- Alt boot bank partition. This 250MB partition is initially empty. The first time you patch ESXi, the new system image is stored here. The partition is also referred to as Hypervisor2.

- Core dump partition. This 110MB partition is normally empty, but the VMkernel will store a memory dump image if a system failure occurs. The partition can be managed with `vicfg-dumppart` from the vCLI.

■ Store partition. This 286MB partition is used to store system utilities such as the ISO images for VMware Tools and floppy disk images for virtual device drivers. The partition is also referred to as Hypervisor3.

When you are installing ESXi Installable on a disk with at least 5GB of storage, ESXi also creates a 4GB scratch partition. This partition is mounted as /scratch and is used to store the output from vm-support and to store upgrade files, and is set as the default location for the advanced parameter Syslog.Local.DatastorePath. If you are installing ESXi to boot from a storage area network (SAN), you can allocate a 5GB logical unit number (LUN) for the boot disk. Note that if you're using a scripted installation, the installer requires an additional 1GB of space as it attempts to create a datastore.

When your ESXi host first starts, SYSLinux is loaded. SYSLinux looks at the file boot.cfg, which is located both on Hypervisor1 and Hypervisor2. SYSLinux uses the parameters build, updated, and bootstate to determine which partition to use to boot ESXi. The following is a typical boot.cfg file:

```
kernel=b.z
kernelopt=
modules=k.z --- s.z --- c.z --- oem.tgz --- license.tgz --- m.z --- vpxa.vgz
    --- state.tgz --- aam.vgz
build=4.1.0-235786
updated=2
bootstate=0
```

After a new installation, ESXi boots from Hypervisor1, which is mounted by ESXi as /bootbank. Hypervisor2 is mounted as /altbootbank and is initially empty. When you patch or upgrade your ESXi host, a completely new firmware image for ESXi is loaded on the host and stored in /altbookbank. The boot parameters are updated so that when ESXi next starts, it will recognize Hypervisor2 as containing the version of ESXi that should be booted. That partition is mounted as /bootbank, whereas Hypervisor1 becomes the new /altbootbank. The partition roles are reversed the next time you patch your ESXi host. With this design, your host boot partitions always contain two complete images that can be used to boot ESXi. If you patch a host and a problem is detected when ESXi starts to boot, the system automatically reverts to the previously installed version of ESXi.

Tip: Update activities on ESXi generate a log file called esxupdate.log. This file can be found in /store/db.

If you experience problems with ESXi after installing a patch, you can manually revert to the prior version with the following process. Begin by rebooting the ESXi host. At the initial

Figure 11.4   The Loading VMware Hypervisor screen displaying a warning message.

Loading VMware Hypervisor screen, press Shift+R. The warning message shown in Figure 11.4 is displayed, where you can press Shift+Y to revert back to the prior version. The screen then displays an option to view the log for the event. Press Esc to view the log or press Enter to continue booting. If the operation was successful, the log displays the message Fallback hypervisor restored successfully. You can then press Esc to exit the log screen or press Enter to continue the boot process. The version of ESXi that you experienced problems with becomes /altbootbank and will be overwritten the next time you apply a patch. If you attempt to repeat the process to revert to the boot version, because the bootstate parameter is set to 3, you will receive the error No valid fallback hypervisor found. If you need to boot ESXi to that version again, you can reapply the ESXi patch or change the parameter bootstate to 0. If you're applying customizations from a third party, each patch causes a change in the boot bank used. If you apply two or more patches, you won't be able to revert to the prepatch state using this method. You instead need to run a repair installation and restore a system configuration backup.

After SYSLinux determines which system image to boot, boot.cfg is read to determine the files that are used to boot the VMkernel. The files that ESXi uses are loaded into memory and then not accessed again on storage until the host is rebooted. It is possible, although not recommended, to remove the boot device from an ESXi host that has completed the boot process. For the most part, the host will function properly, only having difficulty with system processes that access the boot media such as system backups and that access VMware Tools ISO images. Likewise, changes made to the ESXi memory file system are lost when a host reboots. As you will see in the following section, the ESXi system backup process backs up the necessary system state files, but if the random access memory (RAM) disk fills up due to a technical issue, that problem will not persist after a reboot.

There are three significant file types that ESXi uses to boot. First are the Executive files tboot.gz (Trusted Platform Module files), vmkboot.gz (small core), and vmkernel.gz, which make up the VMkernel are loaded into memory as executables. These files exhibit no presence within the ESXi memory filesystem. Second, a series of Archive files with the extension vgz, called tardisks, are mounted and extracted to form the filesystem. Those files include system. vgz, vpxa.vgz, aam.vgz, extmod.tgz, and oem.tgz. These packages use the vSphere Installation Bundle (VIB) format. system.vpz contains core system files, vpxa.vgz contains files for the vCenter Agent, and aam.vgz contains the High Availability system files. VIB updates from third parties may also be listed. The files in these VIBs are extracted in a progressive manner. If a duplicate file is found in both system.vgz and oem.tgz, the file in oem.tgz is extracted later, as is the version of the file that is used by ESXi. The last file type is the State archive file. This file is called state.tgz with ESXi Installable and local.tgz with ESXi Embedded. The contents in both versions are the same and the archive file contains a backup of the files necessary for the configuration of your ESXi host to persist between reboots. This file is discussed further in the following section.

Boot.cfg Filenames with ESXi 4.1 If you've used ESXi 4.0 or earlier, you may have noted a change in the filenames with ESXi 4.1. The typical boot command prior to ESXi 4.1 would contain the following file list:

```
kernel=vmkboot.gz
kernelopt=
modules=vmk.gz --- sys.vgz --- cim.vgz --- oem.tgz --- license.tgz --- mod.tgz
    --- vpxa.vgz --- state.tgz --- aam.vgz
```

That has changed to the following with ESXi 4.1. This change was made to allow for the inclusion of additional files to the boot command without exceeding the 255 character limit that SYSLinux has for the boot command.

```
kernel=b.z
kernelopt=
modules=k.z --- s.z --- c.z --- oem.tgz --- license.tgz --- m.z --- vpxa.vgz
    --- state.tgz --- aam.vgz
```

When the ESXi filesystem has been extracted into the RAM disk, the end result is similar to the directory listing of the root folder shown in Figure 11.5. The root of the filesystem and most folders —such as bin, etc, and sbin—are stored in memory. Note that ESXi does mount the disk partitions that correspond to bootbank, altbootbank, scratch, and store. As you browse the filesystem, it will appear similar to what you would experience with ESX. /sbin contains a number of esxcfg executables that can be used to configure and manage the host if you are unable to do so via vSphere client or other vSphere application programming interface (API) client.

If you run df -h, you get another view of the filesystem showing the disks that ESXi has mounted, as shown in Figure 11.6. Listed first is visorfs, which is the RAM disk that ESXi has created. The

```
~ # ls -l
lrwxrwxrwx   1 root   root        49 Oct  5 05:17 altbootbank -> /vmfs/volumes/adba427a-4f891c64-538d-162cb07082f8
drwxr-xr-x   1 root   root       512 Oct  5 05:18 bin
lrwxrwxrwx   1 root   root        49 Oct  5 05:17 bootbank -> /vmfs/volumes/1f51bf7e-de0b7349-1b44-d1d6b14336a4
drwxr-xr-x   1 root   root       512 Oct  5 10:19 dev
drwxr-xr-x   1 root   root       512 Oct  5 07:18 etc
drwxr-xr-x   1 root   root       512 Oct  5 05:17 lib
drwxr-xr-x   1 root   root       512 Oct  5 05:17 lib64
-rwx------   1 root   root     16152 Oct  3 02:01 local.tgz
lrwxrwxrwx   1 root   root         6 Oct  5 05:17 locker -> /store
drwxr-xr-x   1 root   root       512 Oct  5 05:17 opt
drwxr-xr-x   1 root   root    131072 Oct  5 10:19 proc
lrwxrwxrwx   1 root   root        23 Oct  5 05:17 productLocker -> /locker/packages/4.1.0/
drwxr-xr-x   1 root   root       512 Oct  5 05:17 sbin
lrwxrwxrwx   1 root   root        49 Oct  5 05:17 scratch -> /vmfs/volumes/4c888c70-4f923173-27f4-00505694000e
lrwxrwxrwx   1 root   root        49 Oct  5 05:17 store -> /vmfs/volumes/3c3693e8-f77a642a-1910-5c6bdcb26d3a
drwxrwxrwt   1 root   root       512 Oct  5 10:01 tmp
drwxr-xr-x   1 root   root       512 Oct  5 05:17 usr
drwxr-xr-x   1 root   root       512 Oct  5 05:17 var
drwxr-xr-x   1 root   root       512 Oct  5 05:17 vmfs
drwxr-xr-x   1 root   root       512 Oct  5 05:17 vmimages
lrwxrwxrwx   1 root   root        18 May 19 00:15 vmupgrade -> /locker/vmupgrade/
~ #
```

Figure 11.5   The VMware ESXi filesystem.

```
~ # df -h
Filesystem     Size     Used Available Use% Mounted on
visorfs        1.3G    312.5M  1023.9M  23% /
vfat           4.0G     3.0M     4.0G   0% /vmfs/volumes/4c888c70-4f923173-27f4-00505694000e
vmfs3          3.0G   295.0M     2.7G  10% /vmfs/volumes/4c885ea0-0e27ec78-a7c8-00505694000e
vfat         285.9M   135.5M   150.4M  47% /vmfs/volumes/3c3693e8-f77a642a-1910-5c6bdcb26d3a
vfat         249.7M   102.0M   147.7M  41% /vmfs/volumes/1f51bf7e-de0b7349-1b44-d1d6b14336a4
vfat         249.7M     4.0k   249.7M   0% /vmfs/volumes/adba427a-4f891c64-538d-162cb07082f8
~ #
```

Figure 11.6   The filesystems mounted for a typical ESXi installation.

four vfat partitions are bootbank, altbootbank, scratch, and store. In this case, the boot disk for ESXi also contains a Virtual Machine File System (VMFS) datastore.

The command vdf is new to ESXi 4.1. It provides some valuable data about the RAM disk. The listing that follows first shows the tardisks that ESXi has extracted to create the filesystem. These entries correspond to the Archive and State file types in boot.cfg, discussed earlier. The Space value listed represents the extracted size of the tardisk, not the compressed size within /bootbank. The first tardisk listed is using 199MB of memory on the host. If the root filesystem is running low of space, you can use vdf to check whether one of the tardisks is using too much memory. The command also displays information about the mounts that are available on the RAM disk. The following output shows four mounts: MAINSYS, tmp, updatestg, and hoststats. MAINSYS is the root folder, whereas tmp is /tmp. hoststats is used to store real-time performance data on the host, and updatestg is used as storage space for staging patches and updates. These four mounts and tardisk mounts correspond to the 1.3GB size of visorfs, shown in Figure 11.6.

```
~ # vdf -h
tardisk         Space   Used
SYS1            199M    199M
```

```
SYS2                 55M      55M
SYS3                 12K      12K
SYS4                 12K      12K
SYS5                  4K       4K
SYS6                 42M      42M
SYS7                 20K      20K
SYS8                 12M      12M

- - - - -
Ramdisk             Size     Used Available Use% Mounted on
MAINSYS              32M       1M       30M   3% --
tmp                 192M       0B      192M   0% --
updatestg           750M       8K      749M   0% --
hoststats            53M       1M       51M   3% --
```

In the output from vdf, you can observe the size of memory that has been allocated to the mounts MAINSYS, tmp, updatestg, and hoststats. updatestg has been allocated 750MB, but is currently using only 8KB of actual memory. You can also view the resource allocation to the visorfs components and other system processes for ESXi using the System Resource Allocation screen as shown in Figure 11.7.

One last command that is useful to explore is vdu. The following example shows the output of that command for /etc. The command summarizes the source of files within a folder structure.

```
~ # vdu -hs /etc
For '/etc':
                tardisk SYS1:    4M      ( 221 inodes)
                       heap :   84K      (  43 inodes)
                ramdisk MAINSYS: 60K      (   6 inodes)
                tardisk SYS6:    6K      (   5 inodes)
                tardisk SYS8:    4K      (   2 inodes)
                tardisk SYS2:   10K      (  22 inodes)
```

As you navigate the ESXi filesystem, similarities to the ESX service console will be evident, but you will note that some of the Linux commands that you may have used, such as nano, are missing. The command interface to the VMkernel is based on BusyBox. BusyBox, a single executable designed for use with a Linux kernel, provides many of the standard tools that you would find in Linux, including cp (copy), kill (kill process), tar, and tail. Given the small size of BusyBox, it is typically used with embedded devices. BusyBox uses the ash shell. If you are monitoring your ESXi host with resxtop, you can observe a single process for BusyBox and one ash process for each Local or Remote TSM session that is in progress.

It is important to note that TSM is intended to be the last method of access to your ESXi host. The first level of management should be via the vSphere API and tools such as the vSphere client, the vCLI, and PowerCLI. The DCUI provides the next level of support; with the DCUI, you can

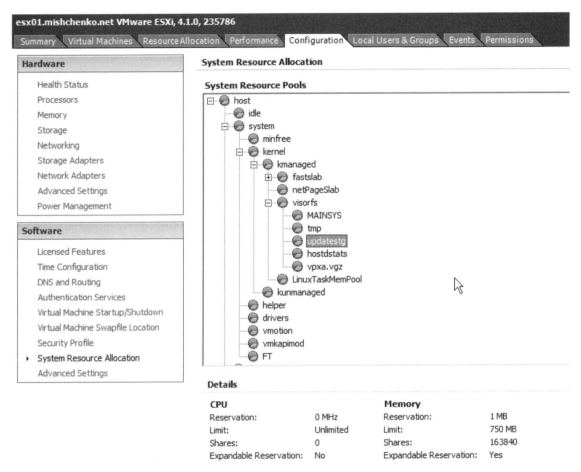

Figure 11.7 You can view resource allocation for the ESXi RAM disk filesystem with the System Resource Allocation screen.

restart the management agents, troubleshoot the management network, and reset the configuration of your ESXi host. The TSM provides the last resort for access, and misconfiguration at this level can have significant consequences on the host. Ideally, TSM access should be made under the guidance of VMware Support. In practice, you may find that you need to perform configuration with TSM, as the vSphere API tools may not include specific capabilities, or problems such as those related to the management network may be difficult to troubleshoot without TSM access. Some of the commands that you may use in TSM are discussed later in the section "Troubleshooting with Tech Support Mode."

Tip: If you're developing a complex installation script that employs the %firstboot section, you can use TSM to work through your script in a test environment. The system tardisk that is loaded for the installation process is the same used to boot ESXi normally. The installation merely adds a specific tardisk to include the necessary files for the installation process. The esxcfg and similar commands that you'll find in TSM also exist when the ESXi installer is booted.

Understanding System Backups and Restores

As discussed in the previous section, ESXi employs a State tardisk to ensure that configuration changes made to the ESXi host persist across a reboot. For ESXi Installable, that tardisk is called state.tgz, whereas for Embedded it is local.tgz. The State tardisk consists of any files in /etc that have been marked with the sticky bit. The initial copy of state.tgz is empty, but files extracted from the other tardisks have the sticky bit enabled and these files are subsequently backed up into state.tgz. For example, the vCenter Agent tardisk vpxa.vgz contains a number of system files that are extracted to /opt/vmware/vpxa, but also the configuration files dasConfig.xml and vpxa.cfg found in /etc/opt/vmware/vpxa. Both files have the sticky bit enabled and are thus backed up into state.tgz. On a subsequent boot of ESXi, these files are extracted from both vpxa.vgz and state.tgz, but as state.tgz is extracted second, those versions of the files overwrite the copies from vpxa.vgz. If you make any changes to files in /etc that do not have the sticky bit enabled, those files are changed only in the RAM disk filesystem and are gone when ESXi is rebooted. The same applies to any files changed, added, or deleted outside of / etc with the exception of mounts that are made to physical partitions such as /bootbank.

To view the contents of state.tgz, you can issue the following commands in TSM or copy the file to a management server for extraction:

```
~ # cd tmp
/tmp # mkdir state
/tmp # cd state
/tmp/state # cp /bootbank/state.tgz state.tgz
/tmp/state # gzip -d state.tgz
/tmp/state # tar -xvf state.tar
local.tgz
/tmp/state # gzip -d local.tgz
/tmp/state # tar -xvf local.tar
```

Extracting vgz Tardisks You can use a similar process as was used with state.tgz to extract the system tardisks (which have the extension .vgz). Given the size of some of the tardisks, it is best to copy the files to datastore or to /scratch. If you extract a tardisk with /tmp and fill that mount, the host should be able to continue to run without any problem. If you fill /, then the host can be rendered unstable.

The following commands can be used to extract the tardisk for the vCenter Agent:

```
~ # cd /scratch
/scratch # mkdir vpxa
/scratch # cd vpxa
/scratch/vpxa # cp /bootbank/vpxa.vgz vpxa.vgz
/scratch/vpxa # vmtar -x vpxa.vgz -o vpxa.tar
/scratch/vpxa # tar -xvf vpxa.tar
```

At every minute past the hour, a backup job defined in /var/spool/cron/crontabs/root is exe-cuted. The backup job runs the script /sbin/autobackup.sh. This script creates a new state.tgz file and copies it to the appropriate location. The script does check the parameters in both boot.cfg files to see whether a reboot is pending from a patch or update installation. If that is the case, then the new state.tgz file is copied to both /bootbank and /altbootbank. autobackup.sh calls another script, /sbin/backup.sh. In part, the function of that script is to make sure that the backups are made in a consistent manner and to ensure file integrity.

Given that there is a period of time between any configuration changes and the scheduled backup, there is a risk of loss of changes should the host experience an unexpected failure. If this occurs, this loss typically affects the registration of virtual machines, as host con-figuration tends to be more static. The time period between backups originated from the need to minimize write operations to flash devices. Excessive write operations can limit the life of those devices. If you restart or shut down an ESXi host, part of the shutdown process includes updat-ing state.tgz. Configuration changes should not be lost when you restart or shut down a host.

Repairing ESXi and Restoring from Backups

The vSphere API allows you to make a configuration backup of your ESXi host. In Chapter 6 the process was shown with the vCLI command vicfg-cfgbackup. You can also back up your host's configuration with the PowerCLI cmdlet Set-VMHostFirmware, as shown in the following example:

```
Get-VMHost esx06.mishchenko.net | Set-VMHostFirmware -BackupConfiguration
    -DestinationPath c:\backups\esx06\
```

The backup file generated has the file name similar to configBundle-esx06.mishchenko.net.tgz. With either method, the vSphere API merely transfers the state.tgz file from the host to the man-agement server. If you extract the backup file that is generated you can view the same files that ESXi bundles into state.tgz to preserve the host's configuration. To restore the configuration backup with PowerCLI, you would issue the following command:

```
Get-VMHost esx06.mishchenko.net | Set-VMHostFirmware -Restore
    -SourcePath c:\backups\esx06\configBundle-esx06.mishchenko.net.tgz
```

The host has to be in maintenance mode before you start the restore and it is rebooted after the restore process has completed.

In some cases, you may not be able to boot your ESXi host due to a corruption of the system partitions, or you may have to revert to a version of ESXi that does not exist in /altbootbank. In such cases, you want to perform a repair installation followed by the restore of the configuration backup. As state.tgz contains the entire configuration of your host, you do not need any further configuration files to restore your ESXi host. To repair your ESXi installation, use the following process:

1. Insert the ESXi 4.1 installation CD into the host's CD-ROM drive.

2. Restart the host and select to boot from the CD.

3. At the installation Welcome screen, shown in Figure 11.8, press R to begin the repair process.

4. Read the VMware end-user license agreement and press F11 to continue.

5. Select the disk that contains the original installation of ESXi and press Enter.

Caution: The ESXi repair process preserves any VMFS datastores that exist on the installation disk as long as those partitions do not exist within the first 900MB of storage. If you do not select the original installation disk, then a new system image is installed and any existing partitions on that disk will be lost.

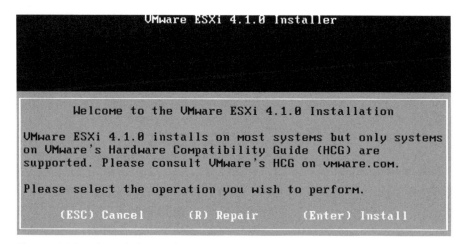

Figure 11.8 The ESXi Repair option is available on the Welcome screen during an ESXi installation.

6. If the disk contains an existing partition, you are prompted to confirm your choice of disk. Press Enter to confirm your choice.

7. Press F11 to begin the repair process.

8. When the repair process has completed, eject the installation CD and press Enter to reboot.

9. After the host has rebooted, make a note of the IP address assigned to the host. You may need to assign an IP address manually if you do not have a Dynamic Host Configuration Protocol (DHCP) server for that network subnet.

10. Restore the host configuration file with the following commands:
    ```
    Set-VMHost -State "Maintenance"
    Set-VMHostFirmware -Restore -SourcePath
        c:\backups\esx06\configBundle-esx06.mishchenko.net.tgz
    ```

11. Start the vSphere client and connect to your vCenter Server. The host will have a state of Not Responding, as the vCenter Agent software does not exist on the host at this point.

12. Right-click on the host and select Connect. This initiates the installation of the vCenter Agent on the host. After the process is complete, the host should show a normal status and any registered virtual machines should no longer have a status of Orphaned.

Accessing System Files with vifs from the vCLI In prior chapters, you have seen examples of using vifs from the vCLI to access both datastore files and host configuration files. vifs can be used to obtain access to the configuration files listed in Table 11.1 and files in /tmp. If you access the URL https://esx06.mishchenko.net/host, you can see a list of files that are accessible with vifs or a Web browser. The files displayed are controlled by the configuration file /etc/vmware/hostd/webAccessibleConfigFiles.xml.

The Permissions column dictates the actions that can be taken on that file. With GET and HEAD permissions, a file can be downloaded either in part or as a complete file. With the PUT permission, you can upload a file from your management computer and replace the file on the host. The configuration files in Table 11.1 can be both downloaded and uploaded back to the host. If your ESXi host does not have access to a domain name service (DNS) server, you can download the hosts file, insert the appropriate host data, and then upload the file back to the host. The log files in the table are read-only and thus have only the GET and HEAD permission. To ensure the security of the host, the private Secure Sockets Layer (SSL) key may not be downloaded from the host. ssl_key has only the PUT permission, so you can replace the file only with a new private key.

Table 11.1 Configuration and Log Files Accessible with vifs

Display Name	Host Filename	Permissions	Description
hostAgentConfig.xml	/etc/vmware/hostd/config.xml	GET/HEAD/PUT	The `hostd` configuration file.
sfcb.cfg	/etc/sfcb.cfg	GET/HEAD/PUT	Configuration file for the small-footprint Common Information Model (CIM) broker.
openwsman.conf	/etc/openwsman/openwsman.conf	GET/HEAD/PUT	Configuration file for the CIM interface.
license.cfg	/etc/vmware/license.cfg	GET/HEAD/PUT	File containing encrypted license data.
vmware.lic	/etc/vmware/vmware.lic	GET/HEAD/PUT	File containing the license serial number assigned to the host.
vmware_config	/etc/vmware/config	GET/HEAD/PUT	Configuration file that controls the services to which `hostd` provides proxy access.
vmware_configrules	/etc/vmware/configrules	GET/HEAD/PUT	File describing some of the constraints on what file paths may be used when powering on a virtual machine.
proxy.xml	/etc/vmware/hostd/proxy.xml	GET/HEAD/PUT	File that controls the security configuration of services that are accessed via `hostd`.
snmp.xml	/etc/vmware/snmp.xml	GET/HEAD/PUT	Configuration file that contains the Simple Network Management Protocol (SNMP) settings for the host.
syslog.conf	/etc/syslog.conf	GET/HEAD/PUT	File containing the syslog settings for the host.
ssl_cert	/etc/vmware/ssl/rui.crt	GET/HEAD/PUT	The public SSL certificate for the host.
ssl_key	/etc/vmware/ssl/rui.key	PUT	The private key to the SSL certificate that the host uses.
hosts	/etc/hosts	GET/HEAD/PUT	The file used for DNS lookups.
motd	/etc/motd	GET/HEAD/PUT	The message of the day file for the host. By default, it contains a warning message about accessing TSM.

(Continued)

Table 11.1 (*Continued*)

Display Name	Host Filename	Permissions	Description
vpxa.cfg	/etc/opt/vmware/ vpxa/vpxa.cfg	GET/HEAD/PUT	The configuration file for the vCenter Agent.
esx.conf	/etc/vmware/esx .conf	GET/HEAD/PUT	The main configuration file for ESXi.
messages	/var/log/messages	GET/HEAD	The VMkernel log file.
ipmi*	/var/log/ipmi*	GET/HEAD	The Intelligent Platform Management Interface (IPMI) files, which contain hardware sensor data. The number of IPMI files varies depending on the IPMI capabilities of the host.
hostd.log	/var/log/vmware/ hostd.log	GET/HEAD	The hostd log file.
vpxa.log	/var/log/vmware/ vpxa/vpxa.log	GET/HEAD	The vCenter Agent configuration file.

Troubleshooting with Tech Support Mode

If you're connecting via Remote TSM, you need a client that supports SSH, and if you want to transfer files, your client should support Secure Copy (SCP). Most Linux distributions include a client with these capabilities. For a Windows computer, you can download Putty from http:// www.putty.org/ to use for your SSH sessions and WinSCP from http://winscp.net/ to transfer and edit files. ESXi includes only vi for editing files, so it is worthwhile to get a client that includes an easy-to-use file editor.

If you start in /bin, you find a number of useful utilities that you can use to manage files and processes within TSM. If you run ls -l, you will note that many of the program names are symbolic links to other programs. kill, gzip, and tail link back to the busybox executable. BusyBox also includes wget, which you can use to download files from a Web server. This command can prove useful to download patch files directly to your host. If you use wget, make sure that you're in a location, such as /scratch or a datastore, with sufficient space to store your downloads.

scp, which links to /sbin/dropbearmulti, is a basic SCP client that you can use to transfer files to and from an SCP-capable server. dropbearmulti is also used to provide SSH connectivity to the Remote TSM. Both ping and ping6 link to /sbin/vmkping. If you're troubleshooting vMotion network issues, you can use either of the commands to check for network connectivity.

There is no separate networking stack as there is with the ESX Service Console, so any network traffic is sent by the VMkernel and thus both `ping` and `vmkping` work the same way on ESXi.

There have been a number of cautions about working with TSM. You should further note that all commands do not operate in a consistent manner. For the most part, if you don't know the command options, you can simply issue the command without any options to see a list of available options. With `/sbin/reboot`, which links to BusyBox, issuing the command without any options will restart your host. To see the options, you have to run `reboot --help`. Likewise, if you execute `/sbin/techsupport.sh`, your screen clears, you see the message `Tech Support Mode Has Been Disabled by the Administrator` and your TSM session is effectively over.

Given that ESXi can be hosted in a virtual machine even on ESXi, there's no significant reason not to set up a test host to use for exploring TSM. Instructions for running ESXi in a virtual machine on VMware Workstation were provided in Chapter 4, "Installation Options." A similar process can be used to host an ESXi virtual machine within your current vSphere environment. Hosting your training environment for ESXi in this manner will provide a method to learn and explore ESXi with no impact on your production environment. With a change to the virtual machine configuration file, documented at the following URL `http://communities.vmware.com/docs/DOC-8970`, it is possible to run a nested virtual machine on your virtual ESXi host.

This caution isn't intended to totally dissuade use of TSM. TSM is supported for troubleshooting, remediation, and in some cases configuration purposes. The official support policy for TSM can be found at http://kb.vmware.com/kb/1017910.

There are a few other commands in `/bin` that are noteworthy. Both `vdf` and `vdu` link to `/sbin/vmkvsitools`. The *vsi* of `vmkvsitools` stands for VMware Sysinfo Interface. As shown in the following output, a number of commands link to `vmkvsitools`. This command can be used to provide a wealth of information about the host's hardware, running processes, and memory. As shown in the Knowledge Base article at http://kb.vmware.com/kb/1024632, the command may be used to gain information that you would have obtained from `/proc` on an ESX host.

```
/bin # vmkvsitools
Usage: 'vmkvsitools [-c/--cache vsicache] cmd args' where cmd is one of
    amldump, bootOption, hwclock, hwinfo, lsof, lspci, pci-info, pidof,
    ps, vdf, vdu, vmksystemswap, vmware
A symlink to vmkvsitools with an above command name can also be used.
```

Lastly in `/bin` is `vim-cmd`, which can be used to control and configure a wide range of aspects of ESXi. `vim-cmd` links to `/sbin/hostd`. When you execute the command without options, the following is displayed:

```
~ # vim-cmd
Commands available under /:
hostsvc/          proxysvc/        supportsvc_cmds/         vmsvc/
internalsvc/      solo/            vimsvc/                  help
```

You can add the commands listed to vim-cmd to see additional commands. vmsvc/ deals with the management of virtual machines. That command displays the following options:

```
~ # vim-cmd vmsvc
Commands available under vmsvc/:
acquiremksticket        get.configoption        power.on
acquireticket           get.datastores          power.reboot
connect                 get.disabledmethods     power.reset
convert.toTemplate      get.environment         power.shutdown
convert.toVm            get.filelayout          power.suspend
createdummyvm           get.guest               power.suspendResume
destroy                 get.guestheartbeatStatus queryftcompat
device.connection       get.managedentitystatus reload
device.connusbdev       get.networks            setscreenres
device.disconnusbdev    get.runtime             snapshot.create
device.diskadd          get.snapshotinfo        snapshot.dumpoption
device.diskaddexisting  get.summary             snapshot.get
device.diskremove       get.tasklist            snapshot.remove
device.getdevices       getallvms               snapshot.removeall
device.toolsSyncSet     gethostconstraints      snapshot.revert
device.vmiadd           login                   snapshot.setoption
device.vmiremove        logout                  tools.cancelinstall
devices.createnic       message                 tools.install
get.capability          power.getstate          tools.upgrade
get.config              power.hibernate         unregister
get.config.cpuidmask    power.off               upgrade
```

As you can see, vim-cmd provides the access to manage all aspects of your virtual machines. The options to manage and configure your hosts are equally numerous. Although this is not the tool to use for day-to-day management, you can leverage vim-cmd in your scripted installs to configure the networking and storage aspects of your hosts.

Within /etc, you find the configuration files for your host. Because the system state backup contains files only from /etc, any configuration changes that you make outside of this folder are temporary. Changes to your host's configuration files within this folder are permanent if the file has the sticky bit enabled. Some of the configuration files within this folder structure are listed in Table 11.1. As the permissions on those files allow you to overwrite the files with vifs, you could also edit these files in TSM. In either case, you would want to ensure that you have made a system backup first. If you use either TSM or vifs to update these configuration files, changes are not verified by the vSphere API and a misconfiguration could render the host unusable.

In the /opt folder structure, you'll find the binaries for any agents you install on the host, such as for the vCenter Agent or for High Availability. Configuration files for these agents are found in /etc. If you change the IP address of your vCenter Server host, you can update the file /etc/opt/vmware/vpxa/vpxa.cfg on your hosts and then issue the command /sbin/services.sh restart to restart the management services on your host. If you need to uninstall any agents from your host manually, you may find an uninstall script in /opt/vmware/uninstallers.

Within /var/logs, you'll find the log files for your host. /var/log/messages is the main VMkernel log file. This includes events from the VMkernel, any agents running on the host, from the hostd daemon, and commands issued in TSM. ESXi maintains a rotation of 10 copies of the messages file and rotates the files when the current file reaches 1MB. The prior copies are compressed to save space within the ESXi RAM disk. If the ESXi installation created a scratch partition on disk, this log file will be mirrored to /scratch/log/ and the log files in that folder will persist across a reboot. However, if you require long-term storage of your host's log files, you should enable the syslog service or use vi-logger from the vSphere Management Assistant (vMA) to capture this log file.

Also in /var/logs is sysboot.log. This file captures the boot process from the time the VMkernel initializes to the completion of the boot process. This file is useful to troubleshoot any problems you experience when your host boots up. In /var/log/vmware, you'll find the hostd log files. Also within subfolders are the logs for agents such as the vCenter Agent service.

Log Files for ESXi and ESX Along with the architectural changes in ESXi come changes in the log files generated by ESXi. Table 11.2 summarizes the similarities and differences in log files between ESXi and ESX.

There are numerous other folders that you can examine and that provide valuable insight into the inner workings of ESXi. The last folder that this section examines is /sbin. Within /sbin, you'll find the commands that will be the most useful to your troubleshooting sessions with TSM. To begin with, a number of esxcfg binaries are included. These closely match the functionality you would find with the vCLI or in the Service Console for ESX. A version of esxcli is also included that tends to be more feature-rich than the version found in the vCLI. For this reason, some Knowledge Base articles will direct you to TSM to perform advanced configuration changes. esxupdate is found in /sbin and can be used to manage patches and updates on the host.

If you're having problems with performance, you can use esxtop. This functions the same as resxtop from the vCLI, but also adds replay mode. With replay mode, you can record and then replay esxtop statistics for a specific period of time. This can be helpful if you need to send the performance data to VMware Support. To record data, you can use the command vm-support -S -i 5 -d 120. The -i parameter sets the query interval, and -d sets the duration of the capture. This generates a support bundle within /var/tmp that contains the performance data and the log

Table 11.2 Comparing the Log Files for ESXi and ESX

Log file	Description	Location on ESXi	Location on ESX
VMkernel log	Log containing everything related to the VMkernel	`/var/log/messages`	`/var/log/vmkernel`
VMKwarning log	Log warnings from the Vmkernel	N/A	`/var/log/vmkwarning`
VMKsummary log	Summary of system activities including uptime	N/A	`/var/log/vmksummary`
Hostd log	Host Management service log	`/var/log/vmware/hostd.log`	`/var/log/vmware/hostd.log`
vCenter Agent log	Log file generated by the vCenter Server Agent service	`/var/log/vmware/vmware/vpx/vpxa.log`	`/var/log/vmware/vmware/vpx/vpxa.log`
Automatic Availability Manager logs	Log file generated by the High Availability service	`/var/log/vmware/aam/vmware_<hostname>-xxx.log`	`/var/log/vmware/aam/vmware_<hostname>-xxx.log`
System boot log	Log file generated during the system boot process	`/var/log/sysboot.log`	`/var/log/boot-logs/sysboot.log`
Software iSCSI log	Log file for the software iSCSI initiator	N/A	`/var/log/vmkiscsid.log`

files from the host. The output from `vm-support` includes instructions to extract the file, as shown in this example:

```
To see the files collected, run: tar -tzf
    '/var/tmp/esx-2010-10-02--02.02.13217.tgz'
```

After you have extracted the tar file, you can issue the following command to replay the data that was captured:

```
esxtop -R vm-support- esx-2010-10-02--02.02.13217
```

The `vm-support` command can also be used to generate support bundles. While the log files `messages`, `hostd.log`, and `vpxa.log` are accessible via a number of methods, the log files for High Availability and other services are not accessible through the vSphere API. All log files for ESXi are available within the support bundle, as well as core dumps, configuration files, and log

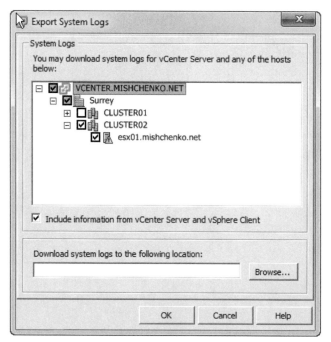

Figure 11.9   Generating a support bundle with the vSphere client.

files for virtual machines. You can generate a support bundle with the vSphere client by selecting File > Export > Export System Logs to display the screen shown in Figure 11.9. Both methods create a support bundle within /var/tmp. With vm-support, you then need to copy that bundle to another computer. If you need to provide VMware Support with a core dump file, such a file can be found in /var/core.

Tip: Generally the ESXi RAM disk mounts should not exceed 90% usage and thus should not run out of space. However, a software bug in a driver for example could cause one of the mounts to fill in which case the following event would be generated. If disk space is a concern on your host you can set up your syslog receiver to monitor for similar events.

```
Oct  1 01:22:08 vmkernel: 0:00:55:09.839 cpu0:4149)BC: 3837: Failed to flush 52
    buffers of size 8192 each for object '1.z' 1 4 1167 0 0 0 0 0 0 0 0 0 0:
    No free memory for file data
```

Conclusion

From the *Spiderman* movies comes the quote, "With great power comes great responsibility." This applies not only to your "spidey senses," but also to your use of ESXi's TSM. When you access TSM, you have complete and unrestricted access to the VMkernel. The commands you issue through TSM are not necessarily filtered for problems or mistakes as the same commands being issued through the vSphere API are. Properly used, TSM is a great tool and it can certainly save the day. However, improperly used, it can have significant negative consequences.

Getting to know TSM means spending time in it exploring the various aspects of the ESXi filesystem and commands that it contains. Given the ease of setting up a virtual ESXi host, that's the best way to get into the TSM without needing to worry about any mistakes. For production use, TSM access should be made under the appropriate circumstances and be audited.

Index

Numerics and Symbols

& (dollar sign), 375
\ (escape character), 332
3DES (Triple DES), 299
32-bit OS, 16
64-bit OS, 16

A

AAM (Automated Availability Manager), 86, 452
accepteula command, 130
account, user, 266
Active Directory. *See* AD
Active Directory Application Mode (ADAM), 155
AD (Active Directory)
  integration
    configuring with host profiles, 184–185
    configuring with vCLI, 185–186
    configuring with vSphere client, 182–184
    prerequisites, 182
    support, 181
  permissions, 186–189
  search list settings, 280
ADAM (Active Directory Application Mode), 155
address
  IP, 34, 42, 50, 355–356
  IPv6, 304
Address Resolution Protocol (ARP), 356–357
Address Space Layout Randomization (ASLR), 248
Administrator permission, 268
advanced performance chart, 218–223
agent, SNMP, 200
alarms
  creating, 207–211
  disabling, 213–214
  editing, 209
  managing, 212–214
  predefined, 207, 209
  resetting, 213
  triggers, 207–208
  vCenter Server, 395–396, 433
alert
  SNMP, 237
  Tech Support Mode (TSM), 433
  vCenter Server, 433
algorithm
  authentication, 298
  encryption, 298–299
  key length requirements, 299
  Secure Hash Algorithm (SHA), 298
Allocate Space permission, 160
architecture, ESXi, 3–6
Archive file, 439
archive utility, 238
ARP (Address Resolution Protocol), 356–357
ash shell, 441
ASLR (Address Space Layout Randomization), 248
Assign Network permission, 161
attack, security, 309–310
auditing
  EVM Control, 91
  logging and, 91
  Tech Support Mode (TSM), 433–435
authentication
  Active Directory integration, 16–17, 336–337
  algorithm, 298
  CHAP, 306–309, 359
  Hash-based Message Authentication (HMAC), 298
  vCLI, 332–333
  vi-fastpass, 335–336
Auto Deploy, 436
Automated Availability Manager (AAM), 86, 452
autopart command, 130

B

backup
  archive utility, 238
  host, 238
  regular interval, 410
  and restoration, 443–447
  vCenter server configuration data, 151–152
  virtual machine, 240–243
balanced performance power management policy, 49
bandwidth, 313
Batch Mode, 364
BIOS settings, 29, 94
boot
  BIOS settings, 94
  device, 94
  PXE
    and ESXi installer, 104
    gPXE enumerating configuration files, 116
    in Linux environment, 110–116
    process of, 100–101
    in Windows environment, 105–110

boot (*Continued*)
    System boot log file, 452
    VMkernel boot options, 121
    VMvisor Boot Menu screen, 128
boot bank partition, 436
boot partition, 437
boot.cfg, 438
bootloader partition, 436
bootstate parameter, 438
bootstrap commands, 129
Browse Datastore permission, 160
brute-force attack, 310
BusyBox, 441, 449

C

CA (certificate authority), 284–285
cap counter, 219
CD, Data Recovery installation, 244
CD-ROM device, 166
certificate, SSL
    certificate authority, 284–285
    ESXi, 285
    pass-phrase, 292
    replacing, 286–293
    security warning, 286
    self-signed, 284
    vCenter Server, 285
    verification, 293
CHAP (Challenge-Handshake Authentication Protocol),
    306–309, 359
child object, 269, 275–276
CIM (Common Information Model)
    broker, 5, 231
    hardware management, 230–231
    management model, 8
    Openwsman client, 231
    plug-in, 5
    providers, adding to ESXi host, 232
    software architecture, 230
    support, adding to generic ESXi installable image, 28
CIM XML (CIM Extensible Markup Language), 230
CIMOM (CIM object manager), 231
Cisco Discovery Protocol feature, 16
clearpart command, 132–133
cluster
    applying host profile to, 58–59
    security and, 314–316
cmdlets, 66
    PowerCLI, 374, 426–427
    PowerShell, 379–380
CMPI (Common Manageability Programming Interface), 231
command
    accepteula, 130
    autopart, 130
    bootstrap, 129
    clearpart, 132–133
    comma-separated value, 66
    dryrun, 132
    esxcli, 352–353
    %firstboot, 137–138
    include, 135
    install, 131
    keyboard, 132–133
    kill, 352

network, 132, 134
paranoid, 132
part, 135–136
partition, 135–136
patching, 426–427
%post, 137
PowerCLI, 65–66
%pre, 135–136
rescan, 362
resxtop, 364–365
rootpw, 131–132
serialnum, 132, 134
shutdown, 346
stop, 352
sudo, 325
svmotion, 353
vCLI, 63–64, 321–322, 324, 329–334
vCLI networking, 354
vicfg-user, 349–351
vifp, 338
vifptarget, 336, 338
vifs, 446–448
vihostupdate, 407–408
vi-logger, 340–342
vmaccepteula, 130
vma-update, 328–329
vmserialnum, 132
vmware-cmd, 351–353
command line-based configuration, 7
comma-separated value (CSV), 66
Common Information Model (CIM)
    broker, 5, 231
    hardware management, 230–231
    management model, 8
    Openwsman client, 231
    plug-in, 5
    providers, adding to ESXi host, 232
    software architecture, 230
    support, adding to generic ESXi installable image, 28
Common Manageability Programming Interface (CMPI), 231
comparison operators, 376
configuration
    command line-based, 7
    data recovery, 241–243
    DHCP stateful, 79
    DNS, 79
    gPXE enumerating configuration files, 115
    host profile, 58–60
    ICMP stateless, 79
    IP, 75
    IPSec, 296–298
    IPv6, 75, 78
    management network, 73–79
    network adapter, 95–96
    SNMP management serve, 203–204
    time, 7, 48
    vCenter Update Manager (VUM), 413–416
    vSphere client, 39–43
    vSwitch security property, 310–313
Configuration tab, 41, 46–48
Configure Network permission, 161
connection management, PowerShell, 378–379
connection options, vCLI, 330–331
console operating system (COS), 2–3
-contains operator, 376

Coordinated Universal Time (UTC), 189
COS (console operating system), 2–3
CPU power, 49
CSV (comma-separated value), 66
custom extensions, removing, 86–87

D

data center object, 275
data management, 197–199
data migration tool, 151–152
data permissions, 159–164
data recovery
    compliance, 240–241
    configuration, 241–243
    Data Recovery installation CD, 244
    File Level Restore (FLR), 244
    plug-in installation, 240
    process, 238–239
    restore point, 244–245
    restoring virtual machine and file with, 244
    virtual machine, 240–243
    Virtual Machine Restore Wizard, 244
data source name (DSN), 148
datastore file management, 7
DBO (database owner) rights, 147
dcui account, 266
DCUI (Direct Console User Interface)
    Change Password screen, 33
    configuration, 32–37
    Configure Management Network screen, 34–35
    configuring and troubleshooting ESXi with, 67–87
    console administration, 5
    custom extensions, removing, 86–87
    IP Configuration screen, 34–35
    keyboard language, 70–71
    Lockdown Mode, 72–73
    management network
        configuration, 73–79
        confirming restart of, 76
        disabling, 80–81
        restarting, 79
        testing, 79.80
    navigation, 68
    network adapters, 75
    permissions, 273–274
    setting root password, 71–72
    Shutdown/Restart screen, 67, 69
    support information, viewing, 82
    system configuration, resetting, 86
    System Customization screen, 33
    system logs, viewing, 82–84
    troubleshooting mode options, 84–86
    TSM access, 430
    vSwitch, restoring, 81–82
    welcome screen, 32, 67–68
Delete Datastore File permission, 160
Delete Datastore permission, 160
Delete Network permission, 161
Dell Remote Access Card (DRAC), 36
Dell servers, 235–237
denial-of-service (DoS) attack, 250
DHCP server, 104, 112–113, 239, 446
DHCP stateful configuration, 79
Diagnostic tool (IPSec), 303

Direct Console User Interface. *See* DCUI
disabling
    Lockdown Mode, 262, 433–434
    management network, 80–81
disk device names, 131
Distributed Management Task Force (DMTF), 230
Distributed Power Management (DPM), 416
Distributed Resources Scheduler (DRS), 12, 80, 346
DMTF (Distributed Management Task Force), 230
DMZ network, 161, 251
DNS configuration, 75
dollar sign ($), 375
DoS (denial-of-service) attack, 250
double-encapsulation attack, 309
DPM (Distributed Power Management), 416
DRAC (Dell Remote Access Card), 36
DRS (Distributed Resources Scheduler), 12, 80, 346
dryrun command, 132
DSN (data source name), 148
dump partition, 347, 436
dvSwitch (vNetwork Distributed Switch), 12

E

editing
    alarms, 209
    host profiles, 58
    permissions, 273
e-mail alert, 199
Embedded installation format, 6, 93–97
    BIOS settings, 94
    network adapter configuration, 95–96
    scratch partition, 98–99
Emulex, 229
Encapsulating Security Payload (ESP), 298
encryption, 298–299
End User License Agreement (EULA), 27, 30
energy usage counter, 219
Enterprise Virtualization Management (EVM) Control, 91
environment variable, 333
-eq operator, 376
escape character (\), 332
ESP (Encapsulating Security Payload), 298
ESX
    ESXi product differences, 12–16
    EXSi common features, 9, 12
    log file, 451–452
    migrating from
        data migration tool, 151–152
        datastore and network permissions, upgrading, 159–164
        license service, installing on vCenter Server host, 158
        Linked Mode feature, 162–164
        performance data, preserving, 168–169
        prerequisites, 145–147
        problem preventing, 166
        process flow, 164–165
        upgrading to vCenter Server 4.1, 147–150
        vCenter Server configuration data backup, 151–152
        vCenter Server configuration data, restoring, 153–156
        virtual hardware upgrade, 177
        virtual machine upgrade, 170–179
        VirtualCenter database to supported version, 150–151
        vMotion migration, 167
        VMware Tools upgrade, 172–179
    release of, 2

esxcli command, 352–353
esx.conf, 448
ESXi
   architecture of, 3–6
   ESX common features, 9, 12
   ESX product differences, 12–16
   file system, 439–440
   installation, 27–32
   log file, 451–452
   management, 6–8
   new features, 16–23
   repair process, 444–446
   SSL certificate, 285
ESXi 3 release, 2
ESXi Configuration Guide, 287
esxupdate.log log file, 437
EULA (End User License Agreement), 27, 30
EVC (vMotion Compatibility), 166
event trigger, 207
events, 56
EVM (Enterprise Virtualization Management) Control, 90
eXecute Disable (XD), 248
Extensible Markup Language (XML), 322
extensions, removing custom, 86–87

F

FastSCP application (Veeam), 88–89
Fault Tolerance (FT), 12, 315
FC (Fibre Channel), 118
FC-HBA (FC Host Bus Adapter), 305
FCOE (Fibre Channel over Ethernet), 19
File Level Restore (FLR), 244
file management, 363–364
File Management permission, 160
file system
   access, 446
   Archive file, 439
   High Availability (HA), 439
   memory, 439
   mounted for typical ESXi installation, 439–440
   partition, 436
   RAM disk, 441–442
   source file within folder structure, 441
   State archive file, 439
   vCenter Agent, 439
   VIB update, 439
   VMFS data store, 440
   WMware ESXi, 439–440
File Transfer Protocol (FTP), 6, 407
firewall, 256–257
%firstboot command, 137–138
FLR (File Level Restore), 244
folder structure, 276, 441
FQDN (fully qualified domain name), 287
FS SAN storage, 305–306
FT (Fault Tolerance), 12, 315
FTP (File Transfer Protocol), 6, 407
fully qualified domain name (FQDN), 287

G

GA (Generally Available) release, 127
-ge operator, 376
Getting Started Wizard, 242

Get-VIEvent query, 396–397
gPXE enumerating configuration files, 116
graphical mode, EXSi installation, 117–120
group permissions, 278
GSX Server, 2
-gt operator, 376

H

HA (High Availability) cluster, 5, 12, 439
hardware
   management
      Common Information Model (CIM), 230–232
      health status, 232–235
   requirements, 25–27
   status, 46
   upgrade, 177
Hardware Compatibility List (HCL), 25–26, 146
Hardware Virtualization (HV), 147
Hash-based Message Authentication (HMAC), 298
HBA (Host Bus Adapter), 229
HCL (Hardware Compatibility List), 25–26, 146
HCL (High Compatibility List), 9
health check, RVTools application, 87–88
health status, monitoring
   when connected to host, 232–233
   when connected to vCenter Server, 234–235
High Availability (HA) cluster, 5, 12, 439
High Compatibility List (HCL), 9
high performance power management policy, 49
HMAC (Hash-based Message Authentication), 298
host
   adding CIM providers to, 232
   backup, 238
   licensing, 50–51
   monitoring health status when connected to, 232–233
   profile, 394–395
   restarting and shutting down, 67
   security profile, 51–52
   shutting down, 346
   troubleshooting, 396
Host Bus Adapter (HBA), 229
host profiles
   applying to cluster, 58–59
   compliance, 58–60
   configuring AD integration with, 184–185
   configuring NTP with, 190–191
   creating new, 58
   editing, 58
   ensuring configuration compliance
      with, 58–60
   overview, 12
   reference host configuration, 57–58
host storage management, 357–362
host update, 29
hostAgentConfig.xml, 447
Hostd log, 452
hostd process, 4, 258
hostd.log, 448
hosts, 447
HTTP, 6, 407
HTTPS, 407
HV (Hardware Virtualization), 147
Hyper-V hypervisor, 248
hypervisor, 247–248

Hypervisor screen, 438
Hypervisor1, 437
Hypervisor2, 437

I–J

iBFT (iSCSI Boot Firmware Table), 19
ICMP stateless configuration, 79
IIS (Internet Information Service), 102
IKE (Internet Key Exchange), 298
include command, 135
indexes, 410
inheritance, permission, 277–278
Input/Output Memory Management Unit (IOMMU), 118
Insight Control, 235–237
install command, 131
installation
    bootstrap commands, 129
    data recovery plug-in, 240
    disk device names, 131
    Embedded format, 6, 93, 97
        BIOS settings, 94
        network adapter configuration, 95–96
        scratch partition, 98–99
    ESXi
        using graphical mode, 117–120
        using scripted mode, 124–126, 128
    EXSi, 27–32
    image storage and access, 99–100
    install command options, 131
    Installable installation format, 6, 99–101
    media depot, 101–104
    OpenSSL protocol, 287
    patch, 405–407
    PowerCLI, 372–373
    PXE booting
        and ESXi installer, 104
        gPXE enumerating configuration files, 116
        in Linux environment, 110–116
        process of, 100–101
        in Windows environment, 105–110
    RMP installer, 173
    sample script, 138–139
    script commands, 128
    script storage options, 128
    script, troubleshooting, 140–142
    SYSLINUX installer options, 117
    vCenter 4.1, 153–156
    vCLI, 321–325
    vMA, 325–328
    vCenter Update Manager (VUM), 409–412
    vSphere client, 37–38
Install-VMHostPatch cmdlet, 424–425
Intel XD (eXecute Disable), 248
Internet Information Service (IIS), 102
Internet Key Exchange (IKE), 298
Internet Protocol (IP), 293
Internet Protocol Security. See IPSec
I/O
    Network I/O Control, 21–22
    Storage I/O Control, 54–55
IOMMU (Input/Output Memory Management Unit), 118
IOPS (I/O operations per speed), 55

IP address, 34, 42, 50, 355–356
IP configuration, 75
IP filter list, 301
IP (Internet Protocol), 293
ipmi*, 448
IPSec (Internet Protocol Security), 20–21
    algorithm key length requirements, 299
    authentication algorithm, 298
    basic description of, 293–294
    communication path setup, 294–295
    configuration, 296–298
    Diagnostic tool, 303
    encryption algorithm, 298
    Internet Layer integration, 293–294
    IP filter list, 301
    IPv6, 295–296, 304
    pre-shared key value, 303
    security association, 296, 298
    security parameter index, 298
    security policy, 296, 299
    setup, 300–303
IPv6 configuration, 75, 78
-is operator, 376
iSCSI Boot Firmware Table (iBFT), 19
iSCSI (Internet Small Computer System Interface), 26, 257, 306–309, 452
ISE (Integrated Shell Environment), 398–399
ISL tagging attack, 309
-isnot operator, 376

K

KB (Knowledge Bus) articles, 12
keyboard command, 132–133
keyboard language, 70–71
kickstart scripts, 128
kill command, 352
Knowledge Bus (KB) articles, 12

L

Lab Manager, 146
LBT (Load-Based Teaming), 22
-le operator, 376
LibXML2 package, 322
license key, 51
license service, 158
license.cfg, 447
-like operator, 376
Linked Mode feature, 162–164
Linux environment
    PXE booting in, 110–116
    SYSLINUX installer options, 117
    vCLI installation, 322–323
Load-Based Teaming (LBT), 22
Local TSM, 430, 432
Lockdown Mode
    basic description of, 260–261
    disabling, 262, 433–434
    enabling, 72–73, 261–262, 264
    ESXi 4.0 versus 4.1, 264–265
    login error message, 262–263
    monitoring for change in, 433
    querying lockdown setting, 264

log file, 437
    accessible with `vifs`, 446–448
    ESXi and ESX comparison, 451–452
logging, 91, 340–342
`-lt` operator, 376
LUN (logical unit number), 14, 26

M

MAC flooding attack, 309
MAC (Media Access Control), 97
Maintenance Mode, 346
Man in the Middle (MiTM) attack, 286
Managed Object Browser (MOB), 370–371
ManageIQ, 91
management
    Common Information Model (CIM), 7–8
    datastore, 7
    ESXi, 6–8
    file, 363–364
    hardware
        Common Information Model (CIM), 230–232
        health status, 232–235
    server management systems, 235–237
    user, 7
Management Information Base (MIB) files,
        203–204, 325
management network
    configuration, 73–79
    confirming restart of, 76
    disabling, 80–81
    restarting, 79
    testing, 79–80
Managing VMware Infrastructure with Windows PowerShell
        (Rottenberg), 390
`-match` operator, 376
maximum transmission unit (MTU), 355
Media Access Control (MAC), 97
media depot, 101–104
memory
    compression, 224–226
    total capacity value, 46–47
    virtual machine value, 47
memory file system, 439
memory management unit (MMN), 17
MIB (Management Information Base) files, 203–204, 325
migrating from ESX
    data migration tool, 151–152
    datastore and network permissions, upgrading, 159–164
    license service, installing on vCenter Server host, 158
    Linked Mode feature, 162–164
    performing data, preserving, 168–169
    prerequisites, 145–147
    problem preventing, 166
    process flow, 164–165
    upgrading to vCenter Server 4.1, 147–150
    vCenter Server configuration
        backup, 151–152
        data backup, 151–152
        restoring, 153–156
    virtual hardware upgrade, 177
    virtual machine upgrade, 170–179
    VirtualCenter database to supported version, 150–151
    vMotion migration, 167
    VMware Tools upgrade, 172–179

MIME type, 115
MiTM (Man in the Middle) attack, 286
MMN (memory management unit), 17
MOB (Managed Object Browser), 370–371
module options, VMkernel, 348
`motd`, 447
Move Datastore permission, 160
Move Network permission, 161
MTU (maximum transmission unit), 355
multicast brute-force attack, 310

N

`-ne` operator, 376
NetQueue network, 16
network adapter, 74, 95–96
`network` command, 132, 134
Network File System (NFS), 6, 26, 256, 306
network interface card (NIC), 17, 26, 354
Network I/O Control, 21–22
network load balance (NLB), 315
network permissions, 159–164
network protocol security, 252–253
network server, 104
network storage security
    FS SAN storage, 305–306
    iSCSI, 306–309
    NFS storage, 306
Network Time Protocol (NTP)
    configuring with host profiles, 190–191
    configuring with PowerCLI, 192–193
    configuring with vSphere client, 189–190
    overview, 5
networking commands, vCLI, 354
new features, ESXi, 16–23
nfs account, 266
NFS (Network File System), 6, 26, 256, 306
NIC (network interface card), 17, 26, 354
NLB (network load balance), 315
No Access permission, 268
`-nomatch` operator, 376
`-notcontains` operator, 376
`-notlike` operator, 376
NPIV (N_Port ID Virtualization), 306
N_Port ID Virtualization (NPIV), 306
NTP Daemon (ntpd), 189
NTP (Network Time Protocol)
    configuring with host profiles, 190–191
    configuring with PowerCLI, 192–193
    configuring with vSphere client, 189–190
    overview, 5

O

object identifier (OID), 203
objects, PowerShell, 374–375
ODBC (Open Database Connectivity), 409
OID (object identifier), 203
Onyx tool, 399–402
Open Virtualization Format (OVF), 43, 326
OpenSSL protocol, 287, 291, 322
Openwsman client, 231
`openwsman.conf`, 447
OVF (Open Virtualization Format), 43, 326

P–Q

paranoid command, 132
parent object, 275–277
part command, 135–136
partition
    boot, 437
    boot bank, 436
    bootloader, 436
    dump, 436
    scratch, 98–99, 437
    store, 437
partition command, 135–136
pass-phrase SSL certificate, 292
password
    classes, 33
    DCUI, 33
    root account, 71–72
    validity, 33
    vSphere client, 41
patching, 239, 437
    baseline, 417–418
    bulletin name, 406
    commands, 426–427
    Install-VMHostPatch cmdlet, 424–425
    media depot, 407–408
    patch installation, 405–407
    with PowerCLI, 424–427
    PowerCLI cmdlets, 426–427
    reboot requirements, 405–406
    remediation, 421–423
    resources, 406
    scanning, 419–421
    staging task, 419, 421–422
    third-party patch source, 414
    update release, 406
    with vihostupdate command, 407–408
    with vCenter Update Manager, 408–420, 423
PCI (Peripheral Component Interconnect), 17
performance charts
    advanced, 218–223
    cap counter, 219
    counters, 223–225
    customizing, 220–222
    energy usage counter, 219
    exporting data in, 222–223
    metric groups, 220
    overview layout, 215–217
    performance counters, 219
    pie charts, 216
    time-based, 216
    usage counter, 219
Peripheral Component Interconnect (PCI), 17
Perl scripts, 324, 366
permissions
    Active Directory (AD), 186–189
    AD search list settings, 280
    Administrator role, 268
    Allocate Space, 160
    Assign Network, 161
    assigning to object on host, 270
    Browse Datastore, 160
    child object, 269, 273, 275–276
    Configuration Network, 161
    data center object, 275

datastore and network, 159–164
    DCUI, 273–274
    Delete Datastore, 160
    Delete Datastore File, 160
    Delete Network, 161
    editing, 273
    File Management, 160
    folder structure, 276
    granting, 273–274
    group, 278
    hierarchy, 275
    host level, 269
    inheritance, 277–278
    managing on VMware ESXi host, 266–273
    managing with PowerCLI, 280
    managing with vCenter Server, 274–280
    Move Datastore, 160
    Move Network, 161
    new role creation, 268–269
    No Access, 268
    parent object, 275–277
    Read-Only, 159, 268
    removing, 273
    Rename Datastore, 160
    resource pool, 270–272
    role-based, 159
    upgrading, 159–164
    validation period, 279–280
    viewing, 273
PFX (Personal Information Exchange) file, 287
pipeline, PowerShell, 375
plug-in
    Common Information Model (CIM), 5
    vCenter Update Manager (VUM), 412
policy enforcement, 91
port
    TCP, 252
    for typical vSphere implementation, 254–255
    UDP, 252
%post command, 137
Power Cycle, 174–175
power management
    policy, 49
    viewing information about, 48
PowerCLI
    accessing, 64
    cmdlet, 374, 426–427
    commands, 65–66
    configuring NTP with, 192–193
    configuring syslog settings with, 195–196
    host configuration with, 390–394
    host profile management with, 394–395
    installation, 372–373
    managing permissions with, 280
    minimum requirements for, 369–370
    overview, 7, 62
    patching with, 424–427
    query time, 389
    querying events related to enabling TSM, 434
    querying health status with, 233
    upgrading VMware Tools using, 177
    vCenter Server alarm integration, 395–396
    virtual machine management, 383–389
    VMware tool interaction, 386–389
    welcome screen, 65

PowerShell
    cmdlets, 379–380
    comparison operators, 376
    connection management, 378–379
    execution policy, 65
    formatting output, 377–378
    objects, 374–375
    pipeline, 375
    variables, 375–376
PowerShell Drives (PSDrives), 380–382
PowerWF application, 402
%pre command, 135–136
Preboot Execution Environment (PXE), 2
processor, 46
proxy.xml, 447
PSDrives (PowerShell Drives), 380–382
PVSCSI (VMware Paravirtualized SCSI), 171
PXE booting
    and ESXi installer, 104
    gPXE enumerating configuration files, 116
    in Linux environment, 110–116
    process for, 100–101
    in Windows environment, 105–110
PXE (Preboot Execution Environment), 2
PXELINUX file, 104, 107–109

query time, PowerCLI, 389
queue depth, 348

R

RAM disk file system, 441–442
ramdisk file system, 193
Raw Device Mapping (RDM), 243
RCLI (Remote Command Line Interface), 2–3, 62
RDM (Raw Device Mapping), 243
RDP (Remote Desktop Protocol), 89
Read-Only permission, 159, 268
recovery
    appliance, 240–241
    configuration, 241–243
    Data Recovery installation CD, 244
    File Level Restore (FLR), 244
    plug-in installation, 240
    process, 238–239
    restore point, 244–245
    restoring virtual machine and file with, 244
    virtual machine, 240–243
    Virtual Machine Restore Wizard, 244
remediation, patch, 421–423
Remote Command Line Interface (RCLI), 2–3, 62
Remote Desktop Protocol (RDP), 89
Remote Supervisor Adapter II (RSA II), 36
Remote TSM, 430, 432
Rename Datastore permission, 160
repair process, ESXi, 444–446
reports, storage, 226–228
rescan command, 362
resource allocation
    available capacity, 53
    CPU summary, 53
    memory total capacity, 53
    reserved capacity, 53
    resource pool, 53–54
    share, limits, or reservation, 54
    Storage I/O Control, 54–56

Resource Allocation tab, 53–54
resource pool, 270–272
Resources pane, 205
restore point, 244–245
restores, 443–447
restoring. *See also* data recovery
    backups and, 443–446
    vCenter Server configuration data, 153–156
    vSwitch, 81–82
resxtop command, 364–365
root account, 266
rootpw command, 131–132
Rottenberg, Hal *(Managing VMware Infrastructure with*
        Windows PowerShell), 390
RPM installer, 173
RSA II (Remote Supervisor Adapter II), 36
RVTools application, 87–88

S

SAN (storage area network), 26, 305–306, 437
SAS (Serial Attached SCSI), 171
scanning patch, 419–421
SCP (Secure Copy), 448
scratch partition, 98–99, 437
script
    installation sample, 138–139
    installation storage options, 128
    installation, troubleshooting, 140–142
    kickstart, 128
    Perl, 324, 366
scripted mode, ESXi installation, 124–126, 128
SDK (software development kit), 87
Secure Copy (SCP), 448
Secure Hash Algorithm (SHA), 298
Secure Shell (SSH), 14, 85
Secure Sockets Layer. *See* SSL
security. *See also* SSL
    attacks, 309–310
    clustering and, 314–316
    ESP (Encapsulating Security Payload), 298
    firewall, 256–257
    host profile, 51–52
    hypervisor, 247–248
    Internet Protocol Security (IPSec)
        algorithm key length requirements, 299
        authentication algorithm, 298
        basic description of, 293–294
        communication path setup, 294–295
        configuration, 296–298
        Diagnostic tool, 303
        encryption algorithm, 298
        Internet Layer integration, 293–294
        IP filter list, 301
        IPv6, 295–296, 304
        pre-shared key value, 303
        security association, 296, 298
        security parameter index, 298
        security policy, 296, 299
        setup, 300–303
    Lockdown Mode
        basic description of, 260–261
        disabling, 262, 264
        enabling, 72–73, 261–262, 264
        ESXi 4.0 *versus* 4.1, 264–265

login error message, 262.263
querying lockdown setting, 264
network protocol, 252–253
network storage
FS SAN storage, 305–306
iSCSI, 306–309
NFS storage, 306
permissions
AD search list settings, 280
Administrator role, 268
assigning to object on host, 270
child object, 269, 273, 275–276
data center object, 275
DCUI, 273–274
editing, 273
folder structure, 276
granting, 273–274
group, 278
hierarchy, 275
host level, 269
inheritance, 277–278
managing on VMware ESXi host, 266–273
managing with PowerCLI, 280
managing with vCenter Server, 274–280
new role creation, 268–269
No Access role, 268
parent object, 275–277
Read Only role, 268
removing, 273
resource pool, 270–272
validation period, 279–280
viewing, 273
traffic shaping policy, 311–312
Trusted Platform Module (TPM), 248–249
user access, 265
virtual machine and, 249–250
virtual machine environments, isolating, 316–318
virtual network
with VLANs, 309–310
vSwitch security property configuration, 310–313
virtual networking layer and, 250–252
VMkernel and, 248–249
Security Alert dialog box, 159
Security Warning dialog box, 286
self-signed SSL certificate, 284
Serial Attached SCSI (SAS), 171
serialnum command, 132, 134
server management systems, 235–237
Service Location Protocol (SLP), 231
session file, 332
sfcb.cfg, 447
SHA (Secure Hash Algorithm), 298
shutdown command, 346
SIM (Systems Insight Manager), 235
Simple Network Management Protocol. See SNMP
Simple Object Access Protocol (SOAP), 399
Site Recording Manager, 146
SLP (Service Location Protocol), 231
SMBIOS (system management BIOS), 230
snapshot technology, 2, 385–386
SNMP (Simple Network Management Protocol), 395
agent, 200
configuring on vCenter Server, 201–203
development, 200
ESX support, 15

management server configuration, 203–204
managing ESXi with, 200–204
snmp.xml, 447
SOAP (Simple Object Access Protocol), 399
software development kit (SDK), 87
Software Installation dialog box, 176
Software iSCI log, 452
software requirements, 25–27
Splunk application, 197–199
SSH (Secure Shell), 14, 85
SSL (Secure Sockets Layer), 6
basic description of, 283–284
certificate
certificate authority (CA), 284–285
ESXi, 285
pass-phrase, 292
replacing, 286–293
security warning, 286
self-signed, 284
vCenter Server, 285
verification, 293
OpenSSL protocol, 287, 291, 322
ssl_cert, 447
ssl_key, 447
staging task, 419–421
State archive file, 439
state trigger, 207
stop command, 352
storage area network (SAN), 26, 305–306, 437
Storage I/O Control, 54–55
storage maps, 228–229
storage reports, 226–228
Storage vMotion, 12
store partition, 437
sudo command, 325
Summary tab, 40
support information, in DCUI, 82
support policy, TSM, 449
svmotion command, 353
SYSLinux, 104, 107, 437
syslog
configuring with PowerCLI, 195–196
configuring with vSphere client, 195
data management, 197–199
syslog.conf, 447
Syslog.Local.Datastore path, 193
Syslog.Remote.Hostname path, 194
Syslog.Remote.Port path, 194
system backups and restores, 443–447
System boot log file, 452
system configuration, 86
system file access, 446
system logs, 56, 82–84
system management BIOS (SMBIOS), 230
System Resource Allocation screen, 441–442
Systems Insight Manager (SIM), 235

T

tardisk, 439–440, 443
TCP Segmentation Offload (TSO), 355
TCP (Transmission Control Protocol), 193, 252
Tech Support Mode. See TSM
template, 384–385

testing
    management network, 79–80
    PowerCLI installation, 372–373
TFTP server, 104, 106, 108, 112–114
Thin Provisioning feature, 9, 207
time configuration, 7, 48
time synchronization, NTP configuration
    with host profiles, 190–191
    with PowerCLI, 192–193
    with vSphere client, 189–190
time-based chart, 216
timeout value, TSM, 430–432
TPM (Trusted Platform Module), 248–249
traffic shaping policy, 311–312
Transmission Control Protocol (TCP), 193, 252
trigger, alarm, 207–208
Triple DES (3DES), 299
troubleshooting
    host, 396
    installation scripts, 140–142
    local tech support, 84–85
    mode options, 84–86
    remote tech support, 84–85
    with Tech Support Mode (TSM), 448–453
Trusted Platform Module (TPM), 248–249
TSM (Tech Support Mode)
    accessing, 429–431
    alert, 433
    auditing, 433–435
    description, 14
    enabling, 434
    Local, 430, 432
    recording user session with, 435
    Remote, 430, 432
    support policy, 449
    timeout value, 430–432
    troubleshooting with, 448–453
    warning message, 435
TSO (TCP Segmentation Offload), 355
Type 1 and 2 hypervisor, 248

U

Ubuntu Server VMware image, 111
UDP (User Data Protocol), 106, 193, 252
Universally Unique Identifier (UUID), 322
update, host, 29
update release, patch, 406
upgrade
    datastore permission, 159–164
    network permissions, 159–164
    vCenter Agent Pre-Upgrade tool,
        157
    to vCenter Server 4.1, 147–150
    virtual hardware, 177
    virtual machine, 170–179
    VMware Tools, 172–179
URL, 61–62
usage counter, 219
user
    creating new, 267
    dcui account, 266
    group, 350
    nfs account, 266
    root account, 266
    vicfg-user command, 349–351

vimuser account, 266
vpxuser account, 266
user access security, 265
User Data Protocol (UDP), 106, 193, 252
user management, 7
"user world" processing, 4
UTC (Coordinated Universal Time), 189
UUID (Universally Unique Identifier), 322

V

VAAI (vStorage API for Array Integration), 19–20
validation period, permission, 279–280
variable, 375–376
vCenter Agent
    file system, 439
    log file, 452
vCenter Agent Pre-Upgrade Check tool, 157
vCenter Server
    alarms, 433
        creating, 207–211
        disabling, 213–214
        editing, 209
        managing, 212–214
        predefined, 207, 209
        resetting, 213
        triggers, 207–208
    configuration data
        backup, 151–152
        restoring, 153–156
    configuring SNMP on, 201–203
    host, installing license service on, 158
    host profiles, 57–60
    managing hosts with, 57–60
    managing permissions with, 27, 275–283
    monitoring health status when connected to, 234–235
    monitoring host with, 205
    performance charts
        advanced, 218–223
        cap counter, 219
        counters, using with Windows environment, 223–225
        customizing, 220–222
        energy usage counter, 219
        exporting data in, 222–223
        metric groups, 220
        overview layout, 215–217
        performance counters, 219
        pie charts, 216
        time-based charts, 216
        usage counter, 219
    release of, 2
    SSL certificate, 285
    storage maps, 228–229
    storage reports, 226–228
vCenter Server 4.1, 147–150, 153–156
vCenter Server alarms, 395–396
vCenter Update Manager (VUM)
    baseline creation, 416–418
    configuration, 413–416
    installation, 409–412
    overview, 12
    patching with, 408–423
    plug-in, 412
    replacing SSL certificate for, 289–290
    scanning and remediation with, 419–424
    upgrading VMware Tools using, 178–179

vCLI
    authentication precedence, 332–333
    changing management network adapter with, 96–97
    command summary, 344–345
    command syntax, 64
    commands, 63–64, 321–322, 324, 329–334
    configuring AD integration with, 185–186
    connection options, 330–331
    file management, 363–364
    host storage management, 357–362
    installation, 321–325
    manual, 344
    networking commands, 354–357
    overview, 7, 62
    performance monitoring, 364–365
    session file, 332
    vicfg-snmp command options, 201
Veeam FastSCP, 88–89
VFAT (Virtual File Allocation Table), 98
vFoglight application (Vizioncore), 90
VGT (Virtual Machine Guest Tagging), 77, 310
vi-admin account, 325
VIB (vSphere Installation Bundle), 28, 232, 439
vicfg-user command, 349–351
View, 146
vi-fastpass authentication, 335–336
vifp command, 338
vifptarget command, 336, 338
vifs command, 446–448
vihostupdate command, 407–408
vi-logger command, 340–342
vimuser account, 266
Virtual File Allocation Table (VFAT), 98
virtual hardware, 177
Virtual Local Area Network (VLAN), 26, 75–77,
        309–310
virtual machine
    backup and recovery, 240–243
    creating, 123, 383
    Hot Add Support, 170
    managing with Web Access, 60–62
    memory, 47
    registering, 351
    retrieving, 352–353
    running ESXi as, 123
    security and, 249–250, 316–318
    snapshot, 385–386
    space usage, 226–227
    starting, 352
    state, 352
    stopping, 352
    tab column format, 206
    upgrading, 170–179
    uptime, 352
    viewing information about, 352
    Virtual Serial Port Concentrator setting, 18
Virtual Machine Communication Interface (VMCI), 171
Virtual Machine Disk (VMDK), 43
Virtual Machine File System (VMFS), 2, 9, 238, 440
Virtual Machine Guest Tagging (VGT), 77, 310
virtual machine monitor (VMM), 4
Virtual Machine Restore Wizard, 244
virtual network security, 97–98, 250–252, 309–313
Virtual Serial Port Concentrator (vSPC), 18
VirtualCenter database, 150–151

virtualization development, 1
Visioncore vFogLight, 90
vi-user account, 325
VLAN (Virtual Local Area Network), 26, 75–77, 309–310
vMA (vSphere Management Assistant), 7, 43
    AD authentication, 336–337
    configuration, 327–328
    increasing storage in, 342
    installation, 325–327
    target server, adding and managing, 338–340
    vi-admin account, 325
    vi-fastpass authentication, 335–336
    vi-logger component, 340–342
    vi-user account, 325
    vma-update command, 328–329
vmaccepteula command, 130
vma-update command, 328–329
VMCI (Virtual Machine Communication Interface), 171
VMDirectPath, 171
VMDK (Virtual Machine Disk), 43
VMFS (Virtual Machine File System), 2, 9, 238, 440
VMkernel, 2
    boot options, 121
    communication for management with, 4
    host name options, 49–50
    IP address, 50
    log file, 452
    module options, 348
    overview, 3–4
    port, adding, 355
    port, IP address, 355–356
    security and, 248–249
    "user world" processes, 4
VMKsummary log, 452
VMKwarning log, 452
VMM (virtual machine monitor), 4
vMotion, 12, 167
vMotion Compatibility (EVC), 166
vmserialnum command, 132
VMvisor Boot Menu screen, 128
VMware Auto Deploy, 436
VMware history, 1–3
VMware Lab Manager, 146
VMware Site Recovery Manager, 146
VMware Sysinfo Interface, 449
VMware Tools, 170, 172–179
VMware View, 146
VMware vSphere Resource Management Guide, 53
vmware-cmd command, 351–353
vmware_config, 447
vmware_configrules, 447
VMXNET Generation 3, 171
vNetwork Distributed Switch (dvSwitch), 12
vpxa process, 5
vpxa.cfg, 448
vpxa.log, 448
vpxuser account, 266
vpxuser process, 5
vShield application, 316–318
vSPC (Virtual Serial Port Concentrator), 18
vSphere
    feature list, 10–11
    login screen, 40
    Storage I/O Control, 54–55
    Web Access, 60–62

vSphere 4.0 Hardening Guide, The, 314, 319
vSphere 4.1 release, 3
vSphere client
    configuration, 39–43
    configuring AD integration with, 182–184
    configuring NTP with, 189–190
    configuring syslog settings with, 195
    home screen, 45–46
    installation, 37–38
    password, 41
    RDP plug-in, 89
    TSM access, 430–431
    upgrade of VMware Tools with, 172–174
vSphere Command Line Interface. *See* vCLI
VSphere Datacenter Administration Guide, The, 268
vSphere Installation Bundle (VIB), 28, 232, 439
vSphere Management Assistant (vMA), 7, 43
vStorage API for Array Integration (VAAI), 19–20
vSwitch
    creating new, 354
    linking to network port, 355
    port group, 354
    restoring, 81–82
    security property configuration, 310–313
    traffic shaping policy, 311–312
VUM (vCenter Update Manager)
    baseline creation, 416–418
    configuration, 413–416
    installation, 409–412
    overview, 12
    patching with, 408–423
    plug-in, 412
    replacing SSL certificate for, 289–290
    scanning and remediation with, 419–424
    upgrading VMware Tools using, 178–179

W

warning message, TSM, 435
Web Access, 60–62
Web Services Management (WSMAN), 230
welcome screen
    DCUI, 32, 67–68
    PowerCLI, 65
-WhatIf command, 379
Windows environment
    PXE booting in, 105–110
    vCLI installation, 324
    WMware performance counters with, 223–225
Windows Workflow Foundation, 402
WinSCP, 448
wmare.lic, 447
WMware Paravirtualized SCSI (PVSCSI), 171
WMware Project Oynx, 399–402
WMware Workstation, 1
WMware Workstation 7, 122
Workstation 7, 122
write operations, 444
WSMAN (Web Services Management), 230
WWPN (worldwide port name), 305

X–Z

x86 server, 1
XD (eXecute Disable), 248
XML (Extensible Markup Language), 322

ZIP file, 407

VMware ESXi: Planning, Implementation, and Security

Aisle B Bay 10 Shelf 6   Item 8

46TF2QoooGG9

Thank you for buying from Goodwill Columbus on Amazon Marketplace.

Ship To
Roger S. Redman
10958 BAROQUE LN
SAN DIEGO, CA 92124-3006

Order Details

Order ID	114-8604498-9951441
Order Date	12/8/2018 12:58:58 PM
Shipping Service	Standard
Buyers Name	Roger S. Redman

SKU / Listing ID	Title / Condition	Location / Comments
46TF2QoooGG9 03154759208210	VMware ESXi: Planning, Implementation, and Security Acceptable	Aisle B - Bay 10 - Shelf 6 - Item 8 This is a paper back book. Front or back cover is slightly bent. The spine is slightly bent. Ships Monday through Friday from Ohio via USPS. Our mission is to help individuals prepare for, find and retain employment.

Goodwill Columbus strives to have each and every customer 100% satisfied with their purchase. If for any reason you are not 100% satisfied please email us at with your concerns.

If we need to make something right, we will, <u>Guaranteed!</u>

Thanks for buying on Amazon Marketplace. To provide feedback for the seller please visit http://www.amazon.com/feedback.